William Nassau Molesworth

History of the Church of England from 1660

William Nassau Molesworth

History of the Church of England from 1660

ISBN/EAN: 9783743399679

Manufactured in Europe, USA, Canada, Australia, Japa

Cover: Foto ©ninafisch / pixelio.de

Manufactured and distributed by brebook publishing software (www.brebook.com)

William Nassau Molesworth

History of the Church of England from 1660

HISTORY

OF THE

CHURCH OF ENGLAND

FROM 1660

BY

Wm. NASSAU MOLESWORTH, M.A.

HONORARY CANON OF MANCHESTER

AUTHOR OF

"HISTORY OF THE REFORM BILL," "HISTORY OF ENGLAND FROM THE YEAR 1830,"
ETC., ETC.

LONDON
KEGAN PAUL, TRENCH & CO., 1, PATERNOSTER SQUARE
1882

(The rights of translation and of reproduction are reserved.)

TO

THE RIGHT REVEREND

THE LORD BISHOP OF MANCHESTER

THIS VOLUME IS DEDICATED,

IN THE HOPE THAT, NOTWITHSTANDING ITS MANIFOLD IMPERFECTIONS,

IT WILL RECEIVE THAT COURTEOUS CONSIDERATION

WHICH ITS AUTHOR HAS FREQUENTLY EXPERIENCED,

AND WHICH HIS WORK GREATLY NEEDS.

PREFACE.

THERE can be no doubt that questions relating to the Church are day by day being brought into greater prominence, and demanding more and more imperatively the attention of the English people and of their representatives. At present there are no fewer than seventeen Bills before Parliament dealing with ecclesiastical questions, and the number is more likely to increase than to diminish in future sessions. It seems to me, therefore, that there is need for a work which will describe with truthful impartiality and energetic brevity the leading influences which have presided over the evolution of the English Church, and have brought her into the relation which she now occupies on the one hand to the State and on the other to the various nonconforming communions, and so help us to forecast some of the varieties of untried being through which she has yet to pass.

This need I have endeavoured to supply in the present volume, by carefully tracing the course of the

English Church from the restoration of the monarchy and the passing of the Act of Uniformity down to a period which most of us remember, and at which all the chief questions that now agitate the Church had already come into distinct prominence, and might be regarded as "burning."

I was not made aware of the existence of the very elaborate essays of Abbey and Overton, until a great part of this book was already in type, and consequently it was altogether out of my power to make any more than mere verbal alterations. I will, therefore, content myself with remarking that their work is of a different character from mine, and intended for a different class of readers.

I wish to take this opportunity of explaining that if I have made use of such terms as Popish, Papist, Puritan, Quaker, etc., which may seem calculated to hurt the feelings of the members or officers of any religious communion whatsoever, I trust it will be evident, from the general tenor of the work, to every reader of it that I have made use of such terms simply because they were in common use in some portion of the period to which my work relates, and because they enabled me to convey my meaning with greater vivacity and clearness, avoiding needless circumlocutions. I would also remind the reader that they are words that belong to periods in which such terms were much more commonly employed than in our day, and were almost regarded as a matter of course.

I shall perhaps be blamed for giving so many minute details of the lives of Sheldon, Sancroft, Penn, Sacheverell, etc. I would, therefore, submit that the opinion we form with regard to the great events in which they took a leading and influential part must in a great degree be determined by the judgments we form of their characters, and consequently of the motives by which we suppose them to have been actuated.

I fear that I shall be still more strongly censured by those persons who regard the stipend of a clergyman as a retaining fee, the acceptance of which binds him to conceal or at least to palliate the abuses of the Church of which he is a minister. Such is not my belief. I regard the emoluments I receive as intended to enable me to be a teacher of truth and righteousness, and that so far from obliging me to conceal or defend the abuses of the communion to which I belong, they make it more imperatively my duty to detect and display them.

W. N. M.

SPOTLAND, ROCHDALE,
April 20, 1882.

CONTENTS.

CHAPTER I.

THE ACT OF UNIFORMITY.

	PAGE
Introductory	1
Prevalent Non-conformity	4
Various Acts of Uniformity	6
Date of the origin of the English Church	7
The post-Reformation Church not a new Church	8
Henry Melvill on the origin of the Church	9
Effect of the Restoration	12
The Presbyterian Established Church	14
Its unpopularity at the Restoration	15
Causes of its unpopularity	16
Return to the old service	20
Hopes of the Presbyterian ministers	21
Reynolds and Baxter offered bishoprics	22
The Restoration of the Church demanded	22
Authority of the king and the primate	23
Position of the primate	25
Juxon appointed to the Primacy	26
Unable to perform the duties of the office	26
Sheldon acts for him	27
Early life of Sheldon	28
The Savoy Conference	30
Opposition of the Presbyterians to a general toleration	31

CONTENTS.

	PAGE
Baxter and Nye	33
Charles in secret communication with the King of France	34
His wish to keep faith with the Presbyterians	35
The Lord Chancellor Clarendon	37
The Savoy Conference assembled	38
The Coronation	39
Sheldon presides at the Savoy Conference	40
His disregard of the warrant under which it was summoned	41
Remonstrances of the Presbyterian divines	42
Failure of the Conference	44
Meeting of Convocation	45
The Act of Uniformity	46
The Act comes into operation on St. Bartholomew's day	49
Expulsion of Presbyterian ministers	50
Conduct of Sheldon	52
Imprisonment of Calamy	53
Measures of severity	54
The Puritans appeal to the king	55
Charles issues a proclamation in favour of toleration	56
His declaration condemned by the Commons	57
Sheldon's letter to Charles	60
His circular letter to his suffragans	62
South, on the proper treatment of Nonconformists	64
Attempts at comprehension of Nonconformists	66
Dr. Gauden's rubric	67
The taxation of the clergy in Convocation	69
Effects of its abolition	70
The High Churchmen of Charles II.'s time	71
Bishop Beveridge's statement of their views	72
His attitude towards the Roman Church	73
The Evangelical party	74
Discontent of Charles	76
Clarendon dismissed	77
Several Papists brought into the Council	78
Fall of Sheldon	79
Episcopacy restored in Scotland	80

	PAGE
Sharp appointed to the Archbishopric of St. Andrews	81
Power possessed by Sheldon	82
His violence	83
His princely generosity	83
His affability	84
His will	85
Pleasant exercise of his archiepiscopal authority	85
His gifts and benefactions	86
Lord Danby's attempt on behalf of the Duke of York	87
The Great Plague	87
Defoe's narrative	88

CHAPTER II.

THE POPISH PLOT.

Coleman, secretary to the Duchess of York	91
Denounced by Titus Oates	91
Burns his papers with one exception	91
Hopes and fears	92
The great fire attributed to the Papists	93
The year 1678, a new point of departure	94
The turn of the tide	95
The prejudice against the Roman Catholics	96
Sir Edmundsbury Godfrey	97
He states his forebodings to Burnet	98
His disappearance	98
Unsuccessful search for him	99
The body found	100
The funeral	100
Disgraceful conduct of Charles II.	101
Trials of the persons denounced by Oates and his confederates	102
Sancroft succeeds Sheldon	103
His early years	103
His friendship for young Bonest	104
His dutiful behaviour to his father	106
He leaves the University	107

	PAGE
Death of his father	107
His works	108
Obtains various preferments	109
Appointed to be Dean of St. Paul's, London	110
Ruinous condition of the Cathedral	110
Letter to Sir Christopher Wren	111
Sancroft's contributions	113
His appointment to the Primacy	113
Prosperous condition of the Church	114
His appointment unexpected	114
Probable explanation of it	115
His advocacy of the royal prerogative	115
Sancroft's attempt to convert the Duke of York	117
Failure of the attempt	118
Sancroft endeavours to augment small livings	119
Alarm of the Protestant part of the nation	121
William of Orange	122
The Church opposed to him	122
Importance of having her assistance	122
Correspondence between Sancroft and Dr. Covel	123
Attempt to exclude James from the succession	123
Sudden illness of Charles	124
Several bishops attend him	125
He receives the Sacrament from a Roman Catholic priest	125
Death of Charles	126

CHAPTER III.

JAMES II.

James proclaimed without resistance	127
Anxiety of the clergy and laity of the Church	128
Sancroft and some of the bishops present an address to James	128
He officiates at the Coronation	129
James causes Roman Catholic services to be performed at Whitehall	130
Prints and distributes the paper found in Charles' box	131
Monks and priests appear in their habits	131
General indignation and alarm	131

The clergy generally preach against Popery	132
Faults on both sides	133
Treatment of Nonconformists in the reign of James II.	135
Trial of Baxter before Jeffreys	136
Baxter convicted	140
Probable policy of Charles and James	141
Declaration of liberty of conscience	141
He promotes Roman Catholics	142
His relations with William Penn	143
Penn and Pennsylvania	144
Penn's letter to the Indians	145
James adopts Penn's views of toleration	147
But also listens to Roman Catholic advisers	148
Folly and obstinacy of James	149
Revives the Court of High Commission	151
Refusal of Sancroft to take part in its proceedings	152
Compton suspended	154
Sancroft disgraced	155
The Prince of Orange	156
Mary writes to Sancroft	157
James exasperates the prejudices of his subjects	158
Sprat, Cartwright, and Crewe	161
The declaration of liberty of conscience	162
Consternation of the Clergy	162
Their difficulties	163
Edward Fowler's courage	164
The bishops	165
Perplexity of Sancroft	166
His difficulties	166
His zeal for the doctrine of passive obedience	167
He writes to the bishops of his province	169
Six bishops obey his summons	171
Petition of the seven bishops	172
Six bishops present the petition to James II.	173
Anger of James	175
He shows symptoms of yielding	177

	PAGE
The petition is printed and sold in the streets of London	177
Action of the Nonconformists	178
Irritation of James	179
General refusal of the clergy to read the king's declaration	180
The seven bishops appear before the king and his Council	181
Sancroft refuses to criminate himself	182
He yields at length, and admits his handwriting under protest	183
The seven bishops are committed to the Tower by warrant	183
The public indignation	184
It is aggravated by other tyrannical acts	184
Especially by the treatment of the Fellows of Magdalen College, Oxford	185
Sancroft's Articles	193
His overtures to the Nonconformists	196
His schemes of comprehension	198
Uneasiness of Lord Chancellor Jeffreys	200
The king consults the bishops	208
The advice they give to the king	203
Critical position of the bishops	206
The Prince of Orange	207
Birth of a son to James	208
William conceals his designs	209
Delicacy and difficulty of Sancroft's position	211
Advice given to James by the bishops	212
Pusillanimous indecision of James	213
Rapid progress made by William	213
He enters the metropolis and takes possession of the throne	214
Sancroft retires to Lambeth	214
The position of Sancroft and the other Nonjurors	215

CHAPTER IV.

WILLIAM AND MARY.

Effects produced on the clergy by the Revolution	217
Proclamation of the new sovereigns	218
Sancroft refuses his blessing to Mary	219

	PAGE
He rebukes Wharton	219
William's forbearance towards the Nonjurors	220
Sympathy of many of the clergy with the Nonjurors	222
Fresh schemes of comprehension	222
William devolves on Mary the care of Church affairs	224
Selects Burnet and Tillotson	225
His confidence in Burnet	226
Tillotson designated by William to be Archbishop of Canterbury	227
His qualifications for the office of Archbishop	227
Is put forward to be prolocutor	229
The three Bills	229
The defeat of Tillotson	230
Address of the Convocation	233
Compton's dissatisfaction	234
The new oath of allegiance	236
Expulsion of the Nonjurors	238
Sherlock	239
Deprivation of Sancroft	240
Tillotson's magnanimity	242
His death	243
His reputation as a preacher	244
Tenison, Archbishop of Canterbury	245
Decisions of Chief Justice Holt	246
Illness and death of Queen Mary	247
Tenison's funeral sermon	248
Bishop Ken's severe reply	248
Unpopularity of William	253
Tenison's early history	254
Changes in the province of York	255
Archbishop Sharp	256
The crown patronage	257
The S.P.C.K. and the S.P.G.	257

CHAPTER V.

THE GOOD QUEEN ANNE.

	PAGE
Anne's accession	259
Her religious and political principles	259
Defoe	260
Tenison disgraced	261
Effects of this change	262
The Occasional Conformity Bill	262
Tenison's speech on the Bill	264
Queen Anne's bounty	265
Popularity of the Queen	267
Her intimacy with the Duchess of Marlborough	268
They quarrel	268
Abigail Hill	269
Henry Sacheverell	270
His impeachment	275
His trial	277
He is found guilty	278
The sentence	278
Riotous conduct of the Sacheverell mob	278
Sacheverell's progress	279
The excitement spreads through the kingdom	280
Triumph of the Church party	281
Sacheverell preaches before the Commons	283
The Schisms Bill	285
Proposed union of the Anglican and Prussian Churches	287

CHAPTER VI.

THE GEORGES.

The Test and Corporation Acts	290
Walpole's ejaculation	292
Suspicions of a plot	292
Atterbury arrested	293
He is examined	293

	PAGE
Bill of pains and penalties	293
Convocation suppressed	295
Neglect of education	297
Wesley	299
The Church affected by Wesleyanism	300
The Evangelical party	301
General spirit of persecution	302
Lord Mansfield's exceptional liberality	303
The Lord George Gordon riots	304
Lord Mansfield's courageous conduct	305
The riots suppressed	306
New position of the Church	307
Cobbett's history of the Reformation	309
The effects it produced	312
Archbishop Howley	313

CHAPTER VII.

THE OXFORD TRACTS.

The Canterbury party	317
The Oxford Tracts	319
Effects produced in the metropolis	321
The Court of Delegates	323
The tract No. 90	325
The Rev. W. G. Ward	327
Surplice riots	331
Dr. Hampden	333
Lord J. Russell's reply to the bishops	335
The election of Dr. Hampden to the see of Hereford	337
The confirmation of the election	338
The question once more raised before the Court of Queen's Bench	339
The case of Dr. Lee	340
The Gorham case	341
Induction of Mr. Gorham	345
Bishop Blomfield's Bill	346
The Papal aggression	348

	PAGE
The Durham letter	350
The Ecclesiastical Titles Bill	353
The popular feeling	355
Gradual development of Ritualism	355
Cardinal Wiseman	357
St. George's in the East	358
The Broad Church party	359
Position of the Evangelical party	362
Controversy between the Evangelicals and the Tractarians	364
Essays and reviews	366
Bishop Colenso	369
The Rev. Charles Voysey	372
Esthetic developments of Tractarianism	375
Ritualistic evolution	376
The Church Union and the Church Association	378
Five distinct parties in the Church	381
Maurice and Kingsley	383
Appropriation of pews	385
The free and open Church system	386
Mr. Herford	387
The Grammar Schools	389
The National Society	390
Bell and Lancaster	391
Dr. Kay	392
Dr. Hook	393
The Education Act	394
Tithes and Church Rates	395
Conclusion	396

HISTORY

OF THE

CHURCH OF ENGLAND.

CHAPTER I.

THE ACT OF UNIFORMITY.

THE object of this work is to endeavour to trace the sequence and concatenation of the ecclesiastical events through which this country has passed since the year 1660, and which have brought it and its Church into the position which they now occupy. We take our point of departure from the restoration of the Stuarts and the passing of the Act of Uniformity, which was the legislative expression of the ecclesiastical principles of the party that triumphed with Charles II. This celebrated Act was founded on a succession of statutes of a somewhat similar character, but more especially on one that had been passed in the reign of Edward VI., and another which was adopted in the reign of Elizabeth. The first of these enactments was entitled, "An Act for the Uniformity of Common Prayer and Service in the Church, and the Administration of the Sacraments." The second was styled, "An Act for the Uniformity of Common Prayer and Service in the Church, and Administration of the Sacraments." The chief object aimed at in these two Acts, as well as in the others above referred to, was to secure an entire uniformity of profession and practice throughout the realm. The multiplicity of the statutes by which these objects were sought to be attained show at once the importance that our forefathers attached to them, and the great difficulty they found in securing them. We shall find all their efforts to obtain doctrinal and practical agreement meeting with continual insuccess, and all their attempts to attain uniformity ending in an increasing and ever-divergent multiformity.

But although we take the Act of Uniformity as our point of departure, and endeavour to trace the changes which were brought about by the continual effort to enforce a compulsory conformity, yet our chief aim will be to follow out the course of the national religion as it has been exhibited in the national Church, which, at the time of the Restoration and throughout the two centuries which followed it, has probably been the body to which the majority have belonged—if not by active attachment to its doctrine and worship, at least by a tacit acquiescence in them. The religion which has not only been established in a nation by law, but which has been during two centuries accepted by the majority of its population, is perhaps the most essential characteristic of the nation in which it has flourished for so long a period. It is the foundation on which all else that distinguishes it is based. Its civilization, its science, its philosophy, its art, its industry,—all depend on its religion. But here we must make a very important distinction. The established religion of a country is one thing, the real religion of its inhabitants is quite another thing. By the latter, I mean the love, hope, faith, and reverence that characterize its inhabitants.

To write such a history as this in any country would be a work of the highest importance, but also of supreme difficulty, if not absolute impossibility; and therefore, without attempting to take a flight so ambitious, I propose to confine myself to the humble and less arduous task of endeavouring to trace the history of the national Church of this country, disentangling it, as far as it is possible to do so, on the one hand from the general history of England, and on the other hand from that of the various religious communities that have grown up in close contact with it, and which have so far modified its character and influenced its evolution that it is not possible to avoid occasionally touching on them. Even thus simplified, the work I have undertaken is full of difficulty, arising chiefly from the fact that the history of the Church has been so completely identified with the history of the State, and has been so trammelled and so vitiated by its secular associations, as sometimes to seem to be not so much the history of the country's religion as of its irreligion; and yet, in spite of the corrupting influences to which the English Church has been exposed, and the corruption it has suffered through that exposure, I submit that a Church that has stood its ground for so long a time in this country must be regarded, in its defects as well as in its excellences, in its vices as well as in its virtues, as representing roughly the religious character of the nation in which it has flourished. There is, perhaps, no instance in the history of the world in which the connection between Church and State has been so close as it has been in our own case. In no instance has any Church been so completely exposed to the action of the public opinion of the nation, exercised through its legitimate organs; and as we proceed with this history, we shall find that, throughout the whole of the period it is designed to cover, there has been, in spite of some occasional efforts and even some violent reluctances, a steady progress in the subjugation of the Church to the power and influence of the State.

There are probably, in the present day, few persons who are at all aware of the extent to which Nonconformity prevailed in the Church, or the length of time during which it continued to exist even after the passing of the Act of Uniformity, and the great secession which took place in consequence. South, in a sermon preached in Westminster Abbey after the revolution of 1688, thus describes the state of things which prevailed even then. He probably alludes to his own cathedral—that of Westminster, though the description he gives of it was doubtless applicable to many others:—

"In the same cathedral you shall see one prebendary

in a surplice, another in a long cloke, another in a short coat or jacket; and in the performance of the public service, some standing up at the Creed, the Gloria Patri, and the reading of the Gospel,—and others sitting, and perhaps laughing or winking upon their fellow-schismatics, in scoff of those who practice the decent orders of the Church, and from hence the mischief shall pass from the priest to the people, dividing them in irreconcilable parties and factions, so that some shall come to church when such an one preaches, and absent themselves when another does. 'I will not hear this formalist,' says one; and, 'I will not hear that schismatic' (with better reason), says another."

No doubt, the complaints thus uttered on one side were met by complaints equally loud on the other. The Presbyterians, who had been following the usages of the party to which they belonged, complained, and not always with moderation, when they saw the vestments which had disappeared with Laud reappearing with those who shared his beliefs, and hoped soon to regain the estates and the dignities from which they had been ousted at the commencement of the civil war. It was therefore absolutely necessary that the Government of the Restoration should interfere between the contending parties, and endeavour to restore peace to a Church which was so sadly divided; and this the Government endeavoured to effect, first by the Savoy Conference, and then by the Uniformity Bill.

There was a time, anterior to the Reformation, when the society, which now goes by the name of the Established Church, was actually, and as a matter of fact, as it still is in legal fiction, composed of the whole body of the English people—a time when all accepted its teachings and conformed to its Liturgy. There might, it is true, even in those ages, have been now and then an eccentric exception in the person of some disregarded protester, who ventured to call in question what the Church had hitherto received and taught.

Such cases were very rare, and the people generally were so incapable of comprehending the arguments employed, that their influence was almost inappreciable, and may be disregarded by the historian. The rising of Wycliffe into prominence marks the time when doubts and suspicions began to be entertained by considerable numbers of persons, and when doctrines and practices hitherto received with implicit faith began, for the first time in the history of the Church, to be called in question. In consequence of this tendency to doubt and inquire, the national mind in this country was set astir, criticisms, often of a hostile character, were ventured, and institutions which, up to this time, had been regarded as too sacred to be subjected to any kind of examination, were now put on their defence, and so a public opinion was gradually formed which enabled the statesmen of that day to effect and maintain a reformation which, a short time before, would have been repelled with unanimity, and almost with horror.

But the various Acts of Uniformity to which we have referred, if they had no other effect, at least showed how anxious the nation and its rulers were not to carry their innovations beyond a certain point, and to maintain a tolerably exact uniformity; and proved how difficult it was to restrain the waters of controversy when they were once let loose. The men who occupied posts of authority soon found how great was the difficulty, when attempts were made, to maintain an enforced conformity and to keep the great religious revolution over which they were presiding from being carried beyond a certain point. Each Act of Uniformity was, in fact, the taking up of a new ground on the part of those who introduced it, and a tacit admission of the untenability of that which they had occupied before.

An opinion very generally prevails that the English Church may be regarded as dating its existence from the Reformation, as if the ancient Catholic Church of this country had then been legislatively abolished, and a new and reformed Church substituted for it. This, however, is clearly a mistake. The Reformation no doubt altered very considerably the character of the Anglican Church, but did not destroy it. New regulations were made, new duties were imposed—both on the clergy and the laity—new liberties were conferred on both. The professions of faith required of both were considerably modified.

But these changes, while they unquestionably altered the character of the Church, did not affect her existence. The men who had filled the archbishoprics, bishoprics, and other Church offices, were permitted to retain their preferments, provided that they were willing to submit to the altered conditions under which all Church preferments were henceforward to be held. It would be uncandid to deny that the changes to which we have referred were, in many instances, imposed on the reluctant clergy by dint of a very strong pressure from without, but the forms of ecclesiastical independence were scrupulously observed, and care was taken to obtain for them the formal sanction of the Convocation of the province of Canterbury, and, at least, the tacit acquiescence of the Convocation of York. Nothing, therefore, is more certain than the fact that the post-Reformation Church was no new Church, but simply a modified continuation of the pre-Reformation Church. The following statement of the case, by Henry Melvill, who was the leader of the Evangelical party in the earlier part of the present century, is as historically true as it is poetically beautiful :—

"We do not deny," says this able and popular divine, "and this we must state clearly before entering on the errors of Rome, that the Roman Catholic Church is a true and apostolic Church—her bishops and priests deriving their authority in an unbroken line from Christ and His apostles. Accordingly, if a Roman Catholic priest renounce what we count the errors of popery, our Church immediately receives him as one of her ministers, requiring no fresh ordination before she will allow him to officiate at her altars, though she grants not the like privilege to other claimants of the ministerial office. If his ordination be not in every sense valid, neither is our own; for if we have derived ours from the apostles, it has been through the channel of the Roman Catholic Church; so that to deny the transmission of authority in the popish priesthood since the Reformation, would be to deny it before, and thus should we be left without any ordination which could be traced back to the apostles. Hence, there is no question that, on the principles of an Episcopal Church, the Roman Catholic is a true branch of Christ's Church, however grievously corrupted and fearfully deformed. It is a true Church, inasmuch as its ministers have been duly invested with authority to preach the Word and dispense the sacraments; it is a true Church, moreover, inasmuch as it has never ceased to 'hold the Head, which is Christ,' and to acknowledge the fundamental truth of our religion, that Jesus, God as well as man, died as a propitiation for the sins of the world.

"And all this," he proceeds to say, "was distinctly recognized by the reformers of the English Church, whatever it may have been by those of other countries. They made no alteration in the constitution of the Church; they saw in the Roman Catholic Church the true foundation and framework of a Church, but saw also that on this foundation had been laid, and into this framework had been woven, many gross errors which were calculated to destroy the souls of its members. And it was to the work of removing these errors that they strenuously gave themselves — not wishing to meddle with the foundation, or destroy the framework; but simply to take away those human inventions and superstitious observances, beneath which genuine Christianity was almost hidden, or rather, almost buried. And so blessed were they by God, with singular discretion, as well as courage, that they achieved the noble result of a Church holding all that is apostolic in doctrine, without letting go one jot of what is apostolic in government. They achieved the result, the only result at which as reformers they could lawfully aim, of making the Church, both in creed and in discipline, what the Church had been in primitive times; removing from it whatsoever had not the sanction of Scripture and antiquity, and retaining whatever had. And thus there spread from their labours what might literally be called a reformed Church—not a new Church, as is more strictly the name of many of those which bear the title of reformed—but a reformed Church, the old, the original Church, stripped of those incrustations, and freed from those pollutions which fastened upon it during a long night of ignorance.

"Theirs was the work of renovating an ancient cathedral, majestic even in decay, presenting the traces of noble architecture, though in ruins on this side, and choked with rubbish on that. They did not attempt to batter down the walls, and plow up the foundations of the venerable edifice, and then to erect on the site a wholly modern structure. They were better taught and better directed. They removed, with the greatest carefulness and diligence, the coating from the beautiful pillars, which men had daubed with 'untempered mortar;' and they swept away buttresses which did but disfigure without sustaining the building; and, above all, they opened the windows, which ignorance, or superstition, had blocked up; and then the rich light of heaven came streaming down the aisles, and men flocked to its courts to worship the one God through the one Mediator, Christ. And, therefore, we would again tell you, they were the reformers, and nothing more than the reformers, of the Church. You sometimes hear or read of the fathers of the English Church, the name being given to the reformers. But the name is most falsely applied. The fathers of the English Church are the apostles, and those apostolic men who lived in the early days of Christianity, and handed down to us what was held as truth, when there were the best means of ascertaining and defining it. We acknowledge no modern fathers; it were to acknowledge a modern birth. We claim to be the ancient Church; we fasten on the Roman Catholic the being the modern—the modern, not in constitution, for therein we have the same date, and that date apostolic; but the modern in a thousand innovations on genuine Christianity—Christianity as preached by Christ and Paul—Christianity as exhibited by the writers of the first four centuries of the Church."

I confidently hope that the reader will pardon me for placing before his eyes this long but animated delineation of the position of the Anglican Church in regard to its reformation. Without accepting all its assertions, I think I may present it as exhibiting the view taken of the Reformation by the party of which Melvill was the recognized leader, and of whose opinions he was, by very far, the ablest exponent. The passage shows, in a very striking manner, that the post-Reformation Church was simply a continuation of the Church which had existed before the changes which were made—changes affecting indeed its character, but in nowise compromising its existence.

But the same cannot be said with regard to another period in the history of the Anglican communion. Then there was a distinct solution of continuity, which admits of no denial. At the period of the great rebellion, the State not only separated itself from the Episcopal Church, but violently suppressed it—substituting for it a Presbyterian Church, forbidding, under severe penalties, the use of its Liturgy, and holding it up to the scorn and hatred of the people.

It is not, then, either from Christ and His apostles, nor yet from the period of the Reformation, that we must date the foundation of the present Established Church of England. If we would seek out its origin, we must come down to a much later period in the history of our country, reckoning from the time when the Stuart dynasty was restored in the person of Charles II., and the legislature adopted that last great Act of Uniformity, by which she recalled into renewed existence the Church she had previously abolished.

The English people, when they called Charles II. to occupy the throne, knew little or nothing of the new monarch, but hoped much from him. Had they been aware of his real character they would probably have given him a much less enthusiastic reception. For his vices were not only odious in themselves, but were also of a peculiarly un-English character and complexion. He was a trifler and an idler, destitute of all political and religious principle. In his serious moments he was a Roman Catholic; in his seasons of recreation, in which the greater part of his time was spent, destitute of all religion, a scoffer and a blasphemer. Secretly sold to the French monarch, yet not keeping the bargain he had made with him. Zealous for nothing, yet pretending an earnest zeal for Protestantism whenever he wanted to extract money from the pockets of his subjects. For the present, however, the victorious cavaliers would see nothing but the bright side of the "Merry Monarch." They greatly exaggerated his good qualities. They threw a veil over his vices, and hoped that as he grew older he would conceal or discard them. On the other hand, they magnified his geniality, his affability, his readiness to enter into conversation with all persons who approached him, if only they did not bore him or require him to attend to any serious business. These were qualities which, lying as they did on the surface and being visible to all men, made him popular with those of his subjects who were thrown into his company.

The moment that it became evident that a restoration of the Stuarts in the person of Charles was imminent, the representatives of the two great religious parties into which the nation was then divided, naturally sought to gain the patronage and protection of the returning monarch. The religious communion that was at the time of the Restoration in possession of almost every benefice in England, and was virtually by law established, was the Presbyterian. Its ministers were not only in possession, but most of them had all along been favourable to the exiled family. They therefore lost no time in urging their claims and presenting their congratulations to their returning sovereign, sending some of their ablest preachers to Breda, where Charles then resided, and where he was waiting for an opportunity to pass into England, to offer him their support, and to stipulate in return for his favour and protection.

Charles, who at that time was not in a position to reject their assistance, received them with much courtesy, making them some general promises which satisfied them for the present, and led them to entertain themselves, and to communicate to those who had sent them, the pleasing hope that they would be allowed to retain their benefices, and that the ecclesiastical arrangements then established would not be seriously interfered with.

But while the Presbyterians, who were in possession, were obtaining from the king vague promises of support and assistance, and were being captivated by his affability and politeness, the Episcopalians who had been turned out of the benefices now in possession of the Presbyterians were no less active in pressing their claims, and could confidently reckon on the support and assistance of the inner circle of courtiers by whose advice Charles was for the most part guided, as well as by the great body of the people, and especially of the victorious cavaliers, who had all along been suffering and contending for the altar as well as for the throne. Their feelings were at this moment completely in unison with those of the great body of the nation, who were as much alienated from Presbyterianism as they were now friendly to the prelacy which, but a short time since, they had so violently and, as then appeared, so unanimously rejected.

In truth, an enormous change had come over the country since the time when the tyranny of Laud and the Star Chamber had rendered the Church odious to the nation. The Presbyterian establishment, which had taken such deep root in Scotland, had never been very congenial to the feelings of the great majority of Englishmen, and had now become intensely unpopular. Many causes had contributed to bring about this great change. Perhaps that which was the most decisive of all was their stern repression of all kinds of amusements, not only of those that were sinful and degrading, but also of those that were innocent or even beneficial, and consequently worthy of encouragement. All theatrical performances, all games, everything calculated to raise a good hearty laugh, was proscribed by the dominant sect as unbefitting the character of one who was looking forward to the speedy return of the Saviour to judge the world in righteousness. After having bitterly denounced the tyranny which they had suffered during the reign of Charles I., they had themselves imitated and even surpassed the intolerance of which they had so loudly complained. They had forbidden the use of the Book of Common Prayer, not only in public, not only in the chamber in which two or three might gather together to offer up their supplications to the throne of grace, but even for the private and individual perusal of those who had been accustomed to use that manual of devotion throughout their lives.

Another cause which had powerfully contributed to discredit and depopularize the ministers of the Commonwealth, was their long extemporaneous prayers and sermons. In our day the really extemporaneous prayer or sermon is a thing unknown. The so-called extemporaneous preacher of modern times meditates on the passage of Scripture which he proposes to expound to his hearers, he examines it by the aid of the best lights he is able to throw on it, he consults commentators. He divides and subdivides it under different heads, and arranges it in such a manner that one topic he handles shall naturally follow on that which had gone before it. Not so the Presbyterian preacher of the time of the Commonwealth. Taught to believe that all preparation showed a sinful want of faith in the aid of Christ, regarding the instructions given by the Saviour to His disciples, with reference to the conduct they were to pursue when brought before heathen magistrates, as directions which they were bound to obey in the delivery of their religious discourses, they were careful not to consider beforehand what they should say or what they should speak, but believed themselves bound to trust to the inspiration of the moment and to the fulfilment of the promise that God would give them a mouth and wisdom that none of their adversaries should be able to gainsay or resist. They acted accordingly. They regarded any sort of preparation for their pulpit addresses as involving a sinful want of faith on the part of those who had recourse to such carnal aids. Their prayers and their discourses were therefore literally delivered *ex tempore;* that is to say, were strictly the outcome of the inspiration of the moment in which they were uttered.

The consequences were such as might naturally be expected. It was true that during the first fervours of the puritanical victory, which the conquering party generally ascribed to the direct intervention of God on their behalf—when the history of the children of Israel, and the destruction of Agag and the Amalekites and the other nations that were driven out of Palestine by the victorious tribes, were brought forward continually to illustrate the battles in which Cromwell and his troops were engaged,—when these utterances of the preacher met with a ready response in the minds of his hearers, which imparted a certain interest and unction to the baldest commonplace or the most unredeemed nonsense, such discourses might be tolerated and even approved.

But when the first fervours of victorious Puritanism had burnt themselves out; when discourses and prayers, composed without any sort of forethought, were carried on Sunday after Sunday and for hour after hour, filled, as under such circumstances they unavoidably must have been, with endless repetitions and drivelling commonplace; then it became impossible for any faith, however strong, or any illusion, however complete, to hide the real character of these utterances, or to lead the hearers of them to believe that the discourses which so sorely tried their patience, and which were evidently so little calculated to promote the edification of those who believed it to be a religious duty to listen to them, were dictated by the immediate inspiration of the Holy Spirit, especially when the discourses and prayers delivered under the circumstances we have endeavoured to describe endured for many hours, and sometimes, as on the occasion of their frequent fasts, for whole days together. Under such circumstances, it was impossible even for a Howe, a Baxter, an Owen, or a Calamy to keep alive the attention and interest of their hearers.

But when extemporaneous effusions thus prolonged were poured forth by men less highly gifted, and even by men who were in mind and spirit below mediocrity, it is easy to conceive that South, using that style of insolent scurrility of which he was so consummate a master, did not very much exaggerate when he said, with regard to the prayers and sermons that were framed and delivered under such circumstances, that they were "always notable for two things—length and tautology; two whole hours for one prayer at a fast used to be reckoned but a moderate dose."

Nor will it surprise the reader who knows anything of human nature, to find an unfriendly critic, who had probably been obliged to listen to a good many such sermons, and who still retained a vivid impression of what as an unwilling auditor he had thus suffered, describing them as being "full of incoherence, confusion, endless repetitions, and insufferable nonsense that never failed to hold out even with the utmost prolixity, so that in all their long fasts from first to last, from seven in the morning to seven in the evening (which was their measure), the pulpit was always the emptiest thing in the church," and that he "never knew such a fast kept by them but their hearers had cause to begin a thanksgiving as soon as they had done." Nor shall we be astonished to find the same keen observer of human nature describing the matter of these prayers as being "full of ramble and inconsequence, and in every respect very like the language of a dream;" nor shall we be altogether incredulous when we find the same writer asserting that such was the nature of the prayers so offered up, "that could any one truly and exactly write them out, it would be the shrewdest and most effectual way of writing against them."

Thus by their stern opposition to all those enjoyments and amusements that render life more endurable; by their denunciations, not only of those that were blameworthy, as many of the entertainments of that time unquestionably were, but also of those that were quite harmless; by the severity with which they treated the innocent foibles of their parishioners in private, and by the manner in which they carried out their public religious exercises, the Puritan ministers had gradually alienated the affections and lost their hold on the consciences of their parishioners, and brought them to such a pass that men were ready to hail the triumphant return of the Prayer Book, which only a few years before they had cast off with every expression of disgust and disdain. Taking advantage of the great change which had thus taken place in the public feeling and opinion of the laity, the Episcopalian clergy had already anticipated the action of the Parliament, and, without waiting for any steps to be taken to bring about the restoration of the Stuarts, they had returned to the use of their beloved and proscribed Liturgy, now rendered dearer than ever to them on account of the persecution to which its adherents had been lately exposed.

At the moment of the king's entrance into his palace at Whitehall his triumph was, as it were, consummated by the performance of a solemn service of thanksgiving in honour of the occasion, in which several of the bishops took part. The Presbyterians, meanwhile, saw clearly in what direction the tide of popular feeling was running, and that, to borrow the expression made use of by Mr. (afterwards Archbishop) Sharpe, the people were "doting on the old service," that the king not only used it himself, but also recommended the use of it to others, saying that he would "take it well from those who used it in their churches," leading them still to hope that they would obtain a compromise, which would at all events release them from the obligation to conform to those ceremonies of the Anglican Church to which they entertained a strong objection—the use of the surplice, which they had all along denounced as a rag of popery, the sign of the cross in baptism, the use of the ring in the Marriage Service, and the kneeling at the reception of the sacrament of the Lord's Supper.

Most of the Presbyterian ministers were prepared to accept these concessions, and others of minor importance, and, in case they should be made, to promise that they would not only conform themselves, but that they would do their best to reconcile their people to the forms contained in the Book of Common Prayer, and would recommend it as containing much piety and devotion, and being such as might lawfully be used.

It is alleged, however, that, instead of keeping these promises, they secretly exhorted the ministers of their own persuasion to persist in the use of the Presbyterian Directory. Most of these were prepared to accept a form of worship which had now come to be identified, in the minds of the generality of the nation, with loyalty to the sovereign, and a hearty recognition of the supposed virtues of him who was now generally regarded as "The Royal Martyr," and who enjoyed a kind of worship hardly inferior to that paid to Christ Himself, his picture being, in many instances, set up in the churches, almost as if it had been an object of adoration.*

Meanwhile, great efforts had been made to win over some of the leading Presbyterians, and to induce them to conform to the Liturgy of the Anglican Church.

---

* Pepys writes in his Diary (Lord's day, October 2, 1664), "Walked with my boy through the city, putting in several churches, among others, at Bishopsgate, and there saw the picture [1] usually put before the king's book put up in the church, but very ill painted, though it were a pretty piece to set up in a church."

---

[1] In a note on the word "picture," the editor of Pepys' Diary adds, "Of Charles I.; still to be seen in several churches, and engraved before the Εἰκὼν βασιλική. See *Notes and Queries*, vol. i. p. 137."

Reynolds and Baxter both had bishoprics offered to them, which the former accepted, and the latter refused. Baxter was also appointed to be one of the king's chaplains, and in that capacity preached before his Majesty, and both he and Reynolds took very leading parts in the Savoy Conference, of which we shall presently have occasion to speak more at large, strongly arguing in favour of an altered Liturgy and a modified episcopacy. Baxter was also licensed by Sheldon, then Bishop of London, to preach in that diocese, on condition that he would abstain from saying anything contrary to the doctrine and discipline of the Anglican Church.

The restoration of that Church, as nearly as circumstances would permit, to the position it had occupied before the death of Laud, was imperiously demanded by the great majority of the nation, and was also quite in accordance with the feelings and wishes of those who at the moment had the direction of the ecclesiastical affairs of the kingdom in virtue of the offices they held. They were the king himself, the Lord Chancellor Clarendon, and Sheldon, Bishop of London, who also at that time discharged the duties which Juxon, the Archbishop of Canterbury, was disabled from performing by a dangerous and painful disease.

To the king there belonged an undefined supremacy in regard to matters ecclesiastical, which might be used as an instrument of tyranny, or an encouragement to religion, according to the character and disposition of the person by whom it was wielded, or the circumstances of the times in which it was exerted. In Charles, it found a prince who by policy and disposition was disposed to make a moderate and kindly use of it, but who through indolence was led to yield to the violent counsels and angry passions of the party which had brought him back, and which conceived that it had a right, in return for its zealous services, to dictate the civil and religious polity of the restored monarch.

Then, again, there was the authority of the primate, who was at that time prevented from exercising it by illness and infirmity, but whose place was zealously supplied by the Bishop of London. His authority was, indeed, very limited, but derived an adventitious force from the veneration with which the office was surrounded, from its ancient associations, and the opinions that were held with regard to the powers that belonged to it.

Men had not at that time, as they have in our day, called those powers into question, or subjected them to the test of legal tribunals. And so the man who virtually or actually filled the office of primate possessed a degree of influence which, though it was small indeed in comparison with that which belonged to the king, and almost nullified when opposed to the public opinion of the nation, became an engine of no little power when Lambeth was regarded as the mouthpiece of the clergy, and became the organ whence opinions and aspirations were sounded forth from ten thousand pulpits. The clergy of the Church of England are a mighty but a scattered host. It is very seldom that they can be induced to work together for any common object, but whenever they can be brought under the guidance of one common head, their influence is nearly irresistible. Generally, however, at the period of the Restoration, and for a long time after, the parochial clergy were in full accord with their rulers in Church and State, and it was the common boast of bishops and clergy that the English Church was the most loyal Church in the whole world. As for the primate, owing as he did the position he enjoyed to the favour of his sovereign, he was bound in honour and gratitude, as well as by a sentiment of loyalty, to give all the support he could to the patron by whom he had been raised to the primacy.

Generally, therefore, the sovereign and the archbishop were in hearty accord. Their interests and sympathies lay, for the most part, in the same direction; but we shall see them occasionally in serious disagreement, and even in open opposition, and when that came to be the case, the issue of the struggle that ensued between these two centres of influence was sometimes doubtful. Of this, however, there was no danger and no symptom at the period of the Restoration, when, after the Church had been shaken to pieces, and for a season annihilated, it came to be a very serious question whether it should be reconstructed on the old basis of an almost despotic episcopacy, or, as the Presbyterian clergy generally desired, on the basis of an episcopate in which the bishops should be counselled, and, to some extent, even controlled, by a portion of the presbyters of their dioceses.

The consequence was, that at the time of the Restoration, and for a considerable time after it had been effected, the primate occupied a position of great and extraordinary importance, being almost necessarily called on to regulate a multitude of details which he alone could well manage, and especially under an indolent prince like Charles, who was only too glad to escape from attention to the ecclesiastical or secular duties of his office, in order to enjoy the company of his courtiers and mistresses, and to devolve his powers and responsibilities on whoever offered, or was called on by the nature of his office, to undertake them. And the person on whom he was naturally led to devolve his ecclesiastical authority was the man who filled the place or discharged the duties of primate. It was through the intermediation of the primate, or his representative, that the relations between Church and State were maintained.

He was a sort of perpetual minister of ecclesiastical affairs, whose advice the king was almost bound to seek whenever important ecclesiastical questions were brought under his attention, but most especially at a time when the relations between Church and State were being renewed after a long discontinuity, when the Crown had not only to administer the affairs of the Church as in ordinary times, but to superintend its reconstruction under the very extraordinary and exceptional circumstances in which the Restoration had placed her. For these reasons the choice of a successor to Laud in the primacy, as it was the first in order of time, so, too, it was chief in order of importance among the many questions with which, at his accession to the throne, the restored monarch found himself forced to deal.

On this point, however, there was fortunately no room for doubt or hesitation. Among the ecclesiastics who had survived the Great Rebellion was the man from whose hands the Royal Martyr had received his last sacrament; who had filled the office of Bishop of London, next in real importance to the archbishopric; who had enjoyed the esteem of the unfortunate monarch; who had attended him on the scaffold, and had received his latest confidences.

Naturally, he was the man designated by the unanimous voice of the triumphant cavaliers as having the strongest claim to be raised to the primacy; and when we consider the mildness of Juxon's character, and the moderation of his views, we shall probably conclude that it would have been a fortunate circumstance for the Church and the country if he could not only have occupied the office of primate, but also have discharged the duties that belonged to it, and especially that of guiding the destinies of the Church.

But at the time of the Restoration, he was in the seventy-eighth year of his age, and was suffering, without the smallest hope of alleviation, from a disease which incapacitated him from discharging even the routine duties of the primacy, and impaired the vigour of his mind. It is true that his translation from the see of London to that of Canterbury was a transference from a post of considerable labour to a situation of comparative ease. But even the lighter duties of his new station were too heavy for him. However, Sheldon, who had succeeded him in the see of London, was in the full vigour of his constitution, and readily undertook the work which Juxon's age and infirmities disabled him from discharging. Besides, he had claims on Charles, which probably in that monarch's estimation were superior even to those of Juxon; for he had not only aided the exiled monarch very liberally from his own private resources, but had also raised and remitted to him considerable sums of money, which had been contributed, at his solicitation, by several of the king's friends. The consequence was that, with the single exception of the chancellor, the Earl of Clarendon, Sheldon was, during the earlier years of the reign of Charles II., his trusted adviser in political matters, and in matters ecclesiastical his influence was even greater than that of the chancellor himself. At all events, he had the undisputed control of a great number of details, with which neither Charles nor Clarendon had time or inclination to deal.

Thus it came to pass that throughout one of the most important crises in the history of this Church and nation, the powers of the primacy were either virtually or actually wielded, with scarcely any limitation or control, by a man "to whose merits and memory," according to the opinion of honest Izaak Walton, "posterity—the clergy especially—ought to pay reverence." I am therefore acting on this opinion of the worthy fisherman, by endeavouring to give a short but truthful sketch of the biography of the man who, at the Restoration and for many years after, exerted a most powerful influence over the constitution, the doctrines, and the historical evolution of the Anglican Church.

Gilbert Sheldon was the descendant of an ancient family, which, however, had fallen into such decay that his father, Roger Sheldon, had been obliged to become a servant in the family of Gilbert, Earl of Shrewsbury. In this station he seems to have acquired the respect of his master's family, for the little Gilbert was brought to the baptismal font by two godfathers of whom he might justly be proud—Gilbert, his father's master, known as "The Great Earl of Shrewsbury," from whom he derived his Christian name; and Robert Sanderson, of Gilthwaite Hall, in the town of Rotherham, father of the celebrated Bishop Sanderson. The child thus honoured was born in the hamlet of Stanton, situated in the parish of Ellaston and the county of Stafford, in the year of our Lord 1598. The name of Sheldon has altogether disappeared from the neighbourhood, but the house in which his parents resided was long after his death shown to visitors; and the room in which he first saw the light contained a wooden tablet, bearing the following inscription:—

> "Sheldonus ille præsulum primus pater
> Has inter ortus aspicit lucem Lares
> O tu beata Stantonis villæ casa
> Cui cuncta possunt invidere marmora."

Towards the end of 1613, Sheldon was entered as a

member of Trinity College, Oxford. In 1617 he took the degree of Bachelor of Arts, that of Master in 1620, and in 1622 was elected a Fellow of All Souls' College, and ordained a deacon. Soon after he became chaplain to Lord Keeper Coventry, by whom, after some experience of his capacity, he was recommended to Charles I. as being well versed in political affairs.

After this he mounted, through a rapid series of preferments, up to the deanery of Westminster and the mastership of the Savoy Hospital. From these posts he was ejected, and his place at the Savoy was occupied by a Puritan divine, who died during the Protectorate. Sheldon then took possession of the mastership without opposition, and continued to hold it till his appointment to the archbishopric. He and Dr. Hammond together attended Charles I., while he was a prisoner in Holmby Castle, as his chaplains, and there celebrated the services of the Anglican Church without hindrance. Like too many others, he entered the civil wars a pious, God-fearing man; but came out of them a profane and debauched cavalier, fired with a strong desire to avenge on the defeated Puritans the injuries which they had inflicted on himself and his friends. Much has been made by Sheldon's apologists of a sermon that he preached before Charles on his arrival at Whitehall, on charity and the forgiveness of injuries, but I suspect that the subject of his discourse had been dictated to him by Charles and Clarendon, at a time when it was still thought necessary to endeavour to propitiate the Presbyterians, and to obtain their support to the new settlement.

But whatever his motives may have been, he took a very early opportunity of displaying his utter disregard of the Christian graces and virtues which he had inculcated in this discourse. His real dispositions were speedily manifested on many occasions, but especially at the celebrated Savoy Conference—so called because it was held in the lodge which he occupied in the Savoy Hospital, as master of that institution. This celebrated meeting raised high hopes, which, in the event, were doomed to meet with bitter disappointment, chiefly through Sheldon's interposition.

There is no sort of doubt that Charles and his chancellor, Clarendon, had held out to the Presbyterian divines who waited on them at Breda just before the Restoration, intimations that almost amounted to promises, that they would not only be tolerated, but that changes would be made in the doctrine and discipline of the English Church which would enable them, without violence to their consciences, to retain the benefices they had held during the Protectorate. I see no reason for supposing that Charles and his adviser were insincere, or that they had any intention of evading the promises they had made or disappointing the expectations they had raised. Charles hated Presbyterianism, and was wont to sneer at it as being a religion that was not fit for a gentleman. He had not forgotten the treatment he had received in Scotland while nominally the king, but really the prisoner, of the people of that country. He was heartily sick of the long sermons which the divines of the Presbyterian Church had inflicted on him, and which were not at all sparing in strictures on his conduct. But notwithstanding his detestation of Presbyterianism, he felt that he could not dispense with the assistance of Presbyterians—first, to replace him and then to maintain him on his throne, and to forward the design he secretly cherished of obtaining toleration for the Papists by the assistance of the other denominations of Nonconformists, to whom he proposed to extend the same toleration. But he was too indolent and too careless to give himself much trouble about redeeming his promises or keeping faith with his Nonconforming subjects.

Charles would probably have succeeded in his project of a general toleration, had he not found that the Presbyterians themselves would rather bear the penalties that they endured, than accept a toleration which was to be shared by the Papists. On the other hand, the Independents, under the lead of a minister named Nye, contended for those principles of religious liberty which are now almost universally accepted in this country. As the matter is of the highest importance to the proper understanding of the events of this time, I place the narrative of these important events before the reader in the words of Baxter himself. After referring to the occurrences of St. Bartholomew's Day, which we shall hereafter have to relate, he thus proceeds—

"When I was absent, resolving to meddle with such businesses no more, Mr. Calamy, and the other ministers of London who had acquaintances at court, were put in hope that the king would grant them, by way of indulgence, that which was formerly denied them; and that, before the Act was passed, it might be provided that the king should have power to dispense with such as deserved well of him in his restoration, on whom he pleased; but all was frustrated.

"After this, they were told that the king had power himself to dispense in such cases, as he did with the Dutch and French Churches, and some kind of petition they drew up to offer to the king; but when they had done it, they were so far from procuring their desires, that there fled abroad grievous threatenings against them, that they should incur a *præmunire* for such a bold attempt. When they were drawn to it at first they did it with much hesitancy, and they worded it so cautiously, that it extended not to Papists.

"Some of the Independents presumed to say that the reason why all our addresses for liberty had not succeeded, was because we did not extend it to the Papists; that, for their parts, they saw no reason why the Papists should not have liberty of worship as well as others; and that it was better for them to have it, than for all of us to go without it. But the Presbyterians still answered that the king himself might do what he pleased; and if his wisdom thought meet to give liberty to the Papists, let the Papists petition for it as we did for ours; but if it were expected that we should be forced to become petitioners for liberty to popery we should never do it, whatever be the issue; nor should it be said to be our work.

"On the 26th of December, 1662, the king sent forth

a declaration, expressing his purpose to grant some indulgence or liberty in religion, with other matters, not excluding the Papists, many of whom had deserved so well of him. When this came out, the ejected ministers began to think more confidently of some indulgence to themselves. Mr. Nye also, and some others of the Independents, were encouraged to go to the king, and, when they came back, told us that it was now resolved to give them liberty. On the 2nd of January, Mr. Nye came to me, to treat about our owning the king's declaration, by returning him thanks for it; when I perceived that it was designed that we must be the desirers or procurers of it; but I told him my resolution to meddle no more in such matters, having incurred already so much hatred and displeasure in endeavouring unity. The rest of the Presbyterian ministers also had enough of it, and resolved that they would not meddle; so that Mr. Nye and his brethren thought that it was partly owing to us that they missed the intended liberty. *But all were averse to have anything to do with the indulgence or toleration of Papists, thinking it, at least, unfit for them.*"

There was, no doubt, great reason to fear that Charles would have made an unfair and improper use of the dispensing power which the Independents were willing to grant to him, but which the Presbyterians steadfastly refused, because they would not accept toleration for themselves on the condition that the Papists were to share it with them. And they had some reason for the jealousy they displayed. They saw how persecuting the Roman Church was on the continent; they knew that there was, in this country, a small, but very influential, body of men, who aimed at obtaining for her not toleration only, but predominance; they knew that they enjoyed the favour of their own sovereign, and were in secret and constant communication with the King of France; they did not know altogether, but they partly knew, that not only their own monarch, but several members of both Houses of Parliament, sitting both on what we should call the ministerial, and also on the opposition benches, were the stipendiaries of the King of France, and were prepared to a certain extent to second his designs, and to vote in accordance with the directions given them by his ambassadors.

They probably also knew that some of the most lovely and accomplished ladies of the French court had been sent to promote here the influence and policy of the French monarch. These things were carefully concealed, but, nevertheless, something of what was going on unavoidably transpired. The Papists could not altogether hide their schemes and their hopes; indeed, they sometimes boastfully exaggerated their designs. Under these circumstances, the proposal to grant indulgence to Nonconformists in general had no chance of success. Opposed by the Churchmen, who objected to all toleration except for themselves; opposed by the Parliament, which was not only predominantly cavalier, but was also jealous of a dispensing power, over the exercise of which the legislature would possess no effective control; opposed by the Presbyterians, who would rather suffer persecution themselves than extend toleration to the Catholics, and who had not yet learnt that equal justice to all alike is the best security against the undue and improper ascendancy of any sect or party; opposed by the great majority of the nation, and of its representatives in Parliament; and supported only by a few Catholics and Independents, who were everywhere spoken against, the projected toleration at this time fell to the ground, and a man of greater firmness than Charles possessed might have been excused for yielding to the confederation that was banded against him. Taken up again by a monarch of a temper less yielding than was that of Charles, it brought speedy ruin on him and on his dynasty.

There is, then, every reason to believe that Charles really wished to keep faith with the Presbyterians, if he could have done it without trouble or inconvenience; but his languid desire to help them was counteracted by the opposition of men who were keenly resolute and deeply in earnest—men who were bent on defeating the objects that he had in view; and, therefore, while he, in his careless and indifferent way desired a general toleration, he found himself borne along by the torrent which ran violently in favour of the restoration of the Episcopal Church to the position it occupied at the time when Laud was in the full exercise of his primatial power, without the slightest attempt or desire to win over, to conciliate, or even to compensate the large number of Presbyterian ministers who had been placed in those benefices which had once belonged to the Anglican Church. Each religious party, in its turn victorious, sought to secure its position by the destruction of the rival party.

Very different in character from Charles was his chief adviser, Lord Chancellor Clarendon. He had all along been a warm and decided partisan of the Church of England. He was not only a Churchman, but a High Churchman, deeply imbued with the doctrine of apostolical succession, and with all the other doctrines which are the corollaries of that fundamental proposition, and were the favourite and distinguishing tenets of the High Churchmen of his period. He was strongly attached to the liturgy, and tenaciously adhered to the state of things that prevailed in England before the commencement of the troubles which had driven him into his long exile. Still there were many concessions which High Churchmen, such as he was, might, without any sacrifice of principle, have made to the Presbyterians, and which they, on the other hand, would have accepted with gratitude, if Clarendon had not been overruled by the violence of a party actuated by feelings much stronger than those that animated him, and fully determined to force the Presbyterians out of the positions which they occupied in the Church, cost what it might, without mercy or remorse.

The leader of this extreme party was Sheldon, who was the concentrated embodiment of the feelings, hopes, and alarms of the episcopal bench and of the cavaliers generally. He was not so much a High Churchman as an ecclesiastical Conservative, opposed to all change, regarding the Book of Common Prayer and the other formularies of the Church with a blind and indiscriminating veneration, and therefore determined to resist the adoption of even such moderate concessions as High Churchmen, such as his successor Sancroft, or his friend Clarendon, would have readily yielded. He probably never proposed any innovation; and even when he yielded to the representations of others he only conceded a few merely verbal changes, in order to give some decent appearance of fulfilling the pledges which Charles and Clarendon had given to the Presbyterians at Breda.

Sheldon had passed through the civil war and the protectorate without learning anything from the events he had witnessed or the sufferings he had undergone, and he would not consent to make any changes in order to avoid the great schism with which the Church was then threatened, and which turned out to be much more serious than he and his Episcopalian brethren had expected, but which was greatly aggravated by the obstinacy with which he insisted in carrying out his reactionary ideas.

Clarendon, who was a much more intelligent and reasonable Churchman, and who, at the time, was all-powerful, would probably have restrained the violence of Sheldon had he not been, as was generally supposed, under great obligations to him for the part he had taken in promoting the marriage of the chancellor's daughter to the Duke of York, afterwards James II. Thus Sheldon and the bishops acting with him succeeded in postponing the consideration of the concessions which it was proposed to make to the Presbyterians until the convention of Parliament, which contained a majority of

Presbyterians, had been dissolved and in its place a new Parliament had been elected, the members of which, chosen during the delirious frenzy of the Restoration, were for the most part frantic cavaliers animated by a spirit of fierce and furious hostility to the Presbyterians and a blind attachment to the Episcopal Church and the Book of Common Prayer, but who too often indulged in excesses which sincere Episcopalians and Presbyterians alike condemned.

In the mean time, common decency required that some semblance of an attempt should be made to fulfil the expectations which had been held out to the Presbyterian divines by Charles and Clarendon at Breda. Accordingly an effort was made to arrive at an agreement which might pave the way for a general conformity, and in order to this the matters in dispute between the Episcopalians and the Presbyterians were submitted to the consideration of that assembly of divines which is generally known in history as the Savoy Conference.

This assembly was constituted with a great show of fairness and with unquestionably honest intentions. To twelve of the most eminent of the bishops there were opposed twelve Presbyterian divines who were fully their equals in learning and ability, and as speakers or preachers were very much their superiors. To the principal disputants on each side there were joined nine assistants who were to supply the place of their principals if they should be prevented from attending by age, infirmity, or the pressure of other business. Among the bishops and their assistants were Sheldon, Sanderson,

Gunning, Gauden, and Pearson, the author of the celebrated treatise on the Apostles' Creed; while on the side of the Presbyterians appeared Dr. John Wallis the eminent Savilian Professor of Astronomy, Baxter, and Calamy. The warrant which authorized the commission to hold its sittings was issued on the 25th of March, 1661. It directed the divines appointed to take part in the conference to meet at the lodgings of the Bishop of of London at the Savoy in the Strand, or in such other place as should be thought fitting. It limited the sittings of the commission to four calendar months. The meeting was put off till the 15th of April, in order that it might not interfere with the arrangements that were being made for the coronation, which took place on the 13th of that month. The Archbishop of Canterbury took a part in the ceremony and placed the crown on the king's head, while he and several of his suffragans, arrayed in magnificent copes of cloth of gold, performed the service which, since the Reformation, had been celebrated on such occasions; but though Juxon took the principal part of the ceremony, he was compelled by the painful illness under which he was suffering, to quit the church before it was over, and he took no part in the Savoy Conference. When, after the delay caused by the coronation, that assembly at length commenced its sittings, the divines who composed it proceeded to take into their serious and grave consideration, as by the king's warrant they were required to do, "the directions, rules, and forms of prayer contained in the Book of Common Prayer; and to advise and consult about them—to consider the several objections that should be raised against them, and to make such reasonable and necessary alterations, concessions, and amendments in them, if any, as might seem to be required, but avoiding as much as possible all unnecessary alterations of the forms and liturgy with which the people were acquainted, and which had been so long received in the Church of England." They were directed to report the result of their deliberations to the king. Judging from internal evidence, I should say that these instructions were drawn up by the chancellor, who, in framing them, appeared not to recollect that the liturgy had been so long disused that great numbers of the younger inhabitants of this country had never been acquainted with it, or had almost forgotten it. The persons named in the commission were directed to report the results of their deliberations in order that they, or as much of them as might be approved by His Majesty, might be legally established.

In the absence of Juxon, for the reason already mentioned, Accepted Frewen, Archbishop of York, whose baptismal name proclaimed his puritanical parentage, being next in rank to Juxon, was requested to preside; but he modestly excused himself on the ground of his incompetence to deal with such matters. The chair was then taken by Sheldon, who might fairly claim the presidency, not only as next in rank to the archbishop, but also as being master of the house in which the Conference held its sittings. He lost no time in displaying that uncompromising spirit by which he was all along evidently actuated. Setting his foot at once on that manifest spirit of fairness and moderation which pervaded the instructions given to the members of the Conference, he treated with entire disregard every suggestion in favour of conformity by mutual concession, and imperiously demanded uniformity by compulsion. Instead of meeting the Presbyterian divines in a conciliatory spirit, and affording a patient hearing of the grievances of which they complained, and of the changes they proposed, on that footing of a fair equality which the warrant and all the preparations made for the Conference entitled them to expect, he at once threw them into the attitude of petitioners to the bishops for the amendments they desired to obtain. Taking advantage of the fact that Episcopacy had been abolished without the formal consent of the king, and completely ignoring the expectations which Charles and Clarendon had held out to the Presbyterians at Breda, as well as the conciliatory tone that pervaded the royal warrant by the authority of which the Conference was assembled, he declared on behalf of himself and his brother bishops, that they were perfectly satisfied with the Book of Common Prayer, which he alleged to be the established form of devotion for the kingdom, and which he contended that all must acknowledge never to have been set aside by any lawful authority. He declared that he and his fellow bishops desired no change in it, but on the contrary, believed that it was the most perfect and the most admirable form of prayer that had ever been drawn up. It was not, therefore, for him or for any of his

Episcopal brethren to commence the discussion. It was rather incumbent on those who found fault with any matters contained in the Book of Common Prayer to state their objections to it, and to propose such alterations as they might think it desirable to make in it. He further insisted that nothing should be done until all exceptions, alterations, and additions that it was proposed to make in the Book of Common Prayer should be brought in at once, that the objections of the Presbyterians should be made in writing, and all made together. By this manœuvre the differences of opinion that prevailed among the Presbyterians were brought into most unfavourable contrast with the perfect union that appeared to prevail among the Episcopalians, who all joined together in rallying round the ancient formularies with true ecclesiastico-conservative unanimity.

The Presbyterians saw at once the advantage which this proposed arrangement gave to their opponents, and protested warmly against it. They insisted on the understanding under which they had been invited to take part in the Conference, they implored their opponents not to throw away the opportunity of reconciliation which was offered them. They besought them to confer with them on that footing of friendly equality which was evidently intended by the royal warrant, under the authority of which they had been called together. They presented for the consideration of the Conference, a scheme of modified Episcopacy drawn up by Archbishop Usher, which they were willing to accept, and an entirely new Liturgy compiled by Baxter exclusively from the Bible.

They entreated the bishops not to drive out of the Church a large number of able and faithful ministers for the sake of ceremonies which were admitted on all hands to be non-essential.

All these remonstrances were entirely thrown away on those to whom they were addressed. Sheldon and his associates would yield nothing and listen to nothing. Knowing that they could reckon on the support of both Houses of Parliament, and of the great majority of the nation, the temper of which was at that moment fiercely cavalier, they persisted in their obstinate determination to reject and refuse every proposal of accommodation, thus throwing away an opportunity, which could never be recovered, of obtaining a large comprehension of Presbyterians, who, seeing how strongly the tide of popular sympathy was running against them, were quite prepared to concede a modified Episcopacy, and to yield on many other points, if the bishops would have taken up an attidude less offensive and less overbearing.

But the tactics of Sheldon had produced their intended effect. He had succeeded in uniting the bishops in firm opposition to the changes for which the Presbyterians pleaded, and had sown the seeds of disunion in the ranks of their opponents, who had all along been far from being agreed among themselves as to the nature and extent of the changes they desired, some of them being ready to accept a very small amount of concession, while others would be satisfied with nothing short of a substitution of the Presbyterian Directory for the Book of Common Prayer.

It must also be admitted that some of their leaders, especially Baxter, by their violent language and unreasonable demands, afforded some colourable excuse for the conduct of the other party. As for Sheldon, having succeeded in playing off one section of his opponents against another, and having placed the Presbyterians in a position from which there was no escape for them, he seldom appeared at the Conference, though he secretly directed all its proceedings. And thus a meeting from which much was expected, and from which, if properly conducted, much might have been obtained—a meeting, too, which was set on foot with an honest and sincere desire of effecting a large comprehension of Presbyterians—degenerated into a mere debating society, frequented as a place of amusement by the fashionable loungers of the metropolis. The four months to which the sittings of the Conference were limited, by the terms of the warrant in virtue of which it had been summoned, were consumed in barren discussions, and so this well-intended effort to obtain uniformity, or, at all events, a decided approach to it, by the comprehension of a large number of Nonconformists, was completely frustrated.

Nor is this result perhaps much to be regretted. When we consider how wide the difference must be between a Prayer Book founded on ancient liturgies, and a Directory which represented the religious aspirations and opinions of the seventeenth century, it will probably be generally felt that the attempt to amalgamate two such incongruous orders of ideas, must under any circumstances have proved a failure. But this does not excuse the conduct of Sheldon, and of those who acted under his leadership. It was unquestionably their duty to have met the Presbyterians in a moderate and conciliatory spirit, and with an honest desire to sacrifice things that were not essential, in order to effect an agreement, or, at least, to show that no agreement was attainable. Instead of acting thus, they laboured to defeat the charitable design they had been convened to promote. Even the celebrated ornaments rubric, which, as the Presbyterians affirmed, and the Episcopalians admitted, sanctioned the use of the cope and other obsolete vestments, was deliberately maintained, in spite of the remonstrances of the Presbyterians.

The dissolution of this Conference was followed by the meeting of Convocation, which commenced its sittings on the 8th of May, 1661, and to whose further consideration the Book of Common Prayer was remitted. This meeting was almost equally unsatisfactory in its results. Sheldon presided over it, manifesting the same unconciliatory disposition that he had exhibited during the sittings of the Savoy Conference. It is true that a great number of changes were made. Archbishop Tenison reckoned them up, and stated that they amounted altogether to upwards of six hundred; but most of the alterations thus introduced were merely verbal, and were without exception calculated rather to repel and irritate than to conciliate the Presbyterian recusants.

These changes having been adopted by the Convocation, were submitted to Parliament, and here a sharp struggle ensued between the advocates of comprehension by concession, and the champions of comprehension by compulsion. The latter prevailed, and the changes the Convocation had made were in the following session of Parliament embodied in the celebrated Act of Uniformity, in virtue of which the Church was reconstituted and placed on the basis on which it has stood from that time to our own day.

The Act received the royal assent in the month of May, but did not come into operation till the 24th of August—the Feast of St. Bartholomew—a day which was thus rendered doubly odious in the annals of ecclesiastical persecution, first as being the occasion of the dreadful massacre of the Huguenots in Paris, and secondly as being the date at which, in accordance with the provisions of the Act of Uniformity, a large number of ministers who declined to accept the Prayer Book as revised by Parliament and Convocation, were driven forth from their houses and their benefices. This statute, which from the time of its passing has regulated the worship of the Anglican Episcopal Church, and was intended to bring the whole nation to an exact conformity, not only in the substance, but also in the form of the worship they were henceforth to adopt, passed without any serious opposition; the Nonconformists being at that time too weak to offer any effectual resistance to a measure which represented the views and wishes of a party which was now triumphant, and was determined to use its victory without moderation or indulgence.

This celebrated statute required every minister who at the time of its passing was holding any preferment in the Church, to make the following declaration:—

"I, A.B., do declare my unfeigned assent and consent to all and everything contained and prescribed in and by the book entitled 'The Book of Common Prayer, and Administration of the Sacraments, and other Rites and Ceremonies of the Church, according to the Use of the Church of England, together with the Psalter or Psalms of David, pointed as they are to be sung or said in Churches; and the Form and Manner of Making, Ordaining, and Consecrating of Bishops, Priests, and Deacons.'"

Every minister who neglected or refused to make this declaration before the Feast of St. Bartholomew (August 24th), 1662, was deprived *ipso facto* of all his spiritual promotions.

They who during the Protectorate had been ordained by presbyters were now required to be reordained by bishops.

Every dean, canon, prebendary, all masters, heads, fellows, chaplains in any college, hall, or house of learning or hospital, all public professors, readers in either university, and in every college and elsewhere, and all parsons, vicars, curates, lecturers, and every schoolmaster keeping any public or private school, and every person instructing youth in any private family was required before the above date to subscribe the following declaration:—

"I, A.B., do declare that it is not lawful on any pretence whatsoever to take arms against the king, and that I do abhor that traitorous position of taking arms by his authority against his person, or against those that are commissioned by him, and that I will conform to the Liturgy of the Church of England as it is now by law established." The declaration then went on to renounce the solemn league and covenant as being an unlawful oath imposed on the subjects of this realm against the known laws and liberties of the kingdom.

This declaration was to be subscribed by the persons above mentioned under pain of deprivation, and for schoolmasters and tutors under pain of three months' imprisonment for the first offence, and for every other offence three months' imprisonment and the forfeiture of five pounds to his Majesty.

Any person presuming to consecrate and administer the holy sacrament of the Lord's Supper before being ordained a priest by Episcopal ordination to forfeit one hundred pounds.

None to be received as lecturers or permitted to preach or read any sermon or lecture in any church or chapel unless they shall be approved and licensed by the archbishop or bishop, and shall read and declare their unfeigned assent to the thirty-nine articles, and openly read and declare their assent to the Common Prayer. Otherwise they were to be disabled from preaching, and if they preached while so disabled were to suffer three months' imprisonment for every offence.

A copy of the Prayer Book as altered by the Convocation was to be provided in every parish church, chapel, college and hall, at the cost and charge of the parishioners or society before the Feast of St. Bartholomew, under pain of forfeiting three pounds a month so long as they should be unprovided with it. Notwithstanding this enactment, in many instances the copies of the amended Prayer Book had not reached the persons required by the Act to make the declaration and could not be obtained by them. Some signed without knowing what it was that they pledged themselves to by their signatures. Many, probably like the notorious Vicar of Bray, would have signed anything the Government required them to sign rather than run any risk, however slight, of losing their benefices. Others again signed after a full, careful, and conscientious examination, and full acceptance of the documents to which they attached their signatures; but about two thousand ministers of religion relinquished the benefices and other offices they held rather than make the declarations required of them. They went forth from their parsonages, not knowing whither they were going or how they were to be supported. No allowance was made to these good men from the benefices they thus relinquished, and the consequence was that many of them were reduced to the verge of starvation, or were forced to depend for their subsistence on the alms of those to whom they had formerly ministered, or on the assistance of wealthy and charitable persons who sympathized with their opinions and compassionated their sufferings.

As has been already mentioned, the Act was brought into operation on the 24th of August, St. Bartholomew's day. This day was selected in order that the incoming Episcopalians might receive the revenues of their benefices for the quarter then ending, while the outgoing Presbyterians who had done the work were excluded from all share in the payment for it. This proceeding was as impolitic as it was harsh and cruel. The choice of St. Bartholomew's Day for putting in force the odious provisions of the Act of Uniformity, and driving forth from their parsonages so many upright and conscientious ministers of religion, was rendered yet more hateful by the recollections it brought with it of that still more terrible St. Bartholomew's Day, when the streets and the houses of the French metropolis were deluged with the blood of the co-religionists of those who now suffered, treacherously assassinated for holding beliefs and adhering to practices that were almost identical with those which brought about the expulsion of the ministers who suffered persecution in England on the day of St. Bartholomew and in the year of grace 1662.

If it should be asked, who were the persons who were chiefly responsible, in this country, for the harsh and uncharitable expulsion of so many good and upright men, the answer we are compelled to give to the inquiry is that although the king, Clarendon, and his other advisers were greatly to be blamed, yet the man on whom the responsibility of the proceedings that have been mentioned chiefly rests was unquestionably Sheldon, who at that time acted as archbishop, and employed all the powers that belonged to his high place to force on the expulsion of the nonconforming ministers. It is, no doubt, quite true that, as we have already mentioned, he rarely attended the meetings of the Savoy Conference, or of the Convocation that followed it; but it cannot be denied that he directed all the proceedings of these assemblies, and exerted all the great power which his position gave him, and all the influence he possessed over the minds of Charles and Clarendon, in opposition to those milder and more conciliatory measures which they were evidently inclined to support, and would probably have sanctioned if they had not been goaded forward in the path of severity by the impetuous will and determination of Sheldon and his cavalier followers, who used all the influence they could exert over the king, his chancellor, the Convocation, and the legislature, in order to force them to adopt the Act of Uniformity and other persecuting measures.

To them, therefore, more than to any other persons, attaches the responsibility of having driven forth, in a manner so harsh and unfeeling, some two thousand ministers and other office-bearers—of having deprived the Church of the services of men such as Baxter, Calamy, Howe, and Owen—men who would have done honour to any communion—men whose honest scruples were at least deserving of fair consideration, and whom a little kindlier treatment, and a few slight concessions, which need not have involved any violation of principle, might have induced to conform and to retain the positions they relinquished on the 24th of August, 1662.

Many, no doubt, went out because they felt that by remaining at the posts they occupied they would subject themselves to the imputation of being actuated by dishonourable and interested motives—imputations from which they might easily have been saved by the leaders of the Anglican party, had they desired to respect the scruples of honest and earnest men. But it was otherwise decided, and I repeat that for this decision and the consequences it entailed, Sheldon was more blameworthy than any other person. When the Bill of Uniformity was under the consideration of the Parliament, the Duke of Manchester, in a manner that did him much credit, expressed to the king a fear that the provisions of the Bill were so rigorous that many ministers would not be able to comply with them. Sheldon, who stood by and heard the remark, at once replied, "I fear they will," and the whole of his conduct was in unison with this declaration. When regret was expressed in his presence at the prospect of the loss of so large a number of able ministers, he at once stated that he was quite prepared to supply the places of those who retired with others who would be more acceptable than they had been to the congregations to which they ministered. Nor did he stand alone in his treatment of Nonconformists: there were many others who were willing and ready to countenance and support him in both Houses of Parliament. Calamy having attended, as one of the congregation, a church at which the regular minister, through some accident or mistake, did not appear, many of those who were present solicited Calamy to take the place of the absent preacher, which he, wishing the congregation not to be sent away without any service, good-humouredly consented to do, and, mounting the pulpit, preached to the people with his usual power and earnestness. For this very venial transgression of the law he was sent to Newgate, but while under confinement in that prison he was visited by so great a number of distinguished persons and was the object of so much attention, that the news of his imprisonment at length came to the ears of the king, who, either from good nature or policy, or perhaps from a mixture of both, showed himself on this occasion, as indeed he did on many others, more tolerant and more sensible than the greater part of his advisers, and gave orders that Calamy should be at once released. The precedent was, no doubt, a dangerous one, and one that perhaps could not, with a sovereign of Charles' character, be allowed to pass without some remark. But the course the House of Commons took was probably dictated rather by insolent bigotry than by a desire to protect the Constitution of the country from royal inroads. They presented to the king an address on the subject of Calamy's release, in which they prayed him in future to allow the law to have free course. There can be no doubt that this request was prompted not so much by a feeling of jealousy of this exercise of the royal prerogative, which, under a sovereign such as Charles, would have been a very legitimate and proper feeling, but by the spirit of haughty intolerance that pervaded the cavalier Parliament, and, indeed, the nation in general, which was carried then to such an excess, that had the king and his advisers been more anxious than they really were to fulfil the expectations they had held out at Breda to the Presbyterian delegates, it is more than doubtful whether he would have been permitted to carry out the policy of toleration to which they were then pledged.

The measures of severity which had been adopted had conspicuously failed to produce the uniformity which their authors had expected from them; but their advocates and framers, instead of having their eyes opened by their failure to the folly of the course they had hitherto pursued, and being led to endeavour to retrace their steps, were only induced to adopt measures of still greater stringency and severity. They contended that persecution had hitherto failed because it had not been carried far enough. We will not weary our readers by carrying them through the dreary annals of persecution which form the history of this period—the Conventicle Act of 1664, the Five Mile Act of 1665, or the Test and Corporation Acts of 1673—measures which, though intended for the defence and support of the Church, really belong rather to the general history of the country than to our special department of it. These and other persecuting statutes, which exhibited the triumph of the cavalier party and hastened its downfall, were intended to deprive Nonconformists through all ages of all political power, and, as far as was possible, also of all religious influence; and in virtue of these measures, good men, whose only crime consisted in their steadfast and conscientious adherence to what they believed to be the truth as it is in Jesus, were imprisoned, banished, or even put to death, solely on account of their steadfast adherence to doctrines and practices which a short time before had been sanctioned and promoted by the law of the land, and which they still continued to believe to be true and right; while others had—some, no doubt from conviction, and some from motives of interest—renounced, and had even, in many cases, joined in persecuting those who still held fast the doctrines and practices which they themselves had repudiated.

In the extremity of their sufferings, the Presbyterians not unnaturally turned to the king. He was not by disposition a persecutor. He hated Presbyterianism; but he was not unkindly disposed towards the Presbyterians. His natural good sense, and the scenes he had witnessed during the period of his exile, had taught him the impolicy of alienating from the crown so huge a proportion of his subjects as they represented, as well as some of the most intelligent and industrious persons in his kingdom. Besides this, he had all along secretly cherished the design of ultimately substituting Romanism for Anglicanism through the assistance of the Presbyterians, who, he hoped, would combine with Protestant and Popish Nonconformists in demanding a general toleration for all sects and denominations of Christians.

But he was surrounded by counsellors, whose hatred of Presbyterianism was much stronger than his own, and the more so because they had once been Presbyterians themselves, and whose detestation of Romanism was far fiercer than their hatred of Presbyterianism. When the Duke of Manchester, who represented the little religious liberalism which was to be found among the courtiers, declared in favour of toleration, Clarendon and Sheldon vehemently insisted that the laws should be strictly enforced, and the latter stated that if any relaxation of their severity were permitted he could not maintain his Episcopal authority and the legislature would become the laughing stock of the nation.

In spite, however, of these protestations, Charles acted on his own opinion, and issued a proclamation in which, after referring to the promises he had made at Breda that he would afford liberty to tender consciences and give his consent to any Act of Parliament which might be passed with that view, he added that all these things were still fresh in his memory, and that he was firmly resolved to perform what he had promised; but that as the Parliament had not thought fit to offer him a Bill for the purpose of carrying his designs into effect, he, through his zeal for the maintenance of the true Protestant religion, had given the Establishment the precedence over matters of indulgence to dissenters from it, but this being now done he was glad to renew to all his subjects to whom promises of indulgence applied, the assurance that so far as he was concerned, the penalties inflicted on those who, living peaceably, did not conform to the Church of England through scruple or tenderness of misguided conscience, but who modestly and without scandal performed their devotions in their own way, that he would make it his special care, as far as in him lay, without invading the freedom of Parliament, to incline their wisdom, at the next approaching sessions, to concur with him in making some Act for the purpose, so as to enable him to exercise with more universal satisfaction that power of dispensing which he conceived to be inherent in his royal authority.

Referring to the Roman Catholics, he observed that the services which they had rendered to his father, to himself, and to the Protestant religion, entitled them to some favourable consideration, and therefore he did not intend to exclude them from all benefit of the proposed indulgence, but they must not expect an open toleration. However, he intended to refer the whole matter to the approaching session of Parliament, which he did not doubt would concur with him in the performance of his promises.

In this expectation, if he really entertained it, he was soon undeceived. He repeated the substance of this declaration in the Speech which he delivered at the opening of the Parliament in the commencement of the year 1663; but ultra-loyal as the Commons were, loudly as they protested their readiness to yield an almost passive obedience to their newly restored monarch, there were two things in this declaration of which they strongly disapproved, and to which the majority of them were determined to offer a resolute and uncompromising resistance. These were the claim of dispensing power in the king, and the proposal to offer toleration to the Romanists.

Accordingly, they made the following reply: "We have considered your Majesty's declaration from Breda, and are of opinion that it was not a promise, but a gracious declaration to comply with the advice of your

Parliament, whereas no such advice has been given. They who pretend a right to the supposed promise put their right into the hands of their representatives, who have passed the Act of Uniformity. If any shall say a right to the benefit of the declaration still remains, it tends to dissolve the very bond of Government, and to suppose a disability in the whole legislature to make a law contrary to your Majesty's.

"We have also considered the nature of the indulgence proposed, and are of opinion (1) that it will establish schism by a law, and make the censures of the Church of no consideration; (2) that it is unbecoming the wisdom of Parliament to pass a law in one session for uniformity, and in another session to pass a law to frustrate and weaken it, the reasons continuing the same; (3) that it will expose your Majesty to the restless importunities of every sect who shall dissent from the Established Church; (4) that it will increase sectaries, which will weaken the Protestant profession, and be troublesome to the Government, and in time some prevalent sect may contend for an establishment which may end in Popery; (5) that it is unprecedented, and may take away the means of convicting recusants; (6) that the indulgence proposed will not tend to the peace, but to the disturbance of the kingdom. The best way, therefore, to produce a settled peace is to press vigorously the Act of Uniformity."

These arguments would probably not have had much weight with the king if they had not been supported by others of a more practical kind. The majority that passed these resolutions, and which was pressing for the strict execution of the cruel and unjust provisos of the Act of Uniformity, held the purse-strings of the nation, and would only loose them on condition of the king's giving his assent to their demands. Charles took the money that was granted him, quietly observing that he had been misunderstood. He was unquestionably sincere in his professions of a desire to relieve consciences, but whether from good nature or a secret inclination to introduce Popery is, as Bishop Kennet observes, "not easy to determine."

There can be no doubt that much might at that time be very plausibly urged in favour of the king's proposals. A dispensing power such as James II. claimed, was in point of fact a transfer of the legislation of the country from the king and Parliament to the king alone. But a power to dispense with some of the tyrannical provisions of the Act of Uniformity, strictly limited, honestly carried out, and jealously watched, would not, indeed, square with our ideas of religious liberty, but would, perhaps, have been the best alleviation of the Act of Uniformity that the circumstances of the times and the state of public opinion would permit; and though Charles desired to obtain the dispensing power with a view to employing it in a manner calculated to promote the designs of the Romanists, he would probably have had the good sense to see that it must be exercised with an honest impartiality, of which his obstinate and unfortunate brother was quite incapable.

For in spite of his Romanizing proclivities, Charles

was, in his opinions and practice with regard to religious freedom and toleration, greatly in advance both of his ministers and his Parliament, and though he no doubt listened with pleasure to Romish councils and counsellors, he saw more clearly than most of his advisers the folly and impolicy of the persecuting intolerance, which they strenuously advocated.

The protest of the Commons was not the only one that was drawn forth by the king's declaration. Sheldon had succeeded Juxon, who died in the year 1663, in the primacy, and he took a very early opportunity of delivering his protest against the declaration of indulgence in the following characteristic epistle * :—

"To the King's most excellent Majesty.

"May it please your Majesty,

"I have been too long silent, and am afraid, by my silence, I have neglected the duty of the place it hath pleased God to call me into, and your Majesty's to place me in. And now I humbly crave leave, I may discharge my conscience towards God and my duty to your Majesty. And therefore I beseech your Majesty, give me leave freely to deliver myself, and then let your Majesty do with me what you please. Your Majesty hath propounded a toleration of religion: I beseech you, Sir, take into your consideration, what the act is, next what the consequence may be.

"By your act you labour to set up that most damnable

---

* I found this letter in the British Museum, bound up with a number of anti-Popish tracts of the period.

and heretical doctrine of the Church of Rome, whore of Babylon. How hateful will it be to God and grievous unto your good subjects, the true professors of the Gospel, that your Majesty, who hath often disputed and learnedly written against these wicked heresies, should now shew yourself a patron of those doctrines which your pen hath told the world, and your conscience tells yourself, are superstitious, idolatrous, and detestable.

"Besides, this toleration which you endeavour to set up by proclamation cannot be done without a Parliament, unless your Majesty will let your subjects see that you will take unto yourself a liberty to throw down the laws of the realm at your pleasure. What dreadful consequences these things may draw after them, I beseech your Majesty to consider.

"And above all, lest by this toleration and discontinuance of the true profession of the Gospel, whereby God hath blessed us, and under which the kingdom hath for many years flourished, your Majesty do not draw upon the kingdom in general, and yourself in particular, God's hearty wrath and indignation. Thus in discharge of my duty towards God, to your Majesty, and the place of my calling, I have taken humble boldness to deliver my conscience. And now, Sir, do with me what you please.

"I am your most faithful subject and servant,
"G. CANTERBURY.

"London: printed for S.U.N.T.F.S."

Whatever may be thought of this letter, it is most certain that Sheldon acted in the spirit of it towards all Nonconformists, whether Protestant or Roman Catholic. The Act of Conformity, the Convention Act, the Five Mile Act, and all the other proceedings of the triumphant party had his warm support. He probably had the chief hand in framing them. He certainly was foremost in putting them into execution.

The king and Clarendon were perhaps not sorry to have in the place of archbishop a man who so readily took on himself the responsibility of the odious measures to which they somewhat reluctantly consented, but which he warmly and openly approved. The spirit in which Sheldon urged the carrying out of these Acts, is shown by a circular letter which he issued to the bishops of his province in the year 1670.

In this missive he exhorts them to follow his example and put in force in their respective dioceses the Acts which had been passed for enforcing uniformity. He directs them, first of all "to counsel the ecclesiastical officers and judges and the officers of the clergy of their dioceses in their own particular duties;" he instructs the bishops to "recommend unto them the cure of the people in their respective jurisdiction, and charges that in their several places they do their best to persuade and win all Nonconformists and Dissenters to obedience to His Majesty's laws and unity with the Church, and such as shall be refractory to endeavour to reduce by the Church, or such other good means and ways as shall be best conducing thereto; to which end," adds Sheldon—

"I advise that all and every of the said ecclesiastical judges and officers, and every of the clergy of your diocese, and the churchwardens of every parish by their respective ministers be desired in their respective stations and places that they take notice of all Nonconformists, holders, frequenters, maintainers, abettors of conventicles and unlawful assemblies under pretence of religious worship, especially of the teachers and preachers in them and of places wherein the same are held, ever keeping a more watchful eye on the cities and great towns from whence the mischief is for the most part derived into the lesser villages and hamlets: and whereinsoever they find such wilful offenders that they with a hearty affection to the worship of God, the honour of the king and his laws, and the peace of the Church and kingdom, they do address themselves to the civil magistrate, justices, and others concerned, imploring their help and assistance for preventing and suppressing the same, according to the late said Act in that behalf made and set forth."

These zealous instructions were for the most part zealously carried out. No writer perhaps better expressed or more ably advocated the feelings and opinions of the country clergy and the country squires of his day towards the Nonconformists than their celebrated preacher Robert South, from whose sermon, "On the fatal use of words and names falsely applied," I quote the following passage, which shows the spirit with which he, and those for whom he writes, were animated, and the opposition they encountered from those who openly supported, or secretly sympathized with, the persecuted preachers :—

"Well, but in the next place we will suppose another man, a justice of the peace? and if so, let him not concern himself to lay this or that fanatical preacher by the heels, as the law and his office require him to do. But if he must needs, for shame or fear, sometimes make a show at least of searching after this *precious man*, let him, however, send him timely notice thereof underhand, that so the justice may fairly and judiciously search for that which he is sure not to find, according to that of the poet, *istud quæro quod invenire nolo.** Moreover, if there chance to be a conventicle or unlawful meeting just under his nose, let him not disturb and break it up; for, alas! those that are of it are a sort of *peaceable, well-meaning people, who meet only to serve God according to their consciences.* Possibly, indeed, some of the chief of them may have fought their king heretofore at Edgehill, Marston Moor, Naseby, or Worcester, but that is past long since, and they are resolved never to do so again, till they are better able than at present (to their sorrow) they find themselves to be. And this is some of the *moderation* which is required to a *Justice of Peace*, so called, I conceive, for sitting still, *holding his peace*, and doing nothing.

"But then, lastly, if a Parliament be sitting. Oh! that above all others is the proper time for such as are men of sobriety and zeal, and understand the true interest of the nation (forsooth), to manifest a fellow feeling of the

---

* I seek that which I wish not to find.

sufferings of the brotherhood and in behalf of their old Puritan friends."

After expatiating at some further length on the injuries that had been inflicted on the clergy and churchmen during the late rebellion, he concludes his discourse with the following exhortation :—

"This I say, and will maintain, that the Church of England as to its external state and condition in this world, stands upon no other bottom, and can be upheld by no other methods, but a vigorous execution of her *laws* on the one side, and a constant, uniform, unreserved conformity to them on the other. And all other ways are but the palliated remedies, and the fallacious prescriptions of quacks and mountebanks, and spiritual Pontœus's, such as wise men would never advise nor good men approve of; and such as by skinning over her wounds for the present (though probably not so much as that neither) will be sure to cure them into an after rottenness and suppurations, and infallibly thereby at length procure her dissolution.

"And for my own part, I fully believe that this was the very thing designed by these men all along. For I dare aver, that if that one project of *union* as it was laid, had took place, it would have done more to the breaking our Church in pieces, and to the bringing in of Popery by those breaches, than the Papists themselves have been able to do towards it, since the Reformation. So that whatsoever the danger may have been to our Church heretofore from *Church Papists*, I am sure the great danger that threatens it now is from Church fanatics."

The persons to whom these predictions and exhortations were addressed were only too ready to listen to such incitements to intolerance as we have just quoted, and not only to carry out the work of persecution themselves, but also to brand those who counselled or practised moderation, and displayed any reluctance or hesitation in carrying out intolerant statutes, as enemies of the establishment.

It would, however, be a great mistake to suppose that these proceedings were regarded with satisfaction and complacency by all the clergy of the Church, or that no attempts were made to consider the demands of the Nonconformists in a spirit far more charitable than was displayed in the discourses of South or the proceedings of his numerous followers. There was all along a body of ministers in the Church, and especially in the metropolis, small in number, but weighty in ability and learning, who kept up a constant communication with the Nonconformists, and endeavoured to frame terms in which a scheme of comprehension might be based. The most considerable effort of this description was originated and promoted by Tillotson, Stillingfleet, and some other of the London clergy, who in liberality of sentiment and enlightenment were very far in advance of most of their rural brethren. In the year 1674, this little band held a conference with several leading Nonconformist ministers, for the purpose of arranging some terms of agreement, but they were frowned on by most of the bishops and aspersed by their clerical brethren, who reviled them as traitors to the Church whose bread they were alleged to eat while they lifted up their hands against her.

After many communications on the subject with persons occupying high positions in Church and State, Tillotson, who might be regarded as the leader of the comprehension party, found himself constrained to confess that as circumstances then were the scheme could not pass in either House of Parliament without the concurrence of a considerable part of the bishops and the countenance of His Majesty, which for the present he was obliged to admit he saw little reason to expect.

The only attempt made to conciliate the Nonconformists throughout the whole of the various discussions on comprehension and conformity, if indeed it can be regarded as an attempt at conciliation, was the insertion of a new rubric after the communion office, which ordered that the communion should be received by the communicants kneeling, but at the same time explained "that thereby no adoration was intended, either unto the sacramental bread and wine there bodily received, or unto any corporal presence of Christ's natural flesh and blood, for the sacramental bread and wine remain still in their very natural substances, and therefore may not be adored; for that were idolatry, to be abhorred of all faithful Christians."

The author of these directions was one Dr. Gauden, who, with the help of some fragments of Charles I.'s journal, composed the Εικων βασιλικη, a sort of religious romance which professed to contain that king's secret meditations, and gave a highly favourable representation of his character and conduct during his misfortunes, and which, being believed to be genuine and authentic, contributed in no small degree to raise the character of "The Royal Martyr," to popularize the Stuarts, and thereby help forward the Restoration, to the effecting of which it powerfully contributed. For this service he was rewarded by being appointed first to the bishopric of Exeter, and then to that of Worcester.

His rubric, appended to the communion service, offended the Puritans, who objected to kneeling in the communion at all, and the High Churchmen and Romanists, who believed in the doctrine of the Real Presence which the rubric in question directly contradicted. Sheldon, though he probably sympathized with neither of these parties, objected to the insertion of it, simply because it was an alteration of some importance, but reluctantly yielded. When the Duke of York, afterwards James II., in reference to this direction which he regarded as heterodox, complained to Sheldon for having permitted its insertion, the archbishop replied, "I had nothing to do with the matter; you must thank your friend Gauden for it."

We may here fitly refer to a change of very serious importance, as affecting the relations between the Church and the State, which was very quietly transacted. Up to the year 1664, the beneficed clergy of the Church had been taxed by their representatives in Convocation, as the laity were by their representatives in Parliament.*

* I may here remark that the clergy were only taxed in Convocation for their ecclesiastical benefices. In their personal capacity they were liable, like others, to the ordinary taxation of Parliament.

This separate taxation was regarded by the Government as a great inconvenience, and by the clergy as a serious grievance, for under this arrangement they found themselves forced to pay a much larger share of the taxation of the country than fairly belonged to them. South, in one of his sermons, says that a clergyman of ten pounds a year had been known to be taxed equal to a layman of ten thousand.* This statement should be taken with some abatement, but at all events it makes it probable that the clergy were great losers, in a pecuniary point of view, by the arrangement that subsisted. So ripe was the matter for settlement, that a private conversation between Lord Chancellor Clarendon on the part of the Government and the archbishop and a few of his suffragans on behalf of the clergy, sufficed to decide the question. It has been justly observed that there probably never was so great a Constitutional change that was effected with so little trouble or attracted so little attention.

An Act of Parliament was of course required to give legislative force to the agreement thus made. In this Act it was provided, " that nothing herein contained shall be drawn into an example to the prejudice of the ancient right belonging to the lords spiritual and temporal or the clergy of this realm." Gibson, Bishop of London, remarked with regard to this matter, that it was the greatest alteration in the Constitution that was ever made without an express law, but the passage above cited shows that although the arrangement was made by a

* See South's Sermons, vol. v. Sermon II.

verbal agreement it was sanctioned " by an express law." It is true that the law passed without any public discussion of its provisions.

This agreement dealt a fatal blow to the authority of Convocation. As long as the Government depended on that assembly for a large proportion of its supplies, it was sure not to omit to convene it when the time came for considering the question of raising them, and it could hardly avoid, too, listening to the gravamina* which it might think proper to complain of, or adopting some of the recommendations it might submit ; but when Convocation was deprived of the power of the purse it lost the hold it previously had on the Government. From that time forward it was only convened when the Ministry in power was friendly to the dominant party in the Lower House of Convocation, which was invariably composed of High Churchmen and Tories, or when a Tory majority in the two Houses of Parliament requested the Crown to convene the ancient legislature of the Church.

When we speak of High Churchmen it must be borne in mind that the High Churchman of the time of Charles II. differed very considerably from the High Churchman of the present day. He was known by a strong attachment to the doctrine of apostolical succession, and by an equally strong aversion from the doctrines and practices of the Church of Rome.

The High Churchman of Charles II.'s. reign, as indeed the High Churchmen of all times, have been chiefly

* Grievances.

distinguished by a more or less strong maintenance of the doctrine of apostolical succession. On this subject no one speaks with more authority, no one represents more clearly or more fully the doctrine held by the High Churchmen of his time than Bishop Beveridge—a man as remarkable for the extent of his acquirements as for the sanctity of his life and conversation. He thus lays it down in his published sermon on Christ's presence with His ministers :—

"In the first place," he writes, "I observe how much we are all bound to acknowledge the goodness, to praise, magnify, and adore the name of the Most High God, in that we were born and bred, and still live in a Church wherein the apostolical line hath, through all ages, been preserved entire, there having been a constant succession of such bishops in it as were truly and properly successors to the apostles, by virtue of that apostolic imposition of hands which, being begun by the apostles, hath been continued from one to another ever since their time down to ours. By which means the same Spirit which was breathed by our Lord into his apostles, is together with their office transmitted to their lawful successors, the pastors and governors of our Church at this time."

Closely connected with the doctrine of apostolical succession, and, in fact, a logical deduction from it, as being necessary to give efficiency to it, was the doctrine of baptismal regeneration, which is thus nakedly affirmed by the same high authority in the thirty-fifth sermon of his published works :—

"As baptizing necessarily implies the use of water, so

our being made thereby disciples of Christ as necessarily implies our partaking of His Spirit; for all that are baptized, and so made the disciples of Christ, are thereby made members of His body; and are therefore said to be baptized into Christ (Rom. vi. 5; Gal. iii. 27).

"But they who are in Christ, members of His body, must needs partake of the Spirit that is in Him, their head. Neither doth the Spirit of Christ only follow upon but certainly accompanies the sacrament of baptism when duly administered according to His institution. For as St. Paul saith, 'By one spirit we are all baptized into one body' (1 Cor. xii. 13). So that in the very act of baptism, the Spirit unites us unto Christ, and makes us members of His body; and if of His body then of his Church and kingdom, that being all His body. And therefore all who are rightly baptized with water, being at the same time baptized with the Holy Ghost, and so born of water and the Spirit, they are *ipso facto* admitted into the kingdom of God established upon earth, and, if it be not their own fault, will as certainly attain to that which is in heaven."

Such was, at the period of which we are treating, and has been at all times, with more or less precision of statement, the doctrine of the High Church or orthodox party, which has probably all along, and especially during the reigns of Charles II. and James II., comprehended the great majority of the clergy of the Church of England, and a very large proportion of her laity.

When pressed to reconcile this position with their

adhesion to the Reformation and his repudiation of the Roman Catholic Church, Beveridge thus replied, and in doing so expressed not his own opinions only, but also the views of his High Church brethren generally:—

"When this our English Church, through long communion with the Roman Church, had contracted like stains with her, from which it was necessary that it should be cleansed, they who took the excellent and very necessary work in hand, fearing that they, like others, might rush from one extreme to another, removed indeed those things, as well as doctrines and ceremonies, which the Roman Church had newly and insensibly superinduced, and, as was fit, abrogated them utterly. Yet notwithstanding, whatsoever things had been at all times believed and observed by all churches, in all places those things they most religiously took care not so to abolish with them, for they well know, that all particular churches are to be formed on the model of the Universal Church, according to the general and received rule of ethics, 'every form which agreeth not with its whole is therein base.' Hence, therefore, these first reformers of this particular Church directed the whole line of the Reformation which they undertook, according to the rule of the whole or Universal Church, casting away those things which had been either unheard of or rejected by the Universal Church, but most religiously retaining those which they saw, on the other side, corroborated by the consent of the Universal Church; whence it hath been brought to pass, that although we have not communion with the Roman nor with certain other particular Churches as at this day constituted, yet have we abiding communion with the Universal and Catholic Church, of which evidently ours, as by the aid of God first constituted, and by his pity still preserved, is the perfect image and representation."

The doctrines thus concisely and distinctly stated we shall meet with frequently in the future course of this history. Though sometimes unpopular and sometimes held back, they have in all times been maintained with more or less distinctness and boldness, not only by High Churchmen, but also by many of those who belong to the Evangelical or Low Church party.* The answer made to them by the Puritans was in effect this. If the doctrine of apostolical succession be true, it is of all doctrines the most essential to be maintained, and it would not have been allowed to remain in the uncertainty that now rests upon it, but every link in the chain of succession would have been placed altogether beyond the possibility of doubt or dispute by the good providence of God.

It is impossible to imagine a more distinct assertion of the doctrine of apostolical succession than those found in the passages above quoted or referred to; and I believe these doctrines were never repudiated by the members of the Evangelical party either before the publication of these passages or after. The fact is indisputable; and the reader of Stanley's life of Dr. Arnold will doubtless remember that he attributed the rapid

---

* See quotation from H. Melvill, p. 6.

spread of Tractarianism in a great degree to the support and encouragement which the dogma of apostolical succession received from the Evangelicals. In fact, the Tractarian movement, as any one who studies its history may see, had its origin among men who belonged originally to the Evangelical party, and who were contributors to the *Record* newspaper, which at that time represented the small remnant of earnestness which was then to be found in the Church. Newman's *Apologia pro vita sua* clearly shows that so far as a mind so active and independent as his could be brought to deliver itself up to the bondage of party, Newman began by attaching himself to the Evangelical party. And it was only when the publication of the celebrated Oxford Tracts forced their authors and followers to adopt more definite views and statements that a wide gulf was fixed between the Evangelical party, which had then passed its zenith and was hastening to its decline, and the Tractarian party, which was rising above the horizon and making its influence to be felt through the kingdom. In process of time, the contrast between the two parties came to be distinctly accentuated, and, as we shall see, while the Tractarian party pressed the doctrine of apostolical succession more and more recklessly to all its logical consequences, the Evangelical party, in their general recoil from Tractarianism, receded more and more from this its fundamental tenet, and in their dread of Tractarianism renounced doctrines which their leaders had hitherto regarded as essential. And, indeed, this doctrine, though it has been a rallying point of the members of the Church of England, has never rested on any intelligible basis. Its advocates, so far from being able to produce the irrefragable evidence we have a right to demand of them, can really bring no proof at all of the alleged fact on which it is supposed to rest. And as for the asserted transmission of special grace to those who receive the sacraments at the hands of ministers who have been episcopally ordained, it is confuted by repeated experience, for every day's observation shows that they who are baptized and partake of the Lord's Supper are, generally speaking, neither morally nor religiously better than many of those who have never received them at all.

We now return from this long, but, we trust, not needless digression to pursue the main thread of our history.

Though Charles had the good sense to listen to the remonstrances of the Parliament, and to desist from an attempt so full of danger as that of pressing for a legislative sanction of the dispensing power which he claimed as inherent in his royal prerogative, yet he was far from being satisfied. He had bound himself to the Presbyterians to grant them toleration, and he was disappointed and humiliated at having been defeated in his attempts to redeem this pledge. He had also shown himself anxious to obtain for the Papists toleration in the present and something more than toleration in the future; but instead of effecting his intentions and keeping his promises, the only result that he had been able to obtain was to render the chains of those whom he desired to relieve heavier, and their persecution more cruel. In a word, whilst honestly desiring to establish a policy of general toleration, he found himself, entirely against his own wish, placed in the position of being a persecutor and loaded with the unpopularity which that policy naturally engendered. This unfortunate state of things was mainly due to Clarendon, who was a steadfast High Churchman, and therefore, according to the ideas that prevailed in his day, a resolute enemy of Romanism. It was chiefly through his unconcealed opposition to the declaration of indulgence, more than through any other cause, that the designs of the king his master had been frustrated, and along with much unpopularity that he really deserved he had also to bear much that was quite undeserved. By sacrificing his chancellor, therefore, Charles got rid of a double load of unpopularity—his own and his chancellor's. In a word, Clarendon became the scapegoat who had to bear into exile the burden of his master's sins as well as his own.

The fall of Clarendon was followed by the introduction of several Papists into the king's council, who had now more fully embraced the religion of Rome, as far as he could be said to have any religion at all; and he hoped to be able to induce many of his people to follow his example in this respect, partly on account of the partiality with which he regarded that religion, and still more because he looked on it as the best means of securing for him that arbitrary power which he coveted rather through indolence than through ambition. For, seeing, as he did, how arbitrary and powerful Louis XIV. was, he attributed the difference between himself and his despotic neighbour to the difference which existed between the religious beliefs of the two nations they respectively governed, imagining that if he could but succeed in establishing in England the religion of the Great Monarch, he would thereby obtain his despotic authority.

Charles was, however, too cautious to avow his aims and intentions, and though he steadily kept them in view he carefully concealed them from the knowledge of the people, the legislature, and the greater part of his most trusted advisers. It was reserved for his brother, after his death, to publish abroad to his subjects and to the world the shameful secret that the defender of the faith had really been all along the betrayer of Protestantism.

The disgrace of Clarendon was a heavy blow to the Church, of which he had all along been a staunch member and a warm adherent; and though he had yielded to the persecuting party, and even allowed himself to be made use of by them and to be dragged into measures of scandalous severity. And notwithstanding the inclination he had originally shown to tolerate and even comprehend Nonconformists, he had afterwards been persuaded to think that these so-called bulwarks were necessary to the safety and welfare of the Church. These views he appears to have adopted in his later days out of deference to the arguments and opinions of Archbishop Sheldon; and yet, if Burnet is to be believed, it was with the advice and concurrence of

Sheldon that Charles had determined to dismiss his chancellor.

If so, Sheldon probably had soon occasion to repent the advice he had given, and to regret the fall of one who appears to have all along been his faithful friend and ally. Be that as it may, certain it is that though he was elected to succeed Clarendon in his office of Chancellor of the University of Oxford—an office which we may readily suppose, that, as being one of the most attached sons and liberal benefactors of that university, he would have been delighted to fill—he was nevertheless forced to relinquish it before he had been installed into it, and to share the frowns of the king with the disgraced chancellor.

It is alleged that he had remonstrated with Charles in very plain, not to say coarse terms, on the irregular life he was leading, and that Charles was deeply offended at his home thrusts and pointed remonstrances, and he perhaps also felt, as Pepys appears to have done,* that Sheldon's own life was by no means so correct as to entitle him to rebuke others. Sheldon appears to have made no attempt to regain the king's favour. He was growing old and infirm; he absented himself from the council board, where his presence was no longer desired; he withdrew from all public affairs; he was no longer consulted, as he usually had been up to this time, in the disposal of bishoprics and other church preferments in the patronage of the crown; and

---

* Pepys in several places in his journal refers to reports of this kind which appear to have been current.

spent the remainder of his days in retirement and in the discharge of those duties which his archiepiscopal office obliged him to perform.

While Sheldon was engaged in promoting and superintending the re-establishment of the Episcopal Church in England on the basis on which it had rested before the commencement of the civil war, and in fencing it in the way that he deemed to be most effectual to protect it against the assaults of the various non-conforming communions, Protestant as well as Papist, he had not been unmindful of the ecclesiastical condition of Scotland, in which country the Presbyterian form of Church polity had struck deeper root and was more popular than it had ever been in England, but into which he was resolved to reintroduce the Episcopal system as he had already done in this country.

His principal instrument and most trusted agent in this matter was one James Sharp, a Presbyterian minister, who, as already mentioned, had been deputed by his fellow Presbyterians to support their cause with the king at Breda. Although he exercised his ministry as a Presbyterian, he seems always to have had a leaning to Episcopacy, and when Cromwell was in Scotland and was endeavouring to settle the civil and ecclesiastical affairs of that country on a satisfactory and permanent basis, Sharp tried to persuade him to introduce a modified Episcopacy. So that there can be no doubt that while his conscience allowed him to conform to the Presbyterian system, as established in Scotland during the Protectorate, and supported there by the strong preference of the Scottish people, he did not regard either Episcopacy or Presbyterianism as absolutely essential, but had a mild preference, which the circumstances of the country prevented him from openly avowing, for a moderate Episcopacy.

At first he faithfully discharged the commission he had received from the Scotch Presbyterians; but soon finding that the Government and people of England were strongly determined to maintain the Episcopal system both in England and Scotland, and that all the world was, to use his own expression, "doting" after the Book of Common Prayer, and that the "cassock men"* were swarming everywhere, he complied with the prevailing party, and so was not unnaturally regarded by those who had deputed him to plead their cause at Breda as one who had betrayed the trust reposed in him. Their wrath and indignation was increased when they found that he had not only sanctioned the revival of prelatic Episcopacy, but had accepted the high office of Archbishop of St. Andrew's and had consented, though not without some show of resistance, to be ordained deacon and priest before being consecrated as bishop. Sheldon, who was at this time Bishop of London, but who, owing to the illness of Juxon and the favour of the king, was taking the leading part in the reconstruction of the two churches of England

* The cassock, and on all public occasions the gown and cassock, was at that time the general dress of the English clergy. It had been compulsorily disused during Cromwell's time, but was at once resumed at the Restoration. A clergyman arrayed in his gown and cassock was said to be in full canonicals, that is to say, dressed as directed by the 74th canon.

and Scotland, saw in Sharp a man likely to carry out his plans zealously and successfully. Sharp had filled the office of Professor of Philosophy and other important posts in the University of St. Andrew's with credit and ability, and entered readily into Sheldon's views. But by doing so he drew down on himself a great amount of unpopularity, which adhered to him till it ultimately brought about his cruel murder by some of the zealots of the party which he was supposed, and not altogether without reason, to have deserted and betrayed.

For the present, however, the Royalist and Episcopal party (for the two went together at the moment of the Restoration), was uppermost even in Scotland, and the Presbyterians were exposed to a cruel persecution, which they endured with fanatical resolution. The new bishops were received in Scotland by the dominant party with enthusiastic acclamations. They landed at Berwick-on-Tweed, on their way to Edinburgh, and were met at Cockburnspath, a hamlet about eight miles beyond Dunbar, by a large number of nobility, gentry, and ministers, who escorted them to the Scotch metropolis, where they were welcomed with renewed acclamations. But the fire that seemed to be extinguished was smouldering beneath the ashes, and eventually burst forth into a conflagration that burned up the structure which Charles, Sheldon, Lauderdale, and Sharp, had with much labour and much bloodshed built up in Scotland.

The power which Sheldon exercised was perhaps greater and more uncontrolled than that which had been possessed by any of those who had either preceded or followed him in the chair of St. Augustine. He superintended and to a great extent dictated the reconstruction of the united Churches of England, Scotland, and Ireland, after they had been demolished by the great rebellion, but the power thus successfully exercised was due not to any personal qualities of the man, whose abilities were below mediocrity, but to his official position, which made him the leader of the cavalier party at the moment of its triumph, and enabled him to carry out that policy of ecclesiastical conservatism which was most consonant with his feelings and with the sentiments of those whom he led.

His very violence placed him in harmony with the triumphant party, whose necessary leader he was in all ecclesiastical matters. A more moderate partizan would soon have found himself hopelessly at variance with his followers. Sheldon was successful in his work of reconstruction, because, not having learnt anything from the past, nor foreseen what would happen in the future, he personified the vices, the ignorance, and the unchained passions of the cavalier party. But while we lay bare his faults, we must not neglect to do justice to his good qualities. He was a man of noble and princely generosity. Oxford owes its Sheldonian Theatre, and many other monuments, to his bounty. All the various situations he held in the Church were benefitted by his large-hearted liberality. Though in public he was imperious both in speech and action, in private intercourse he was remarkably courteous, affable, and accessible to all who desired to approach him; and though he was alleged to be insincere, he generally gained the goodwill of those with whom he conversed. His religious opinions were those of the generality of the clergy of his day, and therefore have an historical value which would not otherwise belong to them. They are very plainly laid down in the preamble of his will, which, according to the usual practice of his time, began with a solemnly attested statement of his religious opinions, made in prospect of death, and therefore with more than ordinary care and deliberation.

That of Sheldon is thus introduced:

"In the name of God, Amen. I, Gilbert Sheldon, Archbishop of Canterbury, being in good health of body, and sound and perfect of memory and understanding (God be praised for it), do make and ordain this my last will and testament in manner and form following. I recommend my soul unto the hands of my gratious Redeemer, my only Lord, Saviour, and Master, Jesus Christ, relying only on His goodness and mercy for my salvation, giving Him most humble thanks for allowing me by his gospel and grace to His knowledge and obedience; abhorring all superstition and tyranny in religion, holding fast the true orthodox profession of the catholic faith of Christ, foretold by the prophets and preached to the world by Christ Himself, His blessed apostles and their successors, being a true member of his Catholic Church within the communion of a living part thereof, the holy Church of England, desiring God to confirm me in this faith and in all Christian charity, and His holy fear till my life's end. My body I desire may be decently buried, but very privately, that my funeral may not waste much of what I leave behind me for better uses."

This last cited clause is interesting, inasmuch as it exhibits the archbishop as having anticipated in his own mind those ideas respecting the reduction of funeral expenses which in the present day have been so warmly advocated, and have attracted such general attention.

Of the pleasant manner in which he exercised his archiepiscopal authority as a peacemaker, we have an amusing and interesting instance in the following facetious epistle. It appears that Sheldon had been desired to intervene in a quarrel that had arisen between the dignitaries of Wells. One, Dr. Silleck, archdeacon of the cathedral, had quarrelled with some of his colleagues in the chapter, and had intended, or at least professed to have intended, to have visited Lambeth to give his explanation, if he had not, as he alleged, been prevented from coming by a cold he had taken. Thereupon M. Smyth, probably a chaplain or secretary of the archbishop, writes, under the prelate's direction, the following epistle:—

"My lord being absent from home all this day, hath commanded me in his name, to let you know that, notwithstanding anything your letters may say for you, there is nothing that can seem tolerably to excuse, much less justify, the severity wherewith you have treated your brethren, and by the authority of my lord I tell you this and have told the same to your dean. For your own particular, my lord says you never had a cold that hath done you more service that this in excusing your journey and attendance here for the present, for it hath saved you a very severe and justly deserved chiding, which he says you have no way to keep off but by falling heartily to a speedy composure and reconciliation with your brethren. If you do not you must have better testimony than your own for your cold to keep you at home, and perhaps that shall not serve your turn neither. As you have been a great instrument in railing and keeping up this broil, you will do well to be as forward, at least, to quiet it, and that done to love one another and live in peace and unity will be the best design and policy you can follow. To which his Grace recommends you by the hand of, Sir,

"Your very humble servant,

"M. SMYTH."

This letter appears to have had the desired effect. The archbishop writes to the Dean of Wells, who had complained of the archdeacon's conduct as having been disrespectful, expressing his fear that the quarrel might break out again, and promising that if it came to him the archbishop would see that the dean was not oppressed by his insubordinate archdeacon.

The amount which Sheldon left by will to be devoted to religious and charitable purposes was very large. The learned and accurate Henry Wharton reckoned that he had given away in his lifetime the sum of £32,208 9s. 9d. Another account states that the total amount of his benefactions given away in his lifetime and under his last will, was £72,000. These are noble sums and were applied to noble uses. A man who has died wifeless, childless, and without near relatives, leaves behind him large sums from which death has parted him, and deserves little credit for having devoted them to religious and charitable purposes. But Sheldon did not wait for death, but gave sums which, when we reflect on the value of money in his day, we must acknowledge to have been prodigious in their amount, and that too during his lifetime, and at a period when the revenues of his see had been very seriously impaired by the civil war.

Only a few months before his death, Lord Danby, in the hope of recovering for the king and his brother, the Duke of York, the confidence of the nation, had brought in a Bill which provided that in the case of the succession to the throne of a king who was not a member of the Anglican Church, all appointments to vacant bishoprics should be made by the bishops, and that the king's children should be placed under the tutelage of the Archbishop of Canterbury. This measure was defeated in the Commons by a small majority.

We must not conclude this portion of our work without referring to the Great Plague which broke out in London in the year 1665. Some of the London clergy remained at their posts during the whole period when this dreadful pestilence was raging, but though many ministers of religion, both conformists and nonconformists, fled at the first alarm and never returned till the pestilence had entirely disappeared, there were others who courageously remained at their posts, and continued to minister to the bodies and souls of those who were suffering from the horrible pestilence. Defoe tells us that one clergyman went every evening through the streets of Whitechapel, and with a loud voice, and with hands uplifted towards heaven, fervently recited that solemn suffrage of the Church liturgy, " Spare us, good Lord, spare thy people whom thou hast redeemed with thy most precious blood." The same writer also informs us that there were some people who, notwithstanding the danger, did not omit to attend the worship of God even in the most perilous times; "and though it is true that a great many clergymen did shut up their churches, and fled, as other people did, for the safety of their lives, yet all did not do so. Some ventured to officiate, and to keep up the assemblies of the people by constant prayers ; and sometimes sermons or brief exhortations to repentance and reformation, and this as long as any would come to hear them. And Dissenters did the like also, and even in the very churches where the parish ministers were dead or fled ; nor was there any room for making a difference at such a time as this was."

It was, indeed, a lamentable thing to hear the miserable lamentations of poor dying creatures calling out for ministers to comfort them and pray with them, to counsel them and direct them,—calling out to God for "pardon and mercy, and confessing aloud their past sins."

During the time that this horrible pestilence was raging, and when it had reached its greatest height and virulence, there was in presence of the common danger a momentary truce and cessation of hostilities between conformists and nonconformists. The penal laws were not abolished, but they were forgotten; and it was only when the plague had disappeared, and when those who had fled in terror saw that the danger was passed, that men thought of putting them in force. A great number of those who deserted their posts and fled with precipitation from the plague-stricken city, thereby acquired a discredit which stuck to them long after the plague had disappeared. But the general calamity was not sufficiently felt to put an end to the animosities which had existed before, especially those which had so long prevailed between conformists and nonconformists. "The quarrel," says Defoe, "remained. The Church and the Presbyterians were incompatible: as soon as the plague was removed the dissenting ousted ministers, who had supplied the pulpits which were deserted by the incumbents, retired; they could expect no other but that they would immediately fall upon them and harass them with their penal laws, accept their preaching while they were sick, and persecute them as soon as they were recovered again. This even we that were of the Church thought was very hard and could by no means approve of it. But it was the Government, and we could say nothing to hinder it; we could only say, it was not our doing, and we could not answer for it. On the other hand, ... a great many of the clergy, who were in circumstances to do it, withdrew and fled for the safety of their lives; but it is also true that a great many of them staid, and many of them fell in the calamity and in the discharge of their duty."

CHAPTER II.

THE POPISH PLOT.

SEVERAL other events, which had a more or less direct bearing on this history, occurred about the time of Sheldon's decease, and contributed to bring about changes which mark that period as an epoch in the history of this country, and especially in its ecclesiastical history. Among them were the Great Fire of London, the appointment of Sancroft to the primacy of the English Church, and the celebrated Popish Plot, which was the cause of a long series of judicial murders, but which also defeated the hopes and designs of the unscrupulous monarchs and statesmen who were secretly conspiring to introduce Romanism and lawless despotism into this country. That such a design actually existed there can be no doubt. Coleman, who was the secretary of the Duchess of York, and who was also general agent of the foreign Roman Catholics, was denounced by Titus Oates, but had time to burn all his papers, with the exception of one, in which he asked the assistance of the Père la Chaise, the confessor of the King of France, for the striking of the greatest blow against Protestantism that it had ever yet received. There can be no doubt that, as Dryden says, in these charges "some truth there was, though dashed and brewed with lies." What could be more natural than that many foolish and many unscrupulous Catholics, emboldened by the knowledge, or at least by the belief, that Charles was secretly a member of their Church— and by the certainty that the next heir to the crown was her devoted champion, and was prepared to make any sacrifices for her, that both of them were in constant and secret communication with the French monarch; in fact, that there was a great European conspiracy headed by the kings of France and England. All this being more or less known to men who were profoundly ignorant of the state of public opinion and feeling in England, naturally inspired them with hopes which, without being formed into settled plans, took the character of aspirations, and were expressed in correspondence by zealots who imagined that England was on the eve of being reconverted to the ancient faith.. Hopes and fears of this nature have been entertained in our day and have produced great results. How much more likely were they to be cherished at a time when most men were profoundly ignorant of the real weakness of the Romish party in England and elsewhere, and of obstacles that stood in the way of the realization of such ideas. It is only very lately that the English people have discarded the bugbears that terrified our forefathers, have come to perceive how groundless such fears are, and to learn that the best protection against the tyranny of one religious body over the rest is to give equal liberty of teaching to all. What might not be hoped on the one hand and feared on the other, with a Popish king actually on the throne and a Popish successor animated by the spirit of Ignatius Loyola, and determined to strain every nerve to secure the triumph of his religion; and behind him a Popish ally, the richest, the most absolute, the most powerful monarch in the world, and rendered still more powerful through the exaggerated belief that men entertained of the greatness of his resources, who, from policy and ambition as well as from religious zeal, entered warmly into the designs of his English allies, and had promised to afford them his aid by land and by sea, whenever matters should seem ripe for the attempt. Under such circumstances it need cause no surprise that foolish and unscrupulous Catholics like Coleman, should, in their secret conclaves and clandestine correspondence, give expression to their wild dreams of conquest and conversion, and that knaves like Titus Oates, by listening at keyholes and piecing out by imagination scraps of letters and sentences half uttered and half whispered, should have framed that monstrous farrago of fact and falsehood, which is known by the name of the Popish Plot, and which, beginning in delusion, ended in unmitigated perjury. The great fire, which the panic fears and prejudices of the populace generally attributed to the Roman Catholics, increased the greediness with which the supposed discoveries of Oates and his associates were swallowed. Any one who ventured to doubt that it was their work was not listened to for a moment, and it was well for him if he was not arrested and imprisoned. The clergy, required as they were by the first canon to preach against Popery, at least four times a year, zealously discharged this duty, and many of them, by their ignorant and virulent invectives, increased the panic and fanned it into a furious flame. The men who believed that the Romanists had been guilty of the atrocities that were imputed to them, naturally and logically concluded that they would commit crimes even more monstrous, and lived in continual dread of the perpetration of something even more terrible than the destruction of their city. The erection of the monument, with its libellous inscription, seemed to set the seal of the highest authority in the land on the truth of the abominable fiction, for it was naturally supposed that the king would not have permitted the inscription which the pillar bore to be placed on it originally, or afterwards to remain on it, if he were not himself satisfied of the truth of the frightful accusation it conveyed; and this belief was further strengthened, when, as each 5th of November came round, the memory of the treason and plot to blow up king, lords, and commons, was resuscitated, and the haranguers against Popery were able to point to a fact which seemed to afford some warrant for their anti-Papistical declamations.

We look on the period of 1678, which we have now reached, as marking a new point of departure in the history of the Anglican Church, not because of the great fire of London or the Popish Plot, not because the long reign of Sheldon was at length brought to a close and a new primate, mounting the archiepiscopal throne of Canterbury, was labouring hard to infuse new life and vigour into the Church, of which he now became the first minister; but because that date marks, at least approximately, the period when the cavalier or ecclesiastico-conservative reaction having run its course, and reached its highest point, the reflux tide had now become distinctly noticeable. From this time forward, it may be roughly calculated that conformity had attained its culminating point, and that henceforward the history of the English Church presents the spectacle of a series of struggles between free opinion on the one hand, and enforced conformity on the other. The former steadily progressing in spite of all the efforts that were made to arrest its advances, while the latter, beaten from each successive position, but still standing firmly and steadily on the defensive, and retiring from post to post in the hope that each position would prove more defensible than that which had been given up before it. I do not pretend to mark, with any degree of accuracy, the date of the commencement of the long struggle that is still going on between the opposing forces of religious liberalism and religious conservatism. But if I am asked to fix as nearly as possible the time at which the two forces entered into strong and decided antagonism, I should put my finger on the period when the great fire had burnt itself out, and when the torpor which characterized the latter part of Sheldon's life, was exchanged for the zealous activity and well intentioned firmness of Archbishop Sancroft. At all events, I would submit that in following the course of the history of the Church through the year 1678, it becomes evident, to careful observers, that the cavalier movement had spent its force, and that a reaction from its violences had set in. One of the first influences that helped most effectually to bring this about was the celebrated Popish Plot, to which we have already referred, and of which we shall now have occasion to speak more fully.

We have mentioned the strong and violent antipathy which pervaded the minds of the clergy, and through the influence of their sermons and conversation had spread itself through all classes of society, so that the public mind was prepared to accept the most absurd fables that could be invented with regard to the clergy and laity of that persecuted communion, and which it was utterly useless for them to deny, because it was generally believed that no oath was binding on their consciences, and that, wherever the interests of their Church were concerned, they deemed it to be their bounden duty to forswear themselves. The revelations, therefore, made by Oates, fell on a soil well prepared to receive them, and as he was well paid for those which he perhaps believed to be true, he was soon led to build a huge superstructure of falsehood on the small foundation of fact which had proved so gainful to him, and as the trade of informer was soon perceived to be both lucrative and honourable, informers swearing to the most barefaced lies were not wanting. Judges, witnesses, and jurymen, were all carried away by their prejudices, and were led to treat the prisoners who were brought before them with barefaced injustice, in disregard of every dictate of law and equity. Many Romanists, conscious of their innocence, at first treated the charges that were brought against them with contemptuous disregard; but they soon found that the wildest dreams and the most absurd inventions were propagated and believed, not only by ignorant curates or squires "full of port wine and foolish prejudices," but by candid and enlightened men, such as Sharp, Stillingfleet, and Tillotson. Nevertheless, these atrocious perjuries would not have obtained any serious credit if the public alarm had not been stimulated almost into madness by the mysterious and tragical fate of Sir Edmundsbury Godfrey, a magistrate before whom Oates had made an affidavit of the truth of his story. Godfrey was a country gentleman, who had made himself conspicuous by the activity and intelligence he had displayed in the discharge of his magisterial duties. Charles II. is said to have had his attention directed to the conscientious firmness he had displayed in the discharge of his magisterial duties, and to have testified that he was the best justice of the peace in his kingdom. He appears to have been a man of a singularly tolerant disposition, considering the times in which he lived; and though a zealous Churchman, he is said to have been on terms of intimacy with Catholics as well as Protestant Nonconformists. When the plague was at its height in London, and clergymen, dissenting ministers, and physicians were fleeing in terror from the pest-stricken city, Godfrey not only remained at his post, but also tended the sufferers with his own hands, and fed the starving and deserted poor. A malefactor, having taken shelter in a house in which the plague had appeared, the officers of justice were afraid to enter it, Godfrey followed the fugitive and took him into custody. Oates finding that the members of the Privy Council were disposed to treat his tale with contemptuous disregard, applied to Godfrey the day before the meeting of the Council summoned to consider the matter, to take care that public attention should be directed to it. Godfrey appears to have incurred the hostility of the Romanists by what they deemed to be an officious interference on his part, and to have been threatened by some of them in consequence. Meeting Burnet, he held conversation with him for some time on the state of affairs, and told him that he expected to be knocked on the head. At that time it was usual for gentlemen of position to be followed in their walks by a servant, but Godfrey frequently went out without any attendant, and gave as his reason for doing so, that he thought that in London, servants were corrupted by the idleness and ill company they fell into while waiting for their masters; and, although some expressions dropped by Coleman, when brought before him, seem to have caused him some alarm, which, as mentioned above, he had expressed in his conversation with Burnet, he took no precautions, but went out, according to his usual practice, entirely unattended, about a fortnight after the time of his receiving the information that Oates had laid before him. He was last seen alive about one o'clock the same day, near the Church of St. Clement in the Strand. As he was a punctual man, and kept good hours, his servants were much surprised that he did not return home at his usual time on that Saturday evening. Knowing, however, that he had a mother who had reached a considerable age, they thought that perhaps she had suffered some sudden attack of illness, and that he had been sent for to see her. When the Sunday came, and they were still without any tidings of him, they sent to Hammersmith where his mother resided, and were informed that he had not been heard of at her house. Becoming now seriously alarmed, they despatched messengers to his two brothers, who lived in the city, but with no better success. Neither of them was able to account for his disappearance. The council was then summoned to consider the matter, and it was proposed that every house about town should be searched, but this order was stopped by the intervention of the Duke of Norfolk. However, on Thursday night, the body of the unfortunate magistrate was discovered in a ditch, near the Church of St. Pancras, at a spot now completely covered with buildings, but then a desolate place about a mile outside the city. His sword was thrust through his body, but there was no blood on his clothes or person, which seemed to show that this must have been done a considerable time after his death. His shoes were clean. His money was safe in his pocket, whence it was inferred that vengeance and not plunder had been the object of his murderers. There were several drops of white wax on his breeches. From these tokens, Burnet and Lloyd, who went together to view the body, inferred that he had been strangled after making a violent resistance, then carried to the place where his body was found, and that there his body had been transfixed with his sword in order to create an impression that he had committed suicide, while it was inferred from the spots of wax on his clothes that the body had been brought either into a Roman Catholic chapel, or else into a house inhabited by Roman Catholics, the only place in which wax-lights were likely to be burnt.

These facts taken together render it highly probable that Godfrey had been put to death by some Roman Catholics, who, knowing the active part he had taken in the persecution carried on against them, and perhaps being aware that Coleman had communicated to him some important secret in private conversation, assassinated him either through revenge or to prevent him from making further revelations. These suppositions, which not improbably might be well founded, were assumed to be indisputable, and were made use of to goad into madness the panic which already prevailed. Godfrey's body, after lying in state for some days, was interred with a solemnity that increased the prevalent excitement. Eighty clergymen, arrayed in full canonicals, walked before the coffin which contained the mangled corpse of the Protestant martyr. Oates at once rose to be one of the most important men in the whole kingdom. His most absurd and outrageous statements met with ready credence. He himself was richly salaried, and many humble imitators presented themselves in the hope, which was not disappointed, of reaping their portion in the field of perjury, delusion, and imposture, which Oates had found to be so profitable. They succeeded in obtaining the belief of judges and juries to the most outrageous and improbable assertions. It was in vain that the parties accused denied the statements of these perjured villains, or produced witnesses who could contradict them on oath, when every Protestant minister believed and taught his people to believe that a Roman Catholic had no regard for an oath, nay even considered himself bound to swear falsely if the supposed interests of the Church to which he belonged required him to do so.

There is nothing in the disgraceful history of the reign of Charles II. more disgraceful than the conduct he pursued in reference to this plot. He must have known the falsity of the charges that Oates and his accomplices brought forward. He must have seen through the plot from its commencement. He must have been well aware that his own tortuous and unprincipled policy had really supplied the small basis of fact on which a huge fabric of perjury and fiction had been built up; and yet without resistance, and apparently without remonstrance, he attached his signature to the warrants that condemned to a shameful and ignominious death men whom he knew to be far more innocent than himself, and that merely for the sake of avoiding a little trouble and a little interruption of his habits of sauntering and idling. If there was a man in the kingdom who sounded still lower depths of baseness than the merry monarch it was his chancellor, the Earl of Shaftesbury, who, regarding the plot simply as a means of raising himself and the party he led to wealth, place, and power, kept up as long as he could the groundless alarm which the pretended discoveries of Oates and his imitators had produced and the blood they had caused to be shed.*

I cannot, after careful examination, find any reason for supposing that the bishops and other leading members of the Church took any special interest in the various trials to which the plot gave rise. Their abject loyalty and their firm belief in the doctrine of non-resistance, which they regarded as the great glory of the Church, prompted them to support the king through all the tortuous windings that his crooked policy underwent, and of the worst part of which they were altogether ignorant. On the other hand, their panic dread of Romanism, fostered by a hundred wild fables and ridiculous misrepresentations, impelled them to oppose the policy of their sovereign, while they offered a sincere homage to his person and to his royal authority.

The persons who were accused by Oates and his accomplices were tried by Sir William Scroggs, the Lord Chief Justice of the King's Bench. He was a man who fully shared the prejudices of his nation and his time with regard to the Roman Catholics, and in the course of the trials over which he presided, he repeatedly laid it down that Roman Catholics were not to be believed on their oath, and with complacent gravity lectured the innocent and unfortunate victims of abominable perjury on

---

* I have looked through Mr. Christie's apology for Lord Shaftesbury, but without finding in it any occasion to change the opinion here expressed.

the wickedness of the perjuries which he believed them to be prepared to commit. It seems to me that every one who carefully reads the reports of the trials over which Scroggs presided, will be led to the conclusion that he was an honest and good-natured man labouring under the force of invincible prejudices, which were probably shared by all classes of the community, except the unfortunate Catholics, who were the victims of them.

While the nation was seething and boiling under the influence of the furious alarm which the Great Fire and the Popish Plot had produced, Sancroft had quietly succeeded to the post which the death of Sheldon had vacated. Though endowed with very moderate abilities and entirely devoid of ambition, he was placed in a situation of great difficulty, in which he was enabled by his sterling uprightness and integrity to rise to the height of his position, and to fill it, not only with credit, but with honour and renown. A knowledge of his character is necessary to the due understanding of the revolution in which he played so important but at the same time so undesired a part. As his motives have been very differently represented, we shall proceed to lay before our readers, in somewhat full detail, those circumstances of the early life of the youth, which appear to be necessary in order to the formation of a just judgment of the character of the man.

William Sancroft was educated in the grammar school of Bury St. Edmund's, whence in due course he passed on into the Protestant and religious foundation of Emmanuel College, Cambridge. The illness and death of a young college friend, named Arthur Bonest, called forth into distinct light the remarkable sensibility of his nature. Writing to his father, he thus expresses the feelings which the decease of his companion awakened in his susceptible nature: "Besides the abilities, natural and acquired, wherewith God had enriched him,—besides that virtuous disposition, and those many powerful attractives in his carriage, whereby he won the affection of all who knew him, one thing there was which made him deservedly more dear to me than others, and that was his exceeding love to me, which I know to have been so great as few brothers equal, none exceed. I am distressed for thee, my brother Jonathan: very pleasant hast thou been unto me; thy love to me was wonderful, surpassing the love of women. Four days before he died I was with him, and when I had taken my leave of him and was gone out of the chamber, he called for me again, and again bade me farewell in the Lord, and fixing a ghastly eye on me, and putting his bones about my neck (for that was all which was left of his arms), he prayed God to bless me, and told me he should never see me more in this world. I was at his burial, and helped to lay him in his bed of rest; and now there is nothing left for me to do but to love his memory and imitate his virtues, which God give me grace to do. He was mortified to all worldly things long before he died; yet, father, I know he found not more difficulty than to part with me his unworthy friend, so dearly did he love me." His uprightness and integrity were also manifested in a letter written to his father at a time when he was expecting to be elected to a fellowship in his college. He thus expresses his scruples about it in a letter which, as the one just quoted, was written to his father. "My quære is," he writes, "whether this assignment (though but in trust), especially if the trust be not mentioned in the instrument, will not invest me with such an estate in lands as will disable me from taking this preferment in the college. That nobody knows of it, I weigh not; for I desire more a thousand times to approve myself to God and my own conscience than to all the world beside. If it be not done, I pray, sir, think of it before you do it; if it be done, and you find it will touch on the statute, let it be undone. I would not be too scrupulous nor yet too bold with my conscience."

Shortly after the death of his friend, Sancroft was thrown on his own resources, and obliged to depend on his own exertions for finding means to support himself. Many of his friends were anxious to aid him in his efforts for this purpose. The master of Emmanuel College offered him a place in an earl's house, which would have yielded him "thirty pounds a year, his diet in the great chamber, and a gelding to ride about on upon occasion." In return, he was to teach the children grammar—that is to say, to impart to them what at that time was regarded as a liberal education. In reference to this offer, he thus writes to his father: "I durst not accept the place, because I knew not your mind, and that was my answer to our master. However, I am infinitely obliged to him, for I had the first offer of it in the college. I pray, sir, when you have occasion to write to Cambridge, express yourself fully what you would have me to do, if the like case be offered again ; for, though such things happen but seldom, yet if it should come to the same point again, I would do nothing without your direction."

In the year 1645 another offer came, which young Sancroft regarded more favourably. The person who made it was a rich London merchant, who desired to send his son beyond the sea, and wished to find him an able tutor. Respecting this proposal, he thus writes to his father : " I like the person better than had he been, what Mr. Weller mistook him for, noble. For then he would have looked for more respect and attendance, nor should I have had so much influence upon him for his good : briefly, I should then have been a servant, and not a master, or at least a companion ; there would have been much expected, and but little done, for generally these great ones prove unruly abroad."

This offer must have been a tempting one to a young man who had to shift for himself as well as he could. However, he decided to refuse it, whether from obedience to his father, or reluctance to leave his own country, or from some other motive, cannot now be ascertained. At all events, he made up his mind to remain in the university, where he occupied himself as fully as he could with tutorial work. He was thus engaged when the Civil War broke out ; and so he continued to be throughout a great portion of the Protectorate, holding fast his principles, but yielding, as all others were obliged to do, to the laws which abolished the Book of Common Prayer, but which could not prevent him from making such uses of it as are alluded to in the following extract :—

"The universities," he writes to his father, "we give up for lost; and the story you have in the country, of Cromwell's coming among us, will not be long a fable: and now 'tis grown treason (which in St. Paul's time was duty) to pray for kings and all that are in authority. The doors of the church we frequented will be shut up, and conscientious men will refuse to preach, where they cannot, without danger of a pistol, do what is more necessary—pray according to their duty. For my part, I have given over all thoughts of that exercise in public till I may with safety pour out my vows for Charles II., the heir, I hope, of his father's virtues as well as kingdoms. In the meantime, there are caves and dens of the earth, and upper rooms and secret chambers, for a Church in persecution to flee to. . . ."

Not long after this letter was written, the father to whom it was addressed, whom he seems to have loved with a warm affection, and by whose counsel and advice he was entirely guided, was taken away from him. A violent fever, aggravated by the misfortunes and anxieties of the times, carried him off in the sixty-ninth year of his age. Sancroft himself caught a severe cough and cold, caused either by the journey or by his attendance at the interment.

The oath, called the engagement, which bound those who took it to be true and faithful to the then established Government, was now enforced with great strictness; and Sancroft, wishing to avoid having it tendered to him, as it would have been against his conscience to take it, retired from the university, and surrendered the preferments he held there, thus acting in the same manner as, under somewhat similar circumstances, he did on a subsequent and much more important occasion.

It was about the time of this retirement that he published the "Fur Predestinatus," which Macaulay alleges to be the most important, and which certainly was the most elaborate, of his writings. It was published anonymously, and seems never to have been acknowledged by Sancroft, who probably wished to avoid giving offence to a party which comprised a large section of the members of the Church. There is, however, a general consensus of authorities which attribute the work to him. Among these is Lord Macaulay, who describes it as "a hideous caricature of the Calvinistic theology." It is in fact an attempt to confute the Calvinistic doctrine of predestination, by exhibiting it in the very words of a great number of eminent divines of that persuasion, whose names are all given, and who certainly enjoyed in their day a considerable reputation among the upholders of Calvinism. Sancroft also published a work in defence of the Vulgate translation of the New Testament. At the time of the Restoration, when the vacant sees were filled up, he was chosen by Dr. Cosin, Bishop-designate of Durham, to be his chaplain, in which capacity he was required to preach at the consecration of his patron and of six other bishops who had been appointed to fill the sees of those prelates who had died during the Protectorate.

He was frequently consulted by Cosin, himself one of the most eminent of all the bishops who have occupied the episcopal bench, and though he did not at this time fill any office in the Church, he enjoyed a high reputation for learning and piety; he was much consulted in the reconstruction of the Church, and probably suggested many of the changes which were made by the Convocation of 1662, and embodied in the Act of Uniformity. Cosin, however, did not long leave him in the dependent state in which the Restoration found him. He took an early opportunity of appointing him to a prebendal stall in the cathedral of Durham, and it appears that Sancroft, finding himself, through this preferment, possessed of a moderate competence, formed the project of entering into the state of matrimony—a design which was warmly encouraged by his patron; but for some reason or other he laid it aside, determining to lead a life of celibacy.

Not long after he was quite unexpectedly elected to the office of master of his own college, and soon began to form earnest projects for the improvement of that "Protestant and religious foundation," by the erection of a new library and chapel; but his appointment, three years after, to the deanery of York put an end to these schemes, and the year after he was transferred to the better endowed but more laborious post of Dean of St. Paul's, London. Here he found a ruined cathedral and a ruined deanery, both of which must be restored, if at all, to a very great extent at the dean's expense. Called on alike by his natural disposition and by the place he occupied to take the lead in the work of reconstruction, he entered on it with zeal and earnestness. He associated with himself those who were most likely to lend assistance in the great and necessary undertaking of restoring or rebuilding St. Paul's Cathedral.

The following letter addressed by him to Dr. (afterwards Sir Christopher) Wren, shows how fully alive he was to his duty in this respect, and how thoroughly he had made himself acquainted with the details of the building. This letter has a peculiar interest for the reader on account of the full and detailed information it affords, as well as the personage to whom it was addressed and the special circumstances under which it was written. It shows how anxious Sancroft was to preserve the old cathedral, and that he only abandoned the hope of being able to do so, when it had become quite manifest that no underpropping would support the venerable edifice, and that it was absolutely necessary that an entirely new building must be substituted for the old one now ruined beyond all hope of repair, and the downfall of which might be attended by widespread destruction if steps were not taken without delay to avert such a calamity. It was under these circumstances that Sancroft indited the following letter to his friend, Dr. Wren.

" To my worthy friend, Dr. Christopher Wren, Professor of Astronomy in Oxford.

"April 25, 1668.

" SIR,

" As he said of old, *prudentia est quædem divinatio,* so science (at the height you are master of it), is prophetic too. What you whispered in my ear at your last coming hither is now come to pass. Our work at the west end of St. Paul's is fallen about our ears. Your quick eye discerned the walls and pillars gone off from their perpendiculars, and I believe other defects too, which are now exposed to every common observer.

"About a week since, we being at work about the third pillar from the west end on the south side, which we had new cased with stone, where it was most defective almost up to the chapitre, a great weight falling from the high wall so disabled the vaulting of the side aisle by it, that it threatened a sudden ruin so visibly that the workmen presently removed, and the next night the whole pillar fell, and carried scaffolds and all to the very ground.

" The second pillar (which you know is bigger than the rest) stands now alone, with an enormous weight on the top of it, which we cannot hope shall stand long, and yet we dare not venture to take it down.

" This breach has discovered to all that look on it, two great defects in Inigo Jones' work: one, that his new case of stone in the upper walls (massy as it is) was not set upon the upright of the pillars, but upon the core of the groins of the vaulting; the other, that there were no key stones at all to tie it to the old work; and all this being very heavy with the Roman ornaments on the top of it, and being already so far gone outwards, cannot possibly stand long. In fine, it is the opinion of all men that we can proceed no further at the west end. What we are to do next is the present deliberation, in which you are so absolutely and indispensably necessary to us, that we can do nothing, resolve on nothing without you.

"It is, therefore, that in my Lord of Canterbury's name, and by his order (already, I suppose, intimated to you by the Dean of Christ Church), we most earnestly desire your presence and assistance with all possible speed.

"You will think fit, I know, to bring with you those excellent draughts and designs you formerly favoured us with; and in the meantime, till we enjoy you here, consider what may be to advise that may be for the satisfaction of His Majesty and the whole nation, an obligation so great and so public that it must be acknowledged by better hands than those of

"Your affectionate friend and servant,

"W. SANCROFT."

In accordance with the announcements contained in this letter, it was determined not only to abandon the project of repairing the church, but also to reconstruct it on that grand scale on which it was actually erected. Although no funds existed for the purpose, it was resolved to commence at once in full confidence that enough would be forthcoming for so noble a purpose. Sancroft himself was a personal contributor of £1400, an enormous sum considering the value of money at that time, besides his share of what was given from the general funds of the chapter. By many efforts and much perseverance he succeeded in obtaining the "Coal Act," in virtue of which a rate levied on all coals brought into the port of London was applied to the rebuilding of the cathedral.

At the same time Sancroft was contributing still more largely to the re-edification of his deanery. It may indeed be said that if he was a bountiful giver he was also a large recipient of ecclesiastical revenues, holding as he did in plurality several other preferments. But it should be remembered that in doing so he was only acting in accordance with the usages of his times, and that the value of church property had been so much reduced by the civil wars and their consequences that the preferments he held were not more than were necessary to enable him to support the hospitalities and other requirements of his position as Dean of St. Paul's.

Sancroft's appointment to the primacy seems not to have been expected either by himself or by others. It took place at a moment when the English Church, after having been tossed by the storms of half a century, seemed at last to have entered a haven of rest and peace. She was strong in the patronage of the sovereign, in the affection of a decided majority of the English nation, in the zealous support of the legislature, in the protection, such as it was, that was afforded her by the various penal statutes by which she was fenced and defended from all external assaults, as well as in the monopoly of all political power which was enjoyed by her children; in the admiring approval of many Dissenters, who, though rejecting some of her ceremonies, and persecuted on account of their nonconformity, still continued to regard her as the great bulwark of Protestantism against the dreaded encroachments of the Roman Catholic Church. Never, perhaps, had she seemed more secure than at the moment when Sancroft was summoned to mount the archiepiscopal throne of Canterbury.

The elevation of Sancroft to the Primacy of all England caused general surprise. He had all along been so quiet, humble, and unassuming; he had kept himself so much in the background; he was so entirely unknown—except for the quiet, but zealous discharge of his decanal duties, and the exercise of his decanal hospitalities—that amidst all the guesses and surmises to which the vacancy of the Primate's place gave rise, his name was not mentioned. It was afterwards, indeed, alleged by Wood and Burnet, that Sancroft owed this high preferment to the interest of the Duke of York and the rest of the Roman Catholic coterie, by which the king was surrounded at this time, and who, it is insinuated, hoped that they would find in Sancroft a pliant accomplice or a time-serving opponent; and there is nothing that is *primâ facie* improbable in the supposition. The Romanists of his day would naturally prefer him to a Low Churchman, and, if they used their influence at all, would use it in favour of a High Churchman rather than a Low Churchman—of a Sancroft rather than a Compton. But this preference, if it really existed, lends no support whatever to the insinuation that Sancroft had afforded the Romanists of his day the least ground for expecting that he was at all likely to give any countenance or support to the views and designs of the Romanists. Taking all the facts with which we are acquainted together, it appears to me that the most probable explanation of the appointment is, that it was made by Charles himself, who, admiring in others the virtues which he himself was far from practising, had a really conscientious desire to promote honest and good men to the high places of the Church; and, accordingly, took entirely into his own hands the appointment of Sancroft to the archbishopric of Canterbury, as on another occasion he took into his own hands the appointment of Ken to the bishopric of Bath and Wells.

There was one qualification possessed by Sancroft which must, no doubt, have recommended him to the favour of both Charles and James. He was an earnest and thoroughly convinced advocate of the royal prerogative, which he took every opportunity of magnifying and exalting. But it must not be supposed that he in any way stood alone in his advocacy of the doctrine of the divine right of kings. The difference between him and some of those who joined him in resisting the absurd tyranny of James, was that while Tillotson and Tennison, and others, abandoned those views when they became unpopular and conflicted with the prejudices of the people, Sancroft clung to and upheld them from first to last, through evil report and good report. And in doing so he only maintained a principle which had been declared over and over again, not only to be permissible, but to be the pride, the boast, and the glory of the Anglican Church, which, it was said, had never in the darkest hour of her adversity swerved from it. From the brief sketch we have given above of the new archbishop's antecedents, it may, I think, be justly concluded, that he was pious, conscientious, humble-minded, affectionate, severely ascetic to himself, while full of indulgence for the follies and weaknesses of others.

If Charles and James, in choosing a successor for Sheldon, really acted from the motives that Burnet attributed to them, they must have speedily discovered their mistake, for one of the first steps taken by Sancroft after his appointment to the primacy, was to wait on the Duke of York, in company with Morley, Bishop of Winchester, to endeavour to persuade him to renounce the Romish opinions he had embraced, and to return to that religion to which his father had been so strongly attached, and for which he was even said to have laid down his life. Sancroft appears to have taken this step at the instigation of the king, or at all events with his concurrence. It seems difficult to imagine that Charles, who was himself secretly a member of the Roman communion, should have sent the newly-appointed archbishop to convert his brother from a religion which he himself believed to be the only true one, to a religion in which he had no faith at all. But it is very easy to understand that a thoroughly unprincipled Roman

Catholic, such as Charles was, would have been glad to have seen his brother profess a religion which he believed to be false but knew to be popular, rather than one which he thought to be true but well knew to be decidedly unpopular. At any rate, he may have hoped that the step which was taken by Sancroft and Morley, avowedly at his instigation, might lead his subjects to look with less suspicion on his motives, and might help to lull the anti-Popish storm that was just then beginning to rage with redoubtable violence. Be this as it may, the character of Sancroft forbids us to suppose that he would have alleged that his proceedings were sanctioned by Charles, unless this was really the case.

Sancroft and Morley accordingly waited on the duke as representatives of the bench of bishops. The duke, having been already informed of the purpose of their visit, listened with respectful patience to a lengthened address from Sancroft, very ill calculated to produce the effect he and Morley hoped for. He then replied that he gave the bishops full credit for their good intentions, but felt that to be pressed on such a point just before the meeting of Parliament was very injurious to his interests, and that he suspected that the persons who had urged them to take this step, at such a moment, intended to do him an injury—a statement which it seems difficult to reconcile with the allegation that the king himself had authorized or ordered this effort to convert his brother back to the Anglican communion. The duke courteously declined to go further into the matter, and begged his episcopal visitors not to take it amiss, or feel surprise that the great pressure of business obliged him to dismiss them. The two prelates then withdrew, having completely failed in their attempt to reconvert the duke.

No sooner had Sancroft been appointed to the primacy than he began to display a degree of zeal and activity in the discharge of his archiepiscopal duties which contrasted most favourably with the indolence and indifference of his predecessor, under whose careless and regardless rule abuses had grown up and flourished in luxuriant profusion. Foremost among these abuses, and most mischievous in its consequences, was the practice that prevailed very commonly of giving to very undeserving persons letters testimonial by means of which they obtained admission to Holy Orders. These testimonies were frequently signed then, as they too often are even now, on no other ground than that they had been signed by others. In order, as far as possible, to put a stop to this flagrant abuse, Sancroft issued a circular addressed to his suffragans, in which he urged them to use greater strictness in ascertaining the characters of those who applied to them for admission to Holy Orders on the strength of testimonials given without due inquiry into the characters of those who had obtained them.

Another matter which occupied the attention of the new primate was the augmentation of the revenues of poor benefices. At the time of the Restoration many of them were so much reduced in value that they might be denominated rather starvings than livings. Through the urgency of Sancroft the matter was at length pressed on the king's notice, and Charles, who gladly seized every favourable opportunity of asserting practically the ecclesiastical supremacy which he continued to claim, but which the House of Commons steadily refused to allow, had, by his own authority, directed the bishops and other Church dignitaries to make reservations from their incomes which were to be applied to the augmentation of the stipends of poor vicars and curates. The Parliament demurred a good deal to a mandate given in a manner so unconstitutional; yet the object was so strongly supported by the clergy, and therefore so popular in the country, that the king's order, objectionable as it was, was subsequently confirmed and sanctioned by an Act of Parliament, the provisions of which, however, had been imperfectly carried out, the persons whose incomes it affected having refused or neglected to obey it.

Sancroft had this matter much at heart. In the situations he had filled before his nomination to the primacy, he had become acquainted with the full extent of the evil which the Act was intended to remedy, and had moved in the matter earnestly but ineffectually. Now that he was primate he acted more energetically and with better results. He sent letters to his suffragans, which he directed them, in their turn, to transmit to their deans, archdeacons, and prebendaries, strictly enjoining them to put the Act in force, and punctually and effectually carry out its requirements; and afterwards he directed that all bishops, deans, and archdeacons should send him particulars of all the augmentations made by them or their predecessors, with the names of the parishes relieved and the sums received for the use of their incumbents, subscribed with their own hands, that he might know what had been done with regard to the matter throughout the whole kingdom, thus anticipating to some considerable extent by a stretch of his own authority the action of the Ecclesiastical Commissioners in the present day, and providing a remedy for a great evil which at that time was tolerably efficacious.

In this and in various other ways did Sancroft employ the authority of his office in improving the efficiency of the Church and raising the character of her ministers. It is true that when he began to exert his primatial authority in a way that interfered with the temporal interests of some of the wealthier clergy, he found it was much more limited than it was generally supposed to be. But at that time its limits had not been brought into question, nor had the powers of the primate been fully ascertained or clearly defined, and therefore claims that had not been subjected to a legal test were often admitted without much examination.

We who have lived to see how powerless the law of the Church often is for the enforcement of discipline, can appreciate the difficulties with which Sancroft had to contend in endeavouring to compel recalcitrant dignitaries to discharge the duties of their various offices faithfully, even when those duties were enforced on them by special legislative enactments. But the aims of Sancroft were so evidently right, he carried with him so entirely the sympathy and support of the great body of the clergy and laity of the kingdom, that he was enabled to rule his diocese and his province much more successfully than many of his predecessors and successors, who, although men of greater ability, did not succeed as fully as he had done in enlisting sympathy and support by the singleness of their aims and the patent honesty of their intentions.

Meanwhile, the Protestant part of the nation began to be seriously alarmed by the Romish proclivities which the Duke of York displayed with offensive and impolitic openness, and began to regard as the head of their party William of Orange, the Stadtholder of Holland, who, as the husband of the eldest daughter of the duke, would probably at some future time occupy the throne, and therefore might without impropriety offer his opinion on questions of grave importance, in the proper solution of which he had a kind of reversionary interest, especially if they were questions that might be regarded as involving the stability of his wife's throne—questions which the imprudence of his father-in-law had suddenly brought into most unexpected prominence.

He was also carrying on a correspondence with the leaders of the Protestant party, who were openly or secretly agitating for the exclusion of the duke his father-in-law from the succession to the throne, either by appointing the Duke of Monmouth, an illegitimate son of the king, to succeed his father, by substituting William for him, or, by the appointment of a regency in the place of James, to get rid of the danger. All these designs were favoured and supported by a large number of the leading nobility. Of course the first was strongly opposed by William, who was generally regarded, and justly too, as the leader of the Protestant party, not only in England, but throughout the whole of Europe. Thus he was engaged in a very active correspondence with many of the English nobility and gentry.

He did not probably at this time contemplate any alteration in the succession, but was disposed to wait patiently for the death of his father-in-law, and in the mean time aimed at forcing the English Government to take its place in the confederacy of which he was the leader, and whose great aim and object was to curb the ambition of the French monarch. One great obstacle in the way of the success of his designs was the attitude assumed by the Church of England, which, while sympathizing strongly with William in many of his views and opinions, was still faithful to its favourite doctrine of passive obedience to the will of the sovereign, and offered a steady resistance to all the efforts that were made to set aside James. It was therefore a matter of the highest importance to William to induce the Church to support him in his designs, and with this view there was no man whose co-operation was so needful to him as that of Sancroft, who by his prejudices, his opinions, and, above all, by his position as primate, was perhaps better able than any other person in the kingdom to influence the course of the English Church in the important struggle which was visibly coming to a head. It was probably with a view to securing his powerful aid that Dr. Covel, who was then chaplain to the Princess of Orange, tried to draw him into a correspondence on the very important question of effecting a union between the Church of England and the foreign Protestant Churches.

The following reply to Dr. Covel shows the spirit in which Sancroft met the overture thus made to him. "Whatever becomes of your project, or mine, or any particular scheme, I can by no means, as our brethren seem to do, give up the whole Protestant cause as lost and desperate and ready to breathe its last. No! God hath by the Reformation kindled and set up a light in Christendom which I am fully persuaded shall never be extinguished. Heaven and earth passeth away, but the word of the Lord endureth for ever." This short extract is valuable, showing as it does that schemes of the nature referred to were rife towards the end of the reign of Charles II.; that one of these projects had been devised by Sancroft and another by William, whose mouthpiece this Dr. Covel probably was, and who felt very strongly the religious and political importance of confederating the Protestants of Europe in one great body against that powerful communion which they all regarded as their common foe, and against Louis XIV. its self-constituted champion.

Meanwhile, the struggle was going on in England. A great effort was made to exclude James from the throne, and it had proved so far successful that he had been compelled to relinquish his office of Lord High Admiral, and to leave the kingdom, though he subsequently returned to Scotland, where he exercised vice-regal power. A Bill for excluding him from the succession was brought in, and was only prevented from being carried by the eloquence of Lord Halifax and the support which the English Church, true even in this extremity to her loyal doctrines, gave to James. Thus leaving him at liberty to mount the throne unfettered by any of those restrictions which the Protestant party sought to impose on him.

In the midst of the struggles which were being carried on with regard to the securities which should be given to the nation against the abuse of authority by a Popish sovereign, the profligate and unprincipled trifler who since the year 1660 had directed the destinies of this country, was suddenly seized with an attack— probably of apoplexy—which threatened the most serious consequences, and at length was evidently about to terminate in his death. The archbishop, attended by several of his suffragans, gathered round the bed of the dying monarch and offered up the prayers contained in the Anglican office for the visitation of the sick. Charles received their exhortations with his usual urbanity, and seemed to join in the supplications that were offered up in his behalf. Two of the bishops then, in accordance with the directions contained in the service they were using, exhorted him to make a special confession of his sins. But Ken, who, from his general High Church proclivities, might have been expected to support them in the exhortation, knowing probably how little edifying that confession was likely to be, and feeling that if heard it would both last a long time and contain much which it was very undesirable should be heard by the promiscuous assemblage of men and women that crowded the chamber of the dying king, interfered, saying that the confession, though permitted, was not a matter of obligation; and then addressing himself to Charles, he said, "Sire, are you sorry for the sins you have committed?" and on receiving an affirmative answer, he pronounced over the dying king that strong and solemn form of absolution which the Anglican Church still retains in her service for the visitation of the sick, and addressed him in a strain of eloquent earnestness that awed and impressed all who were present in the chamber of death.

Still, the king seemed to be uneasy, as though he wanted something more. The bishops pressed the dying man to receive the sacrament according to the form of their Church, but he evaded compliance with this desire. The Duke of York, who was in the secret of his religious opinions, and was standing close to the bedside, whispered to him, "Shall I send for a priest?" "For God's sake do, brother; and quickly, too," was the reply of the dying man. There was some difficulty in finding one, and still more in obtaining all the paraphernalia necessary to the celebration of the sacrament according to the Roman rite. Any priest administering the sacrament to the dying monarch would run the risk of incurring serious and perhaps even capital penalties. At length search was made for one. Huddleston, a priest who had saved the king's life after the battle of Worcester, and in recompense of that service had been specially exempted by name from all the penal statutes against Roman Catholics that had passed during the reign of Charles. This man having been found, with some difficulty the room was cleared of all except a few who were in the secret of the king's real religious beliefs. Huddleston administered to Charles the last rites of the Roman Church. The bishops and courtiers were then re-admitted. All traces of what had occurred during their exclusion from the chamber of death had been removed, and Charles soon after drew his last breath.

CHAPTER III.

JAMES II.

For some time after the demise of his brother, James was in a state of much alarm and anxiety. It was true that he had gained a great victory in the legislature, but it still remained to be seen how his accession to the throne would be endured by that vast majority of his subjects who held his religion in detestation, and regarded all who adhered to it as idolaters, if not as adherents of Antichrist. A very small proportion of them would suffice to overthrow his army, and place Monmouth or Mary on the throne of these realms. He therefore gave orders at once for placing sentinels, and putting the various parts of the city and elsewhere in a posture that would prevent them from being carried by any sudden attack that might be made on them by the partizans and followers of those who had attempted to bring about his exclusion. Then, overwhelmed with fatigue, he retired for a short time to rest. He was soon aroused from his slumbers, in order that he might receive the formal announcement of his proclamation.

The accession of James II. was an anxious moment for the clergy and laity of the English Church. Bowing to an authority that hitherto had always been exerted in their favour, they had, indeed, offered a steady opposition to every attempt that had been made to exclude him from the throne on account of his profession of the Roman Catholic religion; they had gloried in the constancy with which they had stood by him against all the efforts that had been made by Puritans and Presbyterians to prevent him from being proclaimed. And though he belonged to a dreaded and detested communion, he was the undoubted heir to the throne, and as such, on their principles, had a right to claim their support. Accordingly, a body of the bishops and clergy of the Church, with Sancroft at their head, accompanied the members of the Privy Council who came to announce to the king his undisputed accession.

James then delivered an address, in which he promised to maintain and support the Established Church in the possession of all its privileges. Whether it was that the king's speech roused the spontaneous enthusiasm of Sancroft and his suffragans, or whether the proceeding was suggested to him by James, who was naturally desirous to conciliate to himself and to parade before his subjects all the support he could, certain it is that the bishops took a step which was quite unprecedented, by preparing and presenting to the new monarch—in the name of themselves, of their absent episcopal brethren, and the whole state of the clergy—an address filled with the warmest expressions of duty, devotion, and loyalty. When the coronation took place, Sancroft officiated at it, and even stretched his complacency so far as to consent to the omission on this occasion of the communion office, which on all former occasions had formed the most prominent part of the ceremonial, but of which the opinions of the new king and queen prevented them from partaking, though they did not object to the other parts of the service. We are told that this omission afterwards preyed on Sancroft's sensitive mind, and caused him much remorse. It is difficult to understand why it should have had such an effect. Some zealous Protestants thought that he ought to have refused to officiate at all at the coronation of a Roman Catholic sovereign; but surely no reasonable being would contend that he was bound to attempt to force the Anglican rite on persons who thought of it as James and his consort did, and it seems to me that, considering the opinions that Sancroft held and the circumstances in which he was placed, instead of feeling shame and remorse because he had not insisted that James and his consort should partake of the sacrament, he ought rather to have rejoiced that he had escaped being called on to perform an act which the king, the queen, and he himself also, must have regarded as a profanation of the sacrament.

But though James on the occasion of his coronation conformed to the rite of the Church in which he was born, yet he very soon showed that all his preferences were reserved for that Church to which he had been converted. He not only caused its services to be openly celebrated in his palace at Whitehall; he not only diligently attended those services himself in state, but he made it to be seen that he expected his servants to follow the example thus set to them, and that the surest way to win his favour was to embrace his religion.

The king was no doubt perfectly sincere when, at the commencement of his reign, he solemnly promised that he would protect and defend that Church to which he owed his throne, and whose loyalty he expected would be proof against every trial to which he might think proper to subject it. Besides, believing firmly in the truth of the Roman Catholic religion, he thought that in the situation he now occupied it would be no very difficult matter to bring about the conversion of a large number of his subjects to what he supposed to be the truth. He thought that when the arguments in favour of Romanism, which seemed to him to be so conclusive, came before his subjects, backed by the recommendation of their sovereign, they were certain to prevail, and he expected that the conversion of his subjects to the religion he had himself embraced would prove to be a very easy matter. He also regarded the royal supremacy as involving a sort of right on behalf of the sovereign to dictate to his subjects, as Henry VIII. and Elizabeth had done, their religious beliefs and practices. And he hoped that he should meet with no difficulty in persuading the High Church bishops and clergy who were generally, though falsely, accused of a leaning towards Popery, because they did not renounce all the practices of the Romish Church. His first step was to put before

Sancroft and other zealous Anglicans a paper which had been found in the strong box of Charles II., containing the arguments that were generally employed by the advocates of that religious system, and from which it was inferred, and probably with truth, that Charles II. had embraced it; and he challenged Sancroft to give an answer to the arguments this document contained, promising that, if the answer were conclusive, he would comply with his often expressed desire and return into the communion of the Church of England; and not content with displaying these proofs of the insincerity and hypocrisy of his deceased brother, he had them printed, and himself distributed them freely to the crowds that surrounded his carriage when he went out. He soon found, however, that the arguments thus profusely circulated produced no effects. If the ministers of the Church professed a warm loyalty to his person and his office, they despised and detested his religion; and although they still continued zealously to teach the people committed to their care "to submit themselves to every ordinance of man for the Lord's sake, whether to the king as supreme, or unto governors, as unto them that are sent by him for the punishment of evildoers, and for the praise of them that do well," yet, when they were required to be silent with regard to the king's proceedings, and, at least, to treat his religious opinions with respect and deference, they maintained that they could no longer be silent without a sinful dereliction of duty, and that a crisis had arrived which forced them to choose whether they would obey God rather than man.

And as the news of what was doing in London and its immediate vicinity spread through the country; as the monks and friars, for the first time since the reign of Queen Mary, began to appear in the streets of the metropolis and the other great towns of the kingdom, arrayed in the habits of their respective orders, loud and earnest denunciations of Popery resounded from almost every pulpit in the kingdom, and were often couched in language highly offensive to the king and insulting to his religion.

It should be remembered, in justice to James, that he had been brought up as a sailor, and had spent a great part of his life among sailors, and displayed many of the vices and virtues that in his day belonged to that profession in an eminent degree. He was coarse almost to brutality in his language and manners, and especially ignorant of all that it concerned the monarch of a country such as that which he was called to rule to be acquainted with. His ideas with regard to the government of men and the exercise of authority were drawn from the quarter-deck, at a time when the occupants of that position were grossly ignorant and proud of their ignorance. He had therefore no notion of governing the country over whose destinies he was summoned to preside, except by physical force. He was continually repeating that his father had brought everything to ruin by the concessions he had made, and therefore he was resolved to make no concessions whatever. He was very easily duped and very open to flattery. If he is to be blamed for giving his confidence to scoundrels like Sunderland

and brutes like Jeffreys, it should be remembered that both of these worthies had been introduced into office through the carelessness of his brother, and that they were neither more unprincipled nor more cruel than many of their predecessors in office. That he was honest, brave, and sincere admits of no doubt. Indeed, the tenacity with which he clung to his religious opinions, not only throughout his short reign, but also after its unfortunate termination, shows that he possessed these qualities in a degree that was very unusual in his day. There can be little doubt that even after his flight into France he could not have been prevented from recovering his throne if he had only been brought to profess himself a member of the Anglican Church, and to act up to the assurances he had given at his accession. Indeed, it is difficult to say which of the two was the most completely unfitted to be the head of the English Church—the profligate hypocrite who scoffed at all religions, and in his few lucid moments of penitence and reflection preferred that of the Roman Catholics, or the man who ostentatiously and insultingly upheld a religion which ninety-nine out of every hundred of his subjects regarded as blasphemous and idolatrous.

Ye teach of these men in his turn appointed the bishops, every one of whom had been placed on the bench either by Charles or James; and the latter interfered in the internal affairs of the Church of which he was the supreme head in a manner in which none of his predecessors since the time of Mary would have ventured to have done.

Certainly the conduct of James caused more scandal, but more real danger probably arose from the insidious manner in which Charles carried on a carefully concealed and well-concerted plan for the introduction of Popery into this country by the aid of French troops, to be brought over whenever Charles might think that the time had arrived when the country was ripe for the introduction of Popery and Despotism.

Perhaps the open foe was a more honourable and, even, a less dangerous adversary than the man who, at the very time when he was making loud protestations of his zeal for the Protestant cause, was secretly plotting its overthrow.

Charles was an unprincipled dissembler; James, an honest, well-intentioned, obstinate, harsh man, placed in a situation of great difficulty for which he was entirely unqualified. That he should sooner or later come into collision with some large bodies of his subjects was inevitable. His strong religious opinions and zealous religious partisanship brought him into decided antagonism with almost all of them, but especially with the body which at that time was by far the most powerful in the kingdom—the clergy and zealous laity of the Church of England—that is to say, with nine-tenths of his subjects.

It would be unjust and untrue to say that the fault in this matter was exclusively on the side of James. That he acted most unwisely there can be no doubt whatever, but he was less in the wrong than most of his opponents. He had a sincere desire to extend liberty of conscience to men of all creeds, and a grand opportunity for obtaining it was afforded him. Unfortunately, however, instead of being content with seeking to obtain an equal toleration for both Protestant and Roman Catholic Nonconformists, which was what he professed to desire, he now let it be seen that he intended to claim less than a fair toleration for Protestants, and more than a fair toleration for Roman Catholics.

If he had only had to do with none but reasonable men, such as Tillotson and Stillingfleet, he might, perhaps, have been induced to keep within the bounds of a due moderation. But the folly of James came into direct collision with equal or even greater folly, and thus there arose on the one side and the other a violent party feeling by which James was carried away, and which precipitated him into the commission of acts which even his judgment, wrong-headed as he was, would on cool reflection have disapproved. Thus, instead of being the arbitrator between contending factions, he became the heated leader of one party, and that one the weakest both in intellect and in numbers, not probably comprehending a hundredth part of the nation. Exasperated by the strong and growing feeling that prevailed against his religion, he attempted to silence the preachers of Protestantism, on the ground that they were attacking his opinions in a highly disrespectful manner. This might perhaps have been a fair and wise proceeding, if he had imposed on the preachers of Catholicism the same restraints that he imposed on the preachers of Protestantism ; but while the latter had full licence to attack the former were strictly forbidden to defend.

However, at the commencement of his reign James showed a decided disposition to support the Church and crush the Nonconformists. In doing so he seems to have been only carrying out the policy which had prevailed during the reign of his brother, not with due moderation, but with all the violence of a heated partizanship. James at this period probably allowed himself to be influenced by the advice of servile sycophants such as Sunderland, or violent and intolerant bigots like Petre, or such unprincipled preferment hunters as the infamous Jeffreys, in whom he seemed to place unlimited confidence, and whom he had raised from the position of Lord Chief Justice, for which he was quite unfit, to that of Lord Chancellor.

To give an idea of the justice that was meted to Nonconformists at the time of James' accession to the throne, and how unjustly they were treated, we give a brief abstract of the trial of Baxter—one of the most learned and pious of the Nonconformist divines—a man who, as we have already seen, had been chaplain to Charles II. and had been offered and declined a bishopric.

Baxter was ill, and his counsel moved that his trial might be deferred. The Chief Justice angrily replied, "I will not give him a minute's time more to save his life. We have had to do with other sorts of persons, but now we have a saint to deal with, and I know how to deal with saints as well as sinners." Pointing to Oates, who was standing in the pillory in Palace Yard, he exclaimed, "Yonder stands Oates in the pillory, and he says he suffers for the truth, and so does Baxter; but if Baxter did but stand on the other side of the pillory, I would say that two of the greatest rogues and rascals in the kingdom stood there."

The charge against Baxter was that he had reflected on the bishops of the Church, and so was guilty of sedition.

When Mr. Wallop, one of the counsel for the prisoner, opened the case for the defence, the Chief Justice exclaimed, "Mr. Wallop, I observe that you are in all these dirty causes, and were it not for you gentlemen of the long robe, who should have more wit and honesty than to hold up these factious knaves by the chin, we should not be at the pass we are." "My lord," said Wallop, "I humbly conceive that the passages accused are natural deductions from the text." "You humbly conceive" (interrupted Jeffreys), "and I humbly conceive; Swear him. Swear him." "My lord," replied Wallop firmly, "under favour, I am counsel for the defendant, and if I understand either Latin or English the information now brought against Mr. Baxter on such slight ground is a greater reflection on the Church of England than anything contained in the book he is accused of." Jeffreys, growing more and more impatient, replied, "Sometimes you humbly conceive and sometimes you are very positive. You talk of your skill in Church history, and of your understanding Latin and English; I think I understand something of them as well as you; but, in short, I must tell you that if you do not understand your duty better I shall teach it to you."

Wallop, finding that it was useless to contend with the Chief Justice any longer, sat down, and Rotheram, another counsel, who had also been engaged to plead on Baxter's behalf, stood up.

"It is true," said he, "that Mr. Baxter's book contains sharp reflections on the bishops of the Church of Rome, but it speaks respectfully of the prelates of the Church of England."

"Sir," replied the Chief Justice, "Baxter is an enemy to the name and to the thing, the office and the person of bishops."

Rotheram added that Baxter frequently attended divine service, went to the sacrament and persuaded others to do so, as was certainly and publicly known; and had in the very book for the publication of which he had been called in question, spoken very moderately and honourably of the bishops of the Church of England.

Baxter added, "My lord, I have been so moderate with respect to the Church of England that I have incurred the censure of many of the Dissenters on that account."

"Baxter for bishops!" exclaimed the Chief Justice; "that's a merry conceit indeed; turn to it, turn to it."

Rotheram accordingly turned to a passage, in which it was said that great respect is due to those truly called to be bishops among us.

"Aye," interrupted Jeffreys, "that's your Presbyterian cant—'truly called to be bishops!'—that means himself and such rascals called to be Bishops of Kidderminster and such other places—bishops set apart by such factious, snivelling Presbyterians as himself; a Kidderminster bishop, he means."

When Baxter attempted to say a few words on his own behalf, Jeffreys, becoming furious, exclaimed—

"Richard, thou art an old knave ; thou hast written books enough to load a cart, every one as full of sedition, I might say treason, as an egg is full of meat. Hadst thou been whipped out of the writing trade forty years ago, it had been happy. Thou pretendest to be a preacher of the Gospel of peace, and thou hast one foot in the grave. 'Tis time for thee to begin to think what account thou intendest to give. But leave thee to thyself, and I see thou wilt go on as thou hast begun ; but by the grace of God I will look after thee. I know thou hast a mighty party, and I see a great many of the brotherhood in corners waiting to see what will become of their mighty Don, and a doctor of the party (Dr. Bates) at your elbow, but by the grace of Almighty God I will crush you all."

Rotheram was forced to sit down, as his senior Wallop had done before him. Then Allwood stood up. He held his own more pertinaciously against the interruptions and brow-beatings of the Chief Justice, but he was at length obliged to yield as the other counsel had done before him. The two others were silent ; no doubt they thought it best not to irritate any further a judge who raved and raged more like a furious wild beast than an impartial administrator of justice.

Baxter then once more interposed. "I think, my lord," he said, "that I can clearly answer all that is laid to my charge." Then pulling out a written defence he attempted to read it, but the Chief Justice would not listen to a word.

The summing up was a long and violent tirade against Baxter, the greater part of which was ridiculously false and scandalously insulting. At the conclusion of it Baxter said to the Chief Justice, "Do you think that any jury will pretend to pass a verdict on me upon such a trial?"

"Aye," was the reply, "I'll warrant you; don't trouble yourself about that." The opinion of the Chief Justice proved to be correct. The jury promptly found Baxter guilty. He was sentenced to pay a fine of five hundred marks, to lie in prison till it was paid, and be bound to his good behaviour for seven years. Such was the treatment which the most eminent among the Nonconformists received in what was then called a court of justice, and such the man who was chosen to be the keeper of the king's conscience.

The reason why Charles and James permitted such scenes to be enacted probably was that they hoped to drive the Protestant Nonconformists into the arms of the Roman Catholic Nonconformists. This had certainly been the policy of Charles, and was carried on under the new sovereign, who determined to obtain the repeal of the Test Act, if possible, with the sanction and connivance of Parliament, or, if that was refused, then without its assent, by virtue of the dispensing power which had been exercised by some of his predecessors, and which, though it had been formally renounced by Charles, and condemned by the legislature, James affirmed to be an essential part of the royal prerogative.

On the strength of this supposed right, he published his celebrated declaration of liberty of conscience, which was a programme of the policy he intended to adopt, declaring that he would not retain any in his service who were not willing to assist him in carrying out the policy which the declaration proclaimed, and he at once proceeded to obtain a colourable legal sanction for the dispensing power that he claimed by a collusive trial, at which an ignorant and corrupt judge, appointed on account of his known subserviency, gave a decision in his favour.

The first use which James made of the power obtained by these means was such as no one would now blame, though it was strongly censured at the time. Under circumstances that we shall presently have occasion to dwell on more at length, he released from the imprisonment to which they had been condemned for their religious opinions 1500 Quakers and a very much larger number of Roman Catholics. Still he left a considerable number of other Nonconformists to languish in jail. This was, no doubt, partly because they had not, as the Quakers and Catholics had, friends at court to call special attention to their wrongs and sufferings, but still more, perhaps, because at this period he thought of following the policy of his brother, who had allowed the Protestant Nonconformists to remain under persecution in the hope that the sufferings they endured would lead them to combine with the Popish recusants in a general demand for civil and religious liberty. He also took the more questionable step of admitting into the army a large number of Roman Catholic officers.

Still, had he stopped there he probably would have succeeded in his efforts to obtain liberty of conscience for his co-religionists. But not content with the success that had thus far attended his proceedings, he determined to extend the exercise of his dispensing power to the universities and the Church. He argued that the revenues by which they were supported had been given by Roman Catholics, and that it was monstrous that they should be entirely excluded from institutions which owed their very existence to the pious liberality of their Roman Catholic ancestors.

Acting on these views, he allowed a clergyman, named Edward Schlater, a pretended convert to Popery, to retain two livings; Obadiah Walker, a man of considerable learning but an avowed Papist, was chosen to be master of University College, Oxford, and had the mass openly celebrated in his apartments; John Massey, a man of doubtful character and Roman Catholic opinions, was appointed Dean of Christchurch, and thus placed in the most important post in the university; and the sees of Oxford and Chester were filled by Parker and Cartwright, men of some ability, and in many respects as well fitted to fill the office of bishop as most of those who had been appointed to it, but having a strong leaning toward Popery. These appointments roused a feeling in the country of which it is difficult for the men of the present day to entertain an adequate conception, but of which some faint idea may be formed by those who are old enough to remember the feeling that existed in this country while the agitation for Catholic emancipation was being carried on.

Whatever opinion may be formed with regard to the wisdom of James's proceedings, there is no just reason to doubt the honesty of his intentions. Nothing proves this more fully to my mind than the relations he maintained with the celebrated Quaker, William Penn. Penn was the son of Admiral Penn, with whom James had served as a sailor. He had received his naval education under him, and seems to have entertained a very high regard for him. The Admiral repaid the esteem of James with a warm loyalty, left him by his will a considerable sum of money, and placed his Quaker son under his guardianship. At the time of the Admiral's death a considerable sum of money was due to him from the crown, and Charles, who was in great need of money, readily consented to an offer which Penn, made to him to take a large grant of unproductive land in exchange for the debt.

Penn had been led to make this offer by a desire to find a home in the new world for those who, with him, claimed for themselves, and were willing to extend to others, that full liberty of conscience which was nowhere to be obtained in the old world, but which he hoped to be able in the new world to establish in all its completeness.

Charles readily consented to exchange useless land for useful gold, especially as in doing so he gratified the son of one who stood high in his favour. Penn proposed to call his new acquisition Sylvania, on account of the extensive forests and wide spreading trees with which it was almost entirely covered.

Charles, however, politely insisted that it should be called Pennsylvania, in honour of its proprietor. Penn at once took possession of his vast but unproductive property, and proceeded to found on it a new colony which should be governed on principles of pure justice and philanthropy. These principles he not only carried out in his own colony, but applied them also to all his dealings with the various Indian tribes, whose territories were conterminous with the state he had acquired. He embodied them in articles which he laid down for the regulation of his own property, and in a letter which he sent the Indian tribes, he explained to them the manner in which he intended to act in all his future relations with them, as the following extracts from these documents will sufficiently show.

The documents themselves, as well as the success which under prodigious difficulties both from opponents in America and enemies in England attended Penn's efforts, show that few men have ever lived to whom the much abused title of statesman can be applied with more justice than to William Penn, who without armies or navies, and without weapons of offence or defence, succeeded in founding and governing a large colony, and regulating its domestic and foreign relations in a manner that, notwithstanding interference to which we have referred, would probably have been perfectly successful.

"Art. I. In reverence to God the Father of life and spirit, the Author as well as Object of all divine knowledge, faith, and worship, I do for me and mine declare and establish for the first fundamental of the government of this country, that every person that doth or shall reside therein shall have and enjoy the full possession of his or her faith, and exercise of worship towards God in such way and manner as every such person shall in conscience believe is most acceptable to God. And so long as every such person useth not this Christian liberty to licentiousness, or the destruction of others, that is to say to speak loosely and profanely or contemptuously of God, Christ, or Holy Scriptures, or religion, or commit any moral evil or injury against others in their conversation, he or she shall be protected in the enjoyment of the aforesaid Christian liberty by the civil magistrate."

The principles embodied in this article were those which Penn had always taught, and which he laboured to impress both on his own people and on the Indians who inhabited the country in which his territory was situated. To them he addressed a letter, which, as it explains the principles on which he invariably acted towards them on all occasions, I lay before the reader—

"London, the 18th of the 8th month, 1681.

"My friends,—There is a great Power that both made the world and all things therein, to whom you and I and all people owe their being, and to whom you and I must one day give an account for all that we do in the world. This great God hath written His law in our hearts, by which we are commanded to love and help and do good to one another, and not to do harm and mischief one unto another.

"Now this great God hath been pleased to make me concerned in your part of the world, and the king of the country where I live hath given me a great province therein. But I desire to enjoy it with your love and consent, that we may always live together as neighbours and friends. Else what would the great God do to us; who hath made us not to devour and destroy one another, but to live soberly and kindly together in the world? Now I would have you well observe that I am sensible of the unkindness and injustice that hath been too much exercised towards you by the people of these parts of the world, who have sought themselves, and to make great advantages by you rather than to be examples of justice and goodness unto you, which I hear hath been matter of trouble to you, and caused great grudgings and animosities, sometimes to the shedding of blood, which hath made the great God angry.

"But I am not such a man, as is well known in my own country. I have great love and regard towards you, and I desire to win and gain your friendship by a kind, just, and peaceable life; and the people I send are of the same mind, and shall in all things behave themselves accordingly. And if in anything any shall offend you and your people, you shall have a full and speedy satisfaction for the same by an equal number of just men on both sides, that by no means you may have just occasion of being offended against them. I shall shortly come to you myself, at what time we may more largely and freely confer and discourse of these matters. In the mean time I have sent my commissioners to treat with you about land, and a firm league of peace. Let me desire you to be kind to them and the people, and receive these presents and tokens which I have sent you as a testimony of my good will to you, and my resolution to live justly, peaceably, and friendly with you.

"I am your loving friend,

"W. PENN."

When Penn returned to England after having settled his colony in the manner we have seen, he waited on James, who by this time had ascended the throne, to lay before him an account of the cruelties that were being exercised against the Nonconformists under the operation of the persecuting laws that had been enacted in the reign of Charles, and which had hitherto been very rigorously enforced. It was through the influence that these representations had on James that, as we have already had occasion to mention, 1500 Quakers and a still larger number of Roman Catholics, who were under confinement on account of their religious opinions, were set at liberty. James felt that there was not the slightest danger that his Government would be altered either by Quakers or Roman Catholics.

But Penn was not contented with having gained this

point. He wanted to convince James that he might without danger, and indeed with a great gain of strength to his Government, carry the indulgence he had shown much farther by extending it to Nonconformists of all denominations. James, who had received Penn with great cordiality, and had followed his advice to such an extent as we have seen, listened attentively to his arguments in favour of general toleration, and began to act on them very freely.

Unfortunately, however, for himself and for the cause of religious liberty in this kingdom, there were other and very different advisers to whose representations he also listened. He allowed himself to be much influenced by the little coterie of violent Roman Catholics of which Father Petre was the mouth-piece and the treacherous Earl of Sunderland was the tool.

Carried hither and thither by these contradictory influences, he determined to silence those clergymen who were continually abusing his religion and thereby undermining his authority, and he was thus led to enter with passionate violence into the schemes of his Roman Catholic advisers, and more especially of those among them who offered him the most violent counsels and were prepared to run every risk in carrying out the advice they gave him, and so urged him forward on a course which the more prudent of his co-religionists justly feared would end in his overthrow and the ruin in this country of the religion he had embraced.

He began his career of folly by republishing directions which had been issued in the reign of his brother, by which the clergy were prohibited from preaching on controversial topics. This prohibition had proved altogether ineffectual when coming from Charles, who, at the time of its issue, was generally believed to be a zealous Protestant. It was little likely to be better obeyed when it proceeded from an avowed Papist, and was obviously intended to favour the propagation of the abhorred doctrines of Popery. By this means, instead of stopping the preaching of controversial doctrines, James only caused the clergy to preach them more frequently and more earnestly than ever, and thus effectually prevented the calm and dispassionate consideration of those principles of toleration which he had learnt from Penn, and which, if they had only been introduced with a little more prudence, might have obtained general support and acceptance.

But James obstinately set himself not to yield anything until he had brought matters to such a point that he found himself obliged to yield everything, and so gave way when it was too late. He kept on repeating his favourite maxim that concession had been the ruin of his father and that he would concede nothing. He determined to impose his directions on the clergy, and the more strenuously he insisted on obedience to them the more firmly and generally did they resist. To force his views on ten thousand men of education, who regarded themselves as bound in honour and conscience to withstand them, was an height of folly amounting almost to insanity. Nevertheless he persisted.

No tribunal was then in existence before which the offenders could be tried for their disobedience to the king's commands. The Court of High Commission which, in his father's time had discharged its functions with odious severity, and had perhaps done more than anything else to bring about the ruin of both Church and king, had been abolished by an Act of the Long Parliament, and no one desired the revival of an institution which had rendered itself so unpopular that even the most violent cavaliers deprecated the thought of a return of its tyranny.

But Jeffreys and some of the Popish parasites by whom James was surrounded, and to whose counsels he had surrendered his own understanding, advised him to revive this obsolete and unpopular tribunal, which they maintained had never been legally abolished, and without which they alleged, with some show of truth, that the royal supremacy over the Church could not be exercised. They maintained that it was only by issuing a new commission of a similar character to that which had been abolished that the supreme authority claimed for the king over the Church could be exerted. Jeffreys, who felt that his credit at court was sinking, suggested this plan to save himself from being dismissed, and the Jesuits supported his advice as a means of humbling the Protestant Church.

The Commission was accordingly issued. It contained the names of persons who professed to be friendly and even devoted to the Established Church. Lord Chancellor Jeffreys was appointed to preside at its sittings, and nothing could be determined unless he was present and consenting. This regulation was, however, annulled, so far at least as the presence of the chancellor was concerned. But he was all along the chief authority in the commission which had been called into existence by his advice.

The king could reckon confidently on the absolute servility of this bold, bad, but able man. With him were appointed to sit personages who might be expected to discharge with mildness and moderation the duties that were imposed on them. They were the Archbishop of Canterbury, Crewe, Bishop of Durham, Sprat, Bishop of Rochester, the Lord Chief Justice Herbert, the Earl of Rochester, Lord Treasurer, and the Earl of Sunderland, Lord President. Great and extraordinary powers were conferred on this tribunal. Its members were authorized to visit and inspect all bishops' dioceses; to change whatever statutes they might think proper to alter, even in colleges which had been founded by the bounty of private individuals; to punish, suspend, fine, etc. In a word, all the powers that had belonged to the Star Chamber and the Court of High Commission, and the exercise of which had done more than anything else to bring Charles I. to the block, were given to it.

The first blow it received was the refusal of Sancroft to take part in its proceedings or to be present at its deliberations. He truly alleged his age and infirmities as reasons why he desired to be excused from taking his place on it. But it is certain that these impediments would not have prevented him from acting on it if he had not disapproved the constitution of the court. He had very carefully considered the question in all its bearings before declining to take his seat, and had obtained legal advice as to the consequences that might follow his refusal. For his conduct in reference to this matter he has been severely censured by Burnet and Macaulay. But it is indisputably true that at the time of his appointment to a place on the commission he was suffering from an illness which would have rendered his presence at it highly inconvenient to him, and he would probably have been exposed to annoyances which, at the advanced age he had then reached, might have been attended with very serious consequences.

That he had other and even stronger reasons for declining is perfectly true; but they did not invalidate the force of those he actually gave, and he would only have excited the anger of his irascible sovereign, whose wrath he sought to propitiate by the use of language which might be regarded as servile if we did not make due allowance for the almost superstitious veneration with which the person and the office of the sovereign were at that time regarded by churchmen generally, and most especially by the school of divines to which Sancroft belonged.

But his refusal to act under the commission, however mildly and respectfully expressed, discredited the tribunal throughout the nation and incensed James in the highest degree. He knew well the moral effect which this refusal would have, and he showed his anger by directing that, for the future, the archbishop should not be summoned to attend the meetings of the Privy Council, then regarded as the most important body in the state, and which was consulted by the king on all important questions. "If," said James, bitterly, "his Grace of Canterbury is too ill to act under the commission, it will be a kindness to relieve him from taking his place at the council board; therefore for the future let him not be summoned to attend its meetings." He did not, however, venture to strike the name of the archbishop out of the list of privy councillors, but appointed Cartwright, the able Bishop of Chester, to fill the place on the commission which the archbishop had refused to occupy.

The king hesitated for a short time before he ventured to make use of the odious and unpopular tribunal he had brought into existence. There was probably, in his secret councils, a struggle between Father Petre and his followers on the one hand, and Penn on the other. At length, however, the king, irritated by the violence of the clergy, determined to make an example which he hoped would have the effect of showing them that he was resolved to make use of the commission; and the members of that tribunal, acting no doubt under instructions they had received, proceeded in their work with a degree of violence which must have caused Sancroft to congratulate himself on his refusal to sit with them.

The first person brought before them was Sharp, then Rector of St. Giles, London, and afterwards Archbishop of York. He had preached a sermon in his church in which he had used language which the king regarded as insulting both to his person and his religion. The commissioners took cognizance of the matter, and summoning Compton, the Bishop of London, before them, ordered him to suspend Sharp until the king's pleasure should be known. Compton, in reply to this injunction, pleaded that inasmuch as he was the Judge before whom Sharp would in the first instance be tried, he would be doing a clearly illegal act and rendering himself liable to punishment afterwards if he obeyed the mandate of the court. He therefore respectfully declined to comply with the order.

This refusal brought on him the anger of the commissioners or of their master. Sharp was overlooked and Compton was suspended from his episcopal functions, which were exercised by two of his Judges, the Bishops of Durham and Rochester.

Compton, however, though suspended from his bishopric, was allowed still to continue in the enjoyment of his episcopal revenues—an indulgence which did not proceed from leniency on the part of the king or the commissioners, but from a fear that if the matter were brought into the King's Bench (which, if the question of suspension from the revenues of the see were raised, it doubtless would be), the Judges of that court would probably give a decision adverse to the authority of the commission, it being known that the Chief Justice was convinced of its illegality and would act on that conviction if the case came before him. For the present, therefore, the commissioners confined themselves to ecclesiastical censures, and did not attempt to punish the bishop by the infliction of fines.

There can be no doubt that James, acting on the advice of Jeffreys, would have remodelled the Court of King's Bench by placing at the head of it a more pliant Chief Justice than the one who then presided over it, had not events occurred, to which we shall presently have occasion to refer, and which forced James to hold his hand and to endeavour, though too late, to retrace his steps. Meanwhile Sancroft, though under the displeasure of the king, and no longer consulted by him with regard to the disposal of the higher offices in the Church which were in the gift of the crown, continued to offer his recommendations of persons who in his opinion were suited to fill them as from time to time they became vacant. Amongst those whom he thus recommended occurs the name of the celebrated Robert South, whom he suggested as a suitable person to fill the see of Oxford. But his recommendations were slighted, as he no doubt expected that they would be; yet he still felt it to be his duty to continue to offer them.

Several other arbitrary and tyrannical acts were committed by the king, but they belong rather to the political than to the ecclesiastical history of our country. The consequence of these aggressions on the rights of the subject was, that multitudes of those who had been vehement partisans of the doctrines of passive obedience and of the divine rights of kings began to reconsider their theories and to find that a case had occurred which justified resistance to the arbitrary will of the sovereign. The clergy, especially, who had, up to this time, made the proclamation of these doctrines their peculiar boast and glory, became silent with regard to them, or descanted on passages of Scripture which condemned idolatry, when they began to find themselves threatened by the king and his servile advisers at once in their strongest temporal interests, and in their most cherished beliefs. A feeling in favour of resolute resistance was spreading among the clergy, and, by means of their preaching and conversation, throughout the whole kingdom, and that feeling caused men to turn their eyes towards the Prince of Orange, the able leader of the Protestant party in England and throughout Europe.

The Prince of Orange was naturally watching with intense interest the struggle that was going on in England. As his wife was the eldest daughter of James, and her father had no male children, she was next in succession to the throne. He was therefore interested in the struggle that was going on in a threefold capacity, first as being a zealous Protestant, next as being the husband of Mary, and lastly as being the leader of the great struggle which was being carried on throughout Europe against the despotic tyranny and exorbitant pretensions of the French monarch. The consequence was that at the moment we have now reached he was carrying on a correspondence, which was daily becoming more and more active and earnest, with some of the most influential of the nobility and gentry of the kingdom. It is probable that neither he nor his English correspondents anticipated the action which was forced on them by the arbitrary folly of James and by the course of events. They, no doubt, hoped that the union of Protestants in England with Protestants abroad in a determined resistance to the tyranny of James would prevent further violations of the law on his part, and would obtain securities against an exercise of the dispensing power which, if unresisted, would make the King of England as despotic as the sovereign of France.

It was of the highest importance to those who were engaged in carrying out these designs that they should obtain the adhesion of Sancroft, both as being at this conjuncture looked up to by English Churchmen more than any other public man in the kingdom, and as probably marked out to be the next victim of the Ecclesiastical Commission. It was therefore hoped that he would readily associate himself with some of the chief nobility and most influential personages in the kingdom, who were prepared to rally round him, and to afford him help and protection whenever the day of his danger should arrive. It was, probably, from hopes and considerations of this nature that Mary, the wife of William, and the daughter of James, acting no doubt under her husband's desire, despatched a letter to the primate, in which she simply expressed her esteem and veneration for his character, but which was probably written in the hope of drawing him into the secret correspondence which the prince and princess were carrying on with the malcontent party in England, and which soon after resulted in the revolution of 1688. Sancroft, however, steadily resisted the temptation. He not only declined to allow himself to be drawn into the correspondence that was being carried on with the opponents of James, but refused to take any part whatever in their proceedings. The opinions which he had avowed when they seemed to be calculated to promote his own interests and those of the Church of which he was primate, he still continued to uphold now that they were manifestly at variance with both. If he knew anything at all of what was in contemplation, it was merely through vague and uncertain rumours. And he was too wary, as well as too loyal, to enter into a conspiracy against his sovereign, however much he might disapprove, and even feel it his duty to withstand, that sovereign's measures. He therefore returned a reply to the letter of the princess, which, while characterized by his usual courtesy and respect for the royal family, at once put an end to the hopes, if any such had been entertained, that he would be drawn into uniting himself with those who were banded together for the purpose of withstanding the king's proceedings. "All we have endured," he wrote to the princess in his reply to her letter, "cannot in the least shake or alter our steady loyalty to our sovereign and the royal family, in the legal succession of it; yet it embitters the very comforts that are left us, it blasts all our present joys, and makes us sit down with sorrow in dust and ashes." To drive into resistance a loyalty so strong and persistent was a folly of which, probably, few men would have been guilty; but this was what James seemed to be bent on doing. All the projects of resistance that were devised against this unfortunate prince would probably have failed if he himself had not been their most active and persistent promoter.

The chief aim of the king, at the time of which we are now speaking, seems to have been to obtain toleration for the Roman Catholics, and to procure their admission to several of the higher offices in the Established Church, in the hope that by their assistance and exertions the whole nation would ultimately be converted. It was, however, quite evident, even to his understanding, that his object could only be effected by the carrying out of that policy which his brother had introduced, but had felt it necessary to abandon on account of the opposition that was offered to it by the great body of the Presbyterians themselves, who refused to accept a toleration which they would be obliged to share with the Romanists. James, now taking up this scheme, determined with characteristic obstinacy to carry it through. Its chances of ultimate success were small indeed, even if it had been skilfully and discreetly managed. It was certain to fail under the management of a person so foolish and headstrong as James, who seemed to be bent on rushing on to his ruin. In spite of numerous statutes which forbad the company of Jesus and other Roman Catholic orders from entering the kingdom, the sacrifice of the Mass continued to be more and more openly celebrated by them, and monks of all orders, arrayed in their respective habits, paraded the streets of the metropolis, and all the great towns of the kingdom. Instead of respecting prejudices, which, however illiberal they might be, were the prejudices of nineteen out of every twenty of his subjects, and even of those unprincipled men who, in the race for power, were urging him to adopt measures that were certain to bring about his ruin, James did all in his power to exasperate them. At the moment when men's minds were violently excited by his previous proceedings, he published a declaration in favour of liberty of conscience, in which he announced that he intended to carry out the views contained in that proclamation without obtaining the consent of Parliament to this stretch of his prerogative. And in this way he contrived to unite Puritans and their oppressors, Whigs and Tories, the friends of civil and religious liberty, with the advocates of arbitrary power, in one common league of opposition to his proceedings. Nay, many of the Roman Catholics themselves, for whose especial benefit the declaration had been issued, were so justly afraid of the ultimate result of the king's measures, had so keen a recollection of the sufferings they endured, and the dangers they had run in the evil days of the Popish Plot, that they joined in deprecating, and even resisting, a policy which seemed likely to procure them present ease at the cost of ultimate persecution; and this expectation was not disappointed.

But we must now return to the proceedings of the Ecclesiastical Commission.

Sprat, Crewe, and Cartwright have all of them been much blamed for consenting to sit on it, but some of the censures which have been pronounced on them seem to me to be unjustly severe. They could not refuse without incurring the displeasure of their sovereign, and without disregarding commands which, in common with almost the whole body of the clergy, they had all along taught and preached that men ought to obey. All of them, too, were men of note and mark, and decidedly superior to the average bishops of their day. Of Sprat even Macaulay speaks in terms of high commendation; to Cartwright we owe a very valuable and interesting diary published by the Camden Society; and of Crewe, Pepys, who was a very regular attendant at church, and was in the habit of hearing all the best preachers of the day, thus writes in his diary of April 5th, 1667, after listening to his sermon preached on that day: "Dr. Crewe did make a very pretty, neat, sober, honest sermon, and delivered it very readily, decently, and gravely, beyond his years, so as I was exceedingly taken with it, and I believe the whole chapel. He being but young, but his manner of delivery I do like exceedingly." This is by no means the only occasion on which Pepys makes mention of Crewe in terms of high and extraordinary commendation.

James, though decided to proceed, was also anxious to gain his ends by legitimate means, and to avoid being brought into a contest with the Parliament and the nation. He therefore endeavoured to win the leading men of both Houses, and invited them to private interviews, in which he plied them with the arguments for toleration which Penn had taught him, and endeavoured to persuade them to support his measures. These closetings, as they were then termed, were attended with very little success. James was not likely to yield, and the persons whom he thus interviewed were little disposed to tolerate Romanism, and so suspicious of the king's intentions and so thoroughly imbued with dread and hatred of his religion, that most of them came away from these closetings more deeply prejudiced than ever against the king, and more determined than before to offer a steady resistance to his schemes of toleration. The only result he gained was that a few time-servers conformed to his wishes, in the hope of obtaining preferment by an outward compliance with measures which they secretly abhorred, and which they did all in their power to frustrate and defeat. The failure of the efforts thus made by James did not open his eyes to the extent to which the affections and confidence of his subjects were being alienated from him, or to the danger he was running in consequence of their discontent.

On the 27th of April, 1688, he republished his declaration of liberty of conscience; and on the 4th of May in the same year, that is to say only a week later, he issued the following order:—

"At the Court of Whitehall, May 4th.

"It is this day ordered by His Majesty in Council, that His Majesty's late gracious declaration bearing date the twenty-seventh of April last, be read, at the usual time of divine service, on the twentieth and twenty-seventh of this month, in all churches and chapels within the cities of London and Westminster; on the third and tenth of June next in all other churches and chapels throughout the kingdom: and it is hereby further ordered that the Right Reverend the Bishops cause the said declaration to be sent and distributed through their several and respective dioceses to be read accordingly."

The appearance of this document caused great consternation among the clergy. Each clergyman feared that if he resisted he might be crushed by the whole weight of the royal authority falling on him through the arbitrary action of the dreaded High Commission Court. If time had been allowed them for consultation they would have soon discovered that there was such a unanimity in favour of resistance as would have compelled even James and Jeffreys to hesitate, and would have secured individual clergymen from the vengeance of the ill-advised monarch.

The first question which the clergy had to consider in the difficult situation in which they were placed by the order that accompanied the proclamation was, whether they could reckon on the support of the Nonconformists in case they should determine to disobey the king's mandate and refuse to read the declaration in their churches. Their position was one of no slight difficulty. James put himself forward as the champion of civil and religious liberty. There was nothing in the declaration which an honest Anglican could not read with a good conscience. He might not like it; he might think it calculated to do grievous injury to his Church; but he could hardly allege that it placed him in the position of being obliged to say, "I must obey God rather than man." On the other hand, James presented himself to the Nonconformists as the advocate of principles which many among them had long held, and which most of them probably would have joyfully embraced and supported if they had not entertained strong suspicions with regard to the king's ulterior designs. It was, therefore, difficult to foresee how they would act in this great national and religious crisis. There could be no doubt as to the course they would have taken if the dread of Popery had not paralyzed their action. Would they, under existing circumstances, side with James, or join the Churchmen in opposing him? That was an all-important question for the clergy at this conjuncture, but how were they to obtain an answer to it? Scattered as the Dissenters had been by the operation of the Five Mile Act and other penal laws passed in the late reign, it was a difficult matter to collect their opinions within the brief time that remained for consultation. The interval was so short that there was little time for deliberation, and in most cases it seemed that each individual clergyman would have to determine at his own risk, and act on his own individual responsibility, not knowing whether he would stand alone exposed to the king's rage, or could reckon on such an amount of concurrence as would bear him practically harmless. However, the clergy of the metropolis had time to assemble, and many of them came hastily together to deliberate on the course they should determine to pursue. The debate was long and doubtful. At one time it seemed likely that the advocates of passive obedience in London would carry the day, and if they had, no doubt their example would have been to a great extent followed throughout the kingdom; and so the revolution might have been deferred, or, perhaps, even avoided. At this critical conjuncture the boldness of one man decided the matter. At the time when it seemed that a division would take place that would end in a resolution to obey, Edward Fowler, Rector of St. Giles, Cripplegate, a clergyman of high character and great influence, rose and exclaimed, " Let who will read this document, I, for my part, will not." This courageous declaration animated the whole assembly, and they at once pledged themselves one and all to follow Fowler's example. The resolution that embodied this determination was sent round to the incumbents of the London parishes and signed by eighty-five of them.

Still there was another question that arose, and it was regarded as the most important. What will the bishops do? For it was they who would have to bear the brunt of the battle, inasmuch as it was to them that the order to read the declaration was sent, in accordance with the usual practice, that by them it might be transmitted to the clergy, with directions to read it. Here a tremendous responsibility rested on Sancroft, who, as the head of the Episcopal bench, would have to be foremost in acquiescence or resistance, and would give an example to the whole of the Episcopal bench; and the weight of this responsibility was increased by the circumstance that the archbishopric of York was then vacant. Sancroft, as we have seen, was already embroiled with the Court. He knew that a refusal on his part to obey would exasperate the king beyond measure, and that the order to read the declaration would be received with the strongest repugnance, not only by the clergy, but also by the overwhelming majority of the laity. He had, therefore, to decide whether he would obey or resist, with a full knowledge that if he should determine to follow the course that was in consonance with the feelings of the vast majority of his fellow Churchmen, the thunderbolts of royal vengeance would be launched at his devoted head without his being able to foresee whether he would confront them alone, or whether he could reckon on the support of his brethren, many of whom had imbibed those doctrines of passive obedience which he himself had so zealously preached, and of which he was still a firm believer; and with venal judges and packed juries, it was impossible to foresee with what penalties his disobedience to the royal order might be visited. There was no time for calling together any regular assembly of his suffragans to deliberate with him as to the course it was proper for them to take. Almost all of these were, at the moment, absent from London.

James and his advisers probably thought they had played a clever trick by issuing the order at such a time, and under such circumstances. But their cleverness was fatal to the cause it was intended to serve. Had James taken a little longer time for consideration, he might even yet have extricated himself, without much discredit, from the humiliating position into which a succession of blunders, and the advice of corrupt and traitorous ministers, had brought him. But the haste with which he had been urged forward prevented him from retracing his steps.

Another consideration added to the difficulties and perplexities by which Sancroft was beset. He had all along been a most zealous member of that party in the Church which had invariably, up to this time, gloried in its subserviency to the reigning monarch, and which, in return for his favour and protection, had been the earnest defender of the royal prerogative, and the zealous apologist even of its greatest excesses. They had expatiated with especial fervour and frequency on those passages of Scripture in which obedience to the authority of kings and magistrates is most emphatically inculcated. They had exhorted their hearers to submit themselves to every ordinance of man for the Lord's sake; they had reminded them that the powers that be are ordained by God, and that whosoever resisted the power resisted the ordinance of God, and that they who resisted should receive to themselves damnation; and they had proceeded to remind their hearers that St. Paul had laid down these doctrines when Nero was in the place of supreme authority, and they logically inferred that St. Paul would have enforced these doctrines, had he and they lived together under the comparatively mild rule of the Stuart dynasty. They had also boasted that they had adhered faithfully to these doctrines in the adversity as well as in the prosperity of the Church and the sovereign—in the days of the Rebellion as well as in those of the two Charleses. And James well knew all this. He had received again and again protestations of unalterable loyalty and unexcepted obedience from the holders of these doctrines, and now he was testing the sincerity of their professions. We must also remember that these doctrines were not the doctrines of a party, but of the Church. They were not confined to fiery bigots, but were held by the most learned, the most moderate, the most elegant, the most thoughtful of all our divines.

"Are they bad" (says Barrow, writing with regard to kings), "or do they misdemean themselves in their administration of government and justice? We may not by any violent or rough way attempt to reclaim them; for they are not accountable to us, or liable to our correction; *where the word of a king is, there is power: and who shall say to him, What doest thou?* was the preacher's doctrine.

"Do they oppress us or abuse us? Do they treat us harshly, or cruelly persecute us? We must not kick against them, or strive to right ourselves by resistance, For *against a king* (saith the wise man) *there is no rising up;* and *who* (saith David) *can stretch out his hand against the Lord's anointed and be guiltless?* and *they* (saith St. Paul) *that resist shall receive to themselves damnation.*

"We must not so much as ease our stomach, or discharge our passion by inveighing against them. For *thou shalt not speak evil of the ruler of thy people* is a divine law, and to *blaspheme* or revile *dignities* is by St. Peter and St. Jude reprehended as a notable crime.

"We must not be bold or free in taxing their actions, for *is it fit*, saith Elihu, to say to a king, Thou art wicked, and to princes, Ye are ungodly? and to *reproach the footsteps of God's anointed* is implied to be an impious practice.

"We must forbear even complaining and murmuring against them, for *murmurers* are condemned as no mean sort of offenders; and the *Jews* in the wilderness were sorely punished for such behaviour.

"We must not (according to the preacher's advice) so much as *curse them in our thoughts;* or entertain ill conceits and ill wishes in our minds towards them."

It is necessary, in order to understand the conduct of James on this occasion, to remember that the arguments in favour of passive obedience, thus ably and forcibly put by Barrow, were those of the whole Anglican Church, not of Sancroft and Ken only, but also of Tillotson, of Sharp, and of Burnet. They had been laid down by the representatives of all parties and all schools of theology. With a very few exceptions they were universally held; and in this respect the only difference between Sancroft and Tillotson was that the former was ready to suffer the loss of all things rather than renounce them, while Tillotson continued to hold them until they clashed with his interests. But Sancroft had been foremost all along in inculcating them. He had maintained them with unswerving firmness, and though he was prepared respectfully to offer counsel and make remonstrances, he never for one moment entertained the thought of resistance or rebellion. And not only had he himself held the doctrines of non-resistance and passive obedience, but he had also gone beyond others in the proclamation of them. They had grown with his growth, and strengthened with his strength. He had upheld them in his conversation, he had preached them in his discourses, he had dwelt on them with all the fervour of an honest servility. James had warmly declared at his accession that he would defend the Church, because he knew her to be eminently loyal, and he still professed to be determined to adhere to that promise; and he now called on Sancroft and the bishops to show themselves true to the declarations of loyalty they had so frequently made, and to set an example of obedience to their sovereign by issuing a document which, however they might dislike it, and however strong might be the objections they entertained against it, they could hardly maintain that a Christian minister could not read with a good conscience. Besides, documents similar in character, though less offensive to the clergy generally, had often before been read in the churches, if not by the advice of Sancroft and his suffragans, at all events with their full consent and concurrence. If, therefore, he and his brother bishops were only consistent with themselves, they must, notwithstanding the objections they entertained against the declaration, read it themselves, and obey the king's mandate by endeavouring to persuade the clergy also to read it.

Notwithstanding these seemingly unanswerable reasons in favour of obedience to the king's command, Sancroft's antipathy to Popery made him shrink from taking any part in a proceeding which was calculated and intended to promote the cause of a religion which he regarded as idolatrous and superstitious. In his perplexity he sought the advice of his clerical brethren. The clergy of London had, as we have seen, given their decided opinion. By their advice, he despatched letters to the bishops of his province asking them to come up immediately and assist him with their advice in this great emergency. Lest the letters should be interrupted and opened, they were sent by special messengers. Six of his suffragans came up at the summons of the primate, and gravely considered the matter with the ablest of the clergy of the metropolis. The result of their deliberations was embodied in the following petition, which was signed by the archbishop, and the bishops of St. Asaph, Ely, Chichester, Bath and Wells, Peterborough, and Bristol.

"To the King's Most Excellent Majesty.

"The humble petition of William, Archbishop of Canterbury, and of divers of the suffragan bishops of the province, now present with him, in behalf of themselves and others of their absent brethren, and of the clergy of their respective dioceses, humbly sheweth,—

"That the great averseness they find in themselves

to the distributing and publishing in all their churches your Majesty's late declaration for the liberty of conscience, proceedeth neither from any want of duty and obedience to your Majesty, our holy mother the Church of England being, both in her principles and constant practice, unquestionably loyal, and having (to her great honour) been more than once publicly acknowledged to be so by your gracious Majesty; nor yet from any want of due tenderness to Dissenters, in relation to whom they are willing to come to such a temper as shall be thought fit when that matter shall be considered, and settled in Parliament and Convocation; but among many other considerations, from this especially, because that declaration is founded on such a dispensing power as hath often been declared illegal in Parliament, and particularly in the year 1662 and 1672, and in the beginning of your Majesty's reign, and is a matter of so great moment and consequence to the whole nation, both in Church and State, that your petitioners cannot in prudence, honour, or conscience, so far make themselves parties to it as the distribution of it all over the nation, and the solemn publication of it once and again, even in God's house and in the time of His divine service, must amount to in common and reasonable construction.

"Your petitioners therefore most humbly and earnestly beseech your Majesty that you will be graciously pleased not to insist upon their distributing and reading your Majesty's declaration."

This petition was signed by Sancroft himself; by Dr. Lloyd, Bishop of St. Asaph; Dr. Ken, Bishop of

Bath and Wells; Dr. Turner, Bishop of Ely; Dr. Lake, Bishop of Chichester; Dr. White, Bishop of Peterborough; and Sir Jonathan Trelawney, Bishop of Bristol. All of them were men of good reputation and unblemished character. Lloyd did not share the scruples of most of his brethren, and took without hesitation the oaths of allegiance and supremacy to William and Mary. Ken was a man of whom any communion might well be proud, and the circumstances under which his appointment was made reflects credit on Charles, who selected him as well as on himself. When the Merry Monarch visited Winchester, Ken was the prebendary in residence, and he was asked to give up his prebendal house for the use of Nell Gwyn, one of the king's mistresses. Ken promptly replied: Not for his kingdom. Charles, who respected in others virtues that he was far from possessing himself, bore the refusal in his mind, and when the bishopric of Bath and Wells became vacant not long after, conferred it on the man who had rebuked him in a manner which would have given deadly offence to most princes. Ken was in all respects the model of what a Christian bishop ought to be. His prose and poetical writings have come down to our time, and will probably be read and admired as long as the English language endures. He was most industrious in preaching and in catechising the children of his diocese; he was hospitable and kindly courteous to the very poorest. He interposed at the risk of his life to put a stop to the cruelties that were being exercised, after the battle of Sedgemoor, against the poor peasants who had rallied round Monmouth's standard. We have already seen how he conducted himself at the bedside of his dying patron. His character has thus been beautifully described in Dryden's delineation of "The Good Parson."

> "Mild was his accent and his action free;
> With eloquence innate his tongue was armed;
> Though harsh the precept, yet the preacher charmed,
> For letting down the golden chain from high
> He drew his audience upwards to the sky:
> And oft with holy hymns he charmed their ears
> (A music more melodious than the spheres).
>
> * * * * *
>
> He bore his great commission in his look;
> But sweetly tempered awe, and softened all he spoke:
> He preached the joys of heaven, and pains of hell,
> And warned the sinner with becoming zeal;
> But on eternal mercy loved to dwell.
> He taught the gospel rather than the law,
> And forced himself to drive, but loved to draw."

The petition was probably framed by Sancroft himself. It was in his handwriting, but it bore marks of having been carefully altered and amended by the able divines whom he had summoned to his assistance in this trying emergency. It no doubt suffered from the haste with which it must have been composed and revised, for the meeting was held on the Friday evening, and the order given by the king required that the declaration should be read in the churches of the metropolis and its neighbourhood on the following Sunday. It was couched, however, in the most respectful terms, and contained nothing that could be regarded as disrespectful, much less libellous. Sancroft, who was suffering from continued indisposition, and had been forbidden to appear at court, did not accompany his brethren into the king's presence. The rest, however, appeared before James, and after some little difficulty had been raised and overcome, were ushered into the king's presence. They all fell on their knees, while the Bishop of St. Asaph presented the petition. The king, who was unacquainted with its nature, but knew that the men before him had always been strong and even extravagant exalters of the royal prerogative, received the document graciously, and, glancing at the signature, remarked, "This is my Lord of Canterbury's own hand." To which the petitioners, rejoiced to find him in so gracious a mood, and, perhaps hoping to be the bearers of a message of reconciliation to the primate, replied with alacrity, "Yes, sir; it is his own hand." The king then began to examine the document, and as he read on his countenance darkened. There could be no mistake with regard to it. He saw that, mild and respectful as was the language used by the petitioners, they intended to resist his will. For the first time in the history of the Stuarts, the Church and king were openly at variance. For the first time, those who had gloried in being the abject slaves of a despotic ruler, now turned against the royal prerogative. The king read the paper to the end; then, folding it up, he exclaimed, "This is a great surprise to me. Here are strange words; I did not expect this from you. This is a standard of rebellion." The Bishop of St. Asaph, who, as the senior bishop present had been the bearer of the petition, replied, "We have adventured our lives for your Majesty, and we would lose the last drop of our blood rather than lift up a finger against you." James, who doubtless thought that the petition, however respectfully worded, was intended, as indeed it probably was, as an appeal to the nation generally from the king, and one that would have a great effect, repeated with rising anger, "I tell you this is a standard of rebellion; I never saw such a petition." Trelawney, who had distinguished himself by his zealous endeavours to quell the rebellion which Monmouth had raised, fell down again on his knees, and exclaimed, "Rebellion, sir! I beseech you, do not say so harsh a thing of us. For God's sake, do not believe that we are or can be guilty of rebellion. It is impossible that I and my family should be so. Your Majesty cannot but remember that you sent me down to Cornwall to quell Monmouth's rebellion; and I am ready to do what I can to quell another if there were occasion." The Bishop of Chichester added, "Sir, we have quelled one rebellion, and will not raise another." No doubt they were sincere in these protestations of loyalty and submission, though some of them, Trelawney to wit, went over very shortly after to the side of rebellion. The king, too, probably believed in their sincerity, and was in some degree mollified by their abject submission, for he added in a somewhat softened tone, "I will keep this paper. It is the strangest address that ever I saw; it tends to rebellion. Do you question my dispensing power? Some of you have printed and preached for it, when it was for your purpose." After some further altercation with regard to the dispensing power, he dismissed them with these words, which showed the confused state of his mind, and how his thoughts vacillated backwards and forwards between concession and obstinate unbending persistence: "If I think fit to alter my mind, I will send to you;" then, after a short pause, " God hath given me this dispensing power, and I will maintain it. I tell you there are seven thousand men, and of the Church of England too, who have not bowed the knee to the image of Baal."

The king was evidently relenting, and his anger was gradually cooling down: if he had been left to the influence of his own reflections only, he probably would have shrunk from evoking the almost unanimous refusal of the clergy to read the declaration. He could not venture to imprison at once some ten thousand clergymen, at a moment when they had, with a few insignificant exceptions, the whole nation at their back. But he was roused almost to madness when he found that the bishops had hardly left his presence, when the petition they had presented to him, and which had given him so much offence, was printed and openly sold in the streets of London.

Some have supposed that the king had handed it to Sunderland, and that he had published it in order the more effectually to destroy the master on whom he had basely fawned, and whom he now betrayed. No doubt Sunderland was equal to any baseness, but

N

he could hardly have anticipated the effects which the publication of the petition would produce. It is more than probable that some one of those who attended the consultation held at Lambeth, and had heard the reading of the petition, had taken a copy of it, and put it into the hands of the printer in order that the clergy might know that in refusing to read the declaration they would have the support of many of the bishops, and of a large portion—probably a majority—of their clerical brethren. The consequence was, that the declaration was scarcely read anywhere, except by a few sycophants who were ready to sell their souls to the king in the hope of obtaining preferment.

Even the Nonconformists, who were the persons for whose more especial benefit the declaration was issued, refused to swallow the bait that was thrown to them. It was true that some respectable Congregational ministers who had embraced those principles of general toleration which James had imbibed from Penn, and on which the declaration was based, acted consistently with those principles and accepted the policy which the declaration proclaimed, and which they had long since avowed. But Baxter and Howe, and others of the most celebrated Nonconformist ministers, made common cause with the bishops and clergy of the Church, and used the liberty of preaching which the declaration gave them in support of the party of resistance, which they encouraged by assurances of their sympathy and support. These latter carried their flocks with them, while the others were made to feel, by the diminution or extinction of their stipends, the extent to which their conduct was disapproved by those to whom they ministered, and on whose favour and approbation they depended for their support. They paid the penalty which generally has to be borne by those who are in advance of the age in which they live, or the people among whom they dwell.

James was not a man to bear with patience such a defeat as he had suffered. He was violently irritated at the publication of the bishops' address, and in his rage he listened to the dictates of anger, rather than to those of prudence. However, he took more than a week to reflect, and it was not until the 27th of May that he made known his final resolution. On the evening of that day a king's messenger appeared at Lambeth and served on the archbishop a summons to appear before the king in council on the 8th of June, there to answer for a misdemeanour. A similar summons was served on each of the other petitioners.

To this course James had probably been impelled by the more violent of the Romanists who surrounded him, and who looked forward with delighted anticipation to the humiliation and disgrace of the Protestant hierarchy. The wiser portion of them, as we have already pointed out, justly dreaded the danger to which they were exposed through the insane restlessness of the king and some of their other co-religionists who were his most confidential and trusted advisers.

When the 20th of May arrived, scarcely a single clergyman read the declaration, and on the following

Sunday the same thing occurred, with very few exceptions, outside the metropolis and throughout the country. Those who at first had been disposed to yield, now stood firm in their resolution to refuse obedience to the king's mandate. Of all the London clergy only four read it; and out of about ten thousand scattered throughout the kingdom, only about two hundred. Crewe, Bishop of Durham, is alleged to have suspended some two hundred, and yet this man was among the first to cringe to the Government of William and Mary, and in his abject fears to make offers of submission far surpassing those made by any who had signed the petition. At Westminster Abbey, and at many other churches in which the declaration was read, the congregation hurried out of the church as soon as the reading of it commenced. One wit suggested that, though he was forced to read it, the congregation was by no means obliged to stay and listen to it. Even at the Royal Chapel of Whitehall no clergyman remained to read it, and that function was performed by one of the choristers.

The Chief Justice had gone down to Serjeants' Inn for the purpose of enforcing the reading of it there, but the clerk declared that he had forgotten to bring a copy to church, and with that excuse Herbert was forced to be content. Some, indeed, of those whose professions had caused the people to expect that they would be foremost in their opposition to the king's measures, and who afterwards reaped the reward of their supposed zeal in resisting his orders, entirely belied the expectations of their admirers. On the day on which the declaration was appointed to be read, neither Stillingfleet nor Tillotson were present at their respective churches. They had gone down on the Saturday to their country residences, leaving other clergymen to occupy their places, and to bear the brunt of the responsibility of reading, or refusing to read, the king's declaration.

Notwithstanding these alarming indications of public disapproval of the king's measures, the king did not swerve from the course of obstinacy into which he had been drawn by a handful of corrupt or foolish advisers. He hoped to coerce a whole nation; and so he determined, not only to force on his declaration, but to punish those who had so respectfully and submissively remonstrated with him. In accordance with the summons which, had been served on them, Sancroft and the other subscribing bishops appeared before James and his council, and were interrogated by Jeffreys.* They had previously conferred with their able and numerous legal advisers, and had been instructed by them how they should act under any circumstances that were likely to arise, and how to answer the questions that probably would be put to them. Thus prepared, they presented themselves before the king and his counsellors.

Jeffreys first endeavoured to induce them to admit

---

* In this and other places, I mention him by the name by which he has been always known to his posterity, and not by the title of Wem, which was conferred on him. In so doing I follow the example, I believe, of all other historians of the period.

that the signatures to the document complained of were in their handwriting; in fact, required them, contrary to every maxim of law and equity, to criminate themselves. This, Sancroft and the other bishops, acting no doubt on the instructions given them by their counsel, respectfully declined to do. In vain repeated efforts were made to entrap them into making some declaration which would prove the publication of the alleged libel. At length, James, finding all other means useless, commanded Sancroft, on his royal authority, to say whether the signature was his or not.

Being strongly pressed by the king himself, the archbishop thus addressed his sovereign: "Sir, I am called hither as a criminal, which I never was before in my life, and little thought I ever should be, and especially before your Majesty; but since it is my unhappiness to be so at this time, I hope your Majesty will not be offended that I am cautious of answering questions. No man is obliged to answer questions that may tend to the accusing of himself." Lloyd, of St. Asaph, supported the demurrer of the archbishop by adding, "Divines of all Christian Churches are agreed that men, circumstanced as we are, may properly refuse to answer questions that tend to criminate ourselves." Nevertheless, the king continued to press for an answer to his question, stigmatizing their caution as "chicanery." Unwilling to offend their sovereign, who still continued to urge them on this point, and at length gave them an express command, they obeyed it under protest that an admission yielded under such circumstances should not be made use of against them.

They were then sent out, while the king and his council deliberated on the course that should be adopted towards them, and when brought again into the king's presence, Chancellor Jeffreys informed them that they would be proceeded against, with all fairness, in Westminster Hall; and he desired them also to enter into recognizances to appear. But this also, acting on the advice of their zealous and able counsel, who had carefully prepared them with replies to every question likely to be put to them or any course that might probably be adopted with regard to them, they respectfully declined to do, in spite of the pressure put on them by the king, who peevishly remarked, "You believe everybody rather than me." They were committed to the Tower by warrant, signed by fourteen privy councillors, and an Order in Council was also made out, and signed by nineteen, ordering their prosecution by the law officers of the Crown, in the Court of the King's Bench, the majority of the judges of which were creatures of the king, and one of them appointed under that very dispensing power which the petition of the bishops had directly called in question.

Here we pause. The committal of the seven bishops to the Tower, their saintly behaviour during their confinement, their appearance before the tribunal by which they were judged, the alternations of hope and fear, of suspense and delight which agitated the bosoms of the spectators in the court, and the anxious multitude outside—all these have been described with so much particularity of detail, with such surpassing dramatic power, and with so much historic minuteness and impartiality in the pages of Macaulay's history, that it would be an act of folly and presumption in any succeeding historian to attempt to regild the refined gold of the picture which that accomplished writer has given of these events.

The bishops were sent to the Tower on the 8th of June. Only two days after their incarceration, and while they were still in confinement, the queen was delivered of that young prince, afterwards so well known in English history by the title of the Pretender. Consequently the archbishop and other bishops whose testimony would probably have removed the doubts that were thrown on the reality of his birth were precluded from being present, as they doubtless would have been had they not been imprisoned. The public indignation which followed the committal of the seven prelates was aggravated by other equally tyrannical acts of the insensate king committed about the same time, and by the disregard these acts showed of the laws of the country over which he was bound to rule legally and constitutionally; by his appointment of Massey, an avowed Papist, to the deanery of Christ Church, Oxford; by choice of bishops who, if not actually Papists, had a strong leaning in the direction of Popery; by intruding avowed Papists, such as Obadiah Walker, into high offices in the universities, in which the service of the Mass was celebrated in direct defiance of the law; by keeping vacant the see of York, with the intention, as was generally suspected, of ultimately seating a Roman Catholic on the archiepiscopal throne of the northern province; by various other arbitrary and tyrannical acts; but, above all, by the violent and lawless intrusion of a Roman Catholic as head of Magdalen College, Oxford. This affair attracted so much notice, and contributed so largely to bring about the downfall of James, that it is desirable that we should dwell on the event and the circumstances that attended it at some length, and with considerable particularity.

When the news of the avoidance of the presidential office was delivered to James, he determined to put into it a person of the name of Farmer—a man of bad character, and so entirely disqualified for the office into which the king purposed to intrude him, that James himself, obstinate as he was, abstained from pressing his appointment to it. The Fellows of the college, with whom the appointment rested, then sent a petition to James, in which they humbly requested him to allow them to proceed with the election, and they deferred it for two days, in order to give the king time to send them a reply. No answer coming, they proceeded to elect one of their number, named Hough—a man in every way highly qualified for the office to which he was appointed—and he was duly installed into it by Dr. Mew, Bishop of Winchester, and visitor of the college. The king, highly displeased, ordered them to annul the choice they had made, and to admit Dr. Parker, the Bishop of Oxford, to be their president, notwithstanding any statute that might be alleged against this course of proceeding.

To this injunction, twenty-six out of twenty-eight Fellows refused obedience; and, notwithstanding the threats of James, and the earnest exhortations of Penn, they persisted in their resolution not to admit the candidate that the king was endeavouring to thrust on them. James, who at the time when these events occurred was making a royal progress through the country, turned aside to Oxford, hoping that the Magdalen Fellows would yield obedience to the commands of their sovereign personally delivered; but in this expectation he was also disappointed.

Then three commissioners were sent down with positive injunctions to cancel the election of Hough, and to admit Parker in his place. These commissioners were Cartwright, Bishop of Chester, the Lord Chief Justice Wright, who presided at the trial of the seven bishops, and Justice Jenner. They made their public entrance into the city of Oxford, escorted by a large body of soldiers. Cartwright took the lead in carrying into execution the odious and unpopular commission which had been intrusted to them. He and his two associates had come down, not for the purpose of trying the question which the election of Hough and the orders of the king had raised, but for the purpose of forcibly intruding the nominee of the king into an office which he was clearly not entitled to fill.

But we will now leave Cartwright to tell his own story, as he has related it in his diary, published by the Camden Society, which not only gives a very fair account of this transaction, but also throws a pleasant light on the manners of the bishop's time.

"20. We came into Oxon, my Lord Peterborough's regiment receiving us at the town's end, where the lieutenant-colonel and the rest of the officers dined with us.

"21. We went to Magdalen College chapel, where the crowd being great and no preparations made for our sitting, we sent Mr. Atterbury for the proctors, who came accordingly to keep the peace. Mr. Tucker read the king's commission, Mr. Atterbury returned the citation on oath. . . . Dr. Hough desired a copy of the commission in writing, which was denied him, and then he, in his own name, and the greatest part of the Fellows, said he did submit to the visitation as far as it is consistent with the laws of the land and the statutes of the college, and no further; and said he must suffer no alteration in any statute by the king or any other; for which he had taken an oath from which he would not swerve, and for which he quoted the statutes confirmed by Henry the sixth, and their oath in them, that they should submit to no alteration made by any authority.

"Then Dr. Hough's former sentence of deprivation was commanded to be read; to which he replied he was never cited nor heard, and therefore supposed the sentence to be invalid, and refused to submit to it, though he confessed he had notice of it. The college petition to the king to recommend some other in Farmer's room, No. 4, was read; and asking them why they did not stay for an answer to it, Dr. Hough replied, their fifteen days were out before the 15th of April, on which they had no other sent to them; and requiring him to give up the register, he promised we should have it to-morrow morning. . . .

"22. We called in the steward with the books of leases and court-rolls, which were delivered him back till we made further use of them. The butler brought the buttery book, and Dr. Hough being called in again, I told him, Doctor, here is a sentence under seal before us, of the king's commissioners for visiting the universities, by which your election to the presidentship of Magd. Coll. is declared null and void, which you yesterday heard read, and of which you confessed yourself to have legal notice before, it being fixed upon your doors. This sentence, and the authority by which it was passed, you have contemned, and in contempt thereof have kept possession of the lodgings and office to this day, to the great contempt and dishonour of the king and his authority. Are you yet willing, upon second and better thoughts, first, to submit to this sentence passed by the lords upon you or not? secondly, will you deliver up the keys and lodgings, as by a clause in your oath at your admission, you are tied to do, for the use of the president who has the king's letters mandatory to be admitted into that office? To the first he says that the decree of the commissioners is a perfect nullity from the beginning to the end as to what relates to him, he never having been cited, nor having ever appeared before them either in his person or by his proxy; besides, his cause itself was never before them, their lordships never inquiring or asking one question concerning the legality or statuteableness of the election, for which reason he is informed that the decree was of no validity against him, according to the methods of the civil law; but if it had, he is possessed of a freehold according to the laws of England and the statutes of the society, having been elected as unanimously, and with as much formality as any of his predecessors, presidents of the college, and afterwards admitted by the Bishop of Winchester, their visitor, as the statutes of the college require; and therefore he could not submit to that sentence, because he thought he could not be deprived of his freehold but by course of law in Westminster Hall, or by being in some way incapacitated according to the founder's statutes, which were confirmed by King James I. Then the doctor asked whether we acknowledged his title to the presidentship? I replied, No; for we looked upon him as *malæ fidei* possessor, or an intruder. He replied that the Bishop of Winchester made him so, and said that he was satisfied in his own title, and therefore did not think himself concerned to apply to the commissioners till called, and that he expects legal courses should be taken against him if he keep legal possession. To which I replied that the election was undue because the king had laid his hands by mandamus upon the college, which was an inhibition. To the second question he answered there neither is nor can be any president so long as he lives and obeys the laws of the land and the statutes of the place, and therefore he does not think it reasonable to give up his right, nor the keys and lodgings now demanded of him."

Sentence having been given against Hough, he

appeared the following morning with a great crowd of followers, and said: "Whereas your lordships this morning have been pleased, pursuant to the former decree of the lord commissioners, to deprive me of the place of president of this college, and to strike my name out of the buttery book; I do hereby protest against the said proceedings, and against all that you have done, or hereafter shall do in prejudice of me and my right, as illegal, unjust, and null: and I do hereby appeal to our sovereign lord the king in his courts of justice." "Upon which the rabble hummed,* and Dr. Hough was accused by my Lord Chief Justice of bringing them in; upon which he required the peace of him, to which he was bound in £1000 bond, and his two sureties in £500 each, and I gave the doctor this answer: Doctor, we look upon your appeal as to the matter and manner of it to be unreasonable, not admissible, and not to be admitted by us; first, because it is in a visitation where no appeal is allowable; secondly, because our visitation is by commission, under the broad seal of England, which is the supreme authority, and therefore we overrule this your protestation and appeal, and admonish you once for all to avoid the college and obey the sentence. The doctor and Fellows declared their grief for the disorders of the crowd, and disclaimed any hand in it."

Finding that Hough and the Fellows would not yield, the commissioners sent for a smith, who in their presence broke open the outward door of the president's lodge, in the first room of which they found the keys, and left

* This was an expression of their approval.

Mr. Wickens, the Bishop of Oxford's proxy, in quiet possession of the presidential lodge. The whole proceeding was such a flagrant violation of every principle of equity and justice, that it contributed in no small degree to produce that state of public opinion which caused the downfall of James. When that event occurred, Cartwright fled to France, and there joined his fallen patron. Parker died in 1690, and was succeeded by Hough, who, on the death of Tenison, refused the archbishopric of Canterbury, which was then offered to him.

The death of Parker, the intruded Bishop of Oxford caused another vacancy in the office of president of Magdalen, which James hastened to fill again. Instead of profiting by this opportunity of retracing his steps and reconciling himself with his people, he outraged their feelings still further by appointing to the office of president, one Bonaventure Giffard, a Roman Catholic priest with no other recommendation to the office he was illegally thrust into but that of belonging to the unpopular communion. But the obstinacy of James in regard to this and other assertions of the dispensing power which he claimed to exercise, and to exercise in such a manner as to override all laws, had now converted a nation of loyalists into a nation of rebels, and disposed them to believe the absurd stories that were circulated respecting the birth of the Prince of Wales.

The news of the approaching invasion of England by William of Orange at length opened the eyes of James to the folly of the conduct he had been pursuing. Then he retraced his steps with precipitation, and attempted, when it was too late, to regain the loyalty and the affection of his people. His folly, on the one hand, acting on the violent and exaggerated terror of Popery that prevailed throughout his kingdom, and which he had done so much to exasperate, united for the moment men of all creeds and all classes in rallying round the bishops and resisting the violent and lawless proceedings of the unfortunate king.

The attitude of the prelates, firm, yet respectful, increased the sympathy that generally was felt for them, and obtained for the Anglican Church an amount of popularity she has never since enjoyed. The Nonconformists threw their almost undivided influence into the scale, and openly announced their intention to stand by the Church in the contest with the king, in which she was now fully embarked. Sancroft, on the other hand, expressed the general feeling of the Church by showing every disposition to court the alliance thus offered, and to meet the advances of the Dissenters with a cordial reciprocity, striving to give permanence to the friendly feeling which the dread of the common foe had temporarily produced. With this object, he issued to the bishops of his province, and through them to the clergy, the following letter, which I give in full on account of the light it throws on the state of the Church and the dispositions of the clergy at this critical moment :—

"Lambeth, July 27th, 1688.

"SIR,—Yesterday the Archbishop of Canterbury delivered the articles which I send you enclosed to those bishops who are present in this place, and ordered copies of them to be likewise sent in his name to the absent bishops. By the contents of them, you will see that the storm in which he is does not frighten him from doing his duty, but rather awakens him to do it with so much the more vigour; and, indeed, the zeal that he expresses in these articles against the corruptions of the Church of Rome on the one hand, and the unhappy differences that are among Protestants on the other, are such apostolical things, that all good men rejoice to see so great a prelate at the head of our Church, who, in this critical time, has had the courage to do his duty in so signal a manner."

"Some heads of things to be more fully insisted upon by the bishops in their addresses to the clergy and people of their respective dioceses.

"I. That the clergy often read over the forms of their ordination, and seriously consider what solemn vows and professions they made therein to God and His Church, together with the several oaths and subscriptions they have taken and made upon divers occasions.

"II. That, in compliance with these and other obligations, they be active and zealous in all parts and instances of their duty, and especially strict and exact in all holy conversation, that so they may become examples to the flock.

"III. To this end, that they be constantly resident on their cures in their incumbent houses, and keep sober hospitality there, according to their ability.

"IV. That they diligently catechise the children and youths of their parishes (as the rubric of the Common

Prayer Book and the 59th Canon enjoin), and so prepare them to be brought in due time to confirmation when there shall be opportunity; and that they also, at the same time, expound the grounds of religion and the common Christianity, in the method of the catechism, for the instruction and benefit of the whole parish, teaching them what they are to believe, and what to do, and what to pray for, and particularly often and earnestly inculcating upon them the importance and obligation of their baptismal vows.

"V. That they perform the daily office publickly (with all decentcy, affection, and gravity), in all market and other great towns; and even in villages and less populous places, bring people to public prayers as frequently as may be, especially on such days and at such times as the rubrics and canons appoint; on holy days and their eves, on Ember and Rogation days, on Wednesdays and Fridays in each week, especially in Advent and Lent.

"VI. That they use their utmost endeavour, both in their sermons and by private applications, to prevail with such of their flock as are of competent age, to receive frequently the Holy Communion; and to this end, that they administer it in the greater towns once in every month, and even in the lesser, too, if communicants may be procured, or however as often as they may; and that they take all due care, both by preaching and otherwise, to prepare all for the worthy receiving of it.

"VII. That in their sermons they teach and inform their people, four times in the year at least (as the canon requires), that all usurped and foreign jurisdiction is, for most just causes, taken away and abolished in this realm, and no manner of obedience or subjection due to the same, or to any that pretend to act by virtue of it; but that the king's power being in his dominions highest under God, they upon all occasions persuade the people to loyalty and obedience to His Majesty in all things lawful, and to patient submission in the rest; promoting (as far as in them lies) the public peace and quiet of the world.

"VIII. That they maintain fair correspondence (full of the kindest respects of all sorts) with the gentry and persons of quality in their neighbourhood, as being sensible what seasonable assistance and countenance the poor Church hath received from them in her necessities.

"IX. That they often exhort all those of our communion to continue steadfast to the end in their most holy faith, and constant to their professions; and to that end, to take heed of all seducers, and especially of Popish emissaries, who are now in great numbers gone forth amongst them, and more active and busy than ever; and that they take all occasions to convince our own, that it is not enough for them to be members of an excellent Church rightly and duly reformed, both in faith and worship, unless they do also reform and amend their own lives, and so order their conversation in all things as becomes the Gospel of Christ.

"X. And forasmuch as those Romish emissaries, like the old serpent *insidiantur culcaneo*, are wont to be most busy and trouble some of our people at the end of their lives, labouring to unsettle and perplex them in time of sickness and at the hour of death; that, therefore, all who have the cure of souls be more specially vigilant over them at that dangerous season, so that they stay not till they be sent for, but inquire out the sick in their respective parishes, and visit them frequently; that they examine them particularly concerning the state of their souls, and instruct them in their duties, and settle them in their doubts, and comfort them in their sorrows and sufferings, and pray often with them and for them; and by all methods which our Church prescribes, prepare them for the due and worthy receiving of the Holy Eucharist, the pledge of their happy resurrection; thus, with the utmost diligence, watching over every sheep within the fold (especially in that critical moment) lest those evening wolves devour them.

"XI. That they also walk in wisdom towards those that are not of our communion. And if there be in their parishes any such, that they neglect not frequently to confer with them in the spirit of meekness, seeking by all good ways and means to gain and win them over to our communion; more especially that they have a very tender regard to our brethren, the Protestant Dissenters; that upon occasion offered, they visit them at their houses, and receive them kindly at their own, and treat them fairly wherever they meet them, discoursing calmly and civilly with them, persuading them, if it may be, to a full compliance with our Church, or at least that 'whereto we have already attained, we may walk by the same rule, and mind the same thing.' And in order hereunto, that they take all opportunities of assuring and convincing them that the bishops of the Church are really and sincerely irreconcileable enemies to the errors, superstitions, idolatries, and tyrannies of the Church of Rome; and that the very unkind jealousies that some have had of us to the contrary, were altogether groundless. And, in the last place, that they warmly and most affectionately exhort them to join with us in daily fervent prayer to the God of peace for the universal blessed union of all reformed Churches, both at home and abroad, against our common enemies, that all they who do confess the holy Name of our dear Lord, and do agree in the truth of his Holy Word, may also meet in one holy communion, and live in perfect unity and godly love."

This document seems to me to be of the highest value. It shows the care and diligence with which Sancroft was quietly working away to improve the religious efficiency of the Church. It also displays the manner in which he welcomed the advances of the Nonconformists, by proposing such changes as he might concede and they accept without the slightest violation of principle on either side. It is very probable that, in the state of feeling which this document discloses, a scheme of comprehension such as that which had been suggested at the Savoy Conference, and was again brought forward after the Revolution of 1688, might at this moment have been carried out, if the confusion into which the country was thrown by the invasion of William, and the flight of James, had not broken the thread of Sancroft's overtures, put a stop to the scheme of comprehension he had framed, and compelled him to abandon the idea of being able to carry into effect the plan he had devised, and had put an end to the kindly feeling between Nonconformists and Conformists, without which it would be almost impossible to carry any scheme of union and uniformity into effect.

Still, it is due to Sancroft to remember that he had actually desired such a scheme, and was anxious to bring it about, before Dissenters and Churchmen had returned to their old attitude of antagonism. The best account of Sancroft's scheme of comprehension is afforded by a speech delivered by Dr. Wake, then Bishop of Lincoln, and afterwards Archbishop of Canterbury, at the trial of Dr. Sacheverell. "Archbishop Sancroft foreseeing some such revolution as was afterwards happily brought about, began to consider how utterly unprepared they had been, at the restoration of King Charles II., to settle many things to the advantage of the Church, and what a happy opportunity had been lost for want of such a previous care as he was desirous should now be taken for the better and more perfect establishment of it. And he, at the same time, was considering what might be done to gain the Dissenters without doing any prejudice to the Church. The scheme was laid out, and the several parts of it were committed, not only with the approbation, but likewise direction, to such of our divines of the Church as were thought the most proper to be intrusted with it. His grace took one part to himself; another part was committed to Dr. Patrick. The reviewing of the daily service and the Communion Book was referred to a select number of divines, of whom Dr. Sharp, afterwards Archbishop of York, and Dr. Patrick, were two. The design was to improve and enforce the discipline of the Church, to review and enlarge the liturgy, by correcting some things and adding others."

These names prove Sancroft to have been perfectly in earnest in his efforts to effect a comprehension before the occurrence of the revolution, which it might perhaps have prevented. The immense popularity which he enjoyed at that moment, not only with the clergy and laity of the Church, but also with Nonconformists of all classes and denominations, would have secured for any scheme he might sanction a much more favourable consideration than was accorded to the plan of his brilliant successor in the primacy, whose Latitudinarian principles rendered him very unpopular with the clergy, and roused up against his plan—which was probably nearly identical with that which Sancroft would have proposed—an opposition which his high character and great talents could not enable him to override. The calm, quiet, and thoroughly submissive, not to say reverential, opposition which Sancroft offered to the designs of James against the Church would no doubt have brought upon him the heavy displeasure of the insensate king, and might have cost him his see and perhaps even his life.

But the worst of the king's bad advisers were now becoming alarmed at his proceedings. Jeffreys privately told Clarendon, before the bishops had been liberated on bail from the Tower, that he was much troubled at the prosecution; and two or three days after their acquittal he was devising means of entering into a correspondence with them. He expressed himself with regard to the judges in terms of the most vehement and unrestrained condemnation. Clarendon writes, in his diary of the 13th of August—that is to say, a little more than a month after the bishops were released: "The Lord Chancellor (Jeffreys) talked very freely to me of all affairs, called the judges a thousand fools and knaves, said that Chief Justice Wright was a beast." He was, however, still in as high favour as ever at court; and he gleefully told Clarendon that the king and queen were coming to dine with him on Thursday next, and added that he had still good hopes that the king would be moderate when the Parliament met.

A few days after the date of this conversation, the Bishop of Rochester withdrew from the Ecclesiastical Commission, and made a declaration in writing of his reasons for leaving it. Still, in spite of these clear indications of the all but universal disapproval with which his conduct was regarded, the king was still pressing on in his mad career, when certain intelligence reached him, on the 22nd of September, that the Prince of Orange was preparing to invade England. This news made him at length see the folly of which he had been guilty, and forced him to relinquish his designs against the Church, and to solicit the aid and advice of those very bishops whom he had recently sent to the Tower—and especially of the honest, intrepid, and consistent primate, who was ready to stand by him with all loyalty and honour, while the men who for their own ends had urged him on to his ruin were hastening to offer the invader their services and their congratulations.

The unfortunate king now sent repeatedly for Sancroft and the other bishops, but even in the extremity to which he was reduced he dealt only in generalities, and led them to fear that he was leaving an opening for the withdrawal of the concessions that he seemed disposed to make if a favourable turn in his affairs should occur and enable him to do so with any prospect of success. However, he talked freely and courteously with the bishops who waited on him. Sancroft was not present at the first of these interviews, being hindered by illness from accompanying his suffragans; but on a subsequent occasion he waited on the unfortunate prince in company with some of his comprovincial bishops, and read an address to him which, if it had been as frankly accepted on the one hand as it was honestly intended on the other, might at this critical emergency have put a stop to the enterprise of the Prince of Orange, or at least have given the king another opportunity of retracing his steps and reconciling himself with the Church.

The document which the prelates on this critical occasion laid before James is so important in itself, and well adapted to throw light on the events which speedily succeeded its presentation, that we lay it before the reader *in extenso* :—

"May it please your Sacred Majesty,

"When I lately had the honour to wait upon you, you were pleased briefly to acquaint me with what had passed two days before, between your Majesty and these my reverend brethren: by which, and by the account they themselves gave me, I perceived that there passed nothing but in very general terms, and expressions of your Majesty's gracious and favourable inclinations to the Church of England, and of our reciprocal duty and loyalty to your Majesty, both which were sufficiently understood and declared before; and (as one of my brethren then told you) would have been in the same state if the bishops had not stirred one foot out of their own dioceses. Sir, I found it grieved my lords the bishops to have come so far, and to have done so little; and I am assured they came then prepared to have given your Majesty some particular instances of their duty and zeal for your service, had they not apprehended from some words which fell from your Majesty that you were not then at leisure to receive them. It was for this reason that I then besought your Majesty to command us once more to attend you all together; which your Majesty was pleased graciously to allow and encourage. We are here therefore now before you, with all humility, to beg your permission that we may suggest to your Majesty such advices as we think proper at this season, and conducing to your service, and so leave them to your princely consideration."

The king having signified his assent, the archbishop

then proceeded to read the advice which the bishops had jointly agreed to give.

"1. That your Majesty will be graciously pleased to put the management of your government in the several counties into the hands of such of the nobility and gentry there as are legally qualified for it.

"2. That your Majesty will be graciously pleased to annull your commission for ecclesiastical affairs, and that no such court as that commission sets up may be erected for the future.

"3. That your Majesty will be graciously pleased that no dispensation be granted and continued, by virtue whereof any person not duly qualified by law hath been or may be put into any place, office, or preferment in Church or State, or in the universities, or continued in the same; especially such as have cure of souls annexed to them; and, in particular, that you will be graciously pleased to restore the President and Fellows of St. Mary Magdalen College in Oxford.

"4. That your Majesty will be graciously pleased to set aside all licences or faculties already granted, by which persons of the Romish communion may pretend to be enabled to teach public schools, and that no such be granted for the future.

"5. That your Majesty will be graciously pleased to desist from such a dispensing power as hath of late been used, and to permit that point to be freely and calmly debated and argued, and finally settled in Parliament.

"6. That your Majesty will be graciously pleased to inhibit the four foreign bishops who style themselves

Vicars Apostolical, from further invading the ecclesiastical jurisdiction which is by law vested in the bishops of this Church.

"7. That your Majesty will be graciously pleased to fill the vacant bishoprics and other ecclesiastical promotions within your gift, both in England and Ireland, with men of learning and piety; and in particular (which I must own to be my peculiar boldness, for it is done without the privity of my brethren), that you will be graciously pleased forthwith to fill the archiepiscopal chair of York (which has so long stood empty, and upon which a whole province depends), with some very worthy person: for which (pardon me, Sir, I am bold to say) you have here now before you a very fair choice.

"8. That your Majesty will be graciously pleased to supercede all further prosecution of Quo warrantos against corporations, and to restore to them their ancient charters, privileges, and franchises; as we hear God hath put it into your Majesty's heart to do for the city of London; which we intended to have made otherwise one of our principal requests.

"9. That, if it so please your Majesty, writs may be issued with all convenient speed, for the calling of a free and regular Parliament, in which the Church of England may be secured according to the Acts of Uniformity; provision may be made for a due liberty of conscience, and for securing the liberties and properties of all your subjects, and a mutual confidence and good understanding may be established between your Majesty and all your people.

"10. Above all that your Majesty will be graciously pleased to permit your bishops to offer you such motives and arguments as (we trust) may by God's grace be effectual to persuade your Majesty to return to the communion of the Church of England, into whose most Catholic faith you were baptized, and in which you were educated, and to which it is our earnest prayer to God that you may be reunited."

Such was the advice which the archbishop and eight of his suffragans offered to their sovereign; and, if the concessions they recommended had been promptly made, the disasters that overtook James might even yet have been averted. But the unfortunate prince, while really intending to follow in all respects, except a change of religion, the advice given him by the bishops, made his concessions in a manner that caused men to doubt his sincerity, and to fear that if the immediate danger should be removed the horrors of " The Bloody Circuit " would be repeated by Jeffreys or some equally unscrupulous judge. Instead of at once accepting the advice given by the bishops, and acting on it with promptitude, James, fully intending to yield, but desiring to save his dignity and to appear to act spontaneously, yielded article after article separately; and so the concessions which, if made immediately would perhaps have saved him, now served only to accelerate his downfall. The words "too late," which in this century have so often met the tardy and compelled concessions of tottering despotisms, might be regarded as sounding the knell of the deferred graces which James yielded to the advice of his friends and the demands of his enemies, when he was unable any longer to withhold them.

At this juncture of affairs, Sancroft and the bishops who were acting with him found themselves placed in a very critical situation. It was not in the nature of things that the prodigious popularity which their resistance of the king's arbitrary proceedings, and their own noble demeanour while under persecution had obtained for them, could be long sustained; and it was now in fact withering as rapidly as it had sprung up. The people in whose breasts the dread and hatred of Popery had completely annihilated the old cavalier spirit of loyalty, had now one feeling, which was to drive out James and his Jesuits at once and by any means. Their great fear, therefore, was that the bishops, now that the immediate danger was removed, would range themselves on the side of the falling monarch and support the cause with which he was identified.

Nor were these apprehensions unfounded. Sancroft and many of his suffragans still adhered with unshaken tenacity to their old doctrines of passive obedience, non-resistance, and the divine right of kings; and, believing that it was their bounden duty to support the royal authority with all their might, they felt themselves much more in their element when bending the knee before their sovereign, than when combining with Presbyterians and Independents in opposition to him, or receiving the congratulations of acclaiming multitudes. It was not then to be wondered at that when events were following one another with the rapidity that characterizes great revolutions, a sudden revulsion should take place in the feelings with which the bishops were regarded, and that the great services they had rendered to the cause of civil and religious liberty should be forgotten.

But we must now turn back to trace the proceedings of the Prince of Orange. We need hardly say that the events we have narrated had been watched by that astute and ambitious statesman with the liveliest interest; that their bearing on the great European struggle which he was carrying on against the French monarch had not escaped his penetrating glance; and further, that as soon as the birth of a male heir to the English throne took place, he must have felt that if he wished to secure his wife's and his own accession to that throne, he must strike in at once with a feeling that it was now or never.

The birth of the young prince, which seemed to put an end to all prospect of his succession to the English throne in right of his wife on the demise of his father-in-law, made both William and his English correspondents feel that the only hope he had was in busily making his preparations for an immediate invasion of England. From this moment, then, William laboured with secrecy and despatch to hasten forward his preparations, and was soon in a condition to set sail. And so, while James was plunged in blind security, William was diligently surmounting the manifold obstacles and difficulties that stood in the way of his attempt. When at last the appearance of William's fleet in the Channel, and the publication of his manifesto, did not allow James a moment longer to indulge in his dreams of security, he seemed to rely more on prayers to the Virgin Mary, and on the intercessions of his Romish counsellors, than on the measures of concession and the military and naval preparations that an emergency so alarming demanded. Indeed, it is more than doubtful whether, in the extremity to which he was reduced, the utmost promptitude could have saved him from the consequences of his folly and obstinacy. For his party in the country was so disorganized, and the nation generally was so excited by panic fear of the supposed designs of the Papists on the one hand, and on the other by the treason of Lord Churchill and Lord Cornbury—men who were under the greatest obligations to James, and who owed to his bounty and confidence the very posts that enabled them more effectually to betray him; but who, nevertheless were among the first to join the forces of the invader, and to endeavour to make their treason more valuable by taking over with them the troops that were placed under their command to resist the invader. Meanwhile, the poor child, which had already been baptized privately, was now publicly admitted into the Church by the name of James Francis Edward, while the Prince of Orange was advancing as rapidly as possible to seize the crown.

This unfortunate child of unfortunate parents was alleged to have been introduced into the queen's bed, in a warming-pan, by the Jesuits, whose interest it no doubt was to prevent at any cost the accession of Mary to the throne of these realms.

Unfortunately for James, the archbishop was in the Tower at the time of the child's birth; and other witnesses, who enjoyed the confidence of the nation, and whose testimony would probably have dissipated this ridiculous falsehood, were absent when the birth took place; while the queen's bed was surrounded with Papists whose evidence had no weight at all with the nation, who were generally supposed to be privy to the alleged imposture, and whose evidence rather strengthened than weakened the popular belief in this absurd fable.

Thus, while James was repeating to his son-in-law the arguments for toleration he had learnt from Penn, and was trying to carry out a policy so wise by means so exceedingly unwise, William continued to write to him and to conceal his designs till he could no longer wear the mask. To his dissertations in favour of toleration, William replied that he was favourably disposed to toleration, but that he could not consent to remove the securities that had been provided in England against the ambition of Rome. At the same time, his preparations were being carried on more diligently, and his correspondence with the English malcontents became daily more and more active. He addressed to Sancroft his warm but not altogether disinterested congratulations on the result of the trial of the seven bishops. He encouraged the doubts that were cast on the reality of the birth of his infant nephew, and he determined, with the advice of his numerous and influential English correspondents, to attempt an invasion at once; and accordingly, issued a proclamation in which he stated the objects he was coming to effect, and declared that he had decided to come on the invitation of several of the lords spiritual and temporal, and many other persons of rank and importance.

If Sancroft's position had been delicate and difficult before, it had become doubly so now. He was respected and courted by all parties, but he carefully abstained from identifying himself with any of them. He still believed it to be his duty to stand by the king; but he felt that if it should be the will of God to relieve the country from a detestable tyranny, and the Church from a serious and imminent danger, it was not for him to oppose the behests of Providence. James commanded him to draw up a form of prayer against the projected invasion, and Sancroft performed this official duty with so much adroitness as to satisfy the king without offending the partisans of the prince.

Being once more summoned into the royal presence, in company with such of his suffragans as were then in town, the king read to them the passage of the prince's proclamation in which it was stated that he came by special invitation from several lords, spiritual and temporal, and he requested the bishops to sign a paper which contradicted this assertion, so far as they were concerned. Sancroft truly and emphatically denied that he had anything whatever to do with the projected invasion. Compton, who had long been in correspondence with the prince, and who was one of those who had invited him to come over, evaded the question by an unworthy prevarication. However, when James presented the bishops who waited on him a paper which declared that they had not invited the prince to come over, and that they disapproved of the attempt he was making to subvert the present Government, they all refused.

However, they pressed the king to summon a Parliament, and when he alleged the impossibility of compliance with this advice, they suggested that he should convene a meeting of those of the lords, spiritual and temporal, who happened to be in town at the time, in order that they might deliberate freely on the course that it would be advisable to adopt under the very extraordinary circumstances in which they were placed. The general feeling among the bishops—and it probably was shared by Sancroft, if indeed it did not originate with him—was, that the prince should meet his father-in-law, and that they should make such a settlement of the questions at issue between them as would satisfy the nation and effectually provide against a repetition of those arbitrary acts which had caused and enabled the prince to intervene in the manner he was doing in the affairs of this country.

The notion that, after all that had passed between them, such a settlement could possibly have been made, has been held up to derision by a very high authority; but preposterous and absurd as the idea may have been, it certainly was the intention and expectation of many of those who lent their support to William, but who unquestionably would not have listened for one moment to a proposal for the dethronement of James.

The bishops were placed in a very difficult and dubious position. The unfortunate prince whom they honestly desired to serve was acting like a madman, and his best friends were trying to arrest him in his insane career with the least possible injury to his prestige or his authority.

William himself can hardly have contemplated at first the result to which he was at last brought by the logic of events and the unanimity of the nation. Sancroft was one of those who took the lead in pressing the infatuated king to summon a Parliament. To all such advice James replied that he passionately desired to comply with the request, but added, "How is it possible that a Parliament can be free whilst an enemy is in the kingdom, and can secure the return of a hundred members?" Nevertheless, he withdrew his refusal, acting, as he had done throughout, with pusillanimous indecision. Finding that, while William was steadily advancing, his own friends were one by one deserting him and going over to the invader, he burnt the writs he had ordered to be prepared, and thought of nothing but escaping.

On the very day that William was landing with his troops at Torbay, South was preaching to a large congregation in Westminster Abbey. One reads the sermon delivered at such a time with curiosity, to see whether it affords any indication that the preacher was aware of what was going on in that distant part of the kingdom. He could hardly be wholly ignorant of it, and yet his sermon does not contain a single expression which would lead the reader of it to suppose that he was aware of what was occurring. This discourse is only distinguished by more than his usual coarseness of invective against both Puritanism and Romanism.

The only phrase he uses which can be at all construed into an allusion to passing events is one in which he speaks of the "little finger of fanaticism being harder and heavier on the monarchy than the whole loins of Popery," adding the prayer, "God deliver us from them both;" which seems to indicate that he was aware that the two evils which he dreaded the most, and which were the burden of almost all the sermons he delivered between the Restoration and the Revolution, were at that time impending over the kingdom, and likely to come on it with redoubled force. We must give him credit for courage and honesty, when we recollect that James was still reigning, and that though even at that time many hoped that he would be restrained, few expected that he would be dethroned.

Events now followed one another with revolutionary rapidity. James had fled, was again brought back, was placed under the protection of Dutch guards; fled again, and finally made his escape into France, where he was most hospitably received, and entertained by the French king. William advanced with an army composed of Dutch and French soldiers, chiefly commanded by Huguenot officers driven from their own country by the impolitic bigotry of the French king into the ranks of his chief enemy, by whom they were gladly employed in effecting the Revolution of 1688. Meanwhile, most of the bishops and the nobility had hastened to hail the rising sun, and were welcomed with alacrity by the new Government, which sought to enlist as many partisans as possible, without caring to inquire whether they were led to change their views by the basest or the best motives. Even Crewe found himself pardoned in a manner he little deserved and little expected. Lamplugh, who had only just received the archbishopric of York, as a reward for his loyalty to James, was allowed to retain it on the ground of his loyalty to William. Sprat, Cartwright, and Crewe remained undisturbed in their respective sees.

William entered the metropolis, and took possession of his father-in-law's throne, without having been obliged to strike a blow. He was hailed as a deliverer, and, with very few exceptions, his title was universally acknowledged. As for Sancroft, he had always been a divine, and not at all a statesman. He had shunned the regions of party strife, except when the importunities of those who looked up to him for guidance, or the requirements of his station, forced him to descend into them, and he retired again into private life as soon as this uncongenial duty had been performed. He was not the man to join in hailing the rising sun, and he returned to his quiet home at Lambeth, and there calmly awaited the event of the struggle in the commencement of which he had borne so conspicuous, but so undesired, a part. He was dragged from his retirement to attend the council of peers and others, which was held at the Guildhall of London, for the purpose of providing for the peace of the metropolis, imperilled by the momentary dissolution of all government which followed the disappearance of James. When the fallen monarch was brought back to Faversham, Sancroft there waited on him in company with several other bishops.

William, meanwhile, made his entry into the metropolis, at the head of his little army. In conjunction with his wife, he was seated on the throne; but, while he allowed her the title of queen, he took care to seize all the sovereign authority, except such parts of it as he could not safely trust to any one but his wife. Throughout the whole of the events which step by step had led to this result, the position of Sancroft, and those who looked up to him as their leader, was full of difficulty. To side with James was to support the propagation of a religion which they had been taught to regard as impious, blasphemous, and idolatrous. To side with William was to violate the oath of allegiance he had sworn to James, when he placed the crown on his head, and to disavow those doctrines of non-resistance and passive obedience which he had held and taught in common with Tillotson, Burnet, Sharp, Stillingfleet, Compton, and almost the whole body of the clergy. As has been already noticed, the only difference between him and them was, that while they professed to have abandoned these opinions at a time when a continued adherence to them would have involved the loss of all things, he still avowed them. I am far from wishing to insinuate that they who, after having sworn allegiance to James, swore with equal readiness allegiance to William, were less conscientious than they who on this occasion took a different view of their duty. Many of them, I doubt not, were fully satisfied in their own minds of the rightness and propriety of the course they adopted under the very peculiar and wholly unforeseen circumstances in which they were suddenly placed. But they laid themselves open to the suspicion of being actuated by interested motives from which the Nonjurors were certainly free. And if we accord our meed of praise to the honest men who went out with Baxter, or to those who in our day followed Chalmers in his secession from the Scottish Church, we ought not to refuse it to the honest men who, on very different grounds, and under very different circumstances, went out with Sancroft.

CHAPTER IV.

WILLIAM AND MARY.

On no class of persons did the revolution fall more heavily than on the clergy. Very few, indeed, of them were prepared for a change so complete as that which was actually effected. Almost all of them were confounded by the rapidity with which events followed each other; very many of them were prepared for a regency; scarce one of them anticipated that the party of Tillotson and Burnet, which comprised a minority insignificant in numbers, would rise at once to the top, and take the direction of Church affairs. They had witnessed with feelings of deep indignation the desertion of James by those he had most trusted, and even by the members of his own family. And they were by no means without hope that the deposed monarch would speedily return at the head of a French army and reascend the vacated throne. Most of them took up an attitude of expectation, and were silent as the grave, at least in the pulpit, with regard to the important events that were being transacted.

After much discussion, the account of which belongs to constitutional rather than to ecclesiastical history, it was resolved that William of Orange and his wife Mary, the eldest daughter of James, should jointly occupy the vacant throne, with the understanding that, though the government was to be carried on in the names of both, the supreme authority should be vested in William, whose notions of domestic government were very arbitrary.

The new sovereigns were proclaimed on Ash Wednesday—a day then observed with a strictness unknown to later times. Good Churchmen were scandalized to see bonfires blazing, wine-casks broached in the streets, and the church bells ringing out merry peals on the first day of the Lenten fast. But William was not a man to trouble himself about days and seasons; and his wife, though a most devout member of the English Church, yielded to the wishes of her husband, who felt how important, and indeed how necessary, it was not to lose a moment in placing himself in the vacant seat, and vigorously taking hold of the reins of government.

But it was different with Sancroft, who was a rigid observer of the feasts and festivals of the Church, and it is not unlikely that the disregard which the new sovereigns displayed for a day so sacred in his eyes helped to prejudice his mind against them, and especially against William, whose Presbyterian leanings were manifested with impolitic candour and in a manner that greatly shocked and offended many of his new subjects.

Mary, who had been brought up in the doctrines

of the Anglican Church, and was strongly attached to its polity, no doubt shared the feelings of the primate; and, though in obedience to the wishes of her husband, she had taken her part in the ceremony of the proclamation, yet on the same day, she despatched two messengers to Lambeth to ask for the archbishop's blessing, and directed them to attend the daily service at the chapel of Lambeth Palace, in order to ascertain whether her father or her husband and herself were mentioned in the prayers of the day. In answer to the request for his benediction, the indignant primate sternly replied, "Tell her first to ask her father's blessing, for without that mine would be useless."

After having undergone this rebuff, the messengers of Mary then proceeded to execute the other part of the commission they had received, and with that view to attend the evening service celebrated in the chapel of the palace at which Sancroft was present. A Mr. Wharton, a man of great celebrity as a scholar, was the chaplain in attendance, and it was his duty to say the prayers. Before commencing, he waited on the archbishop, and asked him whether he had any special instructions to give him with regard to the service he was about to perform. Sancroft, whose ill-humour was no doubt excited by the occurrences of the day, curtly answered, "No," meaning that the service should be carried out in the usual manner without any change.

Wharton, who, though much attached to the archbishop, was also a warm partisan of the new Government, had observed the messengers of the queen, and divined the object of their visit to the chapel. He chose to understand the reply of the archbishop as a permission to do as he pleased, and, acting in accordance with this interpretation of Sancroft's directions, prayed for William and Mary. After the conclusion of the service, Sancroft sent for him, and, with a warmth very unusual with him, said to his chaplain, "You must either desist from praying for the new pretended king and queen, or you must cease to officiate in my chapel." But, though Sancroft held these views himself, and did not hesitate to avow and maintain them within the precincts of his own residence, he did not interfere to prevent his chaplains and others over whom his position gave him influence or authority from acknowledging them; only he was determined that by no act, either performed by himself or by those for whose conduct he was directly responsible, would he countenance what he considered to be an unlawful usurpation.

William and his advisers were unwilling to break with those whose steadfast resistance to the arbitrary acts of James had brought about the revolution that placed him on the throne; and wisely so, for it is probable that if Sancroft and his followers had met the new Government, not with the passive obedience which in accordance with their principles they yielded to it, but with a watchful and jealous antagonism, they might have placed it in a position of very serious difficulty and embarrassment. William and his advisers therefore acted wisely as well as kindly in treating the old man with great forbearance. They would, perhaps, have done still better had they, in consideration of the great services he had rendered to their cause, left him to the end of his days in possession of his home at Lambeth, allowing him still to have his prayers there and keep a conscience void of offence. Meanwhile they had induced the Parliament to pass an Act enjoining that the oath to be made by the new sovereigns at their coronation might be administered, according to the discretion of King William, either by the archbishop or the Bishop of London, thus holding out to Sancroft another opportunity of being reconciled to the new Government, of which he did not chose to avail himself. Finding, however, that by persisting in the position he had taken up, he was in danger of incurring the penalties of *præmunire*, he granted a commission to the Bishop of London, together with any three bishops of the province of Canterbury, empowering them to exercise his archiepiscopal functions; but he carefully abstained from himself performing any act or uttering any word that could be construed into a recognition of the sovereignty of William and Mary; and being ultimately forced to quit his residence at Lambeth, and deprived of the revenues of his see, he retired, first to London, and then to Freshinfield, the place in which he was born, and in which, soon after the events just narrated, he died. But the period of his residence there belongs to the private life of Sancroft rather than to our history. By the acts we have related he separated himself from the English Church, and became at once the founder and chief of the little company of the Nonjurors, and died, as he had lived—calm, quiet, and resigned.

There can be no doubt that the great majority of the clergy shared the beliefs which had caused Sancroft to relinquish his high station in the Church, but very few of them were prepared to follow the example which their primate had given them. They complied therefore by taking the oaths and by praying for William and Mary; but they were reproached as time-servers, and felt the reproach the more keenly because they could not deny that appearances were against them. Their parishioners remembered how ardently they had formerly preached in favour of the fallen dynasty, and had professed and inculcated a loyalty which no misconduct could destroy and no provocation shake. The consequence was that throughout the whole of the reign of William the relations of the clergy and the Government were the reverse of cordial, and they were still further embittered by the knowledge that the theological opinions of the king differed considerably from those of the great majority of the clergy; that he disliked many of the practices to which they fondly clung; and that he often displayed his dislike of them with an impolitic openness.

The schemes of comprehension and of the union of the Protestants of England with the Protestants on the Continent, which had been proposed at the Restoration, only to be laid aside, which had been renewed by Sancroft when he was seeking to obtain the co-operation of the Nonconformists with himself, and with those who had joined him in withstanding the attempts of James to Romanize the English Church, were again brought forward soon after the accession of William and Mary, apparently with a better chance of success; for now the party that advocated these changes was in power, and seemed to be in a position that would enable it to effect them. William especially was zealously anxious, not only on political and religious grounds, but also from personal preference, to confront the united Church of Rome with a united reformed Church, which should combine the Protestants, not of England only, but of every country in Europe, in resistance to the powerful and ambitious monarch whose haughty aggressions it had been the great object of his life to withstand.

Though he professed himself to be a zealous Calvinist, he felt that it was essential to the maintenance of his position that he should conform to the Established Church, which comprehended nine-tenths of his subjects, and which, by his coronation oath, he had solemnly bound himself to uphold and maintain. But being inclined, both by education and natural disposition, to prefer the simplest and plainest form of worship, he naturally wished to bring the doctrine and policy of the Church over which he was called to preside to the level of his own ideas, and to assimilate the worship of this country to that which prevailed in his own, as well as among the French and German Protestants. And probably something would have been effected in this way if the wars in which he was engaged throughout nearly the whole of his reign had not prevented him from giving the attention which, from motives of policy, he anxiously desired to devote to the affairs of the Church, and which he did devote to them in the earlier part of his reign. He was, therefore, obliged to devolve the care of ecclesiastical affairs on his wife, who, being a steadfast and attached member of the Church, and opposed to all changes in it, contented herself with administering its affairs without attempting to alter it. William, on the other hand, indulged his ecclesiastical preferences as far as the time at his disposal and his other multifarious occupations and engagements would allow. He promoted the revival of Presbyterianism and the suppression of Episcopacy in Scotland with the concurrence of nearly the whole nation. He appointed Burnet to the bishopric of Salisbury, and afterwards Tillotson to the archiepiscopal see of Canterbury. Both of these prelates were men after his own heart—men who zealously promoted the changes which he desired to introduce, but which, as both he and they were aware, could only be introduced with any hope of success by the authority of Parliament without their being required also to receive the sanction of Convocation, which, as he and they clearly foresaw, would be pretty certain to reject any scheme of Comprehension, however moderate, that might be submitted to it.

Tillotson and Burnet were two of the most eminent writers of their day. The former especially. His discourses were indeed far inferior in depth and solidity to those of Barrow and Jeremy Taylor, which, however, were now looked on as somewhat antiquated in their style. But as specimens of pure limpid English, no preacher and writer of his day could equal them. For more than a hundred years after their publication, his sermons were to be found in every library, and were regarded as writings which should be carefully studied by every one who wished to acquire a thoroughly good English style.

As for Burnet, he was a tall, stout, good-looking, rather impudent Scotchman. A great preacher withal, but far inferior to his friend Tillotson in the elegance of his style. His writings were chiefly historical, and are highly valuable as affording on the whole, perhaps, the best narrative we possess of the events of his day, or, at least, as furnishing the best and most copious materials to the historian of later times. Though, as just remarked, chiefly historical, they abound in very unhistorical blunders, and are written for the most part in a spirit of strong partiality for those who, like himself, belonged to the Whig party, and of great unfairness towards their opponents, in whom he can seldom discern any merit whatever, and many of whom he has very undeservedly censured.

These two men were at first the chief advisers of William in all his ecclesiastical affairs. The appointment of Burnet to the see of Salisbury gave bitter offence to the clergy, who detested him on account of the active share he had taken in conspiring against the late Government, as well as on account of his supposed Presbyterian proclivities. But Burnet had other claims on the patronage of William, besides those that arose from the conformity that was supposed to exist between them in their religious opinions. The knowledge he possessed of England and Scotland had enabled him to give William advice and information that were of the very greatest use to him in his enterprise. He had also been the means of putting him in communication with many of the leading nobility and gentry of the kingdom. He had also drawn up many important State papers for him with rare skill and judgment.

But the greatest service of all that he had rendered to him was that of persuading Mary to lay at the feet of a peevish and overbearing husband, who often treated her with a rudeness bordering on brutality, that crown of England which was expected to be hers by inheritance, which William could only claim in her right and as her husband, and which the English people would have conferred on her if she herself had not insisted on bestowing it on her husband.

Burnet, however, possessed qualifications for the high office to which he was appointed, that fully justified the choice William made of him to fill it. Very few bishops have ever discharged their episcopal duties more zealously than Burnet. In his diligence in visiting his diocese, in preaching, in catechizing the children, in relieving the poor, consoling the afflicted, ministering to the sick, showing courtesy and hospitality to men of all classes and opinions, no English prelate has ever surpassed him. But these very merits excited against him the ire of many of those do-nothing prelates, and in his day they were but too numerous, who scarcely ever visited their diocese, and, sunk in sloth and luxury, delighted in railing at those who displayed some zeal and activity in the discharge of their episcopal duties.

William, who pardoned the many foibles of this worthy divine out of consideration for his many good qualities, continued to consult him frequently, not only on the ecclesiastical, but also the political affairs of the country he was called to govern, and in ruling over which he found very few persons competent to advise him properly. It was at his suggestion that the king selected Tillotson to fill the highest and most important place in the Anglican Church. He had already nominated him to the deanery of St. Paul, London; and when the new dean waited on the king to offer him his thanks for choosing him to fill a position which exactly met his views, William informed him that he was appointed to this new office only for a short time, and that he intended to transfer him shortly to the see of Canterbury.

Tillotson had long been known as an ecclesiastical Liberal—a form of belief which in his day, even more than in our own, was sure to bring down on those who held it the censure, if not the persecution, of many among their clerical brethren. He had been an attentive listener to the debates of the Savoy Conference; he had taken some part in the deliberations of that assembly, and probably had thus imbibed those liberal opinions which in after life he consistently upheld. These opinions were such as even in the present day would have procured for him the reputation of being a very broad Churchman; but in his own day they created a strong prejudice against him in the minds of the majority of both clergy and laity of the English Church.

Nevertheless, the peculiar elegance of his style, which elicited the warm admiration even of Addison, his private worth, the extent and variety of his attainments, his deservedly high reputation as a preacher, had procured for him a degree of consideration among the more highly educated portion of the community, such as perhaps no other English ecclesiastic ever enjoyed. Burnet had strongly and with good reason recommended him to William, as being beyond all comparison the man best qualified to carry out the plans he had formed for effecting a comprehension of Nonconformists, and a union with foreign Protestants.

But it was thought that he could best serve the king's schemes of union and comprehension by remaining for the present in the office to which he had recently been appointed. When these designs were brought before the Legislature, Parliament absolutely refused to take a single step in the matter of toleration, comprehension, or the union of Protestant Churches at home and abroad, without the concurrence of the Convocation. William, Tillotson, and Burnet, all three felt that this stipulation was pregnant with danger to the plans they had so much at heart. But the Parliament would not yield, and they were obliged to submit to the conditions it imposed. Still it was hoped that the great reputation of Tillotson, backed as it was by the whole influence of the Government, would enable his friends to secure his election as prolocutor of the Lower

House, or, failing this, to at least obtain by mutual concessions the adoption of a well-considered, well-digested plan of toleration, and perhaps even of comprehension. In order to pave the way for the adoption of such a plan, a Commission was appointed to draw up a measure, to be submitted to the Ecclesiastical Parliament in the hope that it would pave the way for the deliberate consideration of the proposed measure by the Convocation.

The Toleration Bill—which was a very imperfect measure, only granting a partial relief to some classes of Protestant Nonconformists, while it denied it altogether to the Roman Catholics, was a great boon to very many of the Nonconformist ministers and their congregations, and was readily carried through both Houses of Parliament. Not so the measure on which William's mind was chiefly set—the Comprehension Bill. This Bill had been carefully prepared for the consideration of Convocation by the Commission, though the prestige of that body was somewhat damaged by the withdrawal from it of several of those who had been placed on it in the hope that they would favour the objects that it was intended to promote. The plan embodied in the Bill made the use of the surplice in the performance of divine service, the sign of the cross in the baptism of infants, sitting instead of kneeling in the reception of the Lord's Supper, optional. It also introduced other changes similar in character but of no great moment.

The king, who had this measure much more at heart than any of his ministers, or perhaps any one else in the kingdom, on account not only of its religious, but still more of its political and diplomatic importance, and whose favourite idea it was, made a liberal offer to the contending parties. Taking advantage of a visit he paid to the House of Lords, to give his assent to some Bills that had been recently passed, he offered a compromise. He suggested the repeal of the Test and Corporation Acts, on the understanding that if this proposal should be accepted, the Nonjurors, Sancroft and his friends, should be exempted from taking the oaths, and consequently be left in undisturbed possession of their benefices. This was a liberal offer, and one that ought to have been accepted by those who had urged them to hold out; but their love of persecution was stronger than their love of the Nonjurors and those who had acted with them, and so the Nonjurors were left to their fate. One of them, the Bishop of Worcester, died on the twenty-fourth of July, exhorting his clergy, with his latest breath, to refuse to take the oaths to the new Government.

Towards the close of this year Compton, who by this time was aware that Tillotson had been selected by the king to succeed the archbishop, and that consequently his claims to the primacy were disregarded, waited on Sancroft, in company with the Bishop of St. Asaph, to endeavour to persuade him and the other Nonjurors to take the oaths, or to adopt some other means of avoiding deprivation. They offered several suggestions, all of which Sancroft rejected. Up to this time the clergy generally had stood by the primate; some through hope that James would return again, some through genuine attachment to his principles or to his person. But when it became evident that the new Government was firmly seated, they hastened, at the last moment, to make their peace with it, to prepare apologies for their change of opinion, and save their benefices by taking the oaths to it. The consequence was, as Clarendon in his diary bitterly complains, that there was a "great alteration in the tone of the discourses that were then delivered." The old High Church doctrines were still secretly held, but for a time they had almost disappeared from the sermons of the clergy.

Eventually, of the three Bills which had been introduced into Parliament shortly after the accession of William, and which faithfully represented his views with regard to the Church and religion, as well as the opinions of several of those who had taken a leading and active part in bringing about the late revolution, the Toleration Bill was carried, and the other two were rejected. As already mentioned, the first of these statutes granted a grudging, limited, and imperfect toleration to some denominations of Nonconformists, while it excluded others. But it allowed full liberty of preaching to the great majority of the Nonconformist ministers. In dealing with the other two measures, the Parliament had adopted a resolution that was fatal to their success, when they decided, without a single dissentient voice, to request the king to summon the Convocation of the clergy of the kingdom.

What they meant by this somewhat ambiguous phrase does not very clearly appear. Macaulay, indeed, has laid it down very decidedly, that it was "merely the Synod of the province of Canterbury," and he affirms that "it *never* had a right to speak in the name of the whole clerical body." He appears not to have been aware that the two Convocations have ever been fused into one, or have ever acted together on ecclesiastical questions; and yet the title given in the Book of Common Prayer to the Thirty-nine Articles clearly proves the contrary of that which he alleges. It distinctly affirms that at least on one important occasion the two Convocations sat and acted together, for the title placed at the head of the Articles runs as follows:—" Articles agreed upon by the archbishops and bishops of *both provinces*, and the *whole* clergy, in the Convocation holden at London in the year 1562, for the avoiding of diversities of opinions," etc. Considering the language of the resolution by which the Convocation was summoned to meet, may we not conclude that when the two Houses of Parliament spoke of " the Convocation of the Clergy of the kingdom," they intended such a fusion of the two Convocations as is clearly intimated in the title at the head of the Articles to which we have just referred; in fact, not to a provincial but to a national synod, such as that which is stated to have been held in the year 1562?

The very first act of the Convocation showed what was the spirit that animated the great majority of its members. The choice of a prolocutor was the crucial test which should decide the relative strength of the two contending parties—the party of moderate concession, and the party of resistance to all change. The chosen champion of the latter party was Dr. Jane, a High Churchman, Regius Professor of Divinity in the University of Oxford. That of the latter was Tillotson. Nothing shows more clearly the importance that was attached by the king to this struggle than the retention of Tillotson in the Lower House, long after he had been designated for the archbishopric, in order that he might give the supporters of the Government the aid of his influence and reputation. Both parties, indeed, put forth all their strength in order to secure the victory.

The result of the struggle between them was that Jane obtained fifty-five votes, while only twenty-eight were given to Tillotson. The defeat suffered in this preliminary skirmish was of evil augury for the future success of the proposed changes. Burnet had given up all expectation of being able to effect them. Tillotson, more sanguine than his friend, still continued to hope against hope, but he was speedily undeceived. According to the usual practice of Convocation, the Upper House prepared an address to the Crown, and requested the Lower House to join with them in adopting it. The Lower House refused, and at length finding that by ancient custom the two Houses were bound to combine in this matter, they grudgingly and reluctantly accepted a very cold address, and one that completely destroyed all remaining hopes of success.

After a prorogation, caused by an informality which Compton had detected in the Royal Commission, and which, no doubt, served to irritate the Lower House, already ill disposed towards the new Government, the bishops drew up an address containing the following expressions :—

"We thank your Majesty for the grace and goodness expressed in your message, and the zeal shown in it for the Protestant religion in general, and the Church of England in particular, and for the trust and confidence reposed in the Convocation by the Commission, which marks of your Majesty's care and favour we look upon as a continuation of the great deliverance which Almighty God has wrought for us by your means, by making you the blessed instrument of preserving us from falling under the cruelty of Popish tyranny; for which, as we have often thanked Almighty God, so we cannot forget that high obligation and duty which we owe to your Majesty. And on these new assurances of your favour and protection to the Church, we beg leave to renew the assurance of our constant fidelity and obedience to your Majesty, whom we pray God to continue long and happily to reign over us." William must have been deeply mortified, but the state of his affairs in England and Ireland did not allow him to quarrel with the clergy, so he swallowed the affront, and wisely made a gracious reply.

Compton had contributed a good deal to bring about this defeat of the Government. Deeply disappointed at not being raised to the primacy, while openly pretending to support it, he secretly intrigued against it, and did all he could well venture to do to foment the discontent of his clergy. Indeed, he had some reason to be disappointed and even vexed at the preference shown to

Tillotson over himself. His services to William and the new Government had been of no ordinary kind, and gave him a strong claim on its patronage. He had been the first victim of the tyranny of the ecclesiastical commission. He had been highly serviceable to William, not only by carrying on a correspondence with him, but also by inducing others to conspire. He had brought the Princess Ann into William's camp, and in doing so had doffed the peaceful habit of his order to put on the military uniform which he had worn when a young officer in the army. And he had been amongst the first to swear allegiance to William and Mary.

These were, no doubt, important services, and such as gave him a strong claim on the gratitude of William, but they were hardly such as qualified the man who had rendered them to sit on the primate's throne. But it was not unnatural that he should be vexed when he found that Tillotson, a simple Presbyter, and the son of a Yorkshire clothier, was to be placed by the Government in the seat which he, not unreasonably, considered that he had special and peculiar claims to occupy.

Burnet gives it as his opinion that it was a fortunate circumstance that the Convocation defeated the projected changes, believing, as he did, that the Nonjurors, who had formed themselves into a separate communion, would probably have continued to use the old form of prayer, to which great numbers of persons still continued to be warmly attached, and would thus have drawn after them a very numerous body of persons who at present were content to frequent churches in which the old forms and the old prayers were used, but who were not prepared to agree to any alteration in them, and would at once have passed over into the ranks of the Nonjurors, thus swelling an inconsiderable sect into a communion as numerous as the Church, and probably being joined in their secession by some of the ablest divines, and the most eloquent preachers of their day. In fact, from what we can ascertain with regard to the opinions and intentions of those who were entrusted with this important commission, they would in all probability have changed the service very much for the worse.

But it is now time for us to return to the third measure which William and his advisers had framed, and which related to the oaths of allegiance and supremacy. These necessarily required to be altered in such a manner as to mark the change which the revolution had made in the relations of the sovereign with the Church and the State, which it had been the chief aim of those Englishmen by whose aid those had been effected to alter and define, and thus to avoid the necessity for future revolutions.

It might have been expected that the men of this country would at length have learnt from the events that had happened so recently the lesson of the futility of oaths as a means of propping up an old dynasty, or keeping out an invader. Here was a Parliament composed to a great extent of men who had formerly sworn allegiance to James, had broken that oath, and were now engaged in devising a new oath of allegiance to William, and, in so doing, were preparing to expel from their offices in Church and State, the only men who had shown any sort of regard for the sanctity of the oath they had taken to support the authority of the king, whom they afterwards deposed, against all enemies and under all circumstances. They might be well assured that they who, after having sworn fealty to James, had conspired to depose him, would, if he should be restored, just as readily violate the oaths they had taken to his successor.

It may appear strange, but it is nevertheless the fact, that they who turned out the Nonjurors for regarding an oath which they themselves had broken, never, in all probability, felt any more compunction on account of their perjury than the historian who holds them up to the admiration of their posterity, and it may perhaps be well to remind our readers that every one of the Ministers of William, without exception, have been now detected in carrying on a venal and perfidious correspondence with the banished king, and thereby violating the oath of allegiance they had sworn to William, and dishonourably betraying the confidence he was reposing in them.

One would have expected that after these varied experiences of the inutility of oaths, men would have been disposed to get rid of them entirely. But this was an idea that seems never to have occurred to them, and so instead of abolishing these useless oaths altogether they introduced a Bill to amend and enforce them.

This matter having been at length settled and set by after long and careful debate, the next question that arose was, to what persons the new oaths should be administered, and what penalties should be inflicted on those who refused to take them. It was readily agreed that no one should sit in either House of Parliament, or hold any office conferring on him a share in the Government of the country, without having taken the oaths to the new sovereigns. This was, under all the circumstances, clearly fair and reasonable. But when the question of depriving the holders of academical or ecclesiastical offices of their endowments, and especially the bishops who had recently acted so noble a part, and had contributed so largely and yet so unblamably to the overthrow of the late tyranny, there was a strong and very general desire at least to save Sancroft and those who had acted with him from the penalties they would incur if they should refuse to take the oaths. But although the party that desired to save them was really the largest in the kingdom, the Whigs, who were for the moment triumphant, held the reins of Government, and commanded a majority in both Houses of Parliament. The friends of the Nonjurors were disarmed, scattered, divided, without the means of communicating with their leaders and with one another. Sancroft was not the man to put himself, or to allow himself to be put, at the head of an ecclesiastical agitation. Had Convocation been sitting at the moment when this matter was under discussion, it would probably have furnished a nucleus of resistance which would have been most formidable; but owing to the haste with which the Convention Parliament had been summoned, or to the loss of influence and consideration which the Convocation had suffered since the revolution of 1688 had been taken from it, this assembly, either of set purpose or through careless indifference, had been left in abeyance. And when at length, as already mentioned, William, by the determined demand of the two Houses, found himself obliged to call them together, the time for a successful interposition in favour of the Nonjuring bishops and clergy had passed.

Meanwhile, many of those who refused to take the oaths as long as it seemed doubtful whether the new Government would stand or fall, yielded when they found that the battle of the Boyne and other successes in Ireland and elsewhere had confirmed William's authority, and for the moment destroyed the hopes of the Jacobites. Of those who had first refused the oaths, and had afterwards agreed to take them, the most eminent was Sherlock. He was one of the most eloquent, popular, and, withal, highly respected divines of his day He had relinquished the mastership of the Temple rather than take the oaths, but a new light had since broken in on him; the lost sheep was welcomed back into the fold by the victorious party; he took the oaths, recovered his mastership of the Temple, and as it was the policy of the Government to buy over to their side as many as they could of those who stood aloof from them, he obtained the deanery of St. Paul's, when Tillotson vacated it on his appointment to the primacy.

Whether it arose from a fear of the consequences that might follow the expulsion of Sancroft, or from a respect for his character and a desire to conciliate his friends and supporters, every effort was made by the Government to induce him to adopt a course similar to that which had been followed by many able divines who had been his friends, and had looked up to him for guidance. But Sancroft, though willing to pledge himself not to disturb the existing Government, which indeed had treated him with much more consideration and respect than had been shown to him by King James, absolutely refused to perform any act, or use any prayer that recognized the sovereignty of William and Mary. Therefore William, after waiting for a long time with much patience and forbearance, and after having, as we have already seen, held out an offer to the friends of the Nonjurors which, if it had been accepted by them, would have saved Sancroft and his followers from the consequences of their recusancy, at length required them to take the oaths to the new Government under pain of being deprived of their offices.

One reason which probably determined William to take this decisive step, was that he felt it to be a matter of the highest importance to his Government to have a man in the position of Archbishop of Canterbury, whose sympathies and opinions with regard to the important questions of toleration and comprehension were entirely in harmony with his own, and on whose cordial support to his Government he could confidently reckon. It was for this reason, and with this well-grounded expectation, that he had determined soon after his accession to transfer Tillotson from his deanery to the archbishopric. Therefore it was that, when the newly-appointed dean thanked William for appointing him to a place in which he hoped to be settled for life, William informed him of the higher preferment he destined for him, and insisted on his acceptance of it as absolutely necessary to his service. The choice of Tillotson to succeed Sancroft was very generally approved, and no doubt reconciled the minds of many even of Sancroft's friends to the expulsion of that prelate.

Tillotson felt a genuine reluctance to accept the high promotion thus forced on him. For many reasons he was unwilling to be placed in the position for which the king had designated him. He was no longer the man he had been. He felt the approaches of old age, and an apoplectic fit which he had suffered had not only warned him that the close of his career was approaching, but had also to some extent impaired his faculties. His kindly and benevolent disposition was revolted at the idea of his taking any part in the expulsion from Lambeth of the good old man who was still in possession of the palace, and whose disinterested services to the Church he fully appreciated.

Amiable, virtuous, and highly accomplished Tillotson undoubtedly was. And these were qualities which were well adapted to adorn the archiepiscopal throne in ordinary times. But they were not the qualities which would enable their possessor to take the lead in effecting the alterations which William expected and which Tillotson earnestly desired. It is not by polished sentences and well-balanced periods that men are fired and great changes brought about. Tillotson was always listened to with pleasure, but he did not possess the faculty of kindling in his hearers the enthusiasm which produces energetic action. Men did not go to sleep over his sermons, but they were not deeply stirred by them. And superior as he was to both of his predecessors in almost every respect, he did not exercise anything like the influence over the destinies of the Church that they had exerted. Nevertheless, after long resistance, Tillotson yielded. He called several times on his predecessor at Lambeth to see him, and to explain orally the reasons which had induced him to accept the archbishopric. Sancroft, who was naturally embittered against him, and whose health probably was not equal to the excitement of an interview with Tillotson, declined, not over courteously, to see him.

While the new archbishop was receiving the congratulations and good wishes that were showered on him on the occasion of his elevation to the primacy, he was vehemently abused by the Nonjurors and by many of the clergy who secretly sympathized with them. But instead of showing any vindictive feeling towards his assailants, he interceded for them, and used his influence to protect them from the punishment which some of his friends and admirers wished to have inflicted on them. In this respect he showed himself a model of good sense and right feeling.

"I had notice," he wrote to his friend, Lady Russell, "first from the Attorney-General and Mr. Solicitor, and, then from my lord—that several persons, upon account of publishing and dispensing several libels against me were secured in order to prosecution. Upon which I went to wait upon them severally, and earnestly desired of them that nobody might be punished on my account; that this was not the first time I had experienced this kind of malice, which, how unpleasant soever to me, I thought the wisest way to neglect and the best to forgive it."

Tillotson survived his appointment to the primacy a little more than three years. In 1694, while attending service at the Chapel Royal of Whitehall, he was suddenly seized with a fit, similar to that which, as already mentioned, he had experienced a little before the time of his appointment to the primacy. It is alleged that, if proper remedies had been promptly administered, his life would in all probability have been saved. But he was unwilling to interrupt the service; and when it was concluded, and the physicians were at length summoned to his assistance, they found that he was beyond the reach of their remedies.

It was a matter of great difficulty to supply the place thus rendered vacant. There were many divines of greater learning than Tillotson; there were more vigorous writers; there were administrators who could carry out the work of the province and the diocese with greater energy and ability; but there was none who enjoyed so high a reputation, none who was equally beloved and respected, none who was so much esteemed by High Churchmen, by Low Churchmen, and by Latitudinarians, none who so completely commanded the confidence, both of Protestants at home and Protestants abroad, or could so readily rally them round him, and no one whose judgment and wisdom were so thoroughly trusted by the rude soldier and diplomatist who at that time ruled the destinies of this country. Had he been called to occupy the chair of St. Augustine at a time when his physical and mental faculties were in their full bloom and vigour, he might have succeeded in effecting important changes, though whether for the better or the worse must remain somewhat problematical.

As it was, he left behind him a high reputation as an elegant writer and an impressive preacher. His eloquence never rose to the height of the flights of Barrow, of Jeremy Taylor, or perhaps even of South; but was at least free from many serious defects that marred to some extent the excellence of their discourses. But as an ecclesiastical statesman, as one who for good or for evil impressed on the Church of which he was the first minister something of his own character and beliefs, and guided her into new paths, he cannot take rank with Anselm, Becket, Cranmer, Parker, Laud, Sheldon, or Sancroft.

As a general rule, William did not intervene in the religious controversies of this country; on the contrary, he looked on them with a disregard bordering on contempt. Besides, his imperfect acquaintance with our language disqualified him for the task of deciding between the relative merits of our preachers. He therefore wisely left the appointment to bishoprics and other Church dignities in the hands of his wife, who was the only English native he could fully trust, and who in her turn was guided by those of the clergy whom she thought fit to consult. But on the occasion of the appointment to so important a post as that of the archbishopric of Canterbury, he determined to keep in his own hands a choice which he knew to be of great political as well as ecclesiastical importance; and he thought much more of the former than of the latter. Mary very warmly advocated the claims of Stillingfleet to fill the vacant primacy; and if the choice had rested on purely professional grounds, a better selection could not have been made. He was a man of considerable mark, and had acquired a great reputation as a controversialist, on account of the skilful manner in which he had dealt with the arguments of both Protestant and Roman Catholic antagonists. But William considered that an eager controversialist was not the man to fill the see of Canterbury. He therefore selected for that place Dr. Tenison, Bishop of London, who, before he was raised to the Episcopal Bench, had been a popular London preacher and an active parish priest. As vicar of St. Andrews, Cambridge, he had earned deserved credit by remaining at his post and continuing in the faithful and diligent discharge of his ministerial duties during the prevalence of the plague in that town. His opinions seem to have almost exactly coincided with those of Tillotson and of the king. William had seen very little of him when he appointed him to the primacy. But he was a good judge of men, and found in Tenison what he chiefly looked for, one who quietly administered the affairs of the Church, was not unfriendly nor unkind to Nonconformists, gave very little trouble to the Government, and zealously entered into measures which, being generally in full accordance with his own opinions, he could support heartily and with a good conscience. Accordingly we find him adhering to them, not only when they were approved by the sovereign, as in the reign of William and Mary, but also when they caused him to be regarded with disfavour in that of Queen Anne.

About the time of Tenison's appointment to the see of Canterbury a decision was given in the Court of King's Bench which virtually involved a change of law with regard to the Church of no little importance. It had been enacted in a statute passed in the reign of Elizabeth, that all men should attend their parish church every Sunday. Accordingly a clergyman called Britton brought an action against a person of the name of Standish, who had attended divine service in a church which was not the church of his own parish. Chief Justice Holt, who was in the habit of putting a very liberal construction on the statutes that were brought under his consideration, presided at the trial, and gave judgment in favour of the defendant. "Parishes," he said, "were instituted for the care and benefit of the people and not of the parson; that they might have a certain place to repair to when they thought convenient, and a parson from whom they had a right to receive instructions; and if every parishioner is obliged to go to his parish church, then the gentlemen of Gray's Inn and Lincoln's Inn must no longer repair to their respective chapels, but to their parish churches; otherwise they may be compelled to it by ecclesiastical censures."

This upright judge rendered another great service to the cause of humanity and common sense by interpreting the cruel acts against witchcraft in such a manner as virtually to repeal them, though they were not removed from the statute book for some years. "Eleven poor creatures," says Lord Campbell, "were successively tried before him for this supposed crime, and the prosecution was supported by the accustomed evidence of long fasting, vomiting pins and tenpenny nails, secret teats sucked by imps, devil's marks, and cures by the sign of the cross, or drawing blood from the sorceress, which had led Sir Matthew Hale to condemn several poor creatures; but by Holt's good sense and tact in every instance the imposture was detected to the satisfaction of the jury, and there was an acquittal." This decision had the effect of dealing a blow at an absurd and mischievous superstition which prevailed at this time in the English Church.

Scarcely was Tenison fully installed into his new office, when he was called on to perform the melancholy duty of attending the sick bed of the queen, who was suffering from the direful scourge of small-pox, which at that time frequently baffled and defeated the efforts of the most skilful physicians, and in this instance carried off the queen in spite of all the efforts that were made to save her. Tenison attended her during her illness, and gave to the world a sermon which he preached after her decease, in which he described the course of her illness, and gave a glowing and perhaps somewhat exaggerated account of her demeanour and conduct while lying on the bed of death, breathing a spirit of adulation which, though probably honest, was certainly in very bad taste. This performance drew down on the archbishop the somewhat wrathful censure of the good Bishop Ken, of whose letter I reprint the most important passages, because they show the manner in which Tenison's sermon was viewed, not only by his eminent assailant, but also by a very large body of the clergy, who still sympathized with the Nonjurors, and viewed the conduct of Mary to her father with feelings of strong and decided reprobation.

The letter which Ken addressed to the primate was couched in a strain of bitterness not usual with him. Tenison represented the deceased queen as a subject most happily disposed to work on, and one who had always been very reverent and attentive at sermons, who had an averseness to flatterers, and who would therefore have thankfully received any piece of charitable admonition that the primate might have given her.

"You mention," wrote Ken, "a very religious saying that fell from her: that she had learned from her youth a true doctrine, that repentance was not to be put off to a death-bed. But it was your duty, considering the deceitfulness of all hearts, and the usual infirmities and forgetfulness and indisposition of sick persons, to have supplied all her oversights and omissions, and to have examined the truth of her repentance, *whether she truly repented of her sins;* and where you knew anything of moment, which had escaped her observation, you ought to have been her Remembrancer. I, therefore, challenge you to answer before God and the world: Did you know of no weighty matter which ought to have troubled the princess's conscience, though at present she seemed not to have felt it, and for which you ought to have moved her to a special confession, in order to absolution? Were you assured that she was in charity with all the world? Did you know of no enmity between her and her father? No variation between her and her sister? Was the whole revolution managed with that purity of intention, that perfect innocence and exact justice, that tender charity and irreproachable equity that there was nothing amiss in it, no remarkable failings that might deserve one penitent reflection?

"You cannot, you dare not say it, and if you should, out of your own mouth I can condemn you; for you yourself, in your serious intervals, have passed as severe a censure on the revolution as any of those they call Jacobites could do. You have said more than once, that *it was all an unrighteous thing.* Why did you not then deal sincerely with the dying princess, and tell her so? when you must be sensible that, in steering her conscience wrong, you shipwrecked your own. What was it, sir, that moved you to act thus notoriously against your own conscience? Was it the fear you had of losing the favour of the court, which made you rather venture the indignation of heaven? Even that fear was vain, for it had been no offence against the Government to have persuaded a dying daughter to have bestowed one compassionate prayer on her afflicted father, had he been never so unnatural. Though the case was here quite contrary, for he was one of the tenderest fathers in the world. Besides, her illustrious consort, who manifested so great and worthy a passion for her, would, I dare say, have had nothing omitted which might have been conducible to her eternal happiness; and a conscientious confessor, especially on the death-bed, is one of a thousand who will always be desired, and followed, and revered.

"Believe me, sir, you have given the world reason to conclude that your own conscience misgave you, being sensible that in reproving her you must have reproached yourself. You say that she was so judicious and devout a saint as that degenerate Church of Rome can by no means show us; but surely it would have been prudence in you to have waived that comparison, for should you chance hereafter to blame that Church for canonizing Thomas à Becket (for which she is really blameworthy), it is obvious for her to make this in reply to you, that it is as justifiable in her to saint such a subject as in you to saint such a daughter. You tell us she was one who you are well assured had all the duty in the world for other relations (besides her husband) which, 'after long and laborious considerations, she judged consistent with her obligations to God and to her country.' The consideration, then, which she used to reconcile her judgment to the revolution was, it seems, long and laborious, notwithstanding the assistance of her new associates, it being no easy matter to overcome the contrary remonstrances of nature, and to her own conscience, and to unlearn those evangelical maxims which were carefully taught her by the faithful guides of her youth.

"Others might begin to instil opposite principles into her, others might confirm her, but the finishing stroke was reserved for you. But who do you mean, sir, by 'other relations'? We may guess that you mean her royal father, her mother-in-law, and her brother; but you are at liberty to say you mean any other relations, if you please. You give us ambiguous and general words only, when you should have given us most express and particular. All the duty in the world is a comprehensive term; but wherein, sir, did any part of that duty appear? Why are you not so just to her and to yourself as to give us some of those compassionate and melting expressions of filial duty which fell from her on that subject? Why do you not produce some instances of her 'mildness and mercifulness to her enemies'? who, you know, she treated as such, though their crime was their being her father's friends?

"It would have been much for her honour, would have given great satisfaction to all good people, would have convinced the world that the manner of her death had been in all respects truly Christian, would have been much for your own reputation, and much for the credit of the revolution in which you are as great a zealot as a gainer. If you were so well assured of all that duty, what dreadful negligence were you guilty of in not putting her in mind of it on her death-bed? Methinks, sir, you are not just to her when you give us instances of her charity to several sorts of indigent people and to strangers, which all the world knew, and give no instances of even her natural affection to her own royal father, of which all the world doubted; when, had you suggested that doubt to her as you ought to have done, she would have shown herself a tender-hearted daughter, and would have been extremely afflicted for having been instrumental in her father's calamity.

"It is far from my intention here to dispute the lawfulness of the revolution; yet I may say that I never met with any so bigoted to it who would undertake to justify all the part which she as a daughter had in it: and I am persuaded that it would mightily puzzle you to tell us what those obligations were that she had to God and to her country which were inconsistent with her filial duty."

This rebuke, delivered in a manner that would hardly have been expected in a man of so saintly a character as Ken, was not undeserved. Tenison on other occasions had shown no unwillingness to pick up any gauntlet which a polemical adversary might throw down; but on this attack, though he complained of it in private, he was silent in public—probably because he felt that Ken's accusations were undeniably well founded. There were circumstances in Mary's conduct, especially towards her father, which cannot be excused, and which justify the character given of her by Lady Marlborough, that "she wanted bowels."

Ken's letter produced all the more effect because it appeared at a conjuncture when the authority of William was passing through a most dangerous and trying crisis. He had all along been exceedingly unpopular, especially with the clergy and the Churchmen, who hated him on account of his foreign accent, his Dutch sympathies, and his Presbyterian proclivities. And he had been by no means as careful to conciliate this powerful party as policy and prudence required him to be. Hitherto, however, the popularity of Mary, had to a considerable extent balanced the unpopularity of her husband, and diminished the disaffection with which he had all along been regarded.

But besides this, she had given to the new settlement a sort of colourable legitimacy, of which her death altogether deprived it. It was evident that the Government of William was now entering on a new and perilous path, in which it would require all the skill and care of the king to enable him to maintain his ground, and of which it was impossible to foresee whither it would lead the Government, which depended almost entirely for its continuance on the energy, vigilance, and ability of a king who, with all his great qualities, was now thoroughly depopularized, and fast sinking under the infirmities of a premature old age. Nothing, in fact, could have prevented his overthrow but the weakness and incapacity of his deposed father-in-law, who also was himself burdened with many infirmities, and rapidly sinking into the grave. But we must now return to Tenison's earlier history, from which we have been led away by this disgression.

The year 1683 had been remarkable for a winter of uncommon severity, during which the poor of his parish suffered cruelly, and Tenison gave them very liberal assistance. A short time before, he had preached and published a sermon on the very important subject of discretion in giving alms; and now he had an opportunity, of which he availed himself, of carrying out in his practice the discrimination he had recommended from the pulpit.

But while he was thus engaged in providing sustenance for the bodies of his parishioners, he did not neglect their minds. He endowed a charity school and set up a free public library, the first that existed in the kingdom. He provided for the payment of a librarian, usher, and schoolmaster; but though he placed several volumes in the library, he seems to have made no sufficient provision for the future purchase of books. However, the circumstance deserves notice, inasmuch as this institution shows that the idea of free public libraries was not, as many suppose, the invention of the latter end of the nineteenth century, but was anticipated by Tenison, two centuries ago. He also provided an endowment in land, situated somewhere near Regent Street, and which, therefore, if now applicable to the purposes for which it was designed, would be of immense value, and amply sufficient for all the objects that Tenison proposed to effect; but, unfortunately, it somehow found its way into private hands, and the place of it cannot now be discovered.

In the year 1685 he attended the Duke of Monmouth before his execution, and on the scaffold, and addressed him with a kindness and mildness which softened the rebukes he thought it his duty to press on that unfortunate nobleman.

He was appointed to take part in the review of the liturgy projected by Archbishop Sancroft, but which was prevented by the revolution of 1688 from being carried into effect. The special part of the work assigned to Tenison was to replace words in the liturgy which were hard to be understood, by other and simpler synonyms.

Meanwhile, important changes had taken place in the province of York. On the approach of William to the city of Exeter, Dr. Lamplugh, the bishop of that city, entreated the inhabitants to defend it against the invader, and then fled to James, who complimented him on his devotion to the royal cause, applauded him as a bishop of the old sort, and appointed him to the archbishopric of York, which had been kept vacant for nearly two years. Having gained his archbishopric by his supposed fidelity to James, he retained it by the promptitude of his submission to William; but he died in 1691, having enjoyed his high dignity less than three years.

He was succeeded by Sharp, who had been the first victim of the Ecclesiastical Commission, owing to the boldness with which he preached against Popery, and had offended the Commons by delivering before them, immediately after the revolution, a sermon in which he boldly proclaimed the old doctrines of passive obedience and non-resistance, and by praying for King James. The Whigs, naturally offended by this conduct, not only proposed to refuse the intrepid preacher the usual compliment of a vote of thanks for his sermon, but were also disposed to punish him for his boldness. However, wiser counsels prevailed. He had many friends who admired his worth, remembered the courage he had displayed in preaching against Popery, and saved him from the consequences which his resolute consistency at one time seemed likely to draw down on him. He declined bishoprics of which Nonjurors had been deprived for their refusal of the oath; but when the archbishopric of York, vacated by the death of Lamplugh, was offered to him, he accepted it without hesitation.

As these circumstances clearly indicate, he was a thoroughly honest, narrow-minded, High Churchman, strongly and conscientiously attached to the doctrines and discipline of the communion in which he held so high a place. At a time when there was a growing disposition to regard Episcopacy as a political rather than a religious institution, he showed the sincerity of his belief in the principles he taught by labouring to extend the Episcopal system to the colonies and possessions of the British Empire. He also seconded with much ardour an effort that was made by Frederic, king of Prussia, to establish throughout his dominions the system of the English Church—an attempt of which we shall presently have occasion to speak more at length.

King William, as we have already seen, finding how utterly unfitted he was to manage the ecclesiastical affairs of this kingdom, had devolved on Mary the care of this department of his Government, which his own tastes and avocations incapacitated him from administering in a manner likely to prove satisfactory. Mary, in the performance of this important duty, had sought the assistance of those bishops and divines in whose judgment and character she had the greatest confidence. After her death William endeavoured to supply her place in this respect by issuing a commission to Tenison and five other prelates, empowering them to appoint to bishoprics and other benefices the patronage of which belonged to the crown.

The death of Mary almost brought William's reign to a virtual close. His constitution, never very strong, visibly began to give way under the pressure of his manifold anxieties. Day by day he became rapidly worse. At last a fall from his horse anticipated by a short time the inevitable effect of his numerous infirmities. During his last illness, Tenison and Burnet, the only English prelates with whose religious feelings he had any sympathy, were in constant attendance on him.

The foundation, in the year 1698, of the Society for the Promotion of Christian Knowledge, and that of the Society for the Propagation of the Gospel in Foreign Parts in the year 1701—the former being designed for the instruction of persons living in this country in the principles of the English Church, and the latter for the propagation of those principles throughout other parts of the world, and more especially in the British colonies and possessions—were indications that the duties and obligations of Christian men in these respects were becoming more thoroughly appreciated and acknowledged; and that, notwithstanding the ignorance, the prejudice, and the persecuting spirit that prevailed, there was at this time much Christianity that was both genuine and earnest. As yet it was perhaps but a day of small things, so far as these societies were concerned; but at any rate it manifested stirrings of spiritual life, which were favourable omens for the future of the English Church.

CHAPTER V.

THE GOOD QUEEN ANNE.

THE death of William, and the consequent accession of his sister-in-law Anne, changed materially the aspect of ecclesiastical affairs. She was grossly ignorant and violently prejudiced. Whatever might be the nature of the instruction which Bishop Compton had imparted, or caused to be imparted to her, she had the manners and ideas of a housemaid. She was a thorough Tory, and, like all the Tories of her day, warmly attached to the High Church party. She was convinced, if indeed she had ever entertained any serious doubt on the subject, of the legitimacy of her young brother, known in history as the Chevalier St. George, the Pretender—or, to distinguish him from his son, who like him asserted his claim to the English throne, the old Pretender—and though she was not willing to make way for him by refusing the throne in his favour, she secretly desired to have him for her successor.

The nation generally entered warmly into her views by returning a thoroughly High Church and high Tory

Parliament. Tenison, Burnet, and the other Whig bishops who had been appointed during the late reign, were looked coldly on at court, and the more so as they continued to uphold the principles which had obtained them their preferment. But they were wholly unable to stem the torrent of loyalty and Toryism which threatened to carry away the little remnant that still adhered to those principles of civil and religious liberty which had been supported and encouraged in the last reign.

The celebrated Defoe, best known in our day as the author of "Robinson Crusoe," was one of the few who steadfastly withstood the prevailing *furore*. He published a pamphlet which bore the title of "The Shortest Way with Dissenters," and in which he set forth the opinions of the extreme High Churchmen, and ironically recommended the persecution of Nonconformists; but in such a manner as led extreme Dissenters, and extreme High Churchmen, to believe that the treatment which he advocated was seriously intended; and when they at length discovered the humorous deception that had been practised on them, they wreaked their vengeance on the witty and unfortunate author of the pamphlet, who had led them to expose their bigotry, or their ignorance, and held them up to the ridicule of the nation. The consequence was that for writing one of the most humorous books in our language, he was condemned "to pay a fine of five marks, to be imprisoned during the queen's pleasure, to stand three times in the pillory, and to find sureties for his good behaviour for seven years."

But though Defoe was thus severely punished by a coalition of the friends and enemies of the Church, his arguments obtained a degree of attention which would not have been accorded to them if they had been presented to the world under a more serious guise.

The accession of Anne to the throne had operated a thorough change in the relations of the sovereign and the Archbishop of Canterbury. As we have seen already, Tenison stood very high in the esteem and confidence of William, and had been placed by him at the head of a commission by which the bishops were named and the patronage of the crown dispensed, so that the whole government of the Church had been transferred to the primate and some of his suffragans, who would naturally be much influenced by his opinion. The esteem and regard which William showed for Tenison seems to have become closer as the end of the king's life evidently approached.

But when Anne succeeded to the throne his position was changed. He placed the crown on her head at the coronation; but he was treated by her with cold civility, and she was guided by persons whose opinions differed most decidedly from those of the primate and of those bishops who had been raised to the Episcopal Bench on account of their attachment to the principles of the revolution. But the loss of court favour was more than compensated by the gain of greater liberty of action in regard to all questions of public importance, and enabled him and his suffragans to express their opinions freely on questions which came before the House of Lords.

The effect which this change had on the conduct of the prelates showed itself in a very marked and striking manner.

Scarcely had Anne mounted the throne before she began to manifest, after her fashion, her zeal for the Church, especially in regard to a Bill introduced into the House of Lords in the year 1704 for the prevention of the practice of occasional conformity—probably at her special desire, and which she supported with all her power and influence. By the Test and Corporation Acts every person who held any post in the State, whether civil or military, or any place in a municipal corporation, was required to receive the sacrament of the Lord's Supper. The object of this enactment was to exclude Nonconformists from having any share in the government of the country. But this object was to a considerable extent defeated by the practice which was commonly denominated "occasional conformity,"—that is to say, by Nonconformists partaking of the sacraments simply and solely for the purpose of qualifying themselves for the tenure of political or municipal office.

The Tory party, which at this time was dominant in the legislature, brought in a Bill to put a stop to a practice which was certainly a most objectionable mode of evading a bad law. The Whigs, however, succeeded in getting rid of the obnoxious measure. They procured the insertion of a clause into the Bill which imposed a fine of twenty pounds on those who left their own churches to attend conventicles. This was, in fact, an interference on the part of the Lords with a money Bill, a procedure which the Commons have always regarded with peculiar jealousy. The Lower House refused to accept the clause; the Lords, on the other hand, insisted on it. They produced many precedents to show that such a power as they now claimed had been frequently exercised before. A conference between the delegates of the two Houses was held in the Painted Chamber, but without effecting an agreement. By this adroit contrivance the Bill was got rid of; but it was supported by Marlborough, Godolphin, and the Tories generally, as well as by Prince George of Denmark, the queen's husband, who, though himself an occasional conformist, reluctantly voted for the measure. Burnet, from whom better things might have been expected, delivered a Liberal speech, which he published, but supported the Bill.

It was brought in a second time the year following, when it was again supported by Godolphin and Marlborough. The former, indeed, objected to it as unseasonable, though he voted for it, as being a measure good in itself; but both of them declared their approval of the Bill by taking the marked step of drawing up and signing a protest against the rejection of it. On the other hand, the Bill was opposed by Tenison, whose view of the question at issue was peculiar, and gives interest to the speech he is alleged to have pronounced on this occasion. It is, no doubt, very imperfectly reported, as were almost all speeches delivered in Parliament at that time and long after; but the following is probably a tolerably correct account of its purport and general tenor:

"I think the practice of occasional conformity, as used by the Dissenters, is so far from deserving the title of a vile hypocrisy, that it is the duty of all moderate Dissenters, on their own principles, to adopt it. However it may be disapproved by some rigid Dissenters, it ought to be encouraged by all good Churchmen as a means to bring them over. The allowing persons of different religion from the established has been practised in all countries where liberty of conscience has been allowed, and we have gone further already in excluding Dissenters than any other country has done; and whatever reasons there were to apprehend danger to our religion from Papists when the Test Act was made, yet there does not seem the least danger to it from the Dissenters now.

"But, on the other hand, I can see very great inconvenience from this Bill at present, as it is brought in this last time; indeed, they have added a plausible clause which, though it was in the first draft of the Bill, was left out in the second, that the Act of Toleration should be always kept inviolate. But the Toleration Act being taken away, all the rest falls with it."

The opinion of the archbishop prevailed. The Bill passed through the House of Commons without much difficulty. It was then carried up to the House of Lords, where, in spite of the opposition of the archbishop, the majority were in favour of it; but, as we have just seen, the opponents of the measure contrived a means of rejecting it, while appearing to be zealously in favour of it. It was once again brought forward; but Marlborough and Godolphin had now openly joined the Whigs, and the Bill was rejected.

About the same time the queen showed her zealous affection for the Church by making a generous sacrifice of a large portion of her income for its benefit, thus constituting the fund that is commonly known by the name of Queen Anne's Bounty. This fund had come down from very ancient times. It was formed by the payment of the whole of the first year's income of all spiritual preferments and a tenth part of them afterwards. Up to the time of the Reformation the fund thus raised was transmitted to the Pope; but after the abolition of the Pope's authority in this country, it was transferred to the crown, and formed part of the royal revenue. Efforts had been made from time to time to restore it to the Church; but Burnet has the merit of having been the first to move effectually in the matter, and to draw the queen's attention to the abuses that had been practised in connection with this fund. He had used his influence with William to procure a change in this respect, and had impressed upon him the increased stability that would be given to his throne by his renouncing in favour of the poorer clergy his claim to the enjoyment of this fund. Nothing, he urged, would tend more to soften their hostility than the relinquishment of a revenue which was so wasted and plundered that it benefited the sovereign very little, while the larger portion of it went into the pockets of the insatiable courtiers by whom he was surrounded, and, what increased his unpopularity, chiefly into the possession of his Dutch followers, whom they hated with a true British animosity.

William at once assented to the policy of the proposed change, and listened attentively to Burnet's representations; but the wars in which he was involved, and the difficulty he had in raising the funds necessary to enable him to carry them on and to pay the debts he had incurred, prevented him from doing more than accord an attentive and careful consideration to the arguments which Burnet brought forward. The queen, however, being herself very economical, on far better terms with her Parliament than her predecessor ever had been, and much more strongly attached than he ever was to the Church, was both better able and more willing to carry out Burnet's suggestion.

The Parliament, too, which was warmly attached to the Church, accepted the offer with zealous readiness, and passed without difficulty the Bills which were required to give effect to the queen's generous intentions. The first proposal had been that the clergy should henceforward be entirely relieved from the payment of firstfruits and tenths. If this had been all that was done many already rich benefices would have been augmented, while many poor ones would have been left almost unaided. A fairer system was therefore adopted, and of this also Burnet deserves the credit. The money raised was formed into a perpetual fund for the augmentation of livings of small value, which was put under the control and management of a body of "Governors of Queen Anne's Bounty," composed of personages holding high office in Church and State, by whom it was to be applied to the purpose for which it was destined. Nor was this the only benefit which the zealous and charitable queen and the Tory Parliament conferred on the poorer portion of the beneficed clergy. Another Bill, introduced and carried in the course of the same year, altered the Statute of Mortmain in such a manner as to allow benevolent and pious individuals to increase the incomes of poor benefices either by deed of gift or by bequest.

The popularity which these benefactions conferred on the queen was prodigious. It was well understood that the " bounty" was bestowed at her expense, and it was felt that if ever queen deserved the appellation of a nursing mother of the Church it was the good Queen Anne. Notwithstanding a too unrestrained partiality for spirituous liquors, indulged in at very improper times and places, she was a good, kind, amiable woman. Instead of gloating, like the majority of her subjects, over the victories which Marlborough was gaining on the Continent, she and her new confidant, Abigail Hill, wept over every order of war she was constrained to sign. Timid, fearful, amiable, and weak, she was born to be the puppet of others, and if she discarded one favourite she directly fell into the hands of another ; and so, while from every pulpit in the land her praises were loudly sounded, the poor goddess at whose shrine all this laudatory incense was offered was the wretched slave of the Duchess of Marlborough, who, from being Anne's humble confidant, had become her insolent and imperious mistress.

Anne had lived on terms of the greatest intimacy with the duchess. Her affection for her had been so strong that she had insisted on discarding in private all those marks of distinction between her friend and herself which in public she was obliged to maintain. They corresponded on a footing of perfect equality, or rather in inversion of their real rank, under the assumed names of Morley and Freeman, the latter being chosen by the duchess as descriptive of the male energy of her character.

In the course of this intimate and confidential correspondence, Anne had displayed her weakness without reserve, in a manner calculated to expose her to the contempt and derision of her subjects, and to put her completely in the power of her former favourite, now become her bitter enemy, on account of the tardy resistance she offered, when this too fervent friendship was converted into bitter enmity, through the insatiable avarice of the duke and the insupportable insolence of the duchess.

The aim of these two worthies was to surround the queen with their creatures, and not to allow any to have access to her except those on whose fidelity to their interests they thought they could implicitly rely. Their ascendancy was apparently assured by a threefold security: first, the fear of exposure by the production of Anne's letters; secondly, the dread that Marlborough might play the part of another Cromwell; or, thirdly, that he might set aside Anne and bring in the Pretender.

The Marlboroughs, at the accession of Anne, were

allied to the Tories and High Churchmen with her, as they had been before the death of William; but they had found that their purposes would be more effectually served by an alliance with the Whigs,—the Liberal party both in Church and State. And they gradually veered round towards that party, forcing the poor feeble queen to go along with them in supporting measures she detested, in censuring those whom she secretly regarded as her friends, and eulogizing those whom she looked on as her implacable enemies.

Meanwhile, a poor dependent of the Marlboroughs, one Abigail Hill, had secretly taken the place in Anne's affections which had been occupied by Mrs. Freeman, and through her the poor queen timidly communicated with some of the Tory party, and especially with Harley, who was regarded as its leader. But even with his aid she probably would not have had the firmness required to enable her to extricate herself from the bondage in which she was held. Lady Marlborough, feeling that her influence over the queen was rapidly waning, tried to recover it by alternate advances and reproaches. When the queen attended in State a solemn service held in the cathedral of St. Paul, the insolent subject gave her mistress her gloves to hold, and when the poor queen quietly submitted to this indignity, she took them back before the congregation with a gesture of disgust intended to convey the impression that the queen's breath was strongly charged with alcohol. In her capacity of mistress of the robes, the insolent termagant had the master-key of all the rooms in the palace, and pursued the queen from one apartment to another with her vehement reproaches and insults.

Abigail Hill was poor, modest, and submissive, with a real attachment for her mistress, whose sorrows she shared. But what could these two poor women do even with the assistance of Harley? The Marlboroughs had everything;—the army, the navy, the whole administration, the majority of both Houses of Parliament was in the hands of their creatures, and probably would have so continued if an event had not happened which showed Anne how confidently she might rely on the help of the nation, in making an effort to shake off the detested thraldom of the Marlboroughs. The event to which we refer was the trial of Dr. Sacheverell.

Henry Sacheverell was descended from an old and highly respectable Derbyshire family, and had consequently inherited a small estate at Callow in that county. His grandfather, John Sacheverell, had been a zealous Puritan minister, had suffered at the Restoration for his religious opinions, and had died in prison. His son, the doctor's father, had taken the opposite side in religion as well as in politics, and sent his son Henry to Magdalen College, Oxford, the Fellows of which had obtained so honourable a reputation by the firm but respectful resistance they had offered to the lawless tyranny of James II. and by which they had in no small degree contributed to bring about his deposition. At this college he shared the chamber of Addison, who entertained a high esteem and regard for him until long after the time when the divergence of their political opinions had forced them into opposite camps. Before this happened, Addison had dedicated to him a poem, which he published, and to which he gave the title of "A Farewell to the Muses." Sacheverell appears to have been an elegant Latin scholar. He translated a part of Virgil's "Georgics," which he dedicated to Dryden, published some Latin poems in the "Musæ Anglicanæ," and seems to have enjoyed a high reputation for scholarship, not only in his own college, but throughout the university. Having been ordained, he became highly popular as a preacher; and consequently in 1705 he was elected by the parishioners chaplain of St. Saviour's, Southwark, and his reputation for pulpit eloquence increasing, he was selected to preach on several important occasions. It is true that the modern reader will find his sermons, like most of the published discourses of that period, exceedingly dull, heavy, and prolix, and such as no one would willingly peruse unless he had some special reason for reading them; but they were delivered with a fervour, an emphasis, and a tone of earnest conviction which carried away his ignorant and prejudiced hearers.

It would be a great mistake to suppose that, because a sermon offends against every principle of good taste, it is necessarily a bad sermon. Discourses like those of Sacheverell, "full of sound and fury," often command more attention than the polished compositions of great writers. The effect produced by them on their auditors is often in an inverse ratio to their real merits. At all events, whatever may be thought of Sacheverell's discourses now, most certain it is that they were listened to with riveted attention by multitudes of approving hearers, and they obtained for him such a reputation that on the 15th of August, 1709, he was selected to preach before the Judge of Assize, and the High Sheriff of the county, at Derby; and on the 5th of the following November, the day on which the frustration of the Gunpowder Treason and the landing of William III. were commemorated, he preached for full three hours before the Lord Mayor and the Corporation of London. The subject of his discourse was perils among false brethren. It was, in fact, a *rechauffé* of the doctrine which we have already seen so ably and eloquently propounded by the learned Barrow;[*] but it was seasoned with violent personalities, and contained an unsparing attack on the Lord Treasurer Godolphin, to whom it referred under the nickname of "Volpone," by which he was generally known.

It was also intended as a reply to the Rev. Benjamin Hoadley, who, in the year 1701, had been chosen lecturer of St. Mildred-in-the-Poultry, at London, and who had warmly supported Whig and Low Church principles, not only in his sermons, but still more elaborately in a work entitled, "The Reasonableness of Conformity to the Church of England," and who, for this and for other services of the same nature he had rendered to the Whig party, had been recommended to the queen for preferment by the House of Commons, and had been presented to the living of Streatham by the Duke of Bedford. Sacheverell by no means confined

[*] See p. 168.

his invectives to Hoadley, but extended his hostile allusions to all the prominent Whigs, and most especially to Burnet and the Whig bishops generally. The discourse was published by the request of the Lord Mayor, who, however, recanted his approval of it when the matter was brought under the notice of the House of Commons.

It would have been well for Lord Godolphin and his party if he had treated the attack made on him with disregard, and had left Sacheverell and Hoadley to fight out their theological battle, trusting that truth would gain the ascendant in the end. Instead, however, of adopting this prudent and proper course, Godolphin flew in a rage when he read the violent and clumsy personalities of Sacheverell, hurried into the queen's presence, and complained bitterly of the insolence of the Tory party, declaring that unless they were severely checked, he and his friend would be driven out of the kingdom. The queen received these appeals very coolly. She detested the Whigs, whom she suspected of a design to set her aside, and put the Electress of Hanover or the Duke of Marlborough in her place.

She had completely transferred her affections from the Duchess of Marlborough to Abigail Hill, who became Mrs. and then Lady Masham, and through her was secretly guided by Harley, though she still listened to the advice of her constitutional ministers, and read the documents they put into her hands, even when they expressed sentiments and opinions which she strongly disapproved. The Whigs, feeling that the ground was

T

slipping away from under them, and yielding to the passionate instances of Godolphin, took a resolution that was fatal to their party, and very nearly brought about a second restoration of the Stuarts. The Duke of Marlborough, who, whatever his other faults and deficiencies might be, was by no means wanting in strong common sense, advised that the prosecution should be dropped; but his necessary return to the continent to take the command of the allied forces, prevented him from enforcing this prudent advice. Lord Somers and the law officers of the crown also recommended the ministers to content themselves with burning the offending sermon by the hands of the common hangman, and imprisoning Sacheverell till the end of the session. But to no such counsels would Godolphin and the violent Whigs listen. They would be contented with nothing short of an impeachment of Sacheverell for high crimes and misdemeanours, and a solemn trial in Westminster Hall.

Accordingly the matter was formally brought before the House of Commons by Mr. Dolben, a son of the Archbishop of York, who proposed that Sacheverell should be impeached at the bar of the House of Lords, and the resolution was seconded by Sir Peter King, Recorder of London, and afterwards Lord Chancellor. It was also resolved that the impeachment should be conducted by Mr. Dolben. The Tories, who were at that time in the minority, offered a very feeble resistance to the party which for the moment was dominant. At that time they probably did not in the least foresee what would be the result of this foolish prosecution. Harley, who made some show of resistance to the proposal, based his opposition to it on the alleged contemptible character of Sacheverell's sermon, which, as he contended, made it not worth while to treat with so much ceremony a discourse of such moderate pretensions, which he described as "a circumgyration of incoherent words without any order." The Whigs, however, breathing vengeance, decided that the eyes of the whole world should be fastened on the preacher of the offending sermon, and that he should receive a punishment which, it was hoped, would effectually silence both him and the Tory party. He was accordingly committed to the custody of the Usher of the Black Rod, but was admitted by the peers to bail, which was readily given by his supporters and admirers.

Westminster Hall was at great expense and with much labour fitted up for the trial. Lord Cowper presided with dignity and impartiality. Opposite to him at the bar stood Sacheverell, between Atterbury and Smallridge, two of the most celebrated divines and preachers of the day, both afterwards bishops, and owing their bishoprics to the part they had taken on this occasion. Conspicuous among those who stood by him on that occasion were many of the queen's chaplains. He was not only defended by able counsel, but he himself, in the full canonicals of gown and cassock, generally worn at that time by the clergy on all public occasions, with snow-white handkerchief and irreproachable gloves, delivered his defence in the bold and confident tone of a popular preacher. This document is generally supposed to have been composed for Sacheverell by his friend Atterbury. It was certainly drawn up with more taste and judgment than are displayed in most of Sacheverell's effusions.

The queen showed an undisguised and almost indecent sympathy with the accused divine. A box had been fitted up for her accommodation, in which she and her attendants could see and hear all the proceedings; and as she went down day after day to the trial in her sedan chair, the people ran alongside it, crying out, " Sacheverell and High Church; we hope your Majesty is for Dr. Sacheverell." There was no doubt on which side the sympathies of the populace were enlisted, and day by day their feelings were expressed with greater and still greater loudness and vehemence. The Whigs, on the other hand, who had already been rendered unpopular through the continuance of the war, of which they were almost the only supporters, were regarded with steadily increasing disfavour, and the cry of " The Church is in danger from atheistic Whig-appointed bishops," tended to increase still more the load of unpopularity that rested upon them.

To cap all, the wage question was mixed up with the other elements of confusion which were at work, the populace taking advantage of the Church and queen disturbance to avenge themselves on the foreign Protestants, of whom the Low Church party had introduced great numbers into the country, and thereby were supposed to have lowered the wages of the working classes throughout the kingdom, but most especially in the metropolis. From all these causes there was a violent effervescence of loyalty to the queen, zeal for the Church, and sympathy for the accused doctor, which became day by day more violent and demonstrative.

Meanwhile the trial, which had commenced on the 27th of February, 1710, went on till the 10th of March, on which day the Lords retired into their own chamber to discuss a technical question which had been raised by Sacheverell's advocates. They contended that in proceedings by impeachments the particular words which were in question should be specified. The judges, who were consulted, gave an affirmative reply, and their opinion was in accordance with the generally understood principles of law and equity; but, on the other hand, it was contended by the managers of the impeachment, that, although this opinion was in accordance with the practice of the Courts of Law, it was in disaccord with Parliamentary precedents. And therefore it was overruled; more through party feeling of those by whose votes this decision was carried, than from a just balancing of the arguments employed on both sides.

Probably long before the conclusion of this ridiculous trial, the Whigs had begun to rue the day when they first entered on it. It had lasted upwards of three weeks when, on the 16th of March, 1710, the Lords retired to their chamber to consider their verdict. The debate was long and sometimes violent, both parties being now fully alive to the political importance of the question at issue. Sacheverell was found guilty by a majority of seventeen voices, but a strong protest against the condemnation was entered on the records of the House of Lords.

The sentence, which was carried by only one vote, was that he should be suspended from preaching for three years, and that his sermon should be burnt by the common hangman, but it did not prevent him from administering the sacraments or performing other functions of his ministry, nor from accepting any benefice to which he might be appointed.

It was hardly to be expected that the mobs, which day after day had escorted the doctor to Westminster Hall with loud shouts for God and Dr. Sacheverell, and were day by day becoming more violent and excited, should, at the termination of the trial, disperse without making some further rejoicings over the virtual triumph they had achieved, especially as they were liberally supplied with drink by the doctor's partisans. Accordingly, after having attended him in the visits of acknowledgment he thought fit to pay to several of his supporters, they began to pull down Nonconformist chapels without encountering much hindrance; but when they proceeded to attack a church which, judging from its external appearance, they supposed to be a Nonconformist chapel, those who had encouraged them began to be alarmed, and the alarm became a panic when it was announced that the Sacheverell mob was marching on the Bank. Then, at length, the military was called out; but the rough soldier who commanded the troops was directed to treat the people leniently. He received these orders somewhat sulkily, exclaiming, "Do you want me to fight them or to preach to them? If you want them to be preached to, you had better find some one more able to do so than I am." Happily there was no need either for fighting or preaching; the mob, having gained its point, was in high good humour, and was easily dispersed. As for Sacheverell, he was appointed to a valuable living, and went down in triumph to take possession of the benefice. His journey was like the progress of a sovereign taking possession of his dominions, or a conqueror returning from a long career of victories. At every town through which he passed he was received with almost royal honours. He was regarded as a martyr or a saint. Presents of money and other valuables were made to him. The principal gentry came out to meet and salute him with every demonstration of respect. The very bed in which he slept was regarded as a venerable relic. Ladies wore his portrait on their rings and fans.

But nowhere was he so enthusiastically welcomed as at Oxford, which was the head-quarters of Toryism and High Churchmanship, and which had lately been bitterly censured by the very same House of Commons that had impeached Sacheverell, its declaration in favour of arbitrary power having been by their order ignominiously burnt by the common hangman.

The excitement spread through the kingdom. The High Church party were triumphant. The poor timid queen and her secret advisers saw that the time had now arrived when she could shake off the detested yoke of the Marlboroughs and their Whig allies. She appointed bishops without consulting her ministers; and when it was objected that the men she named were High Churchmen, she appointed one Dr. Trimnel, who, though a Low Churchman, had managed to obtain her favour. One after another her ministers were dismissed, and Tories put in their places. Gathering courage at length, she ventured on making an appeal to the country. Parliament was dissolved in the midst of the High Church excitement, which the trial and triumph of Sacheverell had produced.

The clergy generally, encouraged by the vast popularity which Sacheverell had achieved, obtained a cheap renown by preaching the doctrines on account of which he had been impeached. Though the Whigs were still a strong party, the Tory mob was everywhere riotous and triumphant. Many popular and influential members of the party in power did not venture to show themselves on the hustings from fear of personal ill treatment. One after another the Whig ministers were dismissed, and their places supplied by ardent Tories; and, to crown all, twelve new peers were introduced into the Upper House, thus giving the Tories a majority in both Houses.

All these changes were not effected without a vehement struggle on the part of the Marlboroughs to retain their ascendancy. But the Queen was now encouraged by the results of the Sacheverell trial, and by the Tory and High Church effervescence which that trial had produced. Besides, she was now guided more and more entirely by Abigail Hill, whose friends and relations were patronized by the queen with a lavish prodigality almost equal to that which had been shown towards her predecessor in the royal favour. The two women wept together over the frightful effusion of blood that had taken place, and were guided chiefly by Harley and the leaders of the Tory party, conspicuous among whom now appeared Henry St. John, afterwards the celebrated Viscount Bolingbroke.

The Church, which had contributed so largely to the triumph of the Tory party, now obtained its reward. The building of St. Paul's being completed, the Commons decided that the duty on coals, which had been appropriated to its erection, should be continued until it amounted to the sum of three hundred and eighty thousand pounds, to be expended in the erection of fifty new churches in the suburbs of London and Westminster.

The Convocation, which in the meantime had assembled, was chiefly occupied in condemning the opinions which had been advanced by Dr. Whiston, Professor of Mathematics in the university of Cambridge, who was accused of advocating Arian doctrines, and who had, in addition, excited the indignation of the Lower House of Convocation by contending that the Apostolical Constitutions were of higher authority than the Scriptures of the New Testament. Foremost among those who denounced and condemned these views was Dr. Sacheverell, who showed how little daunted he was by his recent condemnation, attacking Whiston with his usual vehemence of language, and refusing to admit him to communion—an example which was followed by many of his brethren, but which did not in the least prevent

Whiston from publishing and maintaining his opinions. His enemies, not satisfied with censuring him in the Convocation of the province of Canterbury, also brought him before the court of the vice-chancellor of Cambridge. Being too poor to provide counsel for himself, he was generously and gratuitously defended by Sir Peter King, afterwards lord chancellor, and himself a divine of no little learning, who had been chosen, on account of his theological attainments, to be a manager of the impeachment of Sacheverell. King was also the author of a valuable work on the history of the Apostles' Creed. He argued that the opinions which had been maintained by his client were not Arian, but were deduced from the Apostolical Constitutions. He also urged that the sentence which had been pronounced was irregular, and ought to be annulled; and this was accordingly done—not, however, without some expressions of dissent from several of the delegates, whom King seems to have somewhat arbitrarily silenced.

Another prosecution that was carried on about the same time was directed against Bishop Fleetwood, who, though a Whig and Low Churchman, was patronized by the queen. He had published a volume of sermons, to which he prefixed a preface containing expressions that were regarded as disrespectful to the Government. Some foolish members of the House of Commons, untaught by the lesson afforded by the Sacheverell trial, proposed to impeach him; but the motion was rejected by a majority of 119 to 54. However, the House did not wholly pass over the matter, but resolved that the preface complained of was "malicious and factious, highly reflecting on the present administration of affairs under Her Majesty, and tending to create discord and sedition among her subjects;" and, following the fashion of that day, they directed that the book which contained the incriminated preface should be burnt by the common hangman.

Sacheverell having been condemned by the Whigs, was absolved and honoured by the victorious Tories; over whose election he had himself exercised so powerful an influence. He was invited to preach before the House of Commons, and was thanked for the discourse he delivered. This was the last great event in his career, which ended in undignified squabbles with his parishioners, amidst which history finally takes leave of him.

Meanwhile, Bolingbroke and some of the Tory and High Church ministers were secretly carrying on negociations with the pretender, whom the queen evidently knew to be her brother; though, in order to maintain her title to the throne, during her lifetime, she professed still to entertain some doubts on that point. But her dread of Popery, and her hatred of the House of Hanover, kept her in a state of indecision which would no doubt have been at once terminated, if the prince would have consented to renounce his religion in order to obtain the crown. But this, much to his credit, he steadily refused to do. Even as it was, if his sister had only lived a few months longer, he probably would have succeeded her. Robinson, bishop of Bristol, and afterwards of London, was appointed to the Privy Seal, he being the first clergyman who had held office in any administration since the days of Laud and Juxon. He not only attended the Congress of Utrecht, but took a leading part in its deliberations; and by his conduct at it justified the choice which had been made of him to represent his country at that assembly. Everything was now evidently tending towards the re-establishment of the Tories and the return of the pretender, when the sudden death of the electress of Hanover, hastened by her anxieties with regard to the succession, threatened to bring on a further crisis. While the Jacobites were plotting for the pretender, the friends of the Hanoverian succession naturally desired to have the elector on the spot, in case of the queen's demise, which was now seriously apprehended. This project Anne deprecated and resisted in the most decided manner. The Tory ministry itself was torn by intestine divisions. Harley, now become Earl of Oxford, was zealous for the elector of Hanover; St. John, who had been raised to the peerage under the title of Bolingbroke, favoured the pretender, and he carried with him the sympathies of the queen and the support of the majority of the cabinet, as well as of Atterbury and Swift—two of the ablest men of the day. Atterbury had brought in a Bill, which was entitled the Schisms Bill, and was intended to check the progress of Nonconformity. This measure enacted that every tutor or schoolmaster in Great Britain must, before exercising his functions, sign a declaration that he would conform to the Church of

England, and must obtain a licence to give instruction from the archbishop of his province, or the bishop of his diocese; and that no licence should be granted, unless the person applying for it should produce a certificate stating that he had received the sacrament according to the order of the Church of England within the last year, and had also subscribed the oaths of allegiance and supremacy. The introduction of such a measure proved the success that had attended the efforts of Nonconformists in the cause of education. The carrying of it was a remarkable evidence of the power and prevalence of the Tory party; and Bolingbroke, by whose able and unscrupulous counsels that party was now guided, determined to take advantage of it. The health of the queen was visibly declining, and as she felt her end approaching she became more and more anxious that her brother should succeed her on the throne. A violent altercation took place between the leaders of the two parties, ending in the dismissal of Harley, and the appointment of Bolingbroke to succeed him. This was a clear proof of a determination of the Jacobites to bring in the pretender, and recognize him as the next heir to the throne. And such was Anne's popularity, that if the attempt had been made, it would most probably have succeeded. But the designs were defeated by the demise of the queen, which occurred before Bolingbroke had completed his preparations for the proclamation of the prince. On her death-bed she put the White Staff of the treasurer into the hands of the Earl of Shrewsbury, a zealous supporter of the pretender. But her sudden demise defeated these projects. The supporters of the elector had made all their arrangements in anticipation of the queen's death. The Tories, on the other hand, were divided and undecided. Atterbury, and a few of the bolder partisans of the chevalier, urged their friends to proclaim him. But more timid counsels prevailed, and the elector of Hanover, under the title of George I., ascended without opposition the throne of Great Britain.

The feeling in favour of the prince was, nevertheless, strong and general. The clergy especially had not forgotten their old doctrines of hereditary right, and laboured by their sermons and conversation to spread discontent through the country. The new king made a very unfavourable impression on those who had access to him. He spoke English very imperfectly, he was surrounded by German mistresses, who were described as "trulls, and very ugly trulls." The leader of the disaffected party among the clergy was the able and ambitious Bishop Atterbury, and he was supported by Robinson, now bishop of London, who, as we have seen, had highly distinguished himself in the negotiation of the treaty of Utrecht.

During the reign of Anne an effort, which nearly proved successful, was made to effect a union between the Churches of England and Prussia. In the year 1701, the electorate of Prussia became a kingdom, and Frederic, the first king, wishing to give all possible *éclat* to his newly assumed dignity, had conferred on two of the most eminent ministers of his dominions the title of bishops, in order that they might officiate in that capacity at his coronation ; and this led him to desire to introduce into his kingdom the liturgy, doctrine, and discipline of the Anglican Church. One of his two bishops died, and Dr. Ernestus Jablousky having taken the matter up very zealously, persuaded the king to direct Dr. Ursinus, the surviving bishop, to write to Archbishop Tenison on the subject, and to propose that the English ecclesiastical system should be introduced into Prussia on the First Sunday in Advent. The proposal gave great satisfaction both in England and Prussia, and was warmly welcomed by many influential members of the Anglican Church, among whom may be mentioned Sharp, archbishop of York, who entered very zealously into the matter, and did his utmost to promote it.

The queen herself also supported the scheme, and commanded Lord Raby, her minister at the Prussian court, to express to the Prussian monarch her hearty thanks for the interest he had displayed in regard to the matter. Although the question of a union between the Church of England and the Protestant communions on the continent had often been agitated, no definite plan had ever been put forward until this overture was made. It was well calculated to meet the views both of the High and Low Churchmen of that period, but appears to have been frustrated by the inaction of Archbishop Tenison, whose indolence or indifference disgusted the Prussian monarch, and caused him to desist from his design.

The scheme was therefore dropped, and was never revived again till the year 1841, when, under the auspices of Archbishop Howley, a step was made in the same direction, an agreement having been entered into and sanctioned by Act of Parliament, in virtue of which a Lutheran divine, nominated by the Prussian Government, and a clergyman of the Anglican Church, nominated by the Government of this country, should alternately be consecrated to the see of Jerusalem, with the intention of making this arrangement a first step towards the union of the Churches of England and Prussia. No second step, however, has been taken in this matter, nor is likely to be, the religious ideas of the two countries having diverged too widely to admit of such a union between them as at one time seemed on the point of being effected.

The idea was highly popular both in our own country and in Prussia. Bonet, the Prussian minister at the English court, stated to his Government that a conformity between the members of the Prussian Church would be received with great joy in England. At the same time he gave his opinion that the conformity to be wished for, related more to the government of the Church than to any change in the ritual or liturgy. He added that the clergy in England were strongly in favour of Episcopacy, that they regarded that form of government as being at least of apostolic institution, and were possessed with an opinion that it had been continued in an uninterrupted succession from the times of the apostles to their day; and that, upon this supposition, they alleged that there could be no true ecclesiastical government but under bishops of this order, nor any true ministers of the Gospel but such as had been ordained by bishops; and that if there were other ministers of the Anglican Church that did not go so far as this, yet that all of them made a great difference between those who had received the laying on of hands from bishops, and those who had been ordained by a Presbyterian synod.

Tenison affirmed that the address which was alleged to have been sent to him in favour of this scheme, had never reached him; but it was evident that he was not heartily zealous for it, if, indeed, he was not absolutely hostile to it. On the other hand, Sharp, the archbishop of York, whose Church principles, as has been intimated already, were those which were described by Bonet, zealously supported this scheme of union; but his efforts were vain, for the Prussian monarch, disgusted at finding his advances so negligently treated by the highest authority in the English Church, desisted from his endeavours, and the matter dropped.

CHAPTER VI.

THE GEORGES.

THE successful manner in which George had been proclaimed seemed for a moment to have stunned and silenced the Jacobites, and the Whigs proceeded to take advantage of their prostrate condition, in order to carry measures of a liberal character, especially in reference to religion, by freeing the Nonconformists from some of the fetters with which they had been bound during the ascendancy of the Tories in the latter part of Queen Anne's reign.

The Occasional Conformity Act, passed in the year 1711, and the Schism Act, adopted in 1714, were now repealed. But the Test and Corporation Acts, passed in the reign of Charles II., though allowed to remain, were rendered innoxious by annual suspensions at least so far as they related to offices held under the crown, though they still remained in vigour with regard to offices in municipal corporations, notwithstanding the efforts made by Lord Stanhope to obtain the repeal of them, and the liberal and honourable support that he received from several bishops, especially Willis, Gibson, Kennett, and Hoadley.

The measure carried by their aid was very imperfect, and the exclusion of Dissenters from corporations was continued until the final and entire repeal of the Test and Corporation Act in 1827, through the earnest and persistent exertions of the late Earl (then Lord John) Russell. The imperfect measure which Lord Stanhope advocated was carried through with great difficulty; but a more complete Bill would certainly have been rejected, as the public opinion of the time was decidedly unfavourable to it.

In the year 1719 a very vigorous attempt was made by Lord Stanhope and others to obtain a repeal of the Act. Sir Robert Walpole, the then prime minister, professed to be a warm supporter of the claims of the Nonconformists; but whenever a Bill was introduced for the purpose of satisfying those claims he, with many professions of good will, pleaded that the time when they could be yielded had not yet arrived. Year after year did the friends of civil and religious liberty press the matter, and year after year did the prime minister exhort them to wait patiently for a more favourable opportunity.

In the year 1734 there was a general election, which was very strongly contested. The Dissenters, relying on the sincerity of Walpole's professions, vigorously supported his administration by their votes at the hustings, and contributed in no small degree to gain, or at least to swell, the majority which the Government obtained.

After having rendered this signal service to the Walpole administration, they naturally expected that the convenient season so often promised had at length arrived, but they found that the old pleas for delay were still urged. Then one, Dr. Chandler, a pertinacious advocate of the claims of the Nonconformists, turned upon the minister and rejoined, "You have so repeatedly made this answer to our inquiries, that I trust you will excuse me if I ask you to tell me when the proper time will come?" Walpole, in the heat and excitement of the debate, replied, "Never." This frank declaration very naturally excited the indignation of the Dissenters, and threw them into the ranks of the opposition, but it also obtained for the minister the support of many High Churchmen who had hitherto opposed him on account of the professions he had formerly made of a desire to repeal the Test and Corporation Act, which was still regarded by zealous Churchmen as a bulwark of the establishment not under any circumstances to be dispensed with.

In the year 1722, suspicions of a plot to bring in the pretender were very rife, and were not altogether without foundation. A clergyman of the name of Kelly was arrested, but he managed to keep off the constables with a drawn sword while he burnt with a candle the papers that would probably have proved his guilt.

Many other arrests were made about the same time; but the head and chief of the plan was unquestionably Atterbury, bishop of Rochester, who had for some time been engaged in a plot for bringing back the exiled prince. However, he was no more guilty, in all probability, than multitudes of others, who, more fortunate or more cautious, took the oath of allegiance to George with the unconcealed intention of transferring their fealty to the pretender whenever they thought they could do so without risk. There can be no doubt that a strong feeling of discontent pervaded the minds of great multitudes of Churchmen and Tories at this crisis.

Circumstances were discovered which, though they afforded a moral certainty that Atterbury was implicated in a conspiracy to bring in the pretender, did not amount to a legal proof of his guilt. However, his correspondence was seized, and he himself was examined before the council. He replied to the questions put to him in the words of the Saviour: "If I tell you ye will not believe, and if I also ask you ye will not answer me nor let me go." As he could not in all probability be found guilty on a fair trial, a Bill of pains and penalties was brought in against him and some others. It passed the Commons without opposition, Atterbury having reserved his defence for the House of Parliament of which he was himself a member. When summoned to the bar of the Upper House, he defended himself with resolution and ability, calling many witnesses, prominent among whom were Pope and Gay. The former, however, did not shine in the witness box with the brilliancy of wit he displayed in his writings; and his testimony tended rather to damage than to help the cause of his accused friend. But against Atterbury were ranged many of the peers, the majority of his episcopal brethren, and the whole power and influence of the Government, and by this combination of opponents he was sent out of the kingdom at the very time when Bolingbroke, having made his peace with the Government by the payment of an enormous bribe to the Duchess of Kendal, the king's favourite mistress, was returning from his exile. The two former associates passed through Calais—Lord Bolingbroke to offer his services to the king of England, Atterbury to throw himself into the arms of the pretender, and to become an honoured and trusted adviser of that unfortunate prince.

Other leaders of the party were more fortunate. Oxford, who certainly had steadily adhered to the Hanoverian succession, and had been therefore turned out of the Jacobite ministry, was nevertheless much mixed up with its proceedings, and was accused by the now dominant Whigs on account of his complicity with many of their worst acts. On this account, he had been impeached by the Commons. He was kept confined in the Tower for two years, at the end of which period he was brought up for trial. He was followed by a large crowd of people, who expressed their sympathy with him by shouting for Oxford, Ormond, and High Church; and he escaped punishment through a quarrel between the two Houses as to the mode of procedure, in consequence of which the Commons refused to appear, and Oxford returned home amidst the congratulatory acclamations of his friends. His escape was regarded as a triumph by the High Churchmen and Tories throughout the kingdom.

Meanwhile, from time to time the Convocation assembled. In the Upper House, the Whig bishops appointed by William III. and the Whig administration during the first half of Anne's reign, were in the majority; in the Lower House the Tories and High Churchmen predominated. The consequence was a hopeless antagonism and continual indecent quarrels between the two Houses. The Upper House claimed the right to fix the hours during which the Lower should sit: the Lower House repudiated this pretension. When ordered by the archbishop to prorogue, they nevertheless continued to sit. Atterbury had taken a very active part in asserting what he regarded as the rights of the Lower House, and he continued to maintain his opinions on this matter after his elevation to the Episcopal Bench. Hoadley, who had successively been appointed bishop of Bangor, Hereford, and Winchester, had published works which High Churchmen and Low Churchmen united in regarding as heretical, but which were in high favour with the House of Commons and the Government. They gave rise to a celebrated discussion, carried on by the publication of a vast number of pamphlets, and also by word of mouth in the Lower House of Convocation. The Government, finding that their champion would be outvoted and censured, anticipated this decision by a prorogation of Convocation, with an intention not to summon it again; and, in accordance with this resolution, for upwards of a century it was merely called together as a matter of form, but was not allowed to deliberate. Hoadley was too much engaged with Bangorian controversies, and other ecclesiastical disputes, to pay any attention to his diocese, which he neglected to visit under the pretext that his presence there would be the means of exciting a party fury. In this respect, however, he was no worse than many of his episcopal contemporaries.

The entire and almost unresisted suppression of the ecclesiastical parliament proves the weakness and deadness of the Church at the time when it was carried into effect. Never, perhaps, had any religious communion sunk so low as had the Church of England at this conjuncture. Rich in this world's wealth, probably beyond any other religious communion in the world, in spiritual gifts it was miserably poor. Great multitudes of the bishops and higher clergy were non-resident and utterly careless of their duties, which they delegated to curates, who were often miserably remunerated for the services they rendered.

There was now and then an exception to this rule, in the case of such men as Butler and Paley. But they were rare indeed. The laws that had been enacted to prevent simony were entirely ineffectual, and very few were promoted on account of their merits. Men were often appointed to important positions in the Church by means of bribes given to the king's mistresses, or others who had influence at the court. The highest places in the Church were filled by furious controversialists or corrupt nepotists, who loaded their relatives with rich preferments often held in plurality.

The education of the people was utterly neglected.

The old grammar schools, built and endowed by the piety and liberality of our ancestors, were allowed to fall into ruin and decay, were converted into sawpits, or applied to other uses, while the masters of many of them gave only such instructions as they were obliged by the wills of their founders to impart, and in many instances no instruction at all.

Here, then, we reach a period which is a blank in our narrative, and which we must be content to leave blank, for the simple reason that history traces the evolution of events, and that when there is no evolution, and consequently no progress, there can be no history. Such periods may embrace many facts which stand isolated and alone; but though they decorate the surface of history, they do not enter into the warp and weft of it. Even at the dead period we have now reached, there was probably some movement; but it was so sluggish as to be altogether inappreciable, or like that of a river which, in its manifold windings, often turns towards its source.

It is true that there were archbishops succeeding one another in the chair of Lanfranc, Anselm, Becket, Laud, and Sancroft. Carlyle pertinently asks: "Who was the primate of England at this time?" and he answers with bitter irony, "No man knoweth." Nor was this far from the truth. There were contented Erastians like Wake and Potter carrying on controversies now entirely forgotten, as they well deserve to be. There were men full of decencies and proprieties, like Secker; but who cares now to know what Archbishops Herring, Hutton, or Moore, thought, said, or did? I have searched carefully the seven volumes of Lord Mahon's history for the names of these prelates, but have not succeeded in meeting with any of them. If their works ever possessed any living interest or any practical value, they have long since lost it. They never attempted to guide or elevate the religious destinies of the nation over whose Church they uselessly presided, and the same might be said of the great body of the clergy. Mr. Gladstone has given the testimony of Sydney Smith with regard to the indolence and inefficiency of the clergy of his day. What he said was still more applicable to the clergy of the preceding generation.

From this deathlike stupor the clergy were suddenly aroused by the rapid diffusion of Wesleyan Methodism, through the zealous preaching of the two Wesleys, Whitfield, and others associated with them, who very shortly, and in the face of powerful and persistent opposition, succeeded in forming a sect whose members were nearly as numerous, and at all events, in the first fervour of their conversion, much more earnestly religious than the clergy or laity, the conformists or nonconformists of their day.

It would be uncandid to deny that Wesley at the outset of his career was a zealous Churchman, and not only a Churchman, but a very High Churchman, accepting fully the doctrines which had been held by Laud, by Sancroft, and by the Nonjurors, which, as we shall hereafter have occasion to point out, were revived in a somewhat modified form by the authors of the Oxford tracts; and which, if not absolutely sanctioned by, are at all events not opposed to the teachings of the Prayer-book.

His aim at first was to constitute a body of lay preachers, who were to work in harmony with the clergy. This object he pursued steadily in his earlier years, in spite of much discouragement and vehement opposition from the clergy, with whom he desired to co-operate, and whose friendly sympathy he vainly endeavoured to cultivate. Hence it was that he directed his preachers and followers to attend the services of the Church, to receive the sacrament at the hand of her ordained ministers, and not to hold services or prayer-meetings in or about the time of the regular Church services. Hence, too, he strictly forbade them to assume the clerical garb which he himself wore constantly, unless, which was the case of very few of them, they were, like himself, ordained ministers of the Church. The aim with which he entered on his zealous and successful ministry—and it was one in which to a certain extent he continued to adhere to the last—was that of establishing an order of lay preachers in connection with the established Church.

It is no less clear that in his old age, pressed by his fellow-workers, irritated and disgusted by the cold and unsympathetic treatment, not to say open opposition, he experienced from the great majority of the English clergy, he yielded to a tendency towards separation which prevailed amongst his followers, or which was imposed on him by the necessities of his position, and which in the earlier years of the movement he would have earnestly deprecated and resolutely resisted.

The progress of Wesleyanism affected the Church in

two different and even opposite ways, producing a movement of opposition on the one hand, and of sympathy and admiration on the other. In the first place, it brought many members and ministers of the Church into collision with the Wesleyans. The Church minister was often annoyed to find his people coming under the influence of the new teachers. It was not agreeable to him to see their places of worship crowded while his church perhaps was very thinly attended. He was vexed and irritated when made to feel that his isolated and desultory efforts did not enable him to compete, with any chance of success, with the well-organized machinery of the Wesleyan body. And this natural irritation was yet further increased if, as was at that time but too commonly the case, by his indolence or drunkenness, his immorality, or his incapacity, he had to a great extent forfeited the esteem of his parishioners. And just in proportion to the need that existed in his parish for better teaching and a better example was his objection to the new teachers, and the vehemence with which he persecuted and abused both them and their followers.

But the progress of Methodism affected the Church in another and a very different way. The zeal of the new preachers was contagious. Many of the most eminent among the clergy were more or less influenced by it for good. Without enrolling themselves in the ranks of Methodism or adopting its system, they nevertheless imbibed a large portion of its spirit; and so, joining with the piety and earnestness that characterized the Methodists, the opinions which had been held by the Low Churchmen, they constituted that body which we know by the name of the Evangelical party, which enjoyed a great influence in the Church, and after a desperate struggle against the orthodox party, succeeded in conquering for itself a high position, rose into importance, was animated by an earnest zeal, identified itself more and more closely with the Low Churchmen, gained great popularity, obtained many of the best benefices in the Church, and finally sank even more rapidly than they had risen, lost their first love, and became almost extinct as a great party.

But there was yet another influence at work about the same time, which, though less perceptible, was probably even more potential, so far at least as the Church was concerned. Laymen so devoted yet so enlightened as Nelson, Addison, Dr. Johnson, Burke, Coleridge, Southey, Wordsworth, and Wilberforce—laymen such as perhaps no other communion can boast, must necessarily, by their writings and conversation, have powerfully leavened the Church of which they were members, and have exercised an influence over the evolution of her religious life, even greater than that which was produced within her pale by the preachings of Wesley and Whitfield and the Evangelical clergy. This influence, less noticeable indeed, and less easy to estimate, must from the nature of the case have produced important results. The kingdom of God cometh not with observation—and the evolution which stirs the depths most powerfully is by no means always that which shows itself most conspicuously on the surface.

There was one great defect which at this time characterized almost all the communions into which the religious world was divided. Whether Methodists or Nonconformists of other denominations, High Churchmen or Low Churchmen, orthodox or evangelicals, they were all ready to combine for the purpose of perpetuating the scandalous disabilities which had been laid on the Roman Catholics. Even the most ardent advocates of civil and religious liberty, the moment that the Catholic Church was in question seemed to cast away their principles, and to become the advocates of the most abominable tyranny and the most flagrant injustice.

It is pleasant, therefore, at this period of discreditable persecution, to note the conduct of those very few of our countrymen who, in spite of prejudice and clamour, firmly withstood the prevalent intolerance. Conspicuous among the few who in that day espoused the cause of civil and religious liberty, was the celebrated Lord Mansfield, who in very many instances advocated and promoted it with all the authority which belonged to his office as first judge of the land, and which resulted from his high character.

In a question regarding the affirmation of a Quaker, he declared that he wished it to be put on the same footing as the oath of another person, on the sensible ground that a different construction of the law was not only injurious to Quakers, but also prejudicial to the rest of the king's subjects, who might want their testimony in order to the establishment of the truth, in cases in which they were in some respects concerned. On another occasion, when an attempt had been made to extort money from a Nonconformist by appointing him to the office of sheriff, which he could not fill without receiving the sacrament according to the rites of the established religion, and then to fine him because he refused to accept it, the matter was brought before Lord Mansfield, who exposed the character of the transaction and defeated this shameful scheme of extortion. He was not only just to the persecuted Nonconformists, but also, as we have already intimated, showed the same liberality towards the Roman Catholics; nay, perhaps sometimes stretched the law in order to prevent the perpetration of flagrant injustice on persons of that religion, and to do a great right did a little wrong. A Bill had been passed in the early part of the reign of William and Mary, that contained clauses condemning a Roman Catholic priest to fine and imprisonment for life if he said mass, and that disqualified a Papist from becoming the proprietor of land either by inheritance or purchase.

A Bill being introduced for the repeal of these odious provisions, he gave it his heartiest support. The attempts thus made, by Lord Mansfield and others, to obtain for Roman Catholics some diminution of the penalties to which they were subject, caused a new outbreak of the spirit of bigotry. It commenced in Scotland, where the general assembly of the Scotch Presbyterian Church adopted several highly intemperate resolutions and addresses, thus producing serious riots, in which several Roman Catholic places of worship were set on fire and destroyed.

The perpetrators of these violent proceedings were not without their associates and defenders even in the legislature. Lord George Gordon, a half-crazy zealot, headed a procession of ultra-Protestants to the House of Commons, and there presented several petitions against the concessions that were made to those whom he denounced as the followers of Antichrist. He declared that the people of Scotland were ripe for insurrection, and, with the exception of a few Papists, were ready to withstand the powers of the Government. The mob that followed him resolved to present their petition themselves, and made their way, without meeting with any resistance, into the lobby of the Houses of Parliament. Lord Chancellor Thurlow was prevented by illness from attending, and Lord Mansfield occupied his place on this trying occasion.

He was regarded by the howling mob, on account of his liberal and charitable principles, with peculiar malevolence, and was violently assailed. With great difficulty, he made his way to the woolsack, his torn robe and dishevelled wig showing with what savage ferocity he had been attacked. Several other peers came in, bearing marks of more or less violent ill-treatment. The Archbishop of York and the Bishop of Lincoln, falsely suspected of a leaning towards Popery, were with great difficulty rescued from the mob. In the halls of the legislature all was terror and confusion. Some proposed that the guards should be called out. Others ridiculously contended that the peers themselves should go forth in procession, the mace carried before them, headed by Lord Mansfield—now seventy-five years of age—in order to rescue some of the peers who were in the hands of the rioters, and whose lives were endangered. Only six constables could be found at the moment to deal with the mob, which continually increased in numbers and audacity.

One by one the peers stole away, leaving Lord Mansfield unprotected, except by a few officers of the House and his servants. Fortunately, he managed to reach his own residence without having experienced further ill-treatment, but the mob speedily followed and set it on fire. He again made his escape, while it was being consumed with all its contents, including the very valuable library he had for many years been collecting at great expense, and for which he generously forbore to claim, as he might have done, reimbursement at the public cost.

Lord Mansfield, though the chief, was by no means the only sufferer by these excesses. Many Roman Catholic places of worship were burnt by the rioters, as well as many private houses. The King's Bench, the Fleet prison, and the new Bridewell were destroyed. The Bank was attacked, but the rioters were repulsed by a strong body of soldiers who had been posted there to defend it. Two hundred and ten of the rioters were killed by the soldiers, and two hundred and forty-eight wounded. But these were by no means the whole of the casualties. Many of the unfortunate wretches had intoxicated themselves to such a degree that they perished in the flames which they themselves had kindled. No such riots have ever taken place in this country either before or since these events occurred. Lord George Gordon was arraigned for high treason on the 5th of February, 1781, in Westminster Hall, but was acquitted on the technical plea that nothing he had done in the *county of Surrey* could be construed into an overt act of high treason. He was subsequently committed to Newgate for libel, and died in prison.

I am not able to say how far the Church was mixed up with these violences, or sympathized with their authors and abettors. The Protestant fanaticism which produced them was very generally diffused through all ranks and classes of persons, and there seems to be no reason for supposing that the clergy and members of the English Church were distinguished from their fellow-citizens, either by a greater liberality of sentiment or by more violent anti-papal prejudices.

It cannot, however, be denied that, from the period of which we are now treating, down to the passing of the Catholic Emancipation Act, the clergy of the Church were foremost in inveighing against the Roman Catholic religion, while great numbers of the Nonconformists, though still more widely separated from them in opinion and practice than the Churchmen, warmly advocated the extension to them of those principles of religious liberty of which they had been permitted to enjoy the benefit; and though many of them were still blinded by the prejudices of education, their conduct in this respect contrasted very favourably with that of many members of the Established Church.

On the other hand, there was found among the clergy of the Church one who stood nearly alone in maintaining these principles, but who advocated them with a mixture of wit, wisdom, and honesty that almost redeemed the Church to which he belonged from the reproach of intolerance that rested on her; and in writings that ought to be for ever memorable, maintained the cause of truth and justice, though unhappily with little apparent success. But the seed he had sown in due time brought forth its proper fruit, though the sower of that seed failed to obtain the credit and the recognition due to services so great as those which Sydney Smith rendered to the cause of civil and religious freedom.

At this time, the Church was divided into two parties—the orthodox, or High Church, and the evangelical, or Low Church—the former very numerous, but lifeless, the latter showing great zeal and activity in proclaiming its peculiar doctrines; the one very careful in its compliance with the directions of the Book of Common Prayer, the other conforming indeed to it, but doing so reluctantly, and preferring very much extempore prayers as well as (so-called) extempore sermons. But the High Churchmen of this time had taken up a very different position from that which had been occupied by the High Churchmen of the reigns of Charles II., James II., William and Mary, and Anne.

As was not untruly remarked by the late Bishop Blomfield, the doctrine of the apostolical succession had gone out with the Nonjurors. The High Churchmen and Low Churchmen of the time of the Georges had tacitly renounced that doctrine, or, at all events, had ceased to rely on it in their conflicts with the Methodists and other Nonconformists.

They now urged her claims to respect and attention, not only on her supposed apostolical and primitive descent, but on the fact of her being *by law established.* This phrase they continually used, until the time when Cobbett came forward with his racy, vigorous, trenchant style, and taking this watchword out of their mouths, turned it against them, employed it with an almost savage ferocity, of which we cannot give our readers a better idea than by citing the words with which this able, but unscrupulous, controversialist commenced his history of the Reformation, by which he expected and intended to bring about the overthrow of the Established Church, and so satiate the hatred with which he regarded her.

The time at which he came forward was one which afforded ample ground for his fierce and fiery invective. There were at that time scandals of all kinds in the Church: drunkenness and other misconduct among the clergy; simoniacal sales of bishoprics, and other high dignities of the Church, by Mrs. Clark, the mistress of the Duke of York—the champion and idol of the Orange Protestant party, and others who, on account of their profligacies and immoralities, were no less unfit to have part and lot in such matters. It would be a great mistake to infer from these facts that the Church was worse at this time than it was before. It was, probably, slightly better. Its moral sores were less virulent, but they were open to the gaze of the world, through the greater publicity which now began to be afforded by the newspaper press. But what, it may be asked, was the Archbishop of Canterbury and his suffragans doing while these abominations were being committed? There were archbishops duly succeeding one another in the seat of St. Augustine. But, as we have already observed, they were primates only in title, leaving the religious affairs of the country to shift very much for themselves, and the Church to drift on as it could, while they were gorging their relatives with the spoils of the Church, and loading them with the wealthiest preferments that belonged to her. Such was the state of things when Cobbett came into the field.

This able writer, calling himself a Protestant, undertakes to prove that what is commonly called the Reformation was no *reformation*, but a *devastation*. He affirms that the Catholic Church originated with Jesus Christ Himself; that He selected PETER to be the head of His Church, etc. At the commencement of his work he writes thus:—"Now, my friends, a fair and honest inquiry will teach us that this (the Reformation) was an alteration greatly for the worse; that the REFORMATION, as it was called, was engendered in beastly lust, brought forth in hypocrisy and perfidy, and cherished and fed by plunder, devastation, and by rivers of innocent blood; and, as to its more remote consequences, they are some of them now before us in that misery, that beggary, that nakedness, that hunger, that everlasting wrangling and spite, which now stare us in the face, and stun our ears at every turn, and which the 'Reformation' has given us in exchange for the ease and happiness and harmony and Christian charity enjoyed so abundantly and for so many ages by our Catholic forefathers." After enlarging, in a series of letters, on these topics, and after giving passages containing a very highly coloured representation of the state of England and France in the fifteenth century, he thus proceeds: "Go and read this to the poor souls who are now eating seaweed in Ireland; who are detected in robbing the pig-troughs in Yorkshire; who are eating horseflesh and grains (draff) in Lancashire and Cheshire; who are harnessed like horses and drawing gravel in Hampshire and Sussex; who have threepence a day allowed them by the magistrates in Norfolk; who are all over England worse fed than the felons in the jails. Go and tell them, when they raise their hands from the pig-trough, or from the grain-tub, and, with their dirty tongues, cry 'No Popery;' go, read to these deluded wretches this account of their Catholic forefathers, who lived under what is impudently styled 'Popish superstition and tyranny,' and in these times we have the audacity to call the dark ages."

This is the conclusion of his book:—"I have now performed my task. I have made good the positions with which I began. Born and bred a Protestant of the Church of England, having a wife and numerous family professing the same faith, having the remains of most dearly beloved parents lying in a Protestant churchyard, and trusting to conjugal or filial piety to place mine by their side, I have in this undertaking had no motive but a sincere and disinterested love of truth and justice. It is not for the rich and powerful of my countrymen that I have spoken; but for the poor, the persecuted, the proscribed. I have not been unmindful of the unpopularity and prejudice that would attend the enterprise; but when I considered the long—long triumph of calumny over the religion of those to whom we owe all that we possess that is great and renowned; when I was convinced that I could do much towards the counteracting of that calumny; when duty so sacred bade me speak, it would have been baseness to hold my tongue; and baseness superlative would it have been, if, having the will as well as the power, I had been restrained by fear of the shafts of falsehood and of folly. To be clear of self-reproach is amongst the greatest of human consolations; and now, amidst all the dreadful perils with which the event that I have treated of has, at last, surrounded my country, I can, while I pray God to save her from still further devastation and misery, safely say that, neither expressly nor tacitly, am I guilty of any part of the cause of her ruin."

These specimen passages may give the reader some faint idea of the strong, coarse, savage invective with which their author assailed the ministers and defenders of that Church "by law established," of which he professed to be a member. His works circulated in immense numbers, chiefly among the poorer classes, and containing a great deal of truth, though mingled with much sophistry and much falsehood, produced a tremendous effect. They were the more successful on account of the vexations caused in the agricultural districts by the collection of the tithe, much of which was levied in kind, and almost all of which, owing to the manner in which it was raised, was a source of constant irritation between the clergy on the one hand, and the farmers and agricultural labourers on the other. The legal and parliamentary establishment of the Church, which a short time before had been put forth as a boast, now came to be regarded almost as a disgrace, and ceased to be urged.

Meanwhile, the Catholic emancipation, so long resisted by High Church as well as Low Church, was triumphantly carried through the defection of those who, up to almost the last moment, had been at the head of the opposition to it ; and who now were angrily assailed by the Protestant party, which, considering that it had been betrayed by its leaders, breathed vengeance against those whom they regarded as perfidious traitors, and determined to avenge themselves on them. If anything was wanting at this time to fill up the measure of the unpopularity which the ministers and members of the Church were amassing, it was found in the resistance offered by them to every attempt that was made to effect reforms which were generally felt to be at once inevitable and indispensable, insomuch that if the Government which came into power in the year 1830, and brought in the great Reform Bill, had at that time proposed the disestablishment of the Church, the measure would probably have been carried at that moment with very little opposition.

CHAPTER VIII.

THE OXFORD TRACTS.

ALL sensible men were now alive to the fact that the miserable, slavish Erastianism on which the Church was at this moment resting, was not the rock which would withstand the breakers that were driving in upon her. The minds of the most thoughtful men of that time were revolted by it, and began to seek out a means of placing the Church on a more defensible basis.

Among the foremost of these, as far as the proprieties of his high office would permit, was the Archbishop of Canterbury, Dr. Howley, who, without taking part in the measures he desired to see carried, set a noble example of impartiality and public spirit in the distribution of the vast patronage that then belonged to his see, and surrounded himself with the ablest and most highly reputed divines and theologians of his day.

In the mean time, Calvinism, or something hardly distinguishable from it, was spreading rapidly among both clergy and laity, under the auspices of Simeon Carus and Melvill. It was true that its advocates, though numerous among the younger graduates and the students of the university of Cambridge, were but few in other parts of the kingdom; but they made up for their deficiency in number by the zeal and activity with which they preached their doctrines, and especially their favourite doctrine of conversion. In the earlier years of the nineteenth century their influence began to be felt in a manner that alarmed the old-fashioned dignitaries of the Church, whom the Evangelicals did not hesitate to denounce, dividing the clergy, after their fashion, into those who preached and those who did not preach the Gospel.

Among those who had been most alarmed at the progress they were making, was Dr. Marsh, bishop of Peterborough, reputed to be the most learned and clear-headed theologian of his day. He drew up eighty-three questions, the object of which was to detect the slightest departure from what he held and taught to be the orthodoxy of the Church, and especially to prevent the spread of Calvinism or Evangelicalism in his diocese. He required all persons applying to be ordained or licensed to curacies in his diocese to answer his eighty-three questions. He did not indeed venture to propose them to clergymen who were appointed to benefices, and who might therefore appeal to the tribunals of the country; but persisted in forcing his questions on those who could not obtain that protection. His conduct was brought under the notice of the House of Lords, in which he vigorously defended his proceedings; but his brother bishops, by their silence, evinced their disapprobation of his conduct, and the public opinion of the country was so evidently opposed to him, that he found himself obliged to yield to the pressure that was brought to bear on him, and to content himself with exacting those subscriptions only that were required by the law of the land. The able and humorous article of Sydney Smith on the question thus raised, probably contributed in no small degree to the formation of the public opinion which forced the bishop to yield.

The period to which we have been referring was also rendered remarkable by the agitation carried on throughout it against slavery, which eventuated in the year 1833 in the total abolition of slavery throughout the whole of the British dominions, the liberty of the slaves being purchased by the noble grant of the large sum of £20,000,000 to the slave-holders.

Nothing showed more plainly the concentration of the spiritual and religious life of the Church in the Evangelical party than the attitude assumed by the clergy during the progress of this agitation, and especially during its final throes. For while the Evangelical clergy inside the Church, and the Dissenters outside, warmly co-operated with Wilberforce, Clarkson, Brougham, and others who led the agitation for the emancipation of the negroes, the orthodox majority of the clergy either held themselves altogether aloof from it, or actively opposed it. Their favourite organ, the *John Bull*, distinguished itself by the coarse ridicule and the invective with which its writers covered those who took part in the agitation of this great and noble measure.

Almost contemporaneously with these events, the Test and Corporation Acts, the Catholic disabilities, and other so-styled *bulwarks* of the Church were, one by one, swept away, and the Reform Bill, which opened wide the doors of Parliament to a considerable influx of Nonconformists, becoming year by year more numerous and influential in the Lower House, was now being carried. These events filled with terror the hearts of many of the clergy, and they naturally began loudly to express their alarm. What if the law on which they had hitherto relied should turn against them? What if the Church which they had so often boasted to be by law established should be by law disestablished? Thoughts such as these caused many of them to cast about for a firmer and more logical basis on which the Church might rest, in case the Nonconformists should continue to increase in numbers and power; and this they found in a recurrence, with some modifications, to those doctrines which had been held and taught by the Nonjurors, and which found considerable countenance in the Prayer-book of the English Church. The opportuneness and the naturalness of these views is shown by their almost simultaneous appearance in various quarters. Curiously enough, the first person by whom they were distinctly propounded was the celebrated Edward Irving.

As early as the year 1825, this extraordinary man had adopted the doctrine of baptismal regeneration, the very keystone of the Anglican system, and in a volume of lectures on baptism had pushed that doctrine to its logical consequences. He had also set himself, under the inspiration and teaching of the poet-philosopher, S. T. Coleridge, to resist the advances of that religious liberalism whose inroads both of them regarded with consternation, and which each in his way was prepared to withstand. Together with these he proclaimed openly the doctrines which, as we have seen, had been generally accepted in the Church during the reigns of Charles II. and James II., and which had been still more distinctly adopted by the Nonjurors. It was not a movement taking place in the Church, but it was one that showed whither men's thoughts were tending. There were other movements going on almost simultaneously with this, and all of them tending in the same direction. For instance, the Archbishop of Canterbury, Dr. Howley, as has been already intimated, had surrounded himself with a body of the most eminent divines in the kingdom—Hugh James Rose, reputed to be the greatest theologian of his day; Dr. Molesworth, eminent for his controversial ability; Mr. Lonsdale, afterwards bishop of Lichfield, and then enjoying a great reputation as preacher at Lincoln's Inn; Dr. Mill, recently returned from India after having ably presided over a college founded at Calcutta. All these were working together on the old lines of the pre-Jacobite Church, and urging their views, by preaching and by writing, in the pages of the *British Magazine* and the *Penny Sunday Reader*—the first edited by Hugh James Rose and a numerous band of coadjutors, chiefly clerical; the latter almost entirely written by Dr. Molesworth, in that vigorous, earnest, and emphatic style which distinguished his writings. These were all working together quietly, in constant communication with one another, and with a unity of thought and purpose which made their working very effectual. One result of their labours was an address drawn up by Dr. Molesworth, and presented to the archbishop, praying for the revival of Convocation; which, after a silence of considerably more than half a century, was allowed to hold a debate on the address to the king. It was not much, but it was something gained for the cause; a first step, indicating an attitude of resistance taken up by the Church.

But the deepest, most earnest, and most efficient movement which was taking place at this time was that which was being carried forward at Oxford. It was connected with that carried on by the little knot of able men that the Archbishop of Canterbury had gathered round him through the intervention of Mr. Hugh Rose, who, though a Cambridge man, had formed many acquaintances in the sister university, through his search for writers to assist him in carrying on the *British Magazine*. There the progress of religious liberalism was more pronounced, and the danger which it threatened to the Church more strongly exaggerated. There was an acute feeling that if she was to stand at all, she must be placed on a basis more logical and more satisfactory than the shallow and selfish Erastianism which then prevailed almost universally. The attempting revivers of the old Nonjuring principles published a series of tracts, in which their opinions were very plainly and recklessly asserted, and which presently raised against them a storm of bitter opposition.

The writers of these tracts were J. H. Newman; Keble, Professor of Poetry; Hurrell Froude; William Palmer, of Dublin and University College. These writers were afterwards joined by Dr. Pusey, Regius Professor of Hebrew and canon of Christchurch, whose age, position, and connections caused him to be forthwith placed at the head of the movement with which his name was henceforth inseparably connected. They were also denominated Tractarians, and by facetious adversaries, Newmaniacs. In our day they are called Ritualists; but this name did not come into vogue until long after Dr. Newman had left the Church of England and joined the Roman Church. Their doctrines, by no means new in themselves, were new to the generation to which they were propounded with a boldness that bordered on recklessness, and they created such consternation among Churchmen generally, that many of those who had at first gone heartily with them dropped off in alarm, as fresh and fresh developments of doctrine brought the leaders of the movement visibly nearer and nearer to the Roman Church and to Roman doctrine. And this feeling was further intensified when one after another of them went over to the Romish Church, and at length the real leader of the whole movement joined the Roman ranks, and published, in his celebrated essay on development, the grounds of his resolution to leave the Anglican communion and join the Church of Rome.

The aim with which these writers started, and which many of them continued to maintain, even after Dr. Newman had announced to the world that he found his position in the English Church no longer tenable, was the revival of dogmatic and religious teaching, and, contemporaneously with this, a disposition to look less unfavourably on the doctrines and practices of the Roman communion, culminating at last in an attempt to show that a man holding Romish doctrine might, nevertheless, with a good conscience, sign the Thirty-nine Articles, which were evidently levelled against that doctrine. This attempt was fortified by quotations from the Homilies, of which the thirty-fifth Article says that "they contain a godly and holy doctrine, and necessary for these times, as doth the former Book of Homilies." There can be no doubt that these Homilies contain teaching that is in accordance with the Romish system, while it is equally indisputable that the Articles are framed with a degree of vagueness which was intended to leave many of the questions to which they relate open and undecided. At length the celebrated tract, No. 90, caused the Bishop of Oxford to interpose, and to forbid the continuance of these works. But let Dr. Newman speak for himself in this matter. He thus concludes this celebrated tract: "They (the Articles) are evidently framed on the principle of leaving open large questions on which the controversy hinges. They state broadly extreme truths, and are silent about their adjustment. For instance, they say that all necessary faith must be proved from Scripture; but they do not say *who* is to prove it. They say that the Church has authority in controversies; they do not say *what* authority. They say that it may enforce nothing beyond Scripture; but do not say *where* the remedy lies when it does. They say that works *before* grace *and* justification are worthless and worse, and that works *after* grace *and* justification are acceptable; but they do not speak of all works *with* God's aid *before* justification. They say that men are lawfully called and sent to minister and preach, who are chosen and called by men who have public authority *given* them in the congregation; but they do not add *by whom* the authority is to be given. They say that councils called by *princes* may err; they do not determine whether councils called in the name of Christ may err." These statements are unquestionably true; but it is no less true that if the authors of the Articles could have foreseen the construction which the Tractarians put on their work, they would have taken care to protest against it in the strongest manner, and would most assuredly have so framed the Articles as to have prevented the possibility of their being interpreted in the manner advocated by the Tractarians.

Such was the state of things at Oxford in reference to the Tractarian movement. Another great centre of the spiritual development and activity which the tracts produced was the metropolis. There curates, who as undergraduates had sat under Pusey, Newman, and the other tract writers, preached the doctrines they had imbibed in the universities, and persuaded many of their rectors, and vicars also, to accept and teach them, or at least to tolerate their preaching of them ; and the teaching thus given roused fruitless and foolish opposition, which served only to help forward the propagation of doctrines which were unwisely opposed, and often unjustly stigmatized. Thus, by able and zealous exposition, and by opposition which was often ignorant and injudicious, the Tractarian movement was helped forward, and caused to spread like a leaven through all parts of the kingdom ; and, as it progressed, created more alarm, and met with a more deliberate opposition, ending in the reference of matters in dispute to the legal tribunals of the country, which were very far from being satisfactorily constituted for dealing with questions of this nature.

There were courts in the universities in which certain ecclesiastical questions could be tried, but their members were selected by the Vice-Chancellor of the university in which the supposed offence had been committed, and were liable to be influenced very much in their decisions by his theological bias, so that very little confidence was placed in decisions often given by heated partisans or by incompetent judges. Still more unsatisfactory was the case when a question was submitted, as occurred sometimes at Oxford, to the judgment of the members of Convocation of the university, who came up in numbers from London chambers, or country vicarages, to vote in approval or condemnation of works which they had perhaps never read, and of which they understood nothing but what they had gleaned from some party newspaper. But the tribunal to which all grave questions of this nature were reserved in the last resort, was the

Judicial Committee of the Privy Council, which had been very recently, and, it may be said, quite accidentally, called on to decide them.

Up to the reign of Henry VIII., appeals were made to the Pope in matters ecclesiastical; but when that monarch threw off the Papal authority, the appeals, which had hitherto been heard by the pontiff, were transferred to the archbishops of the two provinces. Subsequently, however, by the 25 Henry VIII. c. 19, it was directed that these appeals should be heard by the king himself in council; and the king was, by this statute, also empowered to issue a commission under the great seal, to hear appeals. The court thus erected was called the Court of Delegates, because its members were delegated by the king to decide cases which business or pleasure prevented him from hearing himself. It was usually composed to a puisne judge from each of the common law courts, and three or more doctors of civil law.

The king was also authorized to issue a commission of review, which was, in fact, an appeal from this court; but this right had become obsolete, and was very rarely exercised. When it was used, the case was referred to the Lord Chancellor. In the reign of King William, and in the first fervours of reforming zeal which attended the carrying of the Reform Bill of 1832, Lord Brougham, amongst other innovations that he made, introduced and carried a measure for the abolition of the Court of Delegates, and the transfer of its appellate jurisdiction to the king in council; and by two succeeding Acts of Parliament the sovereign was empowered to refer all appeals from ecclesiastical courts to the tribunal thus constituted.

Subsequent changes have been made, principally with the object of improving the constitution of the court, and removing objections which had been made to the manner in which its members were summoned. Hitherto there had been little or no resort to the tribunal of final appeal. During her long period of slumbrous inactivity, the Church had not felt the need of such an institution; but now, when her peace was roughly disturbed, and she was torn by violent intestine divisions, the newly constituted court was put into frequent requisition, without much inquiry either with regard to its origin, its history, or its constitution. Heated litigants, who resorted to it, took its authority and its right to decide the questions submitted to it for granted, and it was only when its decisions were adverse to their convictions, that they began jealously to scan and to contest its claims to be an ecclesiastical court.

One of the first questions which the Tractarians had raised, was that of the legality of prayers for the dead, closely connected with the Romish doctrine of purgatory. In the case of Breeks *v.* Woolfrey, it appeared that the respondent had erected a tomb, or headstone, in the churchyard of Carisbrooke, bearing inscriptions, amongst which the following were complained of:—" Pray for the soul of J. Woolfrey;" "It is a holy and wholesome thought to pray for the dead," 2 Maccabees xii. 44, 45.

The question raised by these inscriptions was tried in the Court of Arches, before Sir Herbert Jenner Fust, the judge of that court. It was argued that the doctrine affirmed in the above-cited passages was at variance with the twenty-second and thirty-fifth Articles, which sanctioned and confirmed the seventh Homily, and thereby pronounced prayers for the dead to be erroneous. But the judge decided that though they might be erroneous, they were not unlawful, and therefore he declared the Articles to be inadmissible; and the case was dismissed, with costs to be paid by the losing party. From this decision no appeal was attempted. In this case, therefore, the Tractarians gained the victory.

They were less fortunate when the celebrated tract, No. 90, which had caused the publication of the tracts to be stopped, came in question. It was an attempt made, and no doubt honestly made, by the author, Dr. Newman, to show that the Thirty-nine Articles might, with a safe conscience, be subscribed by persons who accepted all the doctrines of the Church of Rome, against which it was admitted by the author that these Articles were specially levelled. This tract was solemnly condemned by the Vice-Chancellor and the heads of houses of the university of Oxford.

Thus far the new court of appeal had not been resorted to. But the principle of interpretation advanced in tract No. 90 was strongly censured by Dr. Blomfield, bishop of London, who, in the year 1842, delivered a triennial charge of remarkable ability to the clergy of his diocese in St. Paul's Cathedral. This manifesto condemned the practice recommended in the tract, of putting interpretations on the Articles which were not warranted by their plain grammatical sense, and did not convey the intentions and opinions of those by whom the Articles were framed or imposed. Dr. Blomfield, however, spoke of the authors of these tracts with respect, and with a moderation that was not by any means always imitated by those who rushed into the controversy without having studied the writings they denounced. The bishop, on the contrary, spoke with a gravity befitting his high office, reminding those whom he addressed that good as well as evil had resulted from these publications.

In the year following Dr. Pusey preached a sermon in the cathedral of Christchurch, Oxford, in which he was alleged to have advocated the doctrine of transubstantiation. He was accordingly accused before the Board of Heresy of the university, and by it condemned to be suspended from preaching before the university for the space of two years—a sentence against which a protest was drawn up and signed, among many others, by Mr. Gladstone and Justice Coleridge, but which was angrily rejected by the Vice-Chancellor.

Meanwhile, Mr. Newman, after having attempted to revive the monastic system at Littlemore, resigned the vicarage of St. Mary at Oxford, which he had hitherto held, and openly joined the Roman communion, which he now believed and maintained to be the Catholic Church. He was led to take this step by the censure of the Bishop of Oxford (Dr. Bagot), to which his principles forced him to attach an exaggerated importance, and by the strongly expressed disapproval of the great body of the laity and the clergy of the Anglican Church. He had, no doubt, for a long time past been veering round to the position in which at length he finally settled. But the progress that his doctrines had made in the university was proved by the censures pronounced against Dr. Hampden, by the votes of a majority of the members of the Oxford Convocation, on the ground of the heresy which that divine was alleged to have taught. The university authorities, however, upheld and approved his teaching, which does not appear to have transgressed the fair and allowable limits of theological discussion in the Church of England.

Nor did the conflict of opinion which Newman, in leaving the English Church, bequeathed to her, cease here. The Rev. W. G. Ward, a Fellow of Baliol College, had published a work, entitled "The Ideal of a Christian Church," in which he took the same view of the Articles that had been taken in the celebrated tract, No. 90. For this offence he was summoned before the court of the Vice-Chancellor of the university. He was supported in his views by Dr. Pusey, who declared that he signed the Articles, as he had ever done since he had known what Catholic antiquity is, and to which our Church guides us, in their literal grammatical sense, determined, where it is ambiguous, by the faith of the whole Church before East and West were divided.

A great struggle took place. Both parties urged graduates from all parts of the kingdom to come up and vote on this occasion. The friends of Mr. Ward submitted the matter to Sir John Dodson and Mr. Bethell, afterwards Lord Chancellor Westbury. They considered the case which was put before them, and gave it as their opinion that the House of Convocation of the university of Oxford did not possess the power which the resident authorities of the university had invited them to exercise, of depriving Mr. Ward of his degrees in the manner or on the grounds that were proposed ; and that the statute, which proposed to annex a new sense to the subscription to the Articles, was illegal.

In deference to the opinion of these high authorities the proposed statute was withdrawn, but the proceedings against Mr. Ward were still persevered in. The Vice-Chancellor of the university, Dr. Wynter, submitted to the members of the Convocation the following resolution : " That the passages now read from the book entitled 'The Ideal of a Christian Church, considered in comparison with existing practice,' are utterly inconsistent with the Articles of Religion of the Church of England, and with the declaration in respect of these Articles made and subscribed by Mr. George Ward, previously and in order to his being admitted to the degrees of B.A. and M.A. respectively, and with good faith of him, the said Mr. George Ward, in respect to such declaration and subscription."

To this resolution the following amendment was moved by Dr. Grant, of New College: " That the passages now read from the book entitled 'The Ideal of the Christian Church considered' are worthy of grave censure ; but that the Convocation declines to express any opinion upon the good faith of the author, or to exercise the functions of an ecclesiastical tribunal by pronouncing judgment on the nature or degree of his offence."

A division was taken on the question thus submitted, and it proves the strength of the excitement that prevailed on the question, as well as the exertions that had been made to bring up voters from all parts of the kingdom, that the proposition of the Vice-Chancellor was supported by 777 voters, while the number in favour of the amendment was 386. It was then proposed that Mr. Ward should be deprived of the degrees to which he had been admitted in the university. The motion was carried by a much smaller majority; the votes in favour of the resolution were 569, and those against it 511. Among those who voted against the censure of Mr. Ward, were Mr. Gladstone, Dr. Hook, and Dr. Pusey. It was noticed, too, with exultation by the Tractarians, that Mr. Ward was loudly cheered by the undergraduates as he quitted the theatre. There could be no doubt what were the sympathies of the rising generation, which would soon become the risen generation, in the university.

The anti-Tractarians, having collected so large a number of their partisans, resolved to make use of the majority thus assembled to condemn the teaching of the celebrated tract, No. 90. But this attempt was defeated by the two proctors, who, in the university of Oxford, have a veto on all the proceedings of Convocation. When the proposition was made they rose together, and the senior proctor pronounced the sacramental words, "*Nobis procuratoribus non placet,*" which at once put an end to the matter.

Mr. Ward had been appointed to the vicarage of St. Saviour's Church, at Leeds, where, in spite of the public protests of Dr. Hook, the vicar of the old church at Leeds, he continued to preach doctrines and to carry on practices which more and more closely approximated to those of the Roman Catholic Church. At length he and his curates, finding their position in the Anglican Church to be no longer tenable, openly transferred themselves to the Roman communion, and were solemnly received into it by the Rev. Mr. Newman. These successive conversions, or, as they now began to be generally called, "perversions," increased the strong anti-Tractarian panic, and added fuel to the fire which had been kindled by what was termed the Papal aggression, the discussion on which was being at this very time carried on in Parliament with a good deal of vehemence and passionate feeling. In consequence of the line of conduct that was adopted in these discussions by Mr. Gladstone, an attempt was made by those who disapproved of the course he had taken, headed by Dr. Wynter, the vice-chancellor of the university, to prevent the return of that gentleman as a representative of the university in the House of Commons, which, though it failed at this time, ultimately proved to be successful when the representation of the university was contested in the year 1865.

While these things were going on at Oxford, the public opinion of the country had been violently agitated. The feeling, not only against the Tractarians, but also against the High Churchmen, had become very strong, and they were vehemently charged with dishonesty in eating, as was alleged at the time, the bread of the Church while trying to introduce Romish doctrines and practices.

The excitement was highest in the dioceses of Oxford and Exeter, the bishops of which were supposed to favour the new doctrines. In the latter diocese especially the feeling was very violent. At the time of which we are now speaking, it was generally the practice in all churches, except cathedrals, for the preacher to deliver his sermon in a black gown and cassock, the dress prescribed to be worn by the clergy on all public occasions by the canon, and therefore called canonicals. This dress is not mentioned in the communion service, in which the sermon is ordered to be delivered, and therefore there was plausible, or, as many thought, unanswerable reason for supposing that the surplice ought to be used for the sermon, as it was admitted that it ought to be for the other parts of the communion office, there being no order for any change of habit in the course of that service, and the change being supported only by custom. The Rev. Francis Courtenay, perpetual curate of the church of St. Sidwell, Exeter, was one of those who considered that the use of the surplice in the pulpit was enjoined by the rubric, and who had ventured to adopt it. This innovation, which in the present day has been so generally admitted, at that time excited serious and alarming riots, and the mayor of the city made a representation to the Bishop of Exeter of the danger to the public peace that would result if the incumbent of St. Sidwell persisted in wearing the surplice in that part of his ministrations which was carried on in the pulpit. The bishop advised Mr. Courtenay to yield to the wishes of the civil authorities, if he could do so with a good conscience, adding that he himself did not think the matter so free from doubt as to prevent him from acting on his bishop's advice thus given. On the other hand, the Bishop of London, who had urged some of his clergy to preach in the surplice, when he saw that a storm was likely to be raised by the practice, privately and confidentially commanded those who had followed his advice to desist from the practice he had enjoined; but, to the great distress of some of them, refused to allow them to state that they were making the change in submission to the order of their bishop. At this conjuncture of affairs, the aged Archbishop of Canterbury issued an address to the clergy and laity of his province, in which he counselled forbearance and toleration, recommending that where innovations had been introduced without opposition they should be maintained, but that they should not be forced on recalcitrant congregations. He admitted the desirableness of uniformity in the manner of conducting public worship, but urged that diversity in some cases was unavoidable, and was probably contemplated by the framers of our liturgy.

Men's minds were at this moment too violently heated to allow of their listening to these calm and sensible recommendations. Nor were the very High

Churchmen the only sufferers at this time. The very Low Churchmen did not altogether escape. The Rev. J. Shore was prosecuted in the Court of Arches by the Bishop of Exeter. This gentleman had officiated in the diocese of that prelate without a licence, and had afterwards preached in several Nonconformist places of worship, having previously taken the oaths required by the Toleration Act. He therefore pleaded that he was no longer subject to the jurisdiction of the bishop. But Sir Herbert Jenner Fust rejected the plea on the ground of the indelibility of holy orders. Mr. Shore appealed from this decision to the Judicial Committee of the Privy Council, but his appeal was rejected on the technical ground that it had not been sent in at the proper stage of the trial, and for that reason could not be entertained. Mr. Shore was therefore finally confined to prison for contempt of court, in not having paid the cost of the proceedings in accordance with the sentence that had been pronounced against him.

About this time, Lord J. Russell, the then Prime Minister, made two episcopal appointments which were very generally regarded as evidences of a fixed determination on his part to curb and, if possible, to crush the High Church party, and, in doing so, to outrage the feelings and opinions of a large body—probably, a considerable majority—of the clergy. This he did by advising the Crown in the appointment of two bishops, one to the see of Hereford and the other to the newly created bishopric of Manchester. The man whom he selected to fill the first of these two sees was Dr.

Hampden, Regius Professor of Divinity of the university of Oxford. No appointment that could be made was more likely to bring on a struggle than that of the man whom Lord J. Russell had thus selected to fill the see of Hereford.

Dr. Hampden had been appointed, in the year 1836, to be Regius Professor of Divinity in the university of Oxford. He represented, in the university, that religious liberalism which the Tractarians regarded with horror and aversion, and which was in deadly antagonism to their cherished beliefs and to those of the High Church party in general. His appointment to the important post of Regius Professor of Divinity by Lord Melbourne had called forth loud and angry protests, and ended for the time in his being censured by the majority of the Convocation of the university. Several of the bishops also refused to receive for ordination persons who, according to the usual practice, brought certificates of having attended the lectures of the Regius Professor. However, in the year 1842, his friends had succeeded in placing him as chairman at the head of the Theological Board of the university, an act which virtually condoned him. They also attempted to reverse the censure passed on him in 1836; but in this effort they were defeated by a majority of 334 against 219. Nothing daunted by his defeat, Dr. Hampden continued to press his views in antagonism to those of the party by which he had been condemned. He required candidates for the degree of Bachelor of Divinity to write on the following exercises which he gave out to them, and which were evidently intended to exclude those who had adopted the views taught and inculcated by the leaders of the Tractarian party:—

"1. The Church of England does not teach, nor can it be proved from Scripture, that any change takes place in the elements of consecration in the Lord's Supper.

"2. It is a mode of expression calculated to give erroneous views of divine revelation, to speak of Scripture and tradition as joint authorities in the matter of Christian doctrine."

A Mr. Macmullen, who was one of the candidates to whom these exercises were given out, and who entertained the views which they required him to controvert, refused to write on them, and was consequently denied the degree he sought to obtain. From this decision he appealed to the delegates of appeal in congregation, who upheld the action and teaching of the Regius Professor.

In the year 1847, Lord J. Russell appointed him to the bishopric of Hereford. And now, for the first time since the Reformation, a struggle took place between the recommending minister and a large and influential part of the clergy and laity of the Church, who regarded Dr. Hampden's opinions as heretical. A protest against the proposed appointment, couched in respectful language, was signed by several prelates of widely different opinions—by the primate, by the moderately High Church Bishop of London, by the decidedly Low Church Bishop of Winchester; it deprecated the intended appointment of Dr. Hampden on the ground of the condemnation that had been passed on him by the university, and of the strong objection to it which was felt and expressed by the great majority of the clergy. To this protest Lord John Russell made a reply, of which the following is the most essential part:—

"I observe that your lordships do not state any want of confidence on your part in the soundness of Dr. Hampden's doctrine. Your lordships refer me to a decree of the university of Oxford passed eleven years ago, and founded upon lectures delivered fifteen years ago. Since the date of that decree, Dr. Hampden has acted as Regius Professor of Divinity. The university of Oxford and many bishops, as I am told, have required certificates of attendance on his lectures before they proceeded to ordain candidates who had received their education at Oxford. He has likewise preached sermons, for which he has been honoured with the approbation of several prelates of our Church. Several months before I named Dr. Hampden to the queen for the see of Hereford, I signified my intention to the Archbishop of Canterbury, and did not receive from him any discouragement.

"In these circumstances it appears to me, that should I withdraw my recommendation of Dr. Hampden, which has been sanctioned by the queen, I should virtually assent to the doctrine that a decree of the university of Oxford is a perpetual bar of exclusion against a clergyman of eminent learning and irreproachable life; and that, in fact, the supremacy, which is now by law vested in the Crown, is to be transferred to a majority of the members of one of the universities: nor should it be forgotten that many of the most prominent of that majority have since joined the communion of the Church of Rome. I deeply regret the feeling that is said to be common among the clergy on this subject. But I cannot sacrifice the reputation of Dr. Hampden, the rights of the Crown, and what I believe to be the true interests of the Church, to a feeling which I believe to be founded on misapprehension and fomented by prejudice."

The appointment was therefore carried out, in spite of remonstrances from various quarters that were made against it. One of its most determined opponents was the Dean of Hereford, who, in his official capacity, was one of the electors of the bishop, and, as he contended, one whose concurrence was essential to the validity of the election. He had in vain addressed a memorial to the queen against the appointment. A solemn service was held, according to the usual practice in all such cases. The Holy Ghost was invoked to guide the electors to a right decision, and the dean, as he had threatened, gave his vote against the election, as did also one of the canons (Dr. Huntingford). But the majority of the chapter, whether influenced by the dread of the penalties of præmunire, or really convinced that the proposed appointment was one that was proper and desirable, gave their votes in favour of the nominee of the Crown.

But the election, made in the manner we have described, had still to be confirmed at Bow Church, Cheapside, London. The usual preliminaries having been gone through, proclamation was made, calling on all objectors to come forward and make their objections. Thereupon Mr. Townsend, the proctor of the opposing party, stood up and announced that he appeared on behalf of the Revs. R. W. Huntley, J. Jebb, and W. F. Percival, to oppose the election. The Vicar-General, whose duty it was to preside on the occasion, refused to receive the document stating the objection, but after some discussion he consented to hear Dr. Addams, who argued on behalf of the objectors that, under the 25 Henry VIII. c. 20, the Vicar-General was bound to receive the objections. This argument, however, was overruled. And proclamation being again made inviting objectors to come forward, and pronouncing them contumacious for not coming forward, the ceremony concluded amidst the laughter of those who had come to witness this solemn farce. Still the objectors did not consider themselves finally defeated. From the spiritual court they appealed to the Court of Queen's Bench, asking for a mandamus to compel the Vicar-General, on behalf of the Archbishop of Canterbury, to hear the case. The Attorney-General appeared for the Crown to show cause against the rule being granted.

When the question was thus brought before the Court of Queen's Bench the judges there were equally divided in opinion. Two of the puisne justices, Erle and Coleridge, both men of great ability and extensive legal knowledge, viewed the matter as a question of law, and, looking at it in that manner, were of opinion that the mandamus should issue. On the other hand, the Lord

Chief Justice Denman and Judge Patteson regarded the question as one of polity rather than of law. The former thus delivered his opinion: "Looking to the frightful state of theological animosity at present, the granting of the rule would create and perpetuate it for perhaps two years, by the sanction it would give, at the avoidance of every see, to the course of summoning all mankind as objectors to the appointment of the Crown, in an open court, which might, in fact, never be closed. Bearing in mind the discretion of this court, even were it allowed the proceeding complained of to be judicial, and thought that the judge might be compelled to hear objectors, I feel bound to refuse the writ. I have, however, no doubt as to the law. With reference to the able argument of my brother Coleridge, it only confirms me as to the danger of exposing the clear construction of the Acts of Parliament to those who would bring down the forgotten books and wipe off, in this court, the cobwebs from decretals and canons of which it knows nothing."

The mild and amiable Dr. Howley did not survive to consecrate Dr. Hampden. The events we have recorded caused him great anxiety, and probably hastened his decease, which took place on the 11th of February, 1848. He was succeeded by Dr. Sumner, a most amiable, kind-hearted, and pious prelate, with a very decided leaning towards the Evangelical party, which greatly influenced him in the exercise of his patronage, and sometimes caused him to be seriously imposed on by unworthy persons. By him Dr. Hampden was consecrated in the private chapel of Lambeth Palace.

A somewhat similar struggle to that to which Dr. Hampden was exposed was also encountered by Dr. Lee, who was appointed to be the first bishop of the diocese of Manchester. The opposition to the completion of this appointment was based, not as in the case of Dr. Hampden on doctrinal, but on moral grounds. Mr. Gutteridge, a Birmingham surgeon, had openly, in a large public meeting, charged Mr. Lee with drunkenness on certain specified occasions, and even when engaged in the celebration of divine service, and it was strongly contended that before he was consecrated to an office so sacred as that of a bishop he ought to be required to purge himself of this accusation, by bringing an action for libel against his accuser. This argument was strongly urged by Dr. Molesworth, who was the holder of the most important benefice within the new diocese of Manchester. He had addressed a letter on the subject to Archbishop Howley, who, taking the Bishop of London with him, at once drove to the residence of Lord J. Russell, and laid the letter before him. The law officers of the Crown were consulted, and Lord J. Russell, notwithstanding the arguments of the two prelates, insisted on the appointment being at once carried out. In this case Mr. Gutteridge appeared, and, in answer to the summons of the court, tendered his objections, which were refused. He was again called on to offer his objections, and pronounced contumacious for not offering them.

Thus an ecclesiastical farce, similar to that enacted in the case of Dr. Hampden, was gone through with no other result but that of conclusively showing how completely the Church was subjugated to the State. This was a condition of things which had all along existed, but of the existence of which few were aware, and fewer still were willing to admit a fact which daily was becoming more painfully evident. By the great majority of the clergy it was strenuously denied, and the feeling they entertained against the minister who had outraged their most cherished beliefs, contributed in no small degree to bring about the downfall of his ministry; for the clergy, though a scattered, were still a mighty host, and, when brought into combination, as they were by their disapprobation of the minister's proceedings, exercised a very powerful influence.

Men's minds were now heated with controversy, and events consequently followed one another in the Church with unprecedented rapidity. Undeterred by the failure of Dr. Marsh, of Peterborough, to exclude from his diocese men holding Calvinistic views, or at least such of them as sought ordination or licences, the Bishop of Exeter took the bolder course of endeavouring to exclude rectors or vicars entertaining views which he deemed to be heterodox, but which the new Archbishop of Canterbury would probably approve, and certainly would not condemn. The question was raised with regard to the institution of a Mr. Gorham, from whose name the trial is known as the Gorham case. It appears from the judgment given by Sir Herbert Jenner Fust, before whom the question was tried in the first instance, that the Rev. Cornelius Gorham, B.D., was in the year 1846 presented by the Lord Chancellor to the vicarage of St. Just, in the county of Cornwall. On that occasion he produced such testimonials as to his learning, ability, moral conduct, and sound religious principles as satisfied the bishop, who instituted him to the living to which he had been appointed without further examination.

In the year following, Mr. Gorham was presented by the Lord Chancellor to the vicarage of Brampford Speke (in lieu of that of St. Just), and on the 2nd of December he applied to the bishop requesting an early appointment for institution to the benefice. A correspondence ensued between Mr. Gorham and the bishop's secretary, which ended in a refusal on the part of the bishop to institute him without examination, or to countersign the usual testimonial from three beneficed clergymen which is required from every clerk in holy orders presenting himself to the bishop for admission to a living within his diocese; and he assigned as a reason for this refusal that Mr. Gorham had, in his opinion, held and taught doctrines contrary to the discipline and the teaching of the English Church. The Chancellor, nevertheless, persisted in his nomination, and Mr. Gorham, under protest, submitted to the examination required by the bishop. It was commenced on the 17th of December, 1847, and was continued with intervals to the 11th of March, on which day Mr. Gorham, who had been required to answer no fewer than 149 questions, was at length informed that the bishop would decline to institute him, and on the 20th of that month he received a formal statement of reasons for this refusal. The matter was then brought before Sir Herbert Jenner Fust, the judge of the Court of Arches appointed by the late Archbishop of Canterbury.

This trial raised a question of the highest importance, and one that most especially interested two very powerful classes—the patrons of livings who were in danger of losing their patronage, or at all events of having the exercise of it considerably trammelled; and the clergy of the Evangelical party, who might be excluded for the future from preferment in the Church, if the claim of the bishop should be established. We pass over the proceedings in the Court of Arches, which were set aside by the higher court, and go on directly to the trial which took place before the Court of Appeal, the Judicial Committee of the Privy Council. The members of the committee who sat on this occasion were the two archbishops, Lord Chief Justice Campbell, the Bishop of London, Lord Langdale, the Master of the Rolls, Mr. Baron Parke, Sir J. Knight Bruce, Vice-Chancellor, the Right Honourable Dr. Lushington, and the Right Honourable Pemberton Leigh.

The judgment given by these high authorities, and agreed to by all of them, with the exception of the Bishop of London and Vice-Chancellor Bruce, now probably interests no one; but the concluding part of it, which deals with the general reasons on which the decision was based, is of high value, laying down, as it does, principles which will probably be applied in all similar cases, should any such arise, and will guide and influence the decisions of courts of appeal in ecclesiastical cases, however they may be constituted or whatever changes they may undergo.

"Upright and conscientious men cannot in all respects agree upon subjects so difficult; and the only question for us to decide is, whether Mr. Gorham's doctrine is contrary to or repugnant to the doctrine of the Church of England as by law established; and if Mr. Gorham's doctrine is not so contrary or repugnant, it cannot afford a legal ground for refusing him institution to the living to which he has been lawfully presented.

"This court, constituted for the purpose of advising her Majesty in matters that come within its competency, has no jurisdiction or authority to settle matters of faith, or to determine what ought, in any particular, to be the doctrine of the Church of England. Its duty extends only to the consideration of that which is by law established to be the doctrine of the Church of England, upon the true and legal construction of her Articles and formularies. It appears that opinions, which we cannot in any important particular distinguish from those entertained by Mr. Gorham, have been propounded and maintained, without censure or reproach, by many eminent and illustrious prelates and divines, who have adorned the Church from the time when the Articles were first established. The mere fact that such opinions have been propounded and maintained by persons so eminent and so much respected, as well as by very many others, appears to us sufficiently to prove that the liberty which was left by the Articles and formularies has been actually enjoyed and exercised by the members and ministers of the Church of England."

While this decision set at rest the alarms of patrons of livings, and of members of the Evangelical party, it roused the indignation of the High Churchmen, who regarded the doctrine of baptismal regeneration as a fundamental and essential doctrine of the Church, and one that was laid down in the baptismal services with a clearness that it seemed to them impossible to gainsay.

The struggle, therefore, was only begun. The defeated party was determined to die hard, and not to leave a stone unturned, in order to obtain the reversal of a judgment which they regarded as fraught with danger and injustice to the Church. There was an appeal to the Queen's Bench, then to the Court of Exchequer; but all in vain. Each appeal ended in the confirmation of the original judgment. Then the Bishop of Exeter still refusing to induct Mr. Gorham, Archbishop Sumner was called in to perform that function, which, no doubt, he did with hearty readiness, and was excommunicated by the Bishop of Exeter for his pains; and so Mr. Gorham was at last fairly and legally installed in his living of Brampford Speke-cum-Cowley. This controversy having been thus finally set at rest, the opponents of Mr. Gorham next attacked the court by which the case had been decided. They objected to it on various grounds—on the ground of the manner in which its members were selected, on the ground of its composition, of its competence to deal with ecclesiastical questions, of the accidental manner in which, as Lord

Brougham, who brought it into existence, testified, it had chanced to become a court of appeal for the final decision of ecclesiastical questions. Accordingly, the Bishop of London, an able and moderate prelate, greatly respected by men of all parties, brought into the House of Lords a Bill intended to remove the objections which he, in common with many other thoughtful men, entertained against the Court of Appeal, as then constituted. His proposal was to substitute the bishops for the Court of Appeal in cases involving questions of faith and doctrine.

"When matters of fact," he observed, "and clear enunciation of the law are concerned, the present constitution of the Judicial Committee leaves nothing to be desired; but when faith and doctrine are in question, that court is not competent according to the original constitution of the Church. I can conceive questions so new, that members of the Judicial Committee of the Privy Council would not even understand the terms in which they were couched, whilst a prelate of the Church would consider them as the mere alphabet of his theology. It is impossible for an ecclesiastical tribunal to give a decision on any point of doctrine without materially affecting the doctrine itself; a succession of such decisions by a tribunal including members very ignorant of divinity, careless of such matters, or even unsound, would affect the stability of the Church, both as a teacher of truth and as a national institution. It has been the principle of our constitution from the earliest to the present time, that such cases should be left, not only to ecclesiastical, but to spiritual judges. When the Court of Chancery starts a point of common law, it seeks from the Courts of Common Law to know what the common law is; when a point of foreign law is raised, our courts deal with it as a matter of science, to be proved, like other matters of fact, by the testimony of witnesses practically conversant with the subject; when the Court of Admiralty has to decide by the rules of nautical science, it calls in the assistance of the elder brethren of the Trinity House. In the Established Church of Scotland, the final decision of all questions of false doctrine is left with the courts which that Church considers competent to decide these questions. That is exactly the principle that it is desired to introduce in this Bill."

After considering some objections which might be made to the measure he proposed, he appealed to the House to accept it with very unusual earnestness. Overcome by his emotion, he was obliged to pause for a moment, and then, amidst solemn silence, offered up a prayer that He who of old committed to the Church the sacred deposit of His truth, might guide their lordships to a right conclusion. This address concluded amidst warm expressions of sympathy and approval from all parts of the House. Nevertheless, after a long debate, in which the measure was strenuously opposed by the Marquis of Lansdowne, on the part of the Government, a division took place on the question, when the numbers were—for the Bill, 51; against it, 84; majority, 33. Thus the question raised in the Gorham case was finally set at rest, but the party spirit it had excited was again vehemently roused by what was at the time termed the papal aggression.

Up to the month of September, in the year 1850, the Roman Catholics of England had been ruled in matters ecclesiastical by bishops *in partibus infidelium*, as they were termed; that is, by bishops who did not bear the titles of the sees over which they really presided, but derived them from places into which Christianity had not yet been introduced. There were eight districts, or vicariates, into which England was then divided; but it was now formally announced that, in the opinion of the Pope and his advisers, the time had come in which the form of ecclesiastical government which freely prevailed in other countries might be restored in England. The Pope further announced that, in forming this judgment, he felt that the circumstances of times and things had rendered the government of the Catholics of England by vicars apostolic no longer necessary; and, indeed, that such a change had taken place as called for the establishment of the ordinary episcopal rule in this kingdom. He added that the vicars apostolic of England had unanimously prayed for it, that petitions in the same sense had been presented to him by very many among the clergy, and by laymen distinguished by their virtues and their birth, and that a desire for the hierarchy was entertained by the greater number of the Catholics of England. In compliance with the wishes thus conveyed, the Pope decreed and ordained that there should be for the future an archdiocese of

Westminster, and dioceses of Southwark, Hexham, Beverley, Liverpool, Salford, Shrewsbury, Newport and Minevia, Clifton, Plymouth, Nottingham, Birmingham, and Northampton. According to this arrangement the kingdom of England would comprise one ecclesiastical province, which would be composed of one archbishop, or metropolitan, and of twelve bishops, his suffragans. It will be noticed that, in this arrangement, care was taken to avoid assuming the names of sees already occupied by bishops of the Anglican communion. Dr. Wiseman was raised to the rank of cardinal, and was appointed to be archbishop of the new diocese of Westminster, and administrator apostolic of the diocese of Southwark.

The letters containing these announcements were couched in the pompous and pretentious style which had come down from the days of Hildebrand, and, though probably not intended to give offence, were calculated to cause very great irritation. The "aggression" would, however, have passed without attracting much dispute, if certain persons in high positions had not drawn attention to it. Foremost among those to whom it gave bitter offence was the Prime Minister, Lord J. Russell. He was already deeply offended at the conduct of the Tractarians, who had taken exception to his episcopal appointments, and to various measures of ecclesiastical liberalism which he had promoted; and now, without consultation with his colleagues, and very much against the opinion of many of them, he issued the following epistle, which, from the circumstance of its being addressed to the then

Bishop of Durham, became famous under the name of the Durham letter. As this document had very important political and ecclesiastical consequences, and exercised a very powerful influence over the course of events in the Church, we give it in its entirety. The bishop's letter has not been published, but its tenor may be inferred from the following reply that it drew from Lord J. Russell :—

"I agree with you in considering the late aggression of the Pope upon our Protestantism as insolent and insidious, and I therefore feel as indignant as you can do upon the subject. I not only promoted to the utmost of my power the claims of the Roman Catholics to all civil rights, but I thought it right, and even desirable, that the ecclesiastical system of the Roman Catholics should be the means of giving instruction to the numerous Irish immigrants in London and elsewhere, who, without such help, would be left in heathen ignorance. This might have been done, however, without any such innovation as that which we have now seen.

"It is impossible to confound the recent measures of the Pope with the division of Scotland into dioceses by the Episcopal Church, or the arrangement of districts in England by the Wesleyan Conference. There is an assumption of power in all the documents which have come from Rome, a pretension of supremacy over the realm of England, and a claim to sole and undivided sway, which is inconsistent with the Queen's supremacy, and the right of our bishops and clergy, and with the spiritual independence of the nation as asserted even in Roman Catholic times. I confess, however, that my alarm is not equal to my indignation. Even if it should appear that the ministers and servants of the Pope in this country have not transgressed the law, I feel persuaded that we are strong enough to repel any outward attacks. The liberty of Protestantism has been enjoyed too long in England to allow of any successful attempt to impose a foreign yoke upon our minds and consciences. No foreign prince or potentate will be permitted to fasten his fetters on a nation which has so long and so nobly vindicated its right to freedom of opinion, civil, political, and religious. Upon this subject, then, I will only say that the present state of the law shall be carefully examined, and the propriety of adopting any proceedings with reference to the recent assumption of power deliberately considered. There is a danger, however, which alarms me much more than any aggression of a foreign sovereign. Clergymen of our Church who have signed the Thirty-nine Articles and acknowledged in explicit terms the Queen's supremacy, have been the most forward in leading their flocks step by step to the very verge of the precipice. The honour paid to saints, the claim of infallibility for the Church, the superstitious use of the sign of the cross, the muttering of the liturgy so as to disguise the language in which it is written, the recommendation of auricular confession, and the administration of penance and absolution,—all these things are pointed out by clergymen of the Church of England as worthy of adoption, and are now openly reprehended by the Bishop of London in his charge to the clergy of the diocese. What, then, is the danger to be apprehended from a foreign prince of no great power, compared to the danger within the gates from the unworthy sons of the Church of England herself? I have little hope that the propounders and framers of the innovations will desist from their insidious course. But I rely with confidence on the people of England, and I will not bate a jot of heart and hope so long as the glorious principles and the immortal martyrs of the Reformation shall be held in reverence by the great mass of a nation which looks with contempt on the mummeries of superstition, and with scorn at the laborious endeavours which are now being made to confine the intellect and enslave the soul."

Scarcely was the ink with which this letter was written dry, before Lord J. Russell received from Cardinal Wiseman explanations which must have satisfied him of the injustice of many of the charges against the Pope that it contained, and must have caused him to regret having launched this element of bitterness amongst a highly excited population, without previous consultation with his colleagues, and at a moment when it was likely to cause serious breaches of the peace. For it was sent out just at the time when the discovery of the Gunpowder Plot was about to be commemorated, and effigies of Guy Fawkes were committed to the flames in memory of the happy escape of James I. and his Parliament. On this occasion, the Pope and his cardinals figured in the place of Fawkes, and were consumed amidst rioting, bonfires, squibs, crackers, rockets, and blazing tar barrels. Fortunately no very serious mischief was done.

After this came presentation of petitions and addresses to the Queen from the city of London, from the two universities, and from various other less influential and important quarters; also rioting at St. Paul's, Knightsbridge, where the practices condemned in the Durham letter were being actively carried on, and ending at length, by the desire of the Bishop of London, in the resignation of Mr. Bennett, the incumbent of that church, who, however, was almost directly after appointed by the Marchioness of Bath, its patroness, to the well-endowed benefice of Frome, in the diocese of Bath and Wells.

The Parliament of 1851 was opened on the 4th of February, and the Speech from the throne gave promise of legislation, such as had been foreshadowed by the Durham letter, but couched in terms as pompous and grandiloquent as if an invasion of the country by the Pope had been intended. In reply, it was justly remarked by Mr. Roebuck that this so-called territorial aggression was no new thing; that it had been begun years ago, and had been sanctioned by the noble lord himself. The measure by which the pledges he had given in the Durham letter and in the Queen's Speech were carried into effect, was introduced into the House of Commons by Lord J. Russell on the 7th of February. This Bill prohibited the assumption of titles taken by Roman Catholics from any place or territory situated within the United Kingdom, and it contained clauses rendering void all acts done by them, and forfeiting to the crown all bequests made to them under such titles. It was admitted by Lord J. Russell, in the speech he delivered in introducing the measure, that the Pope, in the course of an interview that Lord Minto had with him, pointed to the document which announced the "aggression," saying at the same time, " There is something that concerns you ; " but Lord J. Russell asserted that Lord Minto had not looked into the paper, and had not been distinctly invited to do so or to call the attention of the English Government to it. The measure, however, was not destined to go far. The followers of the late Sir R. Peel strongly objected to it, and it soon appeared that without their assistance the Government would be unable to carry it through. Lord J. Russell therefore resigned, and Lord Stanley was called in by the queen to take office ; but finding that he was unable to form a ministry, she consulted the Duke of Wellington, and, acting under his advice, requested Lord J. Russell to reconstruct his administration, which, in compliance with the queen's request, he undertook to do, and succeeded in doing. The Ecclesiastical Titles Bill was once more introduced, but in a very mitigated form ; the clauses which had been chiefly objected to being left out, and the measure being thereby reduced to a simple Parliamentary protest against the assumption of territorial titles by Roman Catholic ecclesiastics. But even after this fundamental modification, the Bill encountered very considerable opposition. Graham, Plunket, Denman, Brougham, Macaulay, all disapproved of it. The first-mentioned of these eminent men exclaimed, when it was brought in for the second reading, " There may have been some movement towards Rome, on the surface of what may be called the higher ranks ;

but the deep under-current of the feeling of this country is essentially Protestant. It is written in their very heart's core; what is more, it is written in their Bible, to which they have access; and while they enjoy those privileges and possess those feelings, we have no occasion for a Bill like this. I say there is no danger in England which justifies it—every feeling in Ireland condemns it. It is a brand of discord cast down to inflame the passions of the people; and with confidence in the wisdom of Parliament, I hope and confidently predict the Bill will never pass into a law."

While these things were being carried on in Parliament, the Protestant feelings of the people outside were strongly agitated. The Tractarian movement, which had been occupied chiefly with questions of doctrine to which the people gave comparatively little heed, was now gradually developing into a ritualistic movement, which appealed to the eyes of men, and produced strong excitement, especially among the working classes, who are more prone to be stirred by ritualistic innovations than by doctrinal novelties.

The bishops observed the progress of this feeling with alarm, and assembled for the purpose of deliberating on the manner in which this new development of Tractarianism should be encountered. And as the result of their deliberations, they issued a manifesto to the clergy, in which they observed that the introduction of the ceremonies which were now beginning to be distinguished by the denomination of ritualistic, were wholly incompatible with any uniformity of worship whatsoever, and at variance with the universal practice of the Catholic Church, which has never given to the officiating ministers of separate congregations any such large discretion in the adoption of ritual observance as the Ritualists claimed for themselves. They exhorted the clergy earnestly to avoid all unnecessary deviations from this rule. The Bishop of Exeter summoned a synod of the clergy of his diocese, which the Dean of Exeter and some members of the chapter declined to attend, but to which thirty out of the thirty-two deaneries into which the diocese was divided sent representatives. It was probably the first diocesan synod held in England since the Reformation. It adopted a protest presented by the bishop in favour of the doctrine of baptismal regeneration, and it censured the Papal appointment of a bishop to the see of Plymouth as schismatical, and therefore void.

On the 4th day of July, the Ecclesiastical Titles Bill reached its final stage, and was somewhat hastily and unexpectedly sent up to the House of Lords. In the course of the explanations which were given, Mr. Gladstone took occasion thus to condemn the Bill: "It is hostile to the institutions of this country, more especially to its established religion, because it would teach it to rely on other support than that of the spiritual strength and vitality which alone can give it vigour; because its tendency is to undermine and weaken the authority of the law in Ireland; because it is disparaging to the great principle of religious freedom on which this wise and understanding people has permanently built its legislation of late years; and, lastly, because it would tend to relax and destroy those bonds of concord and goodwill which ought to unite all classes and persuasions of Her Majesty's subjects."

In the Upper House the measure passed easily, and with little delay. The debate on the second reading occupied two nights; in one night more the Bill went through committee unchanged, and soon after it received the royal assent.

While these things were being transacted in Parliament and in the country, Cardinal Wiseman was treating the demonstrations of which he was the chief object with tranquil disregard. As already remarked, he had written to Lord J. Russell a sensible letter, in which he explained that the substitution of bishops for vicars apostolic and the changes made in the arrangements of the districts or dioceses were purely ecclesiastical arrangements, which ought not to have caused alarm, and were not intended to give offence. Lord J. Russell probably already repented of the precipitation with which he had acted, but it was too late for him to withdraw from the position he had taken up.

In the country, and especially in the Church, great efforts were made to keep up the agitation which the "aggression" and the Durham letter had produced. Many of the bishops took the matter up warmly, and through their archdeacons and other officers obtained numerous addresses; but in spite of all the efforts made to fan the flame, it gradually died out, and the attention of the party which had chiefly stirred the embers was drawn into another direction by the agitation produced by the attempt, ultimately crowned with success, to obtain the admission of Jews into the House of Commons, and consequently to allow them to legislate for the Anglican Church. Another result of the feeling which the Papal aggression had produced was to cause a strong agitation against ritualistic practices assimilating the services of the Church of England to those of the Church of Rome.

At St. Paul's, Knightsbridge, though some concessions were made to the anti-ritualistic feeling, they were by no means sufficient to satisfy the party that had driven out Mr. Bennett, and in other places the practices and the opposition to them were carried on with unabated vigour. The church of St. George's in the East especially was the scene of tumults such as have seldom before or since been enacted in any place of worship. The Rev. Bryan King, the incumbent of this church, had assumed vestments in the communion service, and introduced other obnoxious practices, and thus caused riots which were carried on by roughs who were evidently destitute of every kind of religious principles, and made the practices that had been introduced a mere pretext for the indulgence of the most brutal profanity, shouting, whistling, introducing savage dogs into the church, hustling and insulting the clergy and those who assisted them in the performance of divine service, and disturbing the whole neighbourhood, producing such a state of feeling there that no one wearing the garb of a clergyman could make his appearance in it without danger of being assaulted. These riots rose to such a pitch, and were continued for so long a time, that the Bishop of London, though strongly opposed to the practices which had given rise to this mob violence, felt himself forced to assume an authority that did not belong to him, but which the circumstances of the case imperatively required him to exercise, and ordered the church to be closed for a time, in the hope of thus putting an end to the unseemly brawling of which it had been the scene. In this hope, however, he was disappointed. When the church was reopened, the disturbances were renewed with greater violence and more shocking profanity than ever; and though the vestments and the practices that had originally caused them were discarded, the riots were continued without abatement until the Rev. Bryan King exchanged to another parish.

We have now traced the rise and progress in the Church of the Low Church or Evangelical, and the High Church or orthodox party, and we shall attempt to follow the fortunes of another party which now began to occupy a more and more prominent position, namely, the Broad Church party—a party which has gone far beyond the old Latitudinarianism of Tillotson, Tenison, and their followers.

Throughout the earlier part of the period to which this work relates, the chief religious activity was to be found amongst the Nonconformists, and almost all the stirrings of religious thought which occurred in the country originated entirely with them. Thus the Evangelical movement in the Church was due to the influence which Wesley exerted outside of it, and was, in fact, nothing more than the gradual penetration into the Church of the principles and the feelings which he and his followers had propagated. But from the period of the passing of the Reform Bill of 1832, a great change had taken place in this respect. The intellectual and spiritual energy which seemed to have abandoned the Church when she was in comparative safety reappeared in the hour of her extreme peril. We have already referred to the origin and diffusion of the Tractarian movement, and have pointed out the manner in which it arose out of the great struggle for reform—that it was, in fact, an earnest effort made to withstand the advances of religious liberalism, which, allied as it was with political liberalism, seemed ready, like an all-devouring deluge, to overwhelm and break down the dykes and fences which had hitherto been regarded as the chief securities of the Established Church. We have seen how the Tractarians rallied the forces of the Church in order to make a stand against the assaults which were threatened against her, and which they feared would, if not strenuously withstood, bring about her entire overthrow. We have seen, too, how Tractarianism, by a natural process of evolution, developed into Ritualism, and we shall now proceed to point out how, at once modifying the religious liberalism it so much dreaded, and, on the other hand, being modified by it, by their joint action they produced other important developments of doctrine and worship.

The Tractarian system was, in its nature, both doctrinal and æsthetic, and each of these aspects had helped to obtain for it the adhesion and the energetic support of many youthful and enthusiastic spirits. The doctrinal principle of Tractarianism was the authority of the Church—an authority which was supposed, in the last resort, to depend on the right of dispensing or withholding the two sacraments of Baptism and the Lord's Supper—regarded as being "generally necessary to salvation"—by an ordained priesthood, tracing, as was affirmed, its spiritual descent through a long succession of bishops to those holy men of old on whom the Apostles themselves had laid their consecrating hands—thereby transmitting through all generations of those who succeeded them an authority and a sacredness which retains its full force and efficacy in the present day.

The claim to exercise this authority was based, it was alleged, on the consent of the primitive Church, and comprehended what had been taught always everywhere, and by all (semper ubique et ab omnibus), a statement which of course must be accepted by those who most loudly proclaimed it, with some degree of reserve. It was entirely opposed to the celebrated and then generally received dictum of Chillingworth—"The Bible, and the Bible alone, is the religion of Protestants." Thus the Tractarians who insisted on the authority of tradition were at once brought into collision with the Evangelical party, who, though most of them accepted the doctrine of apostolical succession with its logical consequences, received it as a doctrine based on the authority of Scripture, and not on any patristic or traditional foundation. Thus the celebrated saying just quoted, and which the Evangelical party warmly asserted, was brought into earnest controversy. The Tractarians openly and unreservedly denied it, and they adduced forcible arguments in support of that denial. They maintained that the Scriptures of the New Testament derived their authority from the Church by which the canon of the books it contained was settled. They pointed out that the faith once for all delivered to the saints must have existed as a body of doctrine many years before the first written of the books of the New Testament was published, and that when they were, long after, placed together in one volume, it was the Church which decided, in the case of each book on whose behalf a claim for admission into that volume was set up, whether it should be allowed a place in it, or whether it should be rejected. Thus there arose a fierce controversy between the advocates of the supremacy of the Bible and the maintainers of the supremacy of tradition or Church authority.

The Evangelical party, though greatly shocked at the statements of their Tractarian adversaries, had but little to urge in reply to them. Almost all of them were entirely ignorant of the writings of the Fathers, and most of them contented themselves with urging that the Scriptures were their own best proof, and commended themselves to every man who read them in a right spirit as being the true Word of God. Thus writes Henry Melvill, the most learned as well as the most eloquent leader of the Evangelical party of his day:

"The peasant who, when the hard toil of the day is concluded, will sit by his fireside and read the Bible with all the eagerness and all the confidence of one who receives it as a message from God, has some better ground than common report or the tradition of his forefathers on which to rest his persuasion of the divinity of the volume. The book speaks to him with a force which, he feels, never could belong to a mere human composition. There is drawn a picture of his own heart —a picture presenting many features which he would not have discovered had they not been thus outlined, but which he recognizes as most accurate the instant that they are exhibited—that he can be sure that the painter is none other but He who alone searches the heart. The proposed deliverance agrees so wonderfully and so minutely with his wants; it manifests such unbounded and equal concern for the honour of God and the well-being of man; it provides with so consummate a skill, that, whilst the human race is redeemed, the divine attributes shall be glorified, that it were like telling him that a creature spread out the firmament and inlaid it with worlds, to tell him that the proffered salvation is the device of impostors or the figment of enthusiasts. And thus the pious inmate of the workshop or the cottage 'hath the witness in himself.' * The home-thrusts which he receives from the sword of the Spirit are his evidences that the weapon is not of earthly manufacture. The surprising manner in which texts will start, as it were, from the page and become spoken things rather than written; so that the Bible, shaking itself from the trammels of the printing press, seems to

* 1 John v. 10; Eph. vi. 17.

rush from the firmament in the breathings of the Omnipotent. This stamps Scripture to him as literally God's word; prophets and apostles may have written it, but the Almighty still suffers it, and all this makes the evidence with which the poor man is prepared in defence of Christianity. We do not represent it as an evidence which may successfully be brought forward in professed combat with infidelity. It must have been experienced before it can be admitted; and not being of a nature to commend itself distinctly to the understanding of the sceptic, will be rejected by him as visionary, and therefore received not in proof. But if the self-evidencing power of Scripture render not the peasant a match for the unbeliever, it nobly secures him against being himself overborne. 'The witness in himself,' if it qualify him not, like science and scholarship, for the offensive, will make him quite impregnable so long as he stand on the defensive. And we believe of many a village Christian who has never read a line of the 'Evidences of Christianity,' and whose whole theology is drawn from the Bible itself, that he would be to the full as staunch in withstanding the emissaries of scepticism as the mightiest and best equipped of our learned divines, and that if he could give no answer to his assailants whilst urging his chronological and historical objections, yet by falling back on his own experience, and entrenching himself within the manifestations of truth which have been made to his own conscience, he will escape the giving harbourage for one instant to a suspicion that Christianity is a fable, and hold fast, in all its beauty, and in all its integrity, the truth that ' we have an advocate with the Father, Christ Jesus the righteous, and He is the propitiation for our sins.' "

Innumerable passages containing similar statements are to be found, not only in the sermons of Melvill, but also in the works of all the preachers of the Evangelical school who either preceded or followed him. The arguments they employed might no doubt be urged with some degree of plausibility when applied to the Psalms, to the books of the prophets, and to the New Testament generally, but they could hardly be admitted with regard to such passages as those that contained the narratives of the murders of Sisera or of Eglon, or of Jehu's wholesale massacre of the priests and worshippers of Baal. Actions such as these might be defended as justifiable under the peculiar circumstances in which those who perpetrated them were placed, but could scarcely be urged as carrying on the face of them evidences of the divine origin and inspiration of the books in which they are related. However, the controversy thus originated continued to rage with great violence, and led many of the Tractarians, in their zealous assertion of the authority of tradition, sometimes to use language which tended to disparage the authority of the Scriptures. No one more distinguished himself by a bold—we may almost say reckless—treatment of this subject than Dr. Newman, in his tract on Scripture difficulties, as well as in some of his other writings, and especially in those that appeared shortly before he felt himself constrained to join the Church of Rome. It would be very unjust to a great and good man to attribute to him the authorship of views against which he vehemently and not altogether unsuccessfully contended, but there can be no doubt that the arguments he employed, and which were, in point of fact, necessary to the maintenance of his position, tended to unsettle men's minds with regard to the question of the authority of Scripture, and to facilitate the propagation of views that were silently making their way in the universities and elsewhere, but especially in the university of Oxford.

The study of German theology had for some time past been extending in that university. As early as the year 1840 the writings of Schleiermacher, Kant, Spinoza, and Hegel were being eagerly read, and had produced a disposition to advance much further in the direction of the free criticism of the Scriptures than Dr. Newman had ventured, or would for one moment think of proceeding. The result of the German studies above referred to, soon appeared in a very able article in the *Edinburgh Review*, as well as in lectures published by the late Dean Stanley; in Wilson's Bampton Lectures; in Professor Jowett's works on some of the Pauline epistles; in Professor Baden Powell's " Unity of Worlds ;" and at last in a volume, entitled " Essays and Reviews," which was published in the year 1860.

This book, which raised a storm in the religious world, was made up of seven essays, to each of which the name of its author was prefixed. In the first of them the human race was represented as a single person whose mind was formed by the beliefs and teachings of a long succession of ages, from the earliest period down to our own day, and whose religious and intellectual evolution was still proceeding. The second contained a review of the writings of Baron Bunsen. It declared the Bible account of the origin of the human race to be partly traditional and partly imaginary; that the alleged longevity of the patriarchs is fabulous; that the famous prophecy of Isaiah, commencing with the words, "He is despised and rejected of men," etc., does not apply to the Messiah; that the Book of Daniel was the work of some patriotic bard, written in the days of Antiochus; that justification by faith simply means the peace of the soul; that regeneration is another word for the first strivings of the human soul; that salvation expresses the victory of righteousness over vice and error; that hell is a figure of speech for the remorse that men feel on account of the sins of which they have been guilty, and heaven an image representing the accomplishment of the love of God towards us. It is true that this essay professed to be a review of the works of Bunsen, but it was evident that the author approved and sought to recommend the views of the writer whose work he had undertaken to criticise. In the next essay the principles which Niebuhr had made use of in dealing with the documents on which his "History of Rome" is based, were applied as boldly to the documents from which the history of the Hebrew nation are derived. The sixth contained little or nothing calculated to give offence. The seventh recommended that the Bible should be interpreted and criticised with the same freedom as any other book.

There was little that was original in these essays

either in regard to the ideas they enunciated or in the manner in which they were stated. The substance of them had often previously been put forward by the Unitarians or the deists of the eighteenth century. But what principally attracted attention to this book, and drew forth the warm eulogiums of some, and the indignant denunciations of others, was the fact that these essays were the productions of distinguished members of the national Church—of men holding high positions in the university of Oxford and in our great public schools—of men, in short, who might be regarded as placed by their position at the head of the religious education of the country;—of the Rev. Dr. Temple, headmaster of Rugby, and since appointed to be Bishop of Exeter; of the Rev. Dr. Williams, vice-principal of St. David's College, Lampeter; of the Rev. Baden Powell, Savilian Professor of Astronomy in the university of Oxford; of Mr. Goodwin, a layman eminent on account of his attainments in biblical antiquities; of the Rev. Mark Pattison, at that time the tutor and soon afterwards appointed to be the Rector of Lincoln College, Oxford; and of the Rev. J. B. Jowett, Regius Professor of Greek in the same university. The authors of these essays, in a short preface prefixed to the volume, took the precaution of stating that each was responsible only for what he himself had written and published as his own work; but it was alleged that there was a unity of thought running through all of them which seemed to indicate a general and foreknown agreement of sentiment and opinion among their authors.

While this work was still in the press, and before it had come out, a still more audacious exposition of rationalistic opinions had been published by Dr. Colenso, bishop of Natal in South Africa, under the title of "The Pentateuch and the Book of Joshua Critically Examined." In this work the bishop endeavoured to show that the books mentioned in the above title were full of errors; that a large portion of them were "unhistorical," or, in plain English, fabulous. But we ought to place the bishop's teaching before our readers in his own words. "My labours," he writes, in his introductory remarks, "as a translator of the Bible, and a teacher of intelligent catechumens, have brought me face to face with questions from which I had hitherto shrunk, but from which, under the circumstances, I felt it would be a sinful abandonment of duty any longer to turn away. I have, therefore, as in the sight of the Most High, set myself deliberately to find an answer to such questions, with, I trust and believe, a sincere desire to know the truth, as God wills us to know it, and with a humble dependence on the Divine Teacher, who alone can guide us into that knowledge, and help us to use the light of our minds aright. The result of my inquiry is this, that I have arrived at the conviction—as painful to myself at first, as it may be to the reader, though painful now no longer under the clear and shining light of the Truth—that the Pentateuch, as a whole, cannot possibly have been written by Moses, or by any one acquainted personally with the facts which it professes to describe; and, further, that the so-called Mosaic narrative, by whomsoever written, and though imparting to us, as I fully believe it does, revelations of the Divine will, cannot be regarded as historically true. . . . I wish to repeat here, most distinctly, that my reason for no longer receiving the Pentateuch as historically true, is not that I find insuperable difficulties with regard to the *miracles* or supernatural *revelations* of Almighty God recorded in it; but solely that I cannot, as a true man, consent any longer to shut my eyes to the absolute palpable self-contradictions of the narrative. The notion of miracles or supernatural interferences does not present to my own mind the difficulties which it seems to present to some. I could believe and receive the miracles of Scripture heartily if only they were authenticated by a veracious history; though, if this is not the case with the Pentateuch, any miracles that rest on such an unstable support must necessarily fall to the ground with it. . . . We need only consider well the statements made in the books themselves, by whomsoever written, about matters which they profess to narrate as facts of common history—statements which every clergyman, at all events, and every Sunday-school teacher, not to say, every Christian, is surely bound to examine thoroughly and try to understand rightly, comparing one passage with another, until he comprehends their actual meaning, and is able to explain that meaning to others. If we do this, we shall find them to contain a series of manifest contradictions and inconsistencies, which leave us, it would seem, no alternative but to conclude that many portions of the story of the Exodus, though based probably on some real historical foundation, yet are certainly not to be regarded as historically true."

The work abounds in passages of a similar import to those we have just cited; at the same time, it is only just to Dr. Colenso that we should place before the reader of this work words which he wrote that breathe a more reverential spirit than those we have quoted might lead us to expect from him. "Our belief in the Living God remains as sure as ever, though, not the Pentateuch only, but the whole Bible, were removed. It is written in our hearts by God's own finger, as surely as by the hand of the Apostle in the Bible, that GOD IS, and is a rewarder of them that diligently seek Him. . . . It is, perhaps, God's will that we should be taught in this our day, among other precious lessons, not to build up our faith upon a book, though it be the Bible itself, but to realize more truly the blessedness of knowing that He Himself, the Living God, our Father and Friend, is nearer and closer to us than any book can be—that His voice within the heart may be heard continually by the obedient child who listens to it, and *that* shall be our Teacher and Guide, in the path of duty, which is the path of life, when all other helpers—even the words of the best of books—may fail us."

It may, perhaps, be doubted whether the bishop, having gone thus far, would not by the exigences of a stern logic have been forced to go even further than he had done, and to lose his hold on the small remnants of Christianity which he still clutched desperately; but, at all events, these passages show a great improvement in the spirit in which questions of this nature had been approached by Tindal, Toland, Bolingbroke, and other deistical writers of the eighteenth century.

Far as Dr. Colenso had advanced in the paths of Rationalism, another clergyman had trodden them with still more fearless steps. The Rev. Charles Voysey, vicar of Healaugh, in the county and archdiocese of York, first attracted public attention in the year 1864, by a very strongly worded criticism of the teaching contained in 2 Samuel xxi. and xxiv. These strictures were followed by the appearance of a periodical publication by the same writer, entitled *The Sling and the Stone*, in which sermons preached by Mr. Voysey to his humble congregation at Healaugh, were given to a wider circle of readers. There was hardly a single cherished belief of Christendom which he did not assail; but if he attempted to demolish with one hand, he laboured to build up with the other. He dwelt with great earnestness on the Love and Fatherhood of God over all mankind, and the perfect safety which, as he contended, was enjoyed by all men everywhere, in time and eternity, under the protection of the Supreme Being. He also taught the doctrine of human progress, insisting that men could only learn what God is by being themselves upright, pure, and loving. The spirit in which he wrote and taught may be gathered from the following brief extract from a sermon he preached at St. George's Hall, on Sunday, October 29th, 1871, on the text "What think ye of Christ?" (Matt. xxii. 42). In this discourse he thus delivered himself on the question of the internal evidence we have that the writers of the first five books of the New Testament give us authentic and trustworthy history :—

"Suffice it to say, as a summing up of the careful analysis and criticism of learned men, that these New Testament narratives have some basis in fact; that there really was such a person as Jesus of Nazareth, and that His life was, according to the standard of those times, extremely pure and beneficent; that He made Himself obnoxious to the Jewish authorities of the age, who secured His condemnation by the Roman governor on the accusation that He was dangerous to the empire. These bald outlines are common to all the books and may be treated as historical. But beyond that, a careful reader will observe endless contradictions and discrepancies of such a nature as to exclude the idea that the writers were sufficiently acquainted with the ordinary facts of the life of Jesus to justify the use of the term *historical* in speaking of their conflicting accounts."

As Mr. Voysey not only taught these doctrines, but also proclaimed their entire irreconcilableness with the Christian creed, it was not surprising that the ecclesiastical world should protest loudly against his being permitted to preach them from a church pulpit. Accordingly, the Archbishop of York, his diocesan, was both privately and publicly urged to prevent the continuance of such a scandal. The archbishop for some time resisted the importunities that were addressed to him, but at last gave way, and with evident reluctance took action in the ecclesiastical court of his province against Mr. Voysey. Passing over the preliminary proceedings, we come to the real trial in the final Court of Appeal, which commenced in London on the 24th of June, 1869. Many persons of eminence, and among them Dr. Stanley, the dean of Westminster, contributed to a fund which was raised for Mr. Voysey's defence. He pleaded his own cause, and strove to show that there was nothing in his teaching that contradicted the express words of the Articles or Liturgy. But the court gave judgment against him, and sentenced him to be deprived of his vicarage unless he recanted, which, after all that had occurred, it was not at all likely that he would consent to do.

In following out the course of this history we must now turn our attention to another and very different development, which was being carried forward contemporaneously with that of which we have just related the progress. We have already remarked that Tractarianism had its æsthetic as well as its doctrinal side, and that the former had contributed as much as the latter to give force and impetus to the movement with which it was connected. The writers of the *Tracts for the Times* were for the most part men of great classical attainments and of refined and poetical minds, in whom the imagination had been cultivated at the expense of the reasoning faculties. They were warm admirers of the beautiful in history, in poetry, in sculpture, in painting, and in architecture; and, above all, in the architecture of the Middle Ages, of which their beloved Oxford contained so many beautiful models, which had fallen into unmerited neglect. Their good taste was shocked by the ugly and disfiguring additions which in modern times had been made to our old cathedrals and venerable parish churches, and by the debased and degraded style of those which had been erected during the last and the earlier part of the present century. Thus, to repair and restore the old with pious and conscientious care, and to build new churches in better taste, became one of the chief aims of the Tractarian party, and procured for them the adhesion and support of many, especially among the young students of divinity, who cared little for the doctrines of the apostolical succession or the real presence in the Eucharist, but who were drawn towards the new party by the good taste they displayed in the restoration of old churches, and the erection of new churches, as much as they were repelled by the bad taste and Puritanic prejudices which then characterized the Evangelical or Low Church party.

Under the influence of such feelings, the old highbacked pews, ridiculed by the *Times* newspaper as "lidless boxes," and by Mr. Paget as "dozing pans," together with the "three-deckers," as the recently introduced arrangements of pulpit, prayer desk, and clerk's desk were jocosely termed, were gradually being removed in order to make way for fittings more in harmony with the general aspect of the buildings in which they were placed, and with the worship that was carried on in them.

These changes, however, were not effected without loud and angry protests from those in whose minds the objects removed were associated with ideas of sacredness, and those which replaced them were thought to smack of mediæval superstitions. Still, in spite of all the opposition that was offered to the changes that were introduced, good taste slowly prevailed, and was improved by a careful study of the architecture of those grand temples which stud our land. And so in every part of the kingdom churches began to rise, which vied with the churches of the Middle Ages, if not in size, at least in the splendour of their ornamentation, and were fitted up with a tasteful magnificence which extorted the admiration even of those who feared that the revival of the mediæval ornaments would pave the way for a return to mediæval doctrines.

And they were so far right in this supposition that the two did, as a matter of fact, go together. The developments already effected, by a not unnatural connection, led on to further developments. The taste for mediæval ritual naturally engendered a taste for mediæval doctrine. The men who had discovered so much that was really admirable in the centuries which had been stigmatized as "dark ages," began to think that everything belonging to them was admirable. Societies, such as the Camden Society, were formed for the purpose of studying the history and antiquities of a period which had hitherto been too much neglected. The clergyman who officiated in one of the new and splendid basilicas which had been erected or restored under the auspices of this and other similar societies, began to feel that, arrayed in his surplice of modern cut, he was a sort of living anachronism amidst the mediæval magnificence by which he was surrounded, and sighed for vestments which accorded better with the temple in which, and the altar before which, he was appointed to minister; and he was the more strongly urged to carry out his wishes by the consideration that the vestments he desired to assume tended to distinguish the eucharistic service from the other services of the sanctuary, and thereby to give greater honour and sanctity in the eyes of the multitude to that sacrament which was the very keystone of his system of doctrine, and which, of late years, had fallen into a neglect which he never ceased to deplore. He could also urge that the desire thus awakened seemed to be warranted by the rubric prefixed to the Book of Common Prayer, which directed that the ornaments of the Church, and of the ministers thereof, at all times of their ministration, should be retained, and be in use, as they were in the Church of England, by the authority of Parliament, in the second year of King Edward VI.

Without going into this doubtful question, I may say that eminent lawyers gave it as their opinion that this was really the case. Many clergymen proceeded to act on their interpretation of the above-quoted rubric, introducing several other innovations, or as they termed them, revivals, and gradually increasing the ceremonious pomp with which the services of the Church, and especially her eucharistic services, were performed, thus assimilating them to the worship of the Romish Church. These innovations, though warmly approved by a few, were highly offensive to the great majority of members of the English Church, and the hostile feeling was intensified when it was found that along with them the practice of the confessional was being introduced into many churches in the metropolis and in other parts of the country, and great efforts were made to put a stop to them, both in and out of Parliament.

Meanwhile, two societies had been formed to aid the clergy and laity who were struggling to maintain ritualistic practices and propagate ritualistic doctrine. These societies were the Convocation Society, whose aim was, as its title denotes, to revive the legislative action of Convocation, and the English Church Union, which was chiefly occupied with questions of Church law, and in aiding those who encountered opposition in their attempts to carry out ritualistic changes. The action of this latter society was at once offensive and defensive. The two societies were amalgamated, or rather the Convocation Society was swallowed up in the Union, which, continuing to bear its old name, has carried on its operations down to the present day. It was confronted by another society, composed chiefly of men belonging to the Evangelical party, which assumed the name of the Church Association, and proposed to stamp out Rationalism and Ritualism, but especially the latter, to the destruction of which it has since devoted itself exclusively. For although the former laid its axe to the very root of the Evangelical doctrine, and threatened to extirpate its whole system, yet, as the latter more palpably offended the eye, it excited a much stronger opposition than Rationalism, and roused up a more vigorous resistance. The Church Association attempted to put down Ritualism, not so much by force of argument as by force of money. The ultra-evangelical party, whose peculiar boast it had been that the weapons of their warfare were not carnal, now came into the field relying on the very carnal support of a capital of £50,000, which they were prepared to expend in legal proceedings against their opponents. Accordingly, proceedings were taken by this association in the ecclesiastical courts, and by appeal from them to the Judicial Committee of the Privy Council.

Of course the persons who were thus assailed felt that they contended with their assailants on very unequal ground. Some of them allowed judgment to go against them by default; others pleaded their own cause, or were defended by advocates less wary and experienced than those by whom they were assailed. The prosecutions that were carried on looked like persecutions. The popular breeze, which at first, as we have already seen, had been strongly expressed against the Ritualists, began to veer round in their favour, and this feeling was more strongly evoked by the spectacle of poor clergymen contending almost single-handed against a great and wealthy association. The consequences were such as they ever had been and ever will be as long as the English love of fair play continues to exist. Ritualists suffered, but Ritualism gained ground; the prosecuted parties were regarded as martyrs, and the feeling against them, which at first had been so vehemently expressed, rapidly abated.

Objection, too, was taken to the constitution of the final Court of Appeal, and to the manner in which its members were selected. It was complained that in this matter too much liberty was left to the officer whose business it was to summon them in any case of appeal, and that the men chosen, though able lawyers, were not versed in the law of the Church as it had hitherto been practised in the Court of Arches and the other ecclesiastical courts; that there were many questions to which divines attached much importance, but which lawyers treated, if not with contempt, at all events with careless disregard.

The principle by which the Court of Appeal was guided in its decisions—if any principle is to be traced amidst the varying and conflicting judgments of a tribunal whose members were changed for each successive trial that came before it—was that of an extreme laxity, so far as doctrinal uniformity was concerned, provided that the words of the Articles were not expressly and *totidem verbis* contradicted, and a strictness that Laud himself would have deprecated with regard to ritual uniformity. It has been urged that they were influenced by policy rather than by law. The accusation is probably just, and as we have seen, was not only admitted, but avowed by eminent legists; but for this they are not to blame. It is an inheritance that has come down to them from the Star Chamber and the Court of High Commission, and is a course which is forced on them in consequence of the long discontinuance of legislation on the points submitted to their decision, and in dealing with which they are therefore compelled not only to interpret laws, but in doing so sometimes to make them.

Thus, throughout the period over which this volume extends, there have been no fewer than five distinct and well-defined parties in the Church—the old orthodox High Church party, which throughout the whole period has probably embraced the great majority of the clergy of the Church, and has kept aloof generally from the strifes and prosecutions we have had occasion to refer to; the Evangelical or Low Church party, the more moderate and religious members of which, though distressed by the progress of Ritualism, have, nevertheless, kept themselves aloof from the Church Association; the Broad Church or Rationalistic party, now rapidly and quietly spreading; the Ritualists, comprising a great number among the young and zealous clergy, and comprehending a tolerable sprinkling of elders; and, lastly, the Tractarians, who, notwithstanding the defection of Cardinal Newman, still, under the guidance of Dr. Pusey, adhered to the principles he had inculcated before he joined the Church of Rome, without adopting the further developments which he had deduced from them. These five parties shaded away into one another, and each of them might be subdivided into several different schools, the ultimate ramifications of which it is impossible to trace.

It now remains only that we should briefly touch on the events that arose out of the conflict of these differing and strongly opposed opinions, and as nearly as possible in the chronological order in which those events occurred. In this narrative we shall find, in the case of all parties, triumph alternating with defeat. The Broad Church party was the first to suffer in one of its most eminent and highly regarded members— the Rev. F. D. Maurice, who, as Professor of Divinity at King's College, London, had ventured to express doubts with regard to the correctness of the popular belief in the eternity of future punishments, and had published his opinions on this subject in a volume of Theological Essays. For this offence he was accused before the council of the college, who, after a lengthened consideration of the matter, resolved that the opinions set forth and the doubts expressed in the essay laid before them were of a dangerous tendency, and calculated to unsettle the minds of theological students; and that, therefore, the continuance of Mr. Maurice's connection with the college would be seriously detrimental to it. He was accordingly dismissed from the professorial chair he occupied in the college in the year 1853. Seven years afterwards, he was appointed by the Government to the incumbency of St. Peter's, Vere Street, St. Marylebone, and on the occasion of this well-merited promotion he received an address, which contained deserved congratulations on his appointment, as being a slight and tardy recognition of his eminent services, not only as one of the most learned theologians of the day, but more particularly as a wise, benevolent, and active co-operator with the working classes of the community, upon whose minds he had been eminently successful in bringing the practical truths of the Gospel to bear, and in leading them to regard the Church of our common

Lord and Master Jesus Christ as the great instrument designed by Providence for the regeneration of mankind and the alleviation of society.

These congratulations, and the manner in which they were endorsed, showed the rapid progress which the ideas propounded by Mr. Maurice had made in the interval that elapsed between his condemnation and his promotion.

With the name of Maurice that of Kingsley will always be associated. Both laboured together for the social regeneration of the working classes, and the praise which we have quoted from the congratulations offered to the one might very appropriately be applied to the other. Kingsley outlived Maurice and obtained higher promotion, but died at an early age, so that he did not very long survive his friend and fellow-labourer.

Then came the turn of the authors of "Essays and Reviews," and of Bishop Colenso, which, after a long series of litigations and the waste of much time and money, left both parties pretty nearly where it found them.

The period we have now reached, so far as the history of the Church is concerned, may be characterized as a period of ubiquitous and everlasting discussion. The Church, having her mouth at last opened, seemed determined to avenge herself for the silence to which for centuries she had been condemned. She now broke forth into convocations, Church conferences, Church congresses, diocesan synods, diocesan conferences, ruridecanal conferences, and ruridecanal chapters—talk, endless talk, leading to little if any results, but solacing the clerical mind with the hope that something would at last come of it; but nothing did come worth noting, except missions and quiet evenings, which the multitude regarded with suspicion, being supposed by some to be borrowed from the Methodists, and by others to smack of Romanism. On the other hand, many grave abuses were pointed out and slowly reformed; others still more gross, such as the traffic in advowsons and next presentations, were found to be too deeply implicated with private rights of property to be reformed, Parliament itself having sanctioned the trade and created vested interests in it of enormous pecuniary value, so that all efforts to effect a reform in this respect were found to be hopeless and fruitless, and likely to continue to be so as long as the alliance between Church and State endures. Another class of abuses, which loudly but vainly called for reform, were the simoniacal practices (using the expression in its legal and not in its Biblical sense) that existed in connection with exchanges of livings. All these evils were dwelt on and deplored in the various assemblies of Churchmen that were now so rife. A multitude of impracticable schemes were proposed, but no real remedy suggested. Another great evil which demanded much more attention than it was able to obtain, was the emptiness of many churches situated in the centre of the metropolis, and in the heart of other great towns, where the exceptions, few though they were, showed this to be an evil that might be overcome, and that large congregations might be gathered in some churches, while others close to them were almost empty. A practical attempt made to deal with this evil, by removing the chief cause of it, well deserves the attention of those who would study the history of the English Church.

One flagrant abuse in that Church was the traffic in seats carried on in the buildings set apart for public worship. In many instances the whole of the sitting accommodation was appropriated, often without any law or right. In some cases the persons who had become possessors of the pews alleged that they had a legal claim to them, and put locks on the doors in order to prevent others from entering them without express permission; some of these, again, had sold their pretended rights for considerable sums of money. A gentleman informed the author that, having been appointed warden of an important church, he found locks placed on all the doors. He determined to test the right of those who claimed them. He therefore took a hammer and knocked off every lock, and on the following Sunday showed people into the seats which he had thus thrown open to the parishioners generally. Loud threats were uttered by those who were thus dispossessed of the property they claimed; but nothing was done, because they had no title to show.

In almost all the new churches erected at that time this system was adopted, from the alleged necessity of providing a maintenance for the clergyman. The few free seats left to the generality of the parishioners were generally the coldest places in winter and the hottest in summer; and thus, while a few were scattered here and there through the sacred building, the great majority of the parishioners were either excluded altogether or placed in parts of the church which seemed to be selected, as if to say to the poor, "Stand thou there, or sit here under my footstool." This system was a spreading evil in the Church, and was gradually alienating from her the affections of the population, and would, had it been allowed to go on unchecked, have ended in making her the Church of a minority so small that she must have speedily ceased to exist any longer as a national Church, even in name.

It was in order to stem the progress of this mischief that the movement was originated, which is generally known by the name of the Free and Open Church system. This movement, one of the most important that has been made during the present century, was first introduced by Mr. Herford, the coroner of the city of Manchester, about the year 1857. He had been brought up as a Unitarian, and during the time of his connection with that communion he had distinguished himself by the warm interest he had taken in Sunday schools, and the zeal he had displayed in promoting the establishment of various useful institutions in his native town. In his maturer years he had become a zealous member of the Church of England, but he was distressed to find that she was losing her hold on the mass of the population, and especially on the working classes. He at once began to consider the causes of this alienation, and was soon led to the conclusion that it arose from the state of things which we have mentioned above, and which he justly believed could only be removed by the application of very vigorous remedies.

In the part of the kingdom which he inhabited, the evil had reached its highest pitch. Owing to the rapid growth of population in the manufacturing districts, churches had been built for which no endowment had been provided, and in which the income of the minister depended almost or altogether on pew rents. The consequence was that the mischievous system of exclusion which in other parts of the country existed, if at all, in spite of the law, had in the manufacturing districts been legalized, and throughout them the exclusion of the working classes was more complete, and the distinction between free seats and pews was more ostentatiously invidious than in any other part of the kingdom. Mr. Herford soon perceived that this was the chief cause of the evil which had so much shocked and grieved him, and he devoted himself with indomitable energy and perseverance to the work of endeavouring to remedy it, by insisting that in old parish churches the sittings should be free and open equally to all parishioners, and that as soon as possible this system should be universally adopted.

Mr. Herford did not contend that this system should be at once carried out everywhere. As a lawyer, he was naturally disposed to respect vested interests, even when they had been improperly created. As a well-wisher of the clergy he was anxious that they should be properly supported, and placed in a position of independence by deriving their stipends from fixed endowments rather than from the precarious and uncertain income yielded by pew rents, and he earnestly contended that the offertory collected during the communion service, in accordance with the rubrics of the Church, afforded a means of support for the clergy, which was, for many reasons, very preferable to pew rents. These views he very ably advocated in a periodical started in the year 1852, the scope and aim of which was described with energetic conciseness by the title he gave to it—*The Church of the People;* and, in order to bring his views to a practical test, he actively promoted the erection of churches in which the seats were both free and unappropriated, and, therefore, open to all without distinction. In the year 1857 he set on foot a Free and Open Church Association, with the object of endeavouring to procure the gradual adoption of the system he advocated in churches then in existence, as well as in those which might be erected at any future time; and he laboured with indefatigable diligence to effect this object, by letters in various periodicals, by discussions at Church congresses, by public meetings, and in many other ways.

The system he originated was very widely adopted, not only in his own neighbourhood, but throughout the kingdom. In many old parish churches pews illegally appropriated were restored to the parishioners. In many recently built churches the weekly offertory and the free and open system were introduced in consequence of the energetic advocacy of it by Mr. Herford and those associated with him. In other cases a sort of compromise between the two rival systems has been effected, in virtue of which at least one-half of the church, and that as advantageously situated and in every respect as commodious as the other moiety, has been made free and open to all parishioners without distinction. The labours of Mr. Herford have resulted in a largely increased attendance of the working classes, not only in churches, but also in Nonconformist chapels, in many of which the system he so earnestly advocated has been extensively adopted.

We pass on now to the instruction afforded by the Church to her children. In our day scant justice has been done to the system of education that was established in this country by the reformers of our Church, although evidences of their earnestness in this respect everywhere meet our eyes.

There are few towns, or even villages, which do not possess grammar schools originally founded at the time of the Reformation, and which in their day afforded, according to the ideas of that time, sound and gratuitous instruction. Many of them still continue faithfully to carry out the intentions of their pious founders; others have fallen into decay and neglect, chiefly because they have been endowed, not with an estate, but with a fixed income, which, though amply sufficient at the time of their first establishment, has, through alterations which have taken place in the value of money, become altogether insufficient. Little or nothing had been done for these schools from the time of their original foundation to our day, when at length attempts have been made, and not without success, to place them on a more satisfactory footing, though much more remains to be done in this way than has yet been effected. But the gratuitous character of the instruction afforded by them originally has been very much lost sight of, and persons in easy, if not in affluent, circumstances have usurped the educational advantages which the founders of these institutions chiefly intended for the benefit of the poor.

From the time of their establishment little had been done for the education of the mass of the people in connection with the Church, until, in the year 1812, a society was founded under the name of the National Society, for promoting the education of the poor in the principles of the Established Church throughout England and Wales. It commenced its operations by opening a central school in London, and soon after other schools connected with it, and thence called National Schools, were established in all parts of the kingdom. The society was incorporated under the above-mentioned name on the 23rd of May, 1817, and has from that time been the chief instrumentality through which the Church carries on its educational operations, and by which its relations on this subject with the Government of the day have been managed and regulated. An important step in advance was at length taken, when Bell and Lancaster introduced the monitorial system, the former in connection with the Church, and the latter with the Society of Friends. Bell's system differed little in substance from that of Lancaster, and where it did so differed for the worse.*

* See Sydney Smith's article on Trimmer and Lancaster, in the first volume of his collected works.

However, it was taken up generally by the Church, was adopted very generally in the Church schools, and was a decided step in advance, and the more so as it led to other educational progress of which we shall have occasion to speak presently. About the same time Robert Raikes introduced his system of Sunday schools, which extended very rapidly both in the Church and among Nonconformists. These efforts, made by private individuals or societies, were followed up by a vigorous attempt made by Mr. (afterwards Lord) Brougham to carry a Bill for the extension and improvement of the education then afforded. His plan roused a violent opposition by the Church; nevertheless, it was carried through the House of Commons, but was thrown out by the Lords.

Finding that it was impossible to overcome the opposition offered to every effective measure of education by the bishops and clergy and the Church party, as it was called, for at this time the members of the Church generally were decidedly opposed to the establishment of any real national system of secular education, even when some sort of religious education was superadded to it, so completely did he despair of success that he proposed to place the entire management and control of the education of the country in the hands of the parochial clergy, in the hope that the parish clerks would be appointed by them to become the schoolmasters throughout the country. At length, in the year 1833, the year after the passing of the great Reform Bill, an annual grant of £20,000 was made for the purpose of educating the working classes, the amount awarded in each case being proportioned to the sum raised locally. Loud complaints were made that under this arrangement an unfairly larger share of the grant was obtained by the Church. These views were ably advocated by Dr. Kay, a Manchester physician,* who published a pamphlet on the education question, which excited considerable attention on account of the able and comprehensive manner in which it dealt with the subject. It came into the hands of Lord Melbourne, who at that time was Prime Minister. He at once sent for Dr. Kay, and placed him at the head of the education movement as secretary of the Committee of the Privy Council on Education, which office he held during the ten years that elapsed between 1839 and 1849, and though during his period of office he was violently assailed both by Churchmen and Nonconformists, it was generally admitted, after his withdrawal from the post in which he had been so actively employed, and during his retirement, that he had mediated amidst conflicting sects and schools with honourable impartiality, and that the baronetcy which was conferred on him was a well-deserved tribute to the value of the services he had rendered to the country in the important work of the education of the people, and in paving the way for the introduction of a national system of education.

Another man who rendered very valuable service to the cause of education was the Rev. Dr. Hook, the celebrated vicar of Leeds, who proposed that secular

* Better known to the present generation as Sir J. P. K. Shuttleworth.

instruction should be imparted by the schoolmaster in one room, while religious education was being inculcated either in the same or another, by the clergy and ministers of different communions, to the children to whom their parents choose to send them. The plan was never brought under the consideration of the legislature, but was of very great service in preparing the minds of Churchmen to make concessions on the question of religious education, and especially to extend to the children of Dissenters the rights they so peremptorily demanded for their own children. It also probably suggested the idea of the conscience clause, which, first admitted as exceptional, was gradually extended, and at length made universal in schools aided by the Government.

From this time there has been an ever-growing tendency to limit Parliamentary assistance to secular instruction, not necessarily excluding religious education, but leaving it to be given at such times and places and in such a manner as the parents of the children may direct. Such, at least, has been the tendency of all modern educational legislation, and the result at which, judging from the past, we shall probably arrive is the complete separation of moral and religious education from secular instruction, and the establishment of a national system which shall be secular and compulsory. This tendency, distinctly visible for many years previous, was sufficiently pronounced at the period at which this history terminates.

The educational committee, or the educational department as it was afterwards called, continued to extend its aid to schools connected with different denominations of Christians, until, in the year 1859, it had attained the large amount of £836,000, and had been rendered more efficacious by payment being made for results, which were ascertained as far as possible by such an examination of the scholars as could be made by inspectors appointed to visit the schools, and during the short space of time that could be allotted for the purpose. Under all these changes, which were accompanied by an ever-increasing diminution of the control exercised by religious bodies over the management of the national schools, the Church continued to obtain by far the largest share of the public money appropriated by the Government to educational purposes, under the careful direction and superintendence of the legislature, which gradually prepared the way for the Education Act, introduced and carried through by Mr. Forster, and which has done so much to enable every parent to obtain at least an elementary secular education for his children, with ample security that they shall not be taught any religious tenets which he decidedly disapproves.

Throughout the whole of the period which this work embraces, two imposts were levied for the benefit of the Church—the tithe, which provided for the maintenance of her ministers, and the church-rate, which defrayed the expense of maintaining the fabric of the church, and the services that were carried on in it. These imposts were dealt with on different principles, and underwent altogether different treatment. The Established Church could not continue to exist without ministers, and the great majority of the nation desired its continuance. No serious attempt, therefore, was made to disturb the tithe, only the commutation of it; that is to say, its payment as a rent-charge, instead of in kind, was facilitated by various Acts, which benefited both the payer and the recipient; for while they diminished the amount of the impost, they rendered the collection of it much easier, put an end to much discontent that had prevailed before the commutation was effected, and helped to lighten the burden of odium that rested at this time on the clergy on account of the opposition that the great majority of them had offered to the Reform Bill, the remembrance of which was still fresh in men's minds.

With regard to church-rates, the case was much otherwise. To them and their collection a determined resistance was offered. It began in attempts to diminish the amount collected for the purpose of repairing the churches and providing the things that were required for the due and decent celebration of divine service in them. But the opposition to them was soon carried further. Payment of the rate being refused, it was enforced by seizure of goods and the imprisonment of the recusants. In the great Braintree case, after expensive litigation protracted over many years, it was finally determined, on appeal after appeal, that a rate laid by a minority at a meeting of the parishioners could not be enforced. In Rochdale, the contest was carried to such a pitch that upwards of 13,000 votes were recorded and the military were called out to preserve order. But the victorious party, although they had expended large sums of money on the contest, did not collect a single penny of the rate they had with so much difficulty succeeded in laying. It had become evident that the impost was not worth the trouble and expense incurred in obtaining it, and after the two defeats mentioned above, it was gradually expiring, when Mr. Gladstone's Church Rate Bill virtually abolished it, except in a few secluded villages in which the payment became optional.

We have now followed the fortunes of the English Church up to a period that will still be fresh in the recollection of most of my readers. We have seen her assailed with continually increasing vigour from without, and torn by multiplied divisions and dissensions within. And we are naturally led to ask, in concluding, what will the end be? Will she be overpowered by the increasing numbers of her opponents, or will she find some impregnable Torres Vedras * on which, securely posted, she may sally forth on her assailants and repel them? These are questions which are rapidly coming into the domain of practical politics, with which history does not interfere. But history, while it confines itself chiefly to tracing the course of events that have happened in the past, may help us to guide to some extent the evolution which is taking place in our day, and to anticipate the results to which it is likely to lead in the future. Thus much, at

---

* The heights on which the Duke of Wellington arrested the progress of the French invading army, hurled it back, and ultimately forced it to evacuate the Spanish Peninsula.

all events, we can discern, that we are posting on with portentous rapidity to a crisis in which many of the questions to which we have referred will have to be determined. It is quite time now that men's thoughts should be directed to the consideration of problems which are the most difficult that have ever been presented to the people of this country, and must necessarily exert a most important influence on the whole course of her future development.

INDEX.

A

Abolition of slavery, attitude of the clergy towards the, 315

Absolution of Charles II. pronounced by Ken, 125

Accession of Charles II., 12; of James II., 127; of William and Mary, 218; of Anne, 259; of George I., 286

Act for the augmentation of poor benefices, 119; of Uniformity receives the royal assent, 46; changes suggested by Cosin embodied in the, 109; the Five-mile, 164

Addams, Dr., his argument on Dr. Hampden's election, 338

Addison, his admiration for Tillotson's style, 228; Sacheverell shares his chamber at Magdalen College, 270; effect on the Church of his writings, 301

Address, congratulatory, presented to James by the bishops, 128; of the bishops in convocation to William III., 234

Advice given by Sancroft to his suffragans, 192-197; given by the bishops to James II., 203-205.

Advowsons, traffic in still unreformed, 384

Æsthetics of Tractarianism, 360, 374

Affirmation by a Quaker put on the same footing as an oath from another, 302

Aggression, the papal, 348; not a novelty, 353

Agitation, anti-slavery, 315

Allegiance, necessary alteration of the oath of, 236

Allwood, Mr., counsel for the defence on Baxter's trial, 139

Alms, Tenison's preaching and practice on the subject of, 254

Alterations in the Liturgy proposed by Sancroft, 199

America, Penn's colony founded in, 144

Amusements, repression of, by the Presbyterians, 15, 19

Anglican Church, passive obedience the doctrine of, 167; proposed introduction of its system into Prussia, 287

Anne, Queen, brought as princess by Compton into William's camp, 235; her accession, 259; her relations with Tenison, 261; her zeal for the Church, 262; her popularity, 267; her abject submission to the Marlboroughs, 268; her suspicions of Whig designs, 273; her sympathy with Sacheverell, 276; she frees herself from the Marlboroughs and the Whigs, 279; her independent appointment of bishops, 280; her indecision as to the Pretender, 283; her death apprehended, 284; her death, 285; she supports the scheme for the union of the English and Prussian Churches, 287

Antagonism of James II. towards the English Church, 134

Apostolical constitutions, Whiston's high estimate of their authority, 281

Apostolical succession, doctrine of, held by High and Low Churchmen, 8, 70, 74; a bar to union with Lutheranism, 288; tacit renunciation of the doctrine of, 308; general acceptance of the doctrine of, 361

Appeal, the Court of, the Gorham case brought before, 343; objected to by the High Church party, 345; proposed substitution of the bishops for it in doctrinal cases, 346; its laxity, 380

Appropriation of pews, 385

Archbishops of Canterbury in the time of George I., Carlyle quoted as to the, 297; their nullity in Cobbett's time, 309

Arches, the Court of, the Gorham case brought before, 343

Architecture, study of, by the High Church party, 374

Argument of Charles II. in favour of Romanism, printed and distributed by James II., 131

Arian doctrines, Dr. Whiston accused of advocating, 281

Army, admission of Roman Catholic officers into the, 142

Articles, the Thirty-nine, agreed on by the joint convocations of both provinces, 232; signature of, by those holding Romish doctrines discussed, 320; view taken of them by the Rev. W. G. Ward, 327

Ash-Wednesday, William and Mary proclaimed on, 218

Association, the Church, its objects, 378

Atterbury, Bishop, his part in Sacheverell's trial, 275; is supposed to have composed Sacheverell's defence, 276; he favours the claims of the Pretender, 284; brings in the Schisms Bill, 284; heads the disaffected clergy on the accession of George I., 286; his plots for bringing back the Pretender, 292; his trial, 293; his exile, 294; he asserts the rights of the Lower House of Convocation, 295

Augmentation of poor benefices from the incomes of the higher clergy enacted, 119; effected by Queen Anne's Bounty, 265

Authority of the Church, dispute as to the seat of, 362

B

Bagot, Dr., Bishop of Oxford, his censure of Newman, 326

Bank, the, attacked by the Gordon rioters, 305

Baptism, use of the cross in, 20, 229; of the Pretender, 208; extreme views of Irving on the subject of, 316

Barrow, Bishop, quoted as to passive obedience to kings, 168, 272, note

Bates, Dr., a friend of Richard Baxter's, 139

Bath and Wells, the Bishop of, signs the petition against reading James's declaration, 171; presentation of the Bishopric of, to Dr. Ken, 173

Baxter, Richard, declines a bishopric, but is licensed to preach, 22; his account of the refusal of the Independents to accept general toleration, 31; is present at the Savoy Conference, 39; driven from the Church by the Act of Uniformity, 51; abstract of his trial, 136; brutality of Jeffreys towards him, 139; his sentence, 140; he makes common cause with the Church in rejecting the declaration, 178

Bell and Lancaster, their educational system, 390

INDEX. 401

Benefices, augmentation of poor, enacted, 119; effected by Queen Anne's Bounty, 265

Bennett, the Rev. Mr., presented to the living of Frome, 353

Bethell, Mr., Mr. Ward's case submitted to, 327

Beveridge, Bishop, on apostolical succession, 71; on the Romish Church, 73

Bible, quotation from Melvill as to the value of the, 362; Chillingworth's dictum as to the, 361; Colenso's teaching as to the, 371

Birth of the Pretender, doubts as to the, 208, 209

Bishops, Act for the augmentation of poor benefices from the incomes of the, 119; they present an address to James II. on his accession, 128; doubts felt as to their course with respect to James's Declaration, 165; their appointment by Queen Anne without consultation of ministers, 280; *in partibus infidelium*, rule of, in England, 348; appointment of Romish, in England, with territorial titles, 349; their manifesto as to Tractarianism, 355

——, the seven, their petition, 171; brought before James, 181; committed to the Tower, 183; general sympathy with them, 192; released on bail from the Tower, 200; James confers with them, 203-205; change in the popular feeling towards them, 206; they refuse to sign a paper expressing disapproval of William's invasion, 211

Blomfield, Dr., Bishop of London, on the disappearance of the doctrine of apostolical succession, 307; censures the principle of interpretation advocated in Tract xc., 325; his indirect course respecting the use of the surplice, 332; his Bill for the substitution of bishops for the court of appeal, 346; his Bill thrown out, 347

Bolingbroke, Viscount, a leader of the Tory party, 281; his negotiations with the Pretender, 283, 284; makes peace with the government of George I., 294

Bonest, Arthur, Sancroft's grief for the death of, 104

Bonet, on the union of the English and Prussian Churches, 288

Bounty, Queen Anne's, its origin, 265

Boyne, William's authority confirmed by the battle of the, 239

Braintree case, the, as to payment of church-rates, 395

Brampford Speke, Mr. Gorham's appointment to, objected to, 342

Breda, residence of Charles II. at, 14; promises made to the Nonconformists by Charles at, 30, 38; modification of the promise made at, 56, 57

Breeks v. Woolfrey, case of, 324; case dismissed, 325

Bribe from Bolingbroke accepted by the Duchess of Kendal, 294

Bribery in the Church, 296

Bridewell, the new, destroyed by the Gordon rioters, 305

Bristol, Bishop of, signs the petition against the reading of James's declaration, 171

British Magazine, edited by Hugh James Rose, 317

Britton, Mr., his action against a parishioner for attending service not in his own church, 246

Broad Church party, the, Tillotson a precursor of, 227; its rise, 359; its growth, 381

Brougham, Lord, his co-operation with the Evangelicals on the slavery question, 315; his measure for the abolition of the Court of Delegates carried, 323; he proposes an Education Bill, 391

Burnet, Bishop, censures Sancroft for his refusal to act on the High Commission, 152; holds the doctrine of passive obedience, 169; appointed by William to the

2 D

Bishopric of Salisbury, 224; value of his historical writings, 225; his services to William, 226; his recommendation of Tillotson to William, 228; draws the attention of Anne to the abuses in connection with "first fruits," 265

Bury St. Edmund's, Sancroft educated at, 103

C

Calamy, Mr., his hope of toleration for Nonconformists, 31; at the Savoy Conference, 39; is driven from the Church by the Act of Uniformity, 51; is sent to Newgate for preaching, 52; is released by Charles, 53

Calvinism, rapid spread of, 313; Dr. Marsh's efforts to check, 314, 341

Calvinist, William III. professes himself a, 223

Calvinistic theology caricatured in the *Fur praedestinatus*, 108

Cambridge, Whiston brought before the court of the Vice-chancellor of, 282; advocates of Calvinism numerous in, 314

Camden Society formed, 376; diary by Cartwright, published by the, 161, 186

Campbell, Lord Chief Justice, on the trials for witchcraft, under Holt, 247; is on the committee to try the Gorham case, 343

Candidates for orders questioned by Dr. Marsh, 314

Canterbury, Tillotson appointed Archbishop of, 224, 227; reason of William's choice of Tillotson for the Archbishopric of, 241; William appoints Tenison to succeed Tillotson at, 245; Carlyle as to the *fainéant* Archbishops of, 297; Dr. Sumner succeeds Dr. Howley as Archbishop of, 339

Carisbroke, question raised as to the legality of an epitaph at, 324

Carlyle quoted as to the temporary nullity of the primacy, 297

Cartwright, Dr., made Bishop of Chester, 142; on the Ecclesiastical Commission, 153, 161; on the commission for appointing Parker head of Magdalen College, 186; his diary quoted, 187–189; he flees to France on the abdication of James, 191

Carus, Dr., advance of Calvinism under, 313

Cassock, the general dress of the English clergy, 81, note

Catechising of children practised by Ken, 173; insisted on by Sancroft, 194

Cathedral, St. Paul's, in a ruinous condition on the appointment of Sancroft as Dean, 109; Sancroft's letter to Wren concerning its restoration, 110; its rebuilding completed, 281

Catholic Emancipation, Bill for, carried, 312, 316

Ceremonies of the Anglican Church, objection of the Presbyterians to certain, 20; revival of, 377

Chancellor, the Lord, his nomination of Mr. Gorham to a living objected to, 342

Chandler, Dr., questions Walpole as to the Nonconformists, 292

Charity School endowed by Tenison, 254

Charles I., almost religious devotion to the memory of, 21

Charles II., his character, 12; restoration of, 20; his dependence on the primate in ecclesiastical matters, 25; his reception of the Presbyterian ministers at Breda, 30, 38; suspected of being in the pay of the French king, 34; his hatred of Presbyterianism, 55; his declaration of indulgence, 56; is unable to carry out his policy of general toleration, 77; his faithlessness towards Protestantism,

78; his conduct in reference to Oates's plot, 101; his promotion of good men in the Church, 115; secretly a Romanist, 116, 125; his practical assertion of ecclesiastical supremacy, 119; his illness, 124; his deathbed, 125; he receives the last rites of the Romish Church, 126; a paper containing Romish arguments found in his strong box, 131; his scheme for the introduction of Popery by the aid of French troops, 134; his policy towards Nonconformity, 140; grants land in America to Penn in lieu of a money payment of debt, 144; his honourable appreciation of Ken, 115, 173.

Chester, Cartwright made Bishop of, 142

"Chevalier St. George," Anne's conviction of his legitimacy, 259

Chichester, the Bishop of, signs the petition against James's declaration, 171

Chillingworth, his dictum as to the Bible quoted, 361

Christchurch, John Massey, a Papist, appointed Dean of, 142

Christian Knowledge, Society for the Promotion of, founded, 257

Church of England—its close connexion with the State, 4; its continuity, 7; its position in regard to the Reformation, 11; certain of its ceremonies objected to by the Presbyterians, 20; its restoration demanded on the return of Charles II., 22; question as to the basis of its reconstruction at the Restoration, 22, 35; its relation with the State maintained by the Primate, 25; security of its position at the time of Sancroft's appointment, 114; its adhesion to the doctrine of royal prerogative, 116, 122; proposed union of the foreign Protestant Churches with it, 123, 197; its maintenance of the right of James II., in spite of his creed, 128; James's interference in the affairs of the, 133; at open variance with James, 175; Sancroft's efforts for its efficiency, 197; William's conformity to the, 223; its relations to the sovereign changed by the Revolution, 236; efforts at union between it and the Church of Prussia, 286, 288; its debased condition, 296; effect of Wesleyanism on the, 299; the two great parties in the, 307; its subjugation to the State shown by the appointment of undesirable bishops, 341; five well-defined parties in the, 381; its educational efforts, 390

—— the Established, originally co-extensive with the nation, 5; it dates from the Restoration, 12; James promises to support the, 128; James's wish to procure the admission of Papists to high offices in, 159; William's conformity to, 223; Cobbet's abuse of, 309

—— Post-reformation, its continuity with the pre-reformation Church, 8–12

—— Presbyterian, substituted for Episcopal at the great rebellion, 12; growing unpopularity of the, 15–19; extemporaneous prayers and sermons in the, 16; certain Anglican ceremonies objected to by the, 20; hopes of toleration held out to the, 30, 38; no compensation granted to the ministers of the, 35; at a disadvantage at the Savoy Conference, 42

—— Roman Catholic, its Apostolic character acknowledged by the English Church, 8; its persecuting nature on the Continent, 34; its last rites administered to Charles II., 126; James's hope for the conversion of his subjects to the, 130; James's desire to obtain toleration for the, 135, 159; gradual approach of the Tractarian party to the, 319;

conversions to the, 326, 330; ecclesiastical government of, in England, 348

"Church Association," its anti-ritualistic, and anti-rationalistic object, 378

"Church of the People," a periodical started by Mr. Herford, 388

Church-rates, resistance to the collection of, 395

Church Rate Bill, Mr. Gladstone's, 396

Churches, appropriation of the coal-duties for the building of, 281;
—— splendour of those raised by the Tractarian party, 376
—— Foreign Protestant, various efforts at union between the Church of England and the, 123, 197, 222, 286, 288

Clarendon, Lord Chancellor, his character, 36; his obligation to Sheldon, 37; his fall, 77; quoted as to Jeffrey's condemnation of the judges in the case of the seven bishops, 200; quoted as to the change caused by the Revolution in the tone of discourses, 231

Clark, Mrs., sale of bishoprics by, 308

Clarkson, Mr., co-operation of the Evangelicals with, 315

Clergy, the, their taxation by convocation, 67; a change of disposition towards the crown among them, 156; relations of William's government not cordial with, 222; unpopularity of William with, 253; their maintenance of hereditary right as against George I., 286; roused by Wesleyanism, 298; many of them influenced for good by Methodism, 300; their search for a logical basis for the Church, 316

"Coal Act" prepared by Sancroft's efforts, 113

Coals, appropriation of the duty on to Church purposes, 281

Cobbett, William, his invective on "the Church by law established," 308–312

Coleman, Mr., his complicity in the Popish plot, 91; his communication to Sir E. Godfrey, 100

Colenso, Dr., Bishop of Natal, his work on the Pentateuch published, 369

Coleridge, S. T., the friend of Irving, 317

Coleridge, Mr. Justice, signs a protest against the suspension of Dr. Pusey, 326; his part in the Hampden controversy, 338

Colony founded on philanthropic principles by Penn, 144

Colonies, Archbishop Sharp endeavours to extend episcopacy to the, 256

Commission, Court of, revived, 150; granted by Sancroft to exercise his functions, 221

Commissioners appointed to admit Parker as head of Magdalen College, 186

Committal of the seven bishops to the Tower, 183

Common-prayer, the Book of, use of forbidden by the Presbyterians, 15; restoration of the use of, 19; discussion on, at the Savoy Conference, 39; Sheldon's tactics to avoid alterations in, 41; countenance of the doctrines of the Nonjurors to be found in, 316

Commons, House of, demur to Charles's declaration of indulgence, 58; they refuse to allow Charles's claim to ecclesiastical supremacy, 119

Commonwealth, preaching in the time of the, 16

Communion office omitted at the coronation of James II., 129

Comprehension, a scheme of, framed by Sancroft, 197; schemes of, again brought forward by William, 222; Parliament refuses to act in, without the concurrence of convocation, 228

Comprehension Bill prepared for

the consideration of convocation, 229

Compton, Dr., Bishop of London, declines to suspend Dr. Sharp, and is thereupon himself suspended, 154; he evades the question as to the invitation of William, 210; tries to induce Sancroft to take the oaths, 230; foments the discontent of the clergy, 234; his services to William's cause, 235

Confederacy against the French king headed by William of Orange, 122, 156

Conference between James and the bishops, 201

Confession of sins, Charles II. on his death-bed exhorted to, 124

Confessional, the practice of, introduced into Ritualistic Churches, 378

Congregational ministers, their acceptance of the Declaration, 178

Conscience clause, first idea of, suggested, 393

Convocation, the Book of Commonprayer remitted to the consideration of, 45; taxation of the clergy by, 67; its authority diminished by depriving it of the power of the purse, 70; the Articles of the Church of England framed by both provinces in, 232; Dr. Jane, appointed prolocutor of, 233; address to William by the bishops in, 234; projected changes in, defeated, 235; left in abeyance, 238; the opinions of Whiston condemned by, 281; antagonism of the two houses, and consequent suppression of, 295; Dr. Molesworth draws up a petition for the revival of, 318

Convocation Society formed, 378

Coronation of Charles II., 39; of James II., 129

Coronation Oath, Act passed as to its administration, 221; William bound by it to the maintenance of the Established Church, 223

Corporations, admission of Dissenters to, 291, 316

Correspondence maintained between the ministers of William and James, 237

Cosin, Dr., Bishop of Durham, chooses Sancroft for his chaplain, 108; is consulted as to the reconstruction of the Church, 109

Cowper, Lord, presides at Sacheverell's trial, 275

Council, the king in, his rights in matters ecclesiastical, 323

Court of Appeal, its decision in the Gorham case, 343

—— of Arches, question as to prayers for the dead tried in the, 324

—— of Delegates appointed by Henry VIII., 323

—— of High Commission, evil effects of, 150

Courts for the trial of ecclesiastical causes, their unsatisfactory nature, 322; Bishop Blomfield's proposed change in, 346

Courtenay, Rev. Francis, adopts the use of the surplice in preaching, 331

Covel, Dr., his correspondence with Sancroft, 122

Crewe, Dr., Bishop of Durham, on the Court of High Commission, 151, 161; his ready submission to William and Mary, 180; is pardoned by William, 214

Cross in baptism, objection of the Presbyterians to the sign of the, 20; its use made optional, 229

D

Dark Ages, rehabilitation of the, 376

Dead, prayers for the, question as to the legality of, 324

Deathbed of Charles II. described, 124

Declaration required from ministers under the Act of Uniformity, 47

Declaration of Indulgence issued by Charles, 56
—— of liberty of conscience published by James, 141, 160; republished, 162; debate as to reading it in churches, 165; hardly read anywhere, 178
Defoe, Daniel, quoted as to the behaviour of the clergy during the plague, 88, 89; his ironical recommendation of the persecution of Nonconformists, 260
Delegates, abolition of the Court of, 323
Denman, Lord Chief Justice, his views on the Hampden case, 339
Development, Newman gives the grounds of his secession in his essay on, 319
Diary, Cartwright's, quoted, 187, 189
Diocesan division of England by the Roman Catholics, 349
—— synod held by the Bishop of Exeter, 356
Directory, Presbyterian, persistence in the use of the, 21; attachment to the, 43; its date, 44
Disabilities laid on the Roman Catholics, 302; Lord Mansfield's efforts for their removal, 303; abolition of, 316
Discipline, powerlessness of Church laws for the enforcement of, 120
Disclaimer, Sancroft's, of any Romanizing tendency among the bishops, 197
Discourses, extemporaneous, among the Presbyterians, 16
Dispensations, the bishops appeal against, 203
Dispensing power claimed and exercised by James, 140, 177; its exercise extended to the Universities and Church, 142; in the king declared by Parliament to be illegal, 172
Dissenters, the, Sancroft's readiness to meet their advances, 192; Sancroft's advice respecting, 196; "The Shortest Way with," Defoe's ironical pamphlet, 260; their practice of occasional conformity defended by Tenison, 264; their exclusion from corporations, 291; their co-operation with the anti-slavery party, 315; their admission to corporations, 316; concession to them in educational matters, 393
Divine right of kings, the doctrine of, shaken, 155; still upheld by Sancroft, 206
Dodson, Sir John, Mr. Ward's case submitted to, 327
Dogmatic teaching, revival of, at Oxford, 320
Dolben, Mr., conducts Sacheverell's impeachment, 274
Dryden's delineation of Ken in "The Good Parson," quoted, 174
Durham, Lord John Russell's letter to the Bishop of, 350
Duty on coals appropriated to church building, 281

E

Ecclesiastical affairs confided by William to Mary, 224, 244, 257; Tillotson and Burnet, William's advisers in, 225
Ecclesiastical Commission, its work anticipated by Sancroft, 120; proceedings of, 161; the Bishop of Rochester withdraws from the, 200; the bishop's advise James to annul the, 203; Bishops Compton and Sharp victims of the, 235, 255
Ecclesiastical Titles Bill introduced by Lord John Russell, 353; is sent up to the House of Lords, 356; and passes, 357
Education, success of Nonconformist efforts in the cause of, 285; popular, neglect of, 297; afforded by the Church, 389; Dr. Kay's pamphlet on the question of, 392; probable future system of, 393

Education Act introduced and passed by Mr. Forster, 394
Eikōn Basilikè, portrait of Charles prefixed to the, 21, note; composed by Gauden, 67
Election, general, in 1734, help of the dissenters in, 291
Elector of Hanover, his claims to the throne, 284; his accession as George I., 286
Electorate of Prussia, the, becomes a kingdom, 286
Electress of Hanover, her death, 284
Elizabeth, Queen, Act of Uniformity adopted in the reign of, 1; her dictation to her subjects on religious matters, 130
Ely, Bishop of, signs the petition against the reading of James's declaration, 171
Emancipation, Catholic, carried, 312
Emmanuel College, Sancroft educated at, 103; Sancroft elected head of, 109
Engagement, the, its nature, 107
English Church Union founded, 378
Episcopacy, the Presbyterians willing to accept a modified form of, 43; suppression of, in Scotland, by William, 224; Archbishop Sharp endeavours to extend it to the British colonies, 256
Epitaph at Carisbrooke, question raised as to its legality, 324
Erastianism, reaction against, 313; general prevalence of, 318
Erle, Justice, his part in the Hampden controversy, 338
"Essays and Reviews," publication of, 366; causes of its effect, 368
Eternal punishment, Mr. Maurice suffers for his views on, 382
Eucharist, outward tokens of honour for the, 377
Europe, William of Orange heads the Protestant party throughout, 122, 156
Evangelical party, the, support of the doctrine of apostolical succession by, 74; took its rise from the influence of the Methodists, 300, 359; their anti slavery efforts, 315; favoured by Dr. Sumner, 339; their claims threatened by the Gorham case, 343; their ignorance of patristic writings, 362; their value for the Bible, 362
Evolution, the, of Ritualism, 377
Exeter, Dr. Philpotts, Bishop of, his endeavours for ecclesiastical exclusion, 341; he objects to the nomination of Mr. Gorham to a living in his diocese, 342; holds the first diocesan synod, 356; is thought to favour Tractarianism, 331; his advice to Mr. Courtenay, 332; he prosecutes Mr. Shore, 363
Expulsion of Nonconforming ministers, 49
Ex tempore prayers and discourses of the Presbyterians, 16

F

Farce, the, of "congé d'élire" enacted, 338
Farmer, Dr., James's intention of making him Head of Magdalen College, 185
Fathers, the, ignorance of the Evangelical party concerning, 362
Faversham, the bishops wait on James at, 215
Fellows of Magdalen, the, refuse to appoint Dr. Parker as their head, 186; their rights overruled, 190
Fifth of November, South's sermon on the, 212; Sacheverell's sermon on the, 272; demonstration against the Papal aggression on the, 352
Fine imposed on Defoe for his pamphlet, 260
Fire of London, the great, 91; attributed to the Roman Catholics, 93
"First-fruits" added after the

Reformation to the royal revenue, 265
Five distinct parties existing in the Church, 381
Five Mile Act, probably framed by Sheldon, 62; the dissenters scattered by the, 164
Fleet prison destroyed by the Gordon rioters, 305
Fleetwood, Bishop, prosecution of, 282
Forster, Mr., value of his Education Act, 394
Fowler, the Rev. E., his decision as to reading the declaration, 165
France, influence at the English court of the King of, 34
France, James takes refuge in, 213
Frederick, King of Prussia, his desire to introduce the English Church system, 256, 286; he relinquishes the scheme, 289
"Freeman, Mrs.," the Duchess of Marlborough's assumed name in her intercourse with Anne, 268
Free public library, the first, founded by Tenison, 254
Free and Open Church system originated, 386, 388
French troops, Charles II. proposes to introduce Popery by the aid of, 134; King, William of Orange leader of the struggle against the, 156
Freshinfield, Sancroft retires to, and dies there, 221
Frewen, Accepted, Archbishop of York, declines to preside at the Savoy Conference, 40
Frome, Mr. Bennett appointed to the living of, 353
Froude, Mr. Hurrell, one of the writers of the Oxford tracts, 319
Fur Prædestinatus, published by Sancroft, 108
Fust, Sir Herbert Jenner, judge in the Court of Arches, 324; the Gorham case first tried before, 341-3
Futility of oaths as a means of checking political change, 236

G

Gauden, Dr., Bishop of Exeter, at the Savoy Conference, 39; his post-communion rubric, 67; author of the *Eikōn basilikē, ibid.*
Gay called as witness in Atterbury's trial, 293
George I., his accession, 286; unfavourable impression made by, *ibid.*
George, Prince of Denmark, supports the Bill for the Prevention of Occasional Conformity, 263
German Theology, its effect in Oxford, 366
Gibson, Dr., Bishop of London, quoted as to the abolition of the separate taxation of the clergy, 69
Giffard, Bonaventure, appointed Head of Magdalen by James II., 191
Gladstone, Mr., signs the protest against the suspension from preaching of Dr. Pusey, 326; votes against the censure of Mr. Ward, 329; his representation of Oxford objected to, 330; his condemnation of the Ecclesiastical Titles Bill, 356; his Church Rate Bill passed, 396
Godfrey, Sir Edmundsbury, his high character, 97; his mysterious murder, 99
Godolphin, Lord Treasurer, supports the Bill for the Prevention of Occasional Conformity, 263; he afterwards opposes it, 265; is known as Volpone, 272; his anger at Sacheverell's attack, 273
Good Parson, the, a picture of Ken, 174
Goodwin, Mr., one of the authors of Essays and Reviews, 368
Gordon, Lord George, riots headed by, 304; is arraigned for high treason and acquitted, but dies in prison, 306
Gutteridge, Mr., his charge against Dr. Lee, 340

Gorham, Rev. Cornelius, his case, 341; judgment given by the Court of Appeal in the case of, 343
Gospel in Foreign Parts, foundation of the Society for the Propagation of the, 257
Graham, Mr., on the essential Protestantism of England, 354
Grammar schools, the ruined condition of, 297; their early foundation, 389
Grant, Dr., of New College, his modified censure of Mr. Ward, 328
Grant made by government for education, 392
Guildhall, council held at for maintaining the peace of London on James's abdication, 214
Gunning, Bishop, at the Savoy Conference, 39
Gwyn, Nell, Ken's refusal to give up his house at Winchester for the use of, 173

H

Halifax, Lord, prevents the passing of the Bill for the exclusion of James from the throne, 124
Hammond, Dr., one of the chaplains to Charles I., 29
Hampden, Dr., censure pronounced against by the members of the Oxford Convocation, 327; selected by Lord John Russell for the see of Hereford, 333; his previous course at Oxford, 334; his appointment protested against, 335; his election, 337; consecrated Bishop of Hereford by Dr. Sumner, 339
Hangman, Sacheverell's sermon burnt by the, 278; Oxford declaration of arbitrary power burnt by the, 279; a book of sermons by Bishop Fleetwood burnt by the, 283

Hanover, Anne's hatred of the house of, 283; death of the Electress of, 284; accession of the Elector of as George I., 286
Harley, see Oxford, Earl of
Henry VIII., his dictation to his subjects on religious matters, 130; appoints a Court of Delegates for hearing appeals in matters ecclesiastical, 323
Herbert, Lord Chief Justice, on the Court of High Commission, 151
Hereford, Dr. Hampden selected by Lord John Russell for the see of, 333; the dean of, votes against Dr. Hampden's appointment, 337
Heresy, Dr. Pusey condemned by the Board of, 326
Herford, Mr., originator of the Free and Open Church system, 386
High Church clergy accused of a leaning to Popery, 130
High Churchmen, their varying characteristics in different reigns, 70, 307; public feeling against them, 331
High Church party, Anne's attachment to, 259; their triumph after Sacheverell's trial, 279; determination of Lord John Russell to crush the, 333; their indignation at the Gorham judgment, 345
High Commission, Court of, revised, 150; its extraordinary powers, 151; it is discredited by Sancroft's refusal to act on it, 152
Hill, Abigail, Queen Anne's confidant, 267; Anne communicates with the Tory party by means of, 269; she becomes Mrs. and afterwards Lady Masham, 273; her growing power with Anne, 280
"History of the Reformation," by Cobbett, quotation from, 309
Hoadley, the Rev. Benjamin, his services to the Whig party, 272; discussion on his works the cause of the suppression of convocation, 295
Holt, Chief Justice, his decision as to attendance at church, 246; his

mild interpretation of the acts against witchcraft, 247
Holy orders, laxity in giving testimonials to candidates for, 118; indelibility of, asserted by Sir H. J. Fust, 333
Homilies, accordance of some of their teaching with Romish doctrine, 320
Hook, Dr., votes against the censure of Mr. Ward, 329; but protests against his Romanizing teaching at Leeds, 330; his services to the cause of education, 392
Hough, Dr., appointed by the Fellowshead of Magdalen College, 185; the king desires to cancel his appointment, 186; he refuses to submit to the sentence of deprivation, 187; sentence given against him, 189
Howe, Mr., driven from the Church by the Act of Uniformity, 51; he rejects the Declaration, 178
Howley, Dr., Archbishop of Canterbury, the scheme for the union of the English and Prussian Churches revised under the auspices of, 288; his fairness and public spirit, 313; he works on the lines of the pre-Jacobite Church, 317; his conciliatory advice on the subject of innovations, 332; his death, 339;
Huddlestone, Mr., a Roman Catholic priest sent for to Charles II. when dying, 125
Huguenots, William's army chiefly commanded by, 213
Huntingford, Dr., votes against the election of Dr. Hampden, 337
Huntley, Rev. R. W., opposes the election of Dr. Hampden, 338

I

"Ideal of a Christian Church," published by W. G. Ward, 327
Impeachment of Sacheverell, 274
Imposts levied for the benefit of the Church, 394

Incomes from Church preferment, proposed rectification of, 119; those of the first year transferred at the Reformation from the Pope to the Crown, 265
Indelibility of orders asserted by Sir H. J. Fust, 333
Independents, the, contend for religious liberty, 31; but decline to accept it if also accorded to Papists, 33
Indian tribes, Penn's dealings with, 144; his letter to them quoted, 145
Indulgence, declaration of, issued by Charles, 56; and protested against by Sheldon, 60; to Nonconformists advised by Penn, 148
Innovations, Dr. Howley's conciliatory advice respecting, 332; ritualistic, in Church services, 377
Inscription, libellous, on the monument, 94
Inutility of oaths as political safeguards, 237
Invasion of William of Orange imminent, 200; determined on, 209; and carried out, 214
Ireland, William's successes in, 239
Irving, Edward, revives the doctrines of the Nonjurors, 316

J

Jablousky, Dr. Ernestus, his efforts for the union of the English and Prussian churches, 287
Jacobites, their hopes for a time destroyed by William's Irish successes, 239; their plots for the Pretender, 284; silenced by the accession of George I., 290
James II., episcopal resistance to the tyranny of, 115; efforts to exclude him from the throne, 123; his accession, 127; his promise to support the Established Church, 128; his promotion of Romanism, 130; he prints his brother's arguments in favour of Romanism,

131; his sailor education some excuse for his ignorance, 132; his honesty and tenacity, 133, 143; his character compared with that of Charles II., 134; his wrong-headedness, 135; his determination to obtain the repeal of the Test Act, 140; his declaration of liberty of conscience, 141; his promotion of Papists to ecclesiastical posts, 142; his relations with Penn, 143; he silences the clergy as to controversial topics, 148; his folly, 149, 159; he orders his Declaration to be read in churches, 162; he receives the petition of the seven bishops, 175; his irritation against the bishops' petition, 179; he examines the seven bishops in person, 182; his downfall promoted by his proceedings at Magdalen College, 191; he solicits the aid of the seven bishops, 200; his conference with them, 201; his tardy concession to their requests, 205; his expulsion determined on by the people, 206; his inability to resist the invasion of William, 208; his indecision on William's approach, 212; his reception in France, 213; clerical hopes of his return, 217; Archbishop Sharp prays for him after the Revolution, 256

Jane, Dr., appointed prolocutor of Convocation, 233

Jebb, Rev. J., opposes the election of Dr. Hampden, 338

Jeffreys, Lord Chief Justice, introduced into office by Charles II., 133; James's confidence in him, 136; he is made Lord Chancellor, *ibid.*; his brutal behaviour at Baxter's trial, 137; he silences the counsel for the defence, 138, 139; he advises the revival of the Court of High Commission, 150; and presides over it, *ibid.*; the seven bishops interrogated by him, 181; his condemnation of the judges of the bishops, 199

Jenner, Justice, on the commission for appointing Dr. Parker head of Magdalen College, 186

Jerusalem, see of, alternate presentation of Anglican and Prussian divines to the, 288

Jesuits, the, support the advice of Jeffreys, 150; are forbidden to enter England, 159; the people determine on their expulsion, 206; accused of fraud in the matter of the birth of the Pretender, 208

Jews, their admission into the House of Commons, 358

John Bull, the newspaper, opposes the liberation of the slaves, 315

Johnson, Dr., influence on the Church of his writings, 301

Jones, Inigo, defects in his work at St. Paul's Cathedral, 111

Jowett, Prof. J. B., effect of German studies traceable in the works of, 366; one of the authors of "Essays and Reviews," 368

Judicial Committee of the Privy Council, the last resort in ecclesiastical cases, 323; Mr. Shore appeals to the, 333

Juxon, Dr., Archbishop of Canterbury, his duties fulfilled during his illness by Sheldon, 22, 23; his character, 26; he is unable to take part in the Savoy Conference, 39; his death, 60

K

Kay, Dr., made secretary of the Education Committee of the Privy Council, 392

Keble, Rev. John, one of the writers of the Oxford tracts, 319

Kelly, the Rev. Mr., arrested for complicity in plots for the return of the Pretender, 292

Ken, Dr., Bishop of Bath and Wells, dispenses with special confession from Charles II. when dying, 124; holds the doctrine of passive obedience, 169; signs the petition against the reading of James's declaration, 172; his appointment as bishop honourable to Charles, 115, 173; Dryden's "Good Parson" a picture of, 174; his letter of rebuke to Tenison in reference to the death of Queen Mary quoted, 248–252

Kendal, the Duchess of, accepts a bribe from Bolingbroke, 294

"Kidderminster Bishop," a, Jeffreys sneers at, 139

King, the Rev. Bryan, his introduction of ritualistic practices, 358; leaves St. George's in the East, 359

King, Sir Peter, his part in Sacheverell's trial, 274; his defence of Whiston, 282

King, the, his rights in matters ecclesiastical, 22, 323; divine right of, held by Sancroft, 206

King's Bench, James's intention to remodel the Court of, 155; decision of the Court of, as to attendance at Church on Sunday, 246; prison of, destroyed by the Gordon rioters, 305

King's College, London, Mr. Maurice dismissed by, 382

Kingdom, Prussia becomes a, 286

Kingsley, the Rev. Charles, high estimate of, 383

Kneeling at the reception of the Lord's Supper objected to by the Presbyterians, 20; made optional, 229

Knight-Bruce, Sir James, on the committee for the trial of the Gorham case, 343

L

Lake, Dr., Bishop of Chichester, signs the petition against reading James's declaration, 173

Lambeth, Sancroft retires to, on William's arrival, 214; Mary sends messengers to, 219; Sancroft is forced to quit, 221

Lamplugh, Dr., allowed by William to retain the Archbishopric of York, 214; circumstances of his appointment to York, 255; his death, 255

Lancaster, his educational system in connection with the Society of Friends, 390

Lansdown, Marquis of, opposes Bishop Blomfield's Bill, 347

Laud, Archbishop, the Church made odious by his tyranny, 15

Lay preachers, a body of, formed by Wesley, 299

Lay writers, their influence on the Church, 301

Lee, Dr., his appointment as first Bishop of Manchester objected to, 340

Leeds, Mr. Ward's teaching at, protested against, 330

Leigh, the Hon. Pemberton, on the Committee for trying the Gorham case, 343

Liberalism and Conservatism in religion, struggle between, 95

———, ecclesiastical, an unpopular form of belief, 227

———, religious, Tractarianism, an effort to withstand it, 360

Liberation by James of Quakers and Roman Catholics, 141, 147

——— of the slaves, 315

Liberty of conscience, James's declaration in favour of, published, 141, 160; republished, 162

Library, free, founded by Tenison, 254

Littlemore, Newman tries to revive the monastic system at, 326

Liturgy, the Anglican, its restored use, 20; efforts to induce the Presbyterians to conform to it, 21; a new, proposed by Baxter at the Savoy Conference, 42; alterations proposed in it by Sancroft, 199; projected review of, prevented by the revolution from being carried out, 255

Livings, reduction in the value of, 118; augmentation of small, by Queen Anne's Bounty, 266

Lloyd, Dr., Bishop of St. Asaph, signs the petition against reading James's declaration, 172; takes the oath of allegiance to William and Mary, 173; demurs to James's mode of examining the seven bishops, 182

London, great fire of, attributed to the Roman Catholics, 93

—— and Westminster, fifty new churches to be built in, 281

——, effect of the Oxford tracts in, 320

——, Bishop of. *See* Blomfield, Dr.

Long Parliament, Court of High Commission established by the, 150

Lonsdale, Mr., a fellow-worker with Dr. Howley, 317

Lord's Supper, objection of the Presbyterians to kneeling at the reception of the, 20; the reception of, a test of fitness for office, 262

Lords and Commons, disagreement between, as to the Occasional Conformity Bill, 262

Louis XIV., his influence at the English Court, 34; Charles II. desirous of emulating, 77; champion of the Romish nations, 123; Protestant struggle against the pretensions of, 156; expulsion of the Huguenots by, 213

Low Church party, its identification with the Evangelical, 301, 381

Loyalty to James hard to combine with faithfulness to Protestantism, 131; steadfast, of Sancroft, 158

Lushington, the Rt. Hon. Dr., on the committee for the trial of the Gorham case, 343

Lutheran divine to be appointed alternately with an Anglican to the see of Jerusalem, 288

M

Macaulay quoted as to Sancroft's *Fur predestinatus*, 108; he censures Sancroft for refusing to act on the High Commission, 152; his account of the seven bishops alluded to, 184; quoted as to what was meant by convocation, 231; disapproves of the Ecclesiastical Titles Bill, 354

Macmullen, Mr., refuses to write on the exercises proposed by Dr. Hampden, 335

Magdalen College, Oxford, a Roman Catholic appointed as head of, 185; commissioners sent to, 186; the bishops request the restoration of the president of, 203; Sacheverell educated at, 270

Manchester, Dr. Lee's appointment as Bishop of, objected to, 340

Manchester, Duke of, his apprehensions as to the working of the Act of Uniformity, 52; his religious liberalism, 55

Mandamus asked for to compel the hearing of the objections to Dr. Hampden's election, 338

Manifesto by the bishops as to Tractarianism, 355

Mansfield, Lord, his advocacy of civil and religious liberty, 302; he attempts to obtain a mitigation of penalties against Roman Catholics, 303; obnoxious to the Gordon rioters, 304; his library burnt by the rioters, 305

Marlborough, the Duke of, supports the Bill against occasional conformity, 263; he afterwards opposes it, 265; his victories on the continent, 267; he tries to prevent the prosecution of Sacheverell, 274; his failing power with the Queen, 279; his struggles to regain ascendency, 280

Marlborough, Sarah, Duchess of, her description of the character of Mary, 253; her ascendency over Queen Anne, 267; her in-

solence to the queen, 269; loses the affection of the queen, 273
Marsh, Dr., Bishop of Peterborough, his alarm at the progress of Evangelicism, 314
"Martyr, the Royal," 21
Mary, Queen of William III., writes to Sancroft, 157; her authority as queen limited, 215-218; her rebuff from Sancroft, 219; ecclesiastical affairs confided to her by William, 224, 244, 257; is persuaded by Bishop Burnet to share her throne with William, 226; her illness and death, 247; Ken's censure on her, 249-252; political effect of her death, 253, 257
Masham, *see* Hill
Mass, the, openly celebrated in England, 159; celebrated in the universities, 184
Massey, John, a Papist, appointed Dean of Christchurch, Oxford, 142, 184
Maurice, Rev. F. D., dismissed from King's College, London, 382; high public estimation of him, 383
Mediæval architecture a lure to mediæval doctrine, 376
Melbourne, Lord, Dr. Hampden appointed Regius Prof. of Divinity at Oxford by, 334
Melvill, Henry, as to the continuity of the Church, 8; advance of Calvinism under, 313; quoted, as to the Bible, 362
Methodism, its quickening effect on the Church, 298-300
Mew, Dr., installs Hough as Head of Magdalen College, 185
Mill, Dr., a fellow worker with Dr. Howley, 317
Ministers, Presbyterian, their mission to Charles II. at Breda, 14, 30
Minto, Lord, his interview with the Pope, 354
Molesworth, Dr., a fellow worker with Dr. Howley, 317; draws up a petition for the revival of convocation, 318; his action in the appointment of Dr. Lee to the see of Manchester, 340
Monastic system, Newman's attempt to revive the, 326
Monitorial system of education introduced, 390
Monks and friars, public re-appearance of, 132, 160
Monmouth, Duke of, proposed nomination of, as successor to the throne, 21; Trelawney's efforts to quell the rebellion of, 176; Tenison's attendance at the execuof, 255
Monument, libellous inscription on the, 94
Morley, Dr., Bishop of Winchester, endeavours with Sancroft to effect the conversion of the Duke of York, 116
"Morley, Mrs.," Anne's assumed name in her intercourse with the Duchess of Marlborough, 268
Mortmain, Statute of, altered, 267

N

Natal, Dr. Colenso, the Bishop of, publishes his work on the Pentateuch, 369
National schools, foundation of, 390
Newgate, Calamy imprisoned in, 53; Lord George Gordon dies in, 306
Newman, John Henry, his *apologia pro vita sua* referred to, 74; one of the writers of the Oxford tracts, 319; he leaves the English Church for that of Rome, *ibid.*, 326; quotation as to the articles from his Tract xc., 320; he attempts to revive the monastic system, 326; his tract on Scripture difficulties referred to, 365
Nonconformists, Protestant, attempts to deprive them of political power, 54; James's disposition to crush them, 136; motives for the harsh treatment of, 140; they are

left by James in prison, 141; they refuse to accept the Declaration, 178; are ready to stand by the Church in the contest with the king, 192; Sancroft's desire to conciliate them, 196, 222; relief afforded to them by the Toleration Bill, 229-231; excluded from the government of the country by the Test and Corporation Act, 262; their chapels pulled down by Sacheverell's partisans, 278; more ready than Churchmen to extend liberty to Roman Catholics, 306; their admission to Parliament after the passing of the Reform Bill, 316

Nonconformity, its prevalence within the Church, 4; unequal measure of toleration claimed for Romish and Protestant, 135; the Schisms Bill an attempted check on, 284; Sir R. Walpole's inefficient support of, 291

Nonjurors, their disinterested consistency, 216; founded by Sancroft, 221; William's vain attempt to shield them, 230; expelled for keeping their oath by men who had broken it, 237; their friends disorganized, 238; Tillotson intercedes for them, 242; a recent return to the doctrines of the, 316-318

Non-natural sense, condemnation of the principle of signing the Articles in a, 325

"No Popery" cry, by whom, according to Cobbett, raised, 310

Non-resistance, the doctrine of, held by Sancroft, 167-170; preached by Sharp after the revolution, 256

Nye, an independent minister, his endeavours after religious liberty, 31-33

O

Oates, Titus, the agent of the foreign Roman Catholics denounced by, 91; his supposed discoveries as to the Popish plot, 93; is well paid for his revelations, 96, 100; Jeffrey alludes to him, on Baxter's trial, 137

Oath, popular belief in the Romish disregard of an, 96, 101, 102;
—— taken to the new government by the clergy generally, 231

Oaths of allegiance and supremacy, necessary alterations in, 236

Obedience, passive, to the royal will, a doctrine of the English Church, 122; the doctrine of shaken, 155; taught by Sancroft's party in the Church, 167, 169; Sancroft still maintains the doctrine of, 206, 215; Sharp preaches it after the revolution, 256

Objectors to the appointment of bishops called to come forward, and then denied a hearing, 338, 340

"Occasional conformity," a mode of evading the Test and Corporation Acts, 262; a Bill brought in to prevent it, 262; Tenison's speech on, 264; Bill rejected in 1704, 265; the Act, which passed in 1711, repealed, 290

Offertory, the, considered as a means of support for the clergy, 388

Officers, Roman Catholic, admitted into the army, 142
—— Huguenot, in William's army, 213

Opposition, determined, to the payment of Church-rates, 395

Orange, Prince of, *see* William III.

Ornaments rubric maintained at the Savoy Conference, 45; its authority urged by the Ritualists, 377

Owen driven out of the Church by the Act of Uniformity, 51

Oxford, election of Roman Catholics to high offices in, 142, 184, 185, 191; commission sent to, 186-191; Sacheverell's welcome at, 279; fears excited by the progress of religious liberalism in, 318;

attempts made to prevent the return of Mr. Gladstone as representative of the University of, 330; Dr. Hampden appointed Regius Professor of Divinity at, 334

Oxford, Dr. Bagot, Bishop of, forbids the continuance of the Tracts, 320; he is thought to favour Tractarianism, 331

—— Dr. Parker, Bishop of, 142; he is made President of Magdalen College, 185; his death, 191

—— Robert Harley, Earl of, regarded as head of the Tory party, 269; Anne guided by, 273, 281; he opposes the impeachment of Sacheverell, 275; favours the claims of the Elector of Hanover, 284; is confined in the Tower, 294

—— Tracts, results of their publication, 75; revival of old High Church doctrines by the, 298; their publication, 318; list of writers of the, 319; the publication of, stopped after appearance of Tract xc., 325

P

Paget, Mr., quoted as to pews, 375

Pains and Penalties, Bill of, brought in, 293

Palmer, the Rev. W., one of the writers of the Oxford Tracts, 319

Papal aggression, discussion on the, 330; the Pope's explanation of the, 348

Papists, Charles II. desires to secure toleration for, 31; their schemes and hopes, 34; appointment of, under James, in the Church and Universities, 142, 184, 191

Parishes, Chief Justice Holt as to the institution of, 246

Parke, Mr. Baron, on the committee for the trial of the Gorham case, 343

Parker, Dr., made Bishop of Oxford, 142; is appointed by James president of Magdalen College, 185; his death, 191

Parliament, members of, stipendiaries of the King of France, 34; hostility of towards the Presbyterians, 38, 43; protest of against the declaration of indulgence, 57; effect of the remonstrance of, 76; its consent to James's declaration in favour of liberty not asked, 160; declares the royal dispensing power to be illegal, 172; James pressed by the bishops to summon a, 211; it refuses to act in the question of comprehension without the aid of convocation, 228, 231; character of Queen Anne's first, 259; its dissolution after Sacheverell's trial, 280; Nonconformists admitted to, 316

Partibus infidelium, Bishops *in*, their rule in England, 348

Parties, five, in the English Church, defined, 381

Passive obedience, the doctrine of, 122, 167, 206, 256

Patrick, Dr., part of Sancroft's scheme of comprehension entrusted to, 198

Patteson, Judge, his part in the Hampden controversy, 339

Pattison, Rev. Mark, one of the authors of "Essays and Reviews," 368

Payment for results adopted in state-paid schools, 394

Pearson, Bishop, at the Savoy Conference, 39

Peers, new ones made by Queen Anne, 280

Penn, Admiral, James's naval education received under, 143

Penn, William, James's relations with, 143; documents and letters of, quoted, 145; his representation to James respecting the persecution of Nonconformists, 147

Pennsylvania, so named by Charles II., 144

Pentateuch, Dr. Colenso's work on the, published, 369
Pepys's Diary quoted as to a portrait of Charles I., 21; referred to as to Sheldon's conduct, 79; quoted as to Crewe's preaching, 161
Percival, Rev. W. F., opposes Dr. Hampden's election, 338
Persecution of Nonconformists, Penn remonstrates against the, 147; ironically recommended by Defoe, 260
Perversions to the Romish Church, 330
Peterborough, the Bishop of, signs the petition against the reading of James's declaration, 171; Dr. Marsh, Bishop of, his endeavours to keep Calvinism out of his diocese, 314
Petition of the seven bishops presented to James, 165; quoted, 171; probably framed by Sancroft, 174; sold in the streets of London, 177
Petre, Father, his influence with James, 136, 148
Pews, appropriation of, 385; dependence of the minister's income on the rent of, 387
Pillory, Oates condemned to stand in the, 137; Defoe condemned to the, as punishment for his pamphlet, 260
Plague, the great, 87; Sir E. Godfrey remains in London during the, 97; Tenison remains at his post at Cambridge during the prevalence of the, 245
Plot, the popish, its effects, 91, 96
Plymouth, a Roman Catholic bishop appointed to the see of, 356
Political changes not to be checked by oaths, 236
—— power, attempts to deprive the Nonconformists of, 54, 262
Pope, first-fruits claimed by the, 265; his office of hearing appeals transferred to the Archbishops, 323; he orders a new diocesan division of England, 348; his interview with Lord Minto, 354
——, Alexander, called as witness in Atterbury's trial, 293
Popery, the clergy required to preach against it four times a year, 94; the High Church clergy accused of a leaning towards, 130; general denunciations of, 132; Charles's plan for the introduction of, 134; Sancroft's dread of, 171; popular hatred of, 206, 302
Poverty of the lower clergy, 119
Powell, Professor Baden, result of German studies traceable in the works of, 366; one of the authors of "Essays and Reviews," 368
Præmunire, Sancroft avoids the penalties of, 221
Prayers and discourses extemporaneous among the Puritans, 16
Prayer-book, High Church doctrines not opposed to the, 298; countenance of the doctrines of the Nonjurors in, 316
Prayers for the dead, question raised as to the legality of, 324
Preaching on controversial subjects forbidden, 148; of Methodism, 298
Prerogative, royal, jealousy of, under Charles II., 53; earnestly advocated by Sancroft, 115; James's exertion of the, 160
Presbyterians, the, refuse toleration for themselves if also granted to Papists, 33, 35, 159
Presbyterianism, inclination of William to, 218; promoted in Scotland by William, 224
Pretender, circumstances of his birth, 184, 208; Queen Anne's conviction of his legitimacy, 259; negotiations of ministers with the, 283; plans in his favour defeated by the death of Anne, 285; plots formed for his return, 292
Primacy, limits of its power not defined, 120

2 E

Primate, his power, 23; his position at the time of the Restoration, 25
Privy Council, Sancroft not summoned to attend meetings of the, 153; the judicial committee of the, a last resort in ecclesiastical cases, 323; Mr. Shore appeals to the, 333
Privy Seal, Bishop Robinson appointed to the, 284
Proclamation by William of his object in invading England, 210; of William and Mary on Ash-Wednesday, 218
Prolocutor, the choice of, a test of the temper of convocation, 232; Dr. Jane chosen, 233
Promotion of Christian Knowledge, Society for the, founded, 257
Propagation of the Gospel in Foreign parts, Society for the, founded, 257
Prosecution of the seven bishops, 183; of Bishop Fleetwood, 282; of Ritualists, 379
Protest, parliamentary, against the Roman Catholic assumption of territorial titles in England, 354
Protestants, their alarm at the Romish proclivities of the Duke of York, 121; proposed confederation of, 123, 157; general union of, desired by William III., 223; foreign, introduced into England by the Low Church party, 276
Prussia, efforts of the King of, to introduce the English Church system, 256; first made a kingdom, 286; plans for the union of the Church of England with that of, 287, 288
Public library, free, the first, founded by Tenison, 254
Purgatory, connection of the doctrine of, with prayers for the dead, 324
Puritans, their intolerance, 15; extemporaneous prayers and preaching among the, 16

Pusey, Dr. E. B., leader of the Tractarian movement, 319; is suspended from preaching, 326; in what sense he signed the Articles, 327; he votes against the censure of Mr. Ward, 329

Q

Quakers released from imprisonment under James's declaration of liberty of conscience, 141, 147; Lord Mansfield as to affirmation by, 302; monitorial system introduced into schools in connection with the, 390
Queen Anne's Bounty, its origin, 265
Queen's Bench, appeal of the objectors to Dr. Hampden's election to the court of, 338
Questions, anti-calvinistic, proposed by Dr. Marsh to candidates for holy orders, 314
—— of faith and doctrine, proposed removal of, from lay jurisdiction, 346

R

Raby, Lord, Anne's minister at the Prussian court, 287
Raikes, Robert, introduces Sunday schools, 391
Rate for rebuilding St. Paul's levied on coals, 113
Rationalism, growth of, 372
"Reasonableness of conformity to the Church of England," by Bishop Hoadley, 272
Rebellion of the Duke of Monmouth, 176
Reconstruction of St. Paul's determined on, 112
Reform Bill passed, 316
Reformation, character of the English Church, but not its existence affected by the, 7–9; Sancroft's

belief in the permanence of its work, 123; History of, by Cobbett, quoted, 308, 311; schools founded at the time of the, 389

Regency suggested in the place of James II., 121

Regeneration, baptismal, Bishop Beveridge quoted as to, 71; the doctrine of, held by Irving, 316

Regent Street, land near, left by Tenison as a charitable endowment, 254

Restoration, the, 12; reconstruction of the Church after, 24

—— of churches under Tractarian auspices, 375

Revenue, royal, "first-fruits" added to the, after the Reformation, 265

Revenues of poor benefices, Sancroft's efforts for the augmentation of, 118

Revolution, the, its effects on the clergy, 217; change effected by, in the relations between Church, State and Crown, 236; Ken's censure of Mary's part in, 249

Reynolds, Dr., his acceptance of a bishopric, 22

Ring in the marriage service, objection of the Presbyterians to the use of the, 20

Riots against the Roman Catholics in Scotland, 303; headed by Lord George Gordon, 304; anti-ritualistic at St. Paul's Knightsbridge, 353; and at St. George's-in-the-East, 358

Ritualism, a development of tractarianism, 319, 360; evolution of, 355, 377; agitation against, 358

Robinson, Dr., Bishop of Bristol, appointed to the privy seal, 283; he supports Atterbury and the disaffected clergy, 286

Rochester, Earl of, on the high commission, 151; Bishop of, withdraws from the ecclesiastical commission, 200

Rochdale, contest at, as to Church-rates, 395

Roebuck, Mr., on the Papal aggression, 353

Roman Catholics, Charles II., his favourable consideration of, 57; liberated under James's declaration of liberty and conscience, 141; James's aim to obtain toleration for, 159; no relief granted to them by the Toleration Bill, 229; perpetuation by all parties of the disabilities laid on, 302; Lord Mansfield's efforts for their relief, 303; their places of worship burnt, 304, 305; emancipation of, carried, 312

Romanism, Charles II. embraces, 77, 116, 125, 134; strong antipathy of the clergy towards, 96; tendency of Tractarianism towards, 319, 351

Romish Church, the last rites of, administered to Charles II., 126; James II. hopes for the conversion of his subjects to the, 130; toleration of the, in the time of James, 135; Dr. Newman joins the, 319; Mr. Ward and his curates join the, 330

Rose, Hugh James, a fellow-worker with Dr. Howley, 317

Rotheram, Mr., defends Baxter on his trial, 138

Rubric concerning ornaments maintained at the Savoy Conference, 45; its authority urged by the Ritualists, 331, 377

Russell, Lord John, obtains the repeal of the Test and Corporation Acts, 291; drift of his episcopal appointments, 333; appoints Dr. Hampden Bishop of Hereford, 335; his reply to the protest against this appointment quoted, 336; he insists on the appointment of Dr. Lee to the see of Manchester, 340; his action as to Papal aggression, 349; his letter to the Bishop of Durham quoted, 350; his Ecclesiastical Titles Bill introduced, 353; his resignation and resumption of office, 354; his correspondence with Cardinal Wiseman, 352, 357

Russell, Lady, letter from Tillotson to, quoted, 242

S

Sacheverell, Dr. Henry, history of, 270; preaches an anti-whig sermon, 272; and is impeached for it, 274; he is found guilty, 277; but has his triumph, 279; is invited to preach before the Commons, 283

Sacramental grace, question of, 76

St. Asaph, the Bishop of, signs the petition against the reading of James's declaration, 171; he is the bearer of the petition to James, 175

St. Bartholomew's Day, referred to by Baxter, 31; Act of Uniformity passed on, 46; its memories, 49, 50

St. George's-in-the-East, anti-ritualistic riots at, 358

St. Paul's Cathedral, Sancroft made Dean of, 109; question as to repairing or rebuilding of, 110; its rebuilding completed, 281

St. Paul's Knightsbridge, rioting at, 353; concessions made at, to anti-ritualistic feeling, 358

Sailor, James II. brought up as a, 132

Sale of bishoprics by Mrs. Clark, 308

Salisbury, Dr. Burnet appointed by William, Bishop of, 224

Sancroft, Dr. William, made primate, 91; biographical sketch of, 103; death of his father, 107; made Dean of St. Paul's, 109; and primate, 113; his activity as primate, 118; his difficulties, 120; his influence on the English Church, 122; officiates at James's coronation, 129; James applies to him to answer the Romish arguments of Charles II., 131; he refuses to act on the high commission, 151; Mary wishes to enter into correspondence with him, 157; he declines to do so, 158; holds the doctrine of passive obedience, 167; is the probable framer of the petition against reading the declaration, 174; his readiness to meet the advances of the dissenters, 192; his scheme of comprehension, 198; his loyalty to James, 200; his letter to James quoted, 202; he urges James to summon a Parliament, 212; retires to Lambeth on William's arrival, 214; his rebuke to Mary, 219; abstains from recognizing the sovereignty of William and Mary, 220; his separation from the Church, and his death, 221; unsuccessful efforts made to induce him to acknowledge William's sovereignty, 240; declines to receive the visits of Tillotson, 242

Sanderson, Bishop, at the Savoy Conference, 38

Savoy Conference, its object, 5; leading part in it taken by Baxter and Reynolds, 22; frustration of its aims, 30; account of the, 38; dissolved, 45; scheme of comprehension suggested at the, 197; Tillotson's part in the, 227

Scheme of comprehension framed by Sancroft, 197, 198

Schisms Bill brought in by Atterbury, 284; its provisions, 285; Act repealed, 290

School Charity, endowed by Bishop Tenison, 254

Schools, denominational, state aid to, 394; grammar, founded by the reformers, 389; national, foundation of, 390; Sunday, introduced by R. Raikes, 391

Scripture, Newman's tract on the difficulties of, 365

Scripture, free criticism of, in Oxford, 366; free criticism of, recommended in Essays and Reviews, 367
Schlater, Edward, retention of livings by, 142
Scotland, firm hold of Presbyterianism in, 80; landing of the bishops in, 82; James exercises vice-regal powers in, 123; indignation in, at the attempt at relief of the Roman Catholics, 303
Scroggs, Sir Wm., presides over the trial of those accused by Oates, 102
Secession to the Romish Church of Oxford Tractarians, 319, 330
Secular instruction, tendency of Parliament to limit its assistance to, 393
Sedgmoor, cruelties practised after the battle of, 173
Sermon by South, quoted, 64; clerical taxation mentioned by South in a, 69; on 5th Nov., by South, 212; on 5th Nov. by Sacheverell, 272; ordered to be burnt by the hangman, 278
Sermons, their effect not always proportionate to their merit, 271
Service, daily, and Communion book, proposed review of, 198; decision in the King's Bench regarding attendance at, 246
Settlement suggested between James and William, 211
Seven bishops, the, their petition quoted, 171
Shaftesbury, Earl of, profits by the pretended discoveries of Oates, 101
Sharp, Dr. James, afterwards Archbishop of St. Andrews, quoted as to the affection of the people for the "old service," 20; one of the deputation to Charles at Breda, 80; is made Archbishop of St. Andrews, 81; his murder, 82
Sharp, Dr. John, brought before the High Commission, 153; is appointed Archbishop of York, 255; his resolute consistency, 256; desires the union of the English and Prussian Churches, 287–289
Sheldon, Gilbert, Bishop of London, conditionally licenses the preaching of Baxter, 22; undertakes the work of the primacy during Juxon's illness, 27; biographical sketch of, 28; presides at the Savoy Conference, 40; presides over Convocation, 45; principally answerable for the harsh working of the Act of Uniformity, 50; is made Archbishop of Canterbury, 60; he remonstrates with Charles, 79; his great power, 82; his will quoted, 84; his liberality, 87; he is succeeded by Sancroft, 103, 116
Sherlock, Dr., takes the oaths, having first refused them, 239; is made dean of St. Paul's, *ibid.*
Shore, Rev. J., prosecuted by the Bishop of Exeter, 333
"Shortest way with Dissenters," written by Defoe, 260
Shrewsbury, Earl of, appointed Treasurer by Anne on her deathbed, 285
Simeon, Rev. Charles, advance of Calvinism under, 313
Simony, inefficiency of laws against, 296; still unreformed, 384
Slavery, part taken by the Evangelicals in the abolition of, 315
"Sling and the Stone, The," published by the Rev. Ch. Voysey, 372
Smallpox, Queen Mary dies of, 247
Smallridge, Bishop, his part in Sacheverell's trial, 275
Smith, Sydney, his services to civil and religious liberty, 307; on Dr. Marsh's examination of candidates, 315
Somers, Lord, his advice as to Sacheverell's impeachment, 274
South, Dr. Robert, his sermon quoted as to Nonconformity in the Church, 4; as to the extem-

poraneous discourses of the Puritans, 18; his sermon enjoining intolerance quoted from, 63; quoted as to the taxation of the clergy, 69; is recommended by Sancroft for the see of Oxford, 155; general tone of his sermons, 213

Sprat, Dr., Bishop of Rochester, on the Court of High Commission, 151, 161

Stanhope, Lord, his efforts for the repeal of the Test and Corporation Acts, 290, 291

Stanley, Dean, effect of the study of German theology traceable in the writings of, 366; he contributes to the fund for Mr. Voysey's defence, 374

Stanley, Lord, is unable to form a ministry, 354

Star Chamber, result of its tyranny, 15

State, general subjugation of the Church to the power of the, 4, 341

Statutes, persecuting, 54, 62

Statute of Mortmain altered in favour of poor benefices, 267

Stillingfleet, Archbishop, his desire for agreement with the Nonconformists, 66; his reasonableness, 135; absents himself from his church on the day for reading the declaration, 181; recommended by Mary for the Archbishopric of Canterbury, 245

Succession, Apostolical, doctrine of, maintained originally by Evangelicals, 75

—— Bill proposed for the exclusion of James, 124

—— to the throne, correspondence concerning the, 121

Sumner, Dr. J. B., is appointed Archbishop of Canterbury, 339; is called in to induct Mr. Gorham, 345

Sunday attendance at church, decision respecting, 246

—— Reader, The penny, by Dr. Molesworth, 317

Sunday schools introduced by Robert Raikes, 391

Sunderland, Earl of, James's confidence in, 132; his influence with James, 136, 148; on the Court of High Commission, 151; his readiness to betray the king, 177

Suppression of Convocation, 295

Supremacy, ecclesiastical, practically asserted by Charles II., 119; royal, James's view of, 130; of Bible or Church, controversy as to the, 362; necessary alterations in the oath of, 236

Surplice, objection of the Presbyterians to the use of the, 20; use of the, made optional by the Toleration Bill, 229; riots occasioned by wearing the, 331; action of the Bishop of London concerning the, 332

Synod, diocesan, the first, held by the Bishop of Exeter, 356

T

Talk, clerical, a period of, 383

Taxation, separate, of the clergy, 68

Temple, the, Sherlock at first resigns the mastership of, 239

——, Dr., one of the authors of Essays and Reviews, 368

Tenison, Dr., Archbishop of Canterbury, quoted as to changes in the Prayer-book, 45; he abandons his view of the royal prerogative, 115; appointed Archbishop, 245; Ken's letter of censure to him quoted, 248-252; his early history, 254; his changed relations to the sovereign on Anne's accession, 261; his speech on occasional conformity, 263; scheme for the union of the English and Prussian Churches thwarted by his inaction, 287, 289

Territorial titles of Romish bishops in England, parliamentary protest against, 354
Test Act, James's determination to obtain the repeal of, 140
Test and Corporation Acts, when passed, 54; William suggests the repeal of, 230; evasion of, 262; modified in their action, 290; repealed in 1827, 291, 316
Testimonial letters, laxity in giving, to candidates for orders, 118
Theology, German, its effect in Oxford, 366
Tillotson, Dr., Archbishop of Canterbury, his efforts for agreement with the Nonconformists, 66; is leader of the comprehension party, 67; he abandons his view of the royal prerogative, 115; his reasonableness, 135; holds the doctrine of passive obedience, 169; absents himself from his church on the day for reading James's declaration, 181; his latitudinarianism, 199; his party has the direction of Church affairs, 217; is made Archbishop, 224; an ecclesiastical liberal in belief, 227; champion of moderate concession, 233; reasons for William's choice of him, 240; his wish to shield the Nonjurors, 242; his death, 243
Time-servers, the clergy justly reproached as, 222
Tithe, vexations caused by the collection of, 312; Acts passed by which it became a rent-charge, 395
Toleration, general, aimed at by Charles II., 31; opposition to its concession, 34; failure of Charles's attempts to secure, 76; unequal measure of, granted to Protestant and Romish nonconformity, 135; general, Penn's argument in favour of, 148; if equally extended to Papists it is refused by Presbyterians, 159; James's schemes of, not acceptable, 162; James dissertates on, to William, 209; Toleration Bill, amount of liberty granted by, 229; it is carried, 231
Torbay, William lands at, 212
Tory, Queen Anne a thorough, 259
Tories, the, unite with the Whigs in opposition to James's declaration, 160; they bring in a Bill for the prevention of "Occasional Conformity," 262; Harley regarded as leader of the, 269; their growing strength in Parliament, 280; divisions among them, 284, 286
Tower, the, the seven bishops committed to, 183; they are released from, on bail, 200; Lord Oxford confined in, 294
Townsend, Mr., his official opposition to Dr. Hampden's election, 338
Tracts, the Oxford, published by the revivers of the nonjuring principles, 318; their writers, 319; Tract xc. appears, 320; it is condemned at Oxford, 325; its condemnation by the Oxford Convocation attempted, 329; æsthetic tastes of the authors of, 374
Tractarian movement, its origin, 75, 319; its progress, 322; its aims, 360; restoration of churches under its auspices, 375
Tractarians, a name for the Oxford party headed by Dr. Pusey, 319; their interpretation of the Thirty-nine Articles, 320; question as to the legality of prayers for the dead raised by the, 334
Tradition, the authority of, maintained by the Tractarians, 365
Transubstantiation, the doctrine of, said to have been preached by Dr. Pusey, 326
Trelawney, Sir J., Bishop of Bristol, signs the petition against reading the declaration, 173; his disclaimer of rebellion, 176
Trimnel, Dr., a Low Churchman made a Bishop by Anne, 280

U

Turner, Dr., Bishop of Ely, signs the petition against reading the declaration, 173

U

Ultra-evangelical party, pecuniary force of the, 379
Uniformity, Act of, of Edward VI., 1; of Elizabeth, 2; its object, 4; the Church of England dates from the passing of the, 12; receives the royal assent, 46, 49; its harsh working, 51; changes in it suggested by Cosins, 109
Union proposed between the English Church and the foreign Protestant Churches, 123, 157; of reformed Churches, Sancroft's aspiration after, 197; proposal for, brought forward by William, 222; between the Churches of England and Prussia nearly effected in Anne's reign, 286; and revived under Archbishop Howley, 288
Union, the English Church, the Convocation Society is merged in, 378
University College, Oxford, a Papist chosen Master of, 142
Universities, James exercises his dispensing power with regard to the, 142; appointment of Papists to high offices in the, 184
Ursinus, Dr., writes on the proposed union of the English and Prussian Churches, 287
Ussher, Archbishop, draws up a scheme of modified Episcopacy, 42
Utrecht, congress of, Bishop Robinson's distinguished part in the, 184-186

V

Vestments, obsolete, sanctioned by the ornaments rubric, 45; their use at St. George's in the East, 358; desirableness of, in Tractarian eyes, 377
Vicars-apostolic, appeal against, by the bishops, 204; to be superseded in England by bishops with territorial titles, 348, 357
Vicar-General, the, refuses to receive objections to the appointment of Dr. Hampden, 338
Vice-chancellor of Oxford, Tract xc. condemned by the, 325
Visitation of Magdalen College, Oxford, 186-191
Volpone, nickname of Lord Treasurer Godolphin, 272
Voysey, Rev. Charles, his rationalistic tendencies, 372; ecclesiastical proceedings taken against, 374

W

Wages lowered by the introduction of foreign workmen, 276
Wake, Dr., Bishop of Lincoln, quoted as to Sancroft's scheme of comprehension, 198
Wales, stories respecting the birth of the Prince of, 191, 208
Walker, Obadiah, a Papist, chosen Master of University College, Oxford, 142, 184
Walton, Izaak, quoted as to Sheldon, 27
Wallop, Mr., his defence of Baxter on his trial, 137-139
Walpole, Sir Robert, his inaction in the cause of Nonconformity, 291, 292
Ward, Rev. W. G., publishes "The Ideal of a Christian Church," 327; he is deprived of his degrees, 329
Warming-pan fable of the birth of the Pretender, 208
Wellington, the Duke of, devises the reconstruction of Lord John Russell's ministry, 354
Wells, quarrel between dignitaries at, 85

Wem, the title conferred on Jeffreys, 181, note

Wesley, Rev. Charles, originally a High Churchman, 298; separation from the Church forced on him, 299; his influence in originating the Evangelical movement, 359

Wesleyanism, its effect on the Church, 300

Westminster Abbey, irregularities in, described by South, 5; the declaration read at, 180

Wharton, Mr., Sancroft's chaplain, a partisan of the new government, 219

Whigs, the, and Tories unite in opposition to James's tyranny, 160; they command a majority in both Houses, 238; the Marlboroughs form an alliance with, 269; Sacheverell's attack on them, 273; their growing unpopularity, 276; their majority in the Upper House of Convocation, 295

White, Dr., Bishop of Peterborough, signs the petition against reading James's declaration, 173

Whitehall, Romish services conducted at, 130; the declaration read by a chorister at, 180

Whiston, Dr., accused of advocating Arian doctrines, 281

Whitfield, the results of the preaching of, 298

Wickens, Mr., left in possession of Magdalen College, 191

Wilberforce, Mr., his influence on the Church, 301; co-operation of the Evangelicals with, 315

William III., regarded, while Prince of Orange, as head of the Protestant party, 121; his interest in English struggles, 156; news of his approaching invasion of England, 191, 200; his fleet appears in the Channel, 207; he conceals his designs from James, 209; lands with troops at Torbay, 212; composition of the army of, 213; he enters London peaceably, 214; occupies the throne jointly with Mary, 218; desires to confront Rome with an united Reformed Church, 223; his desire for a Comprehension Bill, 229; he suggests the repeal of the Test and Corporation Acts, 230; is a good judge of men, 245; his unpopularity with the clergy, 253; his death hastened by a fall from his horse, 257

Williams, Dr. Rowland, one of the authors of "Essays and Reviews," 368

Wilson's Bampton Lectures, effect of German theology on, 366

Wiseman, Dr., appointed Archbishop of Westminster, 349; his letter of explanation to Lord J. Russell, 352, 357

Winchester, Ken's courageous behaviour on Charles's visit to, 173

Witchcraft, Chief Justice Holt's mild reading of the Acts against, 247

Worcester, Charles II. saved by a Romish priest after the battle of, 125; Bishop of, a consistent Nonjuror, 230

Wordsworth, Wm., influence on the Church of his writings, 301

Wren, Sir Christopher, letter from Sancroft to, quoted, 111

Wright, Lord Chief Justice, on the commission sent to Oxford, 186; Jeffrey's opinion of him, 200

Wycliffe, result of the spirit of inquiry roused by, 6

Wynter, Dr., Vice-chancellor of Oxford, his censure of Mr. Ward, 328; his disapprobation of Mr. Gladstone's conduct, 330

Y

York, the Archbishop of, with difficulty rescued from the Gordon rioters, 304; Mr. Voysey proceeded against by the, 373

York, the Archbishopric of, kept vacant, 184; Sancroft appeals to have it filled, 204; the circumstances of Lamplugh's appointment to, 214, 255
—— Duke of, Sancroft's appointment to the primacy probably due to the, 114; Sancroft's efforts for the conversion of the, 116; openness of his Romish proclivities, 121; he proposes to send for a priest to the dying Charles, 125

York, Duke of, the champion of the Orange Protestant Party, 308

THE END.

A LIST OF

EGAN PAUL, TRENCH, & CO.'S PUBLICATIONS.

1 Paternoster Square,
London.

A LIST OF
KEGAN PAUL, TRENCH, & CO.'S PUBLICATIONS.

ADAMS (F. O.) F.R.G.S.—THE HISTORY OF JAPAN. From the Earliest Period to the Present Time. New Edition, revised. 2 volumes. With Maps and Plans. Demy 8vo. price 21*s*. each.

ADAMSON (H. T.) B.D.—THE TRUTH AS IT IS IN JESUS. Crown 8vo. cloth, price 8*s*. 6*d*.

THE THREE SEVENS. Crown 8vo. cloth, price 5*s*. 6*d*.

A. K. H. B.—FROM A QUIET PLACE. A New Volume of Sermons. Crown 8vo. cloth, price 5*s*.

ALBERT (Mary)—HOLLAND AND HER HEROES TO THE YEAR 1585. An Adaptation from 'Motley's Rise of the Dutch Republic.' Small crown 8vo. price 4*s*. 6*d*.

ALLEN (Rev. R.) M.A.—ABRAHAM; HIS LIFE, TIMES, AND TRAVELS, 3,800 years ago. With Map. Second Edition. Post 8vo. price 6*s*.

ALLEN (Grant) B.A.—PHYSIOLOGICAL ÆSTHETICS. Large post 8vo. 9*s*.

ALLIES (T. W.) M.A.—PER CRUCEM AD LUCEM. The Result of a Life. 2 vols. Demy 8vo. cloth, price 25*s*.

A LIFE'S DECISION. Crown 8vo. cloth, price 7*s*. 6*d*.

ANDERSON (R. C.) C.E.—TABLES FOR FACILITATING THE CALCULATION OF EVERY DETAIL IN CONNECTION WITH EARTHEN AND MASONRY DAMS. Royal 8vo. price £2. 2*s*.

ARCHER (Thomas)—ABOUT MY FATHER'S BUSINESS. Work amidst the Sick, the Sad, and the Sorrowing. Cheaper Edition. Crown 8vo. price 2*s*. 6*d*.

ARMSTRONG (Richard A.) B.A.—LATTER-DAY TEACHERS. Six Lectures. Small crown 8vo. cloth, price 2*s*. 6*d*.

ARNOLD (Arthur)—SOCIAL POLITICS. Demy 8vo. cloth, price 14*s*.

FREE LAND. Second Edition. Crown 8vo. cloth, price 6*s*.

AUBERTIN (J. J.)—A FLIGHT TO MEXICO. With 7 full-page Illustrations and a Railway Map of Mexico. Crown 8vo. cloth, price 7*s*. 6*d*.

BADGER (George Percy) D.C.L.—AN ENGLISH-ARABIC LEXICON. In which the equivalent for English Words and Idiomatic Sentences are rendered into literary and colloquial Arabic. Royal 4to. cloth, price £9. 9*s*.

BAGEHOT (Walter)—THE ENGLISH CONSTITUTION. Third Edition, Crown 8vo. price 7*s*. 6*d*.

LOMBARD STREET. A Description of the Money Market. Seventh Edition. Crown 8vo. price 7*s*. 6*d*.

SOME ARTICLES ON THE DEPRECIATION OF SILVER, AND TOPICS CONNECTED WITH IT. Demy 8vo. price 5*s*.

BAGENAL (Philip H.)—THE AMERICAN-IRISH AND THEIR INFLUENCE ON IRISH POLITICS. Crown 8vo. cloth, 5*s*.

BAGOT (Alan) C.E.—Accidents in Mines : Their Causes and Prevention. Crown 8vo. price 6s.
 The Principles of Colliery Ventilation. Second Edition, greatly enlarged, crown 8vo. cloth, 5s.

BAKER (Sir Sherston, Bart.)—Halleck's International Law ; or, Rules Regulating the Intercourse of States in Peace and War. A New Edition, revised, with Notes and Cases. 2 vols. Demy 8vo. price 38s.
 The Laws relating to Quarantine. Crown 8vo. cloth, price 12s. 6d.

BALDWIN (Capt. J. H.)—The Large and Small Game of Bengal and the North-Western Provinces of India. 4to. With numerous Illustrations. Second Edition. Price 21s.

BALLIN (Ada S. and F. L.)—A Hebrew Grammar. With Exercises selected from the Bible. Crown 8vo. cloth, price 7s. 6d.

BARCLAY (Edgar)—Mountain Life in Algeria. Crown 4to. With numerous Illustrations by Photogravure. Cloth, price 16s.

BARNES (William)—An Outline of English Speechcraft. Crown 8vo. price 4s.
 Outlines of Redecraft (Logic). With English Wording. Crown 8vo. cloth, price 3s.

BARTLEY (G. C. T.)—Domestic Economy : Thrift in Every-Day Life. Taught in Dialogues suitable for children of all ages. Small cr. 8vo. price 2s.

BAUR (Ferdinand) Dr. Ph., Professor in Maulbronn.—A Philological Introduction to Greek and Latin for Students. Translated and adapted from the German. By C. Kegan Paul, M.A. Oxon., and the Rev. E. D. Stone, M.A., late Fellow of King's College, Cambridge, and Assistant Master at Eton. Second Edition. Crown 8vo. price 6s.

BAYNES (Rev. Canon R. H.)—At the Communion Time. A Manual for Holy Communion. With a preface by the Right Rev. the Lord Bishop of Derry and Raphoe. Cloth, price 1s. 6d.

BELLARS (Rev. W.)—The Testimony of Conscience to the Truth and Divine Origin of the Christian Revelation. Burney Prize Essay. Small crown 8vo. cloth, 3s. 6d.

BELLINGHAM (Henry) M.P.—Social Aspects of Catholicism and Protestantism in their Civil Bearing upon Nations. Translated and adapted from the French of M. le Baron de Haulleville. With a preface by His Eminence Cardinal Manning. Second and Cheaper Edition. Crown 8vo. price 3s. 6d.

BENT (J. Theodore)—Genoa : How the Republic Rose and Fell. With 18 Illustrations. Demy 8vo. cloth, price 18s.

BLUNT (The Ven. Archdeacon)—The Divine Patriot, and other Sermons, Preached in Scarborough and in Cannes. Crown 8vo. cloth, 6s.

BLUNT (Wilfrid S.)—The Future of Islam. Crown 8vo. cloth, 6s.

BONWICK (J.) F.R.G.S.—Pyramid Facts and Fancies. Crown 8vo. price 5s.
 Egyptian Belief and Modern Thought. Large post 8vo. cloth, price 10s. 6d.

BOUVERIE-PUSEY (S. E. B.)—Permanence and Evolution. An Inquiry into the supposed Mutability of Animal Types. Crown 8vo. cloth, 5s.

BOIVEN (H. C.) M.A.—STUDIES IN ENGLISH, for the use of Modern Schools. Third Edition. Small crown 8vo. price 1s. 6d.
    ENGLISH GRAMMAR FOR BEGINNERS. Fcp. 8vo. cloth, price 1s.

BRIDGETT (Rev. T. E.)—HISTORY OF THE HOLY EUCHARIST IN GREAT BRITAIN. 2 vols. Demy 8vo. cloth, price 18s.

BRODRICK (the Hon. G. C.)—POLITICAL STUDIES. Demy 8vo. cloth, price 14s.

BROOKE (Rev. S. A.)—LIFE AND LETTERS OF THE LATE REV. F. W. ROBERTSON, M.A. Edited by.
    I. Uniform with Robertson's Sermons. 2 vols. With Steel Portrait. Price 7s. 6d.
    II. Library Edition. 8vo. With Portrait. Price 12s.
    III. A Popular Edition. In 1 vol. 8vo. price 6s.
    THE SPIRIT OF THE CHRISTIAN LIFE. A New Volume of Sermons. Second Edition. Crown 8vo. cloth, price 7s. 6d.
    THE FIGHT OF FAITH. Sermons preached on various occasions. Fifth Edition. Crown 8vo. price 7s. 6d.
    THEOLOGY IN THE ENGLISH POETS.—Cowper, Coleridge, Wordsworth, and Burns. Fourth and Cheaper Edition. Post 8vo. price 5s.
    CHRIST IN MODERN LIFE. Sixteenth and Cheaper Edition. Crown 8vo. price 5s.
    SERMONS. First Series. Twelfth and Cheaper Edition. Crown 8vo. price 5s.
    SERMONS. Second Series. Fifth and Cheaper Edition. Crown 8vo. price 5s.

BROOKE (W. G.) M.A.—THE PUBLIC WORSHIP REGULATION ACT. With a Classified Statement of its Provisions, Notes, and Index. Third Edition, revised and corrected. Crown 8vo. price 3s. 6d.
    SIX PRIVY COUNCIL JUDGMENTS—1850-72. Annotated by. Third Edition. Crown 8vo. price 9s.

BROWN (Rev. J. Baldwin) B.A.—THE HIGHER LIFE. Its Reality, Experience, and Destiny. Fifth Edition. Crown 8vo. price 5s.
    DOCTRINE OF ANNIHILATION IN THE LIGHT OF THE GOSPEL OF LOVE. Five Discourses. Third Edition. Crown 8vo. price 2s. 6d.
    THE CHRISTIAN POLICY OF LIFE. A Book for Young Men of Business. Third Edition. Crown 8vo. cloth, price 3s. 6d.

BROWN (J. Croumbie) LL.D.—REBOISEMENT IN FRANCE; or, Records of the Replanting of the Alps, the Cevennes, and the Pyrenees with Trees, Herbage, and Bush. Demy 8vo. price 12s. 6d.
    THE HYDROLOGY OF SOUTHERN AFRICA. Demy 8vo. price 10s. 6d.

BROWN (S. Borton) B.A.—THE FIRE BAPTISM OF ALL FLESH; or, the Coming Spiritual Crisis of the Dispensation. Crown 8vo. cloth, price. 6s.

BROWNE (W. R.)—THE INSPIRATION OF THE NEW TESTAMENT. With a Preface by the Rev. J. P. NORRIS, D.D. Fcp. 8vo. cloth, price 2s. 6d.

BURCKHARDT (Jacob)—THE CIVILIZATION OF THE PERIOD OF THE RENAISSANCE IN ITALY. Authorised translation, by S. G. C. Middlemore. 2 vols. Demy 8vo. price 24s.

BURTON (Mrs. Richard)—THE INNER LIFE OF SYRIA, PALESTINE, AND THE HOLY LAND. With Maps, Photographs, and Coloured Plates. Cheaper Edition in one volume. Large post 8vo. cloth, price 10s. 6d.

BUSBECQ (Ogier Ghiselin de)—His Life and Letters. By Charles Thornton Forster, M.A., and F. H. Blackburne Daniell, M.A. 2 vols. With Frontispieces. Demy 8vo. cloth, price 24s.

CANDLER (H.)—The Groundwork of Belief. Crown 8vo. cloth, price 7s.

CARPENTER (Dr. Philip P.)—His Life and Work. Edited by his brother, Russell Lant Carpenter. With Portrait and Vignettes. Second Edition. Crown 8vo. cloth, price 7s. 6d.

CARPENTER (W. B.) LL.D., M.D., F.R.S., &c.—The Principles of Mental Physiology. With their Applications to the Training and Discipline of the Mind, and the Study of its Morbid Conditions. Illustrated. Sixth Edition. 8vo. price 12s.

CERVANTES—The Ingenious Knight Don Quixote de la Mancha. A New Translation from the Originals of 1605 and 1608. By A. J. Duffield. With Notes. 3 vols. Demy 8vo. price 42s.

CHEYNE (Rev. T. K.)—The Prophecies of Isaiah. Translated with Critical Notes and Dissertations. 2 vols. Second Edition. Demy 8vo. cloth, price 25s.

CLAIRAUT—Elements of Geometry. Translated by Dr. Kaines. With 145 Figures. Crown 8vo. cloth, price 4s. 6d.

CLAYDEN (P. W.)—England under Lord Beaconsfield. The Political History of the Last Six Years, from the end of 1873 to the beginning of 1880. Second Edition, with Index and continuation to March 1880. Demy 8vo. cloth, price 16s.

CLODD (Edward) F.R.A.S.—The Childhood of the World: a Simple Account of Man in Early Times. Sixth Edition. Crown 8vo. price 3s.
    A Special Edition for Schools. Price 1s.

The Childhood of Religions. Including a Simple Account of the Birth and Growth of Myths and Legends. Ninth Thousand. Crown 8vo. price 5s.
    A Special Edition for Schools. Price 1s. 6d.

Jesus of Nazareth. With a brief sketch of Jewish History to the Time of His Birth. Small crown 8vo. cloth, price 6s.

COGHLAN (J. Cole) D.D.—The Modern Pharisee and other Sermons. Edited by the Very Rev. H. H. Dickinson, D.D., Dean of Chapel Royal, Dublin. New and Cheaper Edition. Crown 8vo. cloth, 7s. 6d.

COLERIDGE (Sara)—Phantasmion. A Fairy Tale. With an Introductory Preface by the Right Hon. Lord Coleridge, of Ottery St. Mary. A New Edition. Illustrated. Crown 8vo. price 7s. 6d.

Memoir and Letters of Sara Coleridge. Edited by her Daughter. With Index. Cheap Edition. With one Portrait. Price 7s. 6d.

COLLINS (Mortimer)—The Secret of Long Life. Small crown 8vo. cloth, price 3s. 6d.

CONNELL (A. K.)—Discontent and Danger in India. Small crown 8vo. cloth, price 3s. 6d.

COOKE (Prof. J. P.) of the Harvard University.—Scientific Culture. Crown 8vo. price 1s.

COOPER (H. J.)—The Art of Furnishing on Rational and Æsthetic Principles. New and Cheaper Edition. Fcp. 8vo. cloth, price 1s. 6d.

CORFIELD (*Professor*) *M.D.*—HEALTH. Crown 8vo. cloth, price 6s.

CORY (*William*)—A GUIDE TO MODERN ENGLISH HISTORY. Part I.— MDCCCXV.-MDCCCXXX. Demy 8vo. cloth, price 9s.

CORY (*Col. Arthur*)—THE EASTERN MENACE. Crown 8vo. cloth, price 7s. 6d.

COTTERILL (*H. B.*)—AN INTRODUCTION TO THE STUDY OF POETRY. Crown 8vo. cloth, price 7s. 6d.

COURTNEY (*W. L.*)—THE METAPHYSICS OF JOHN STUART MILL. Crown 8vo. cloth, price 5s. 6d.

COX (*Rev. Sir George W.*) *M.A., Bart.*—A HISTORY OF GREECE FROM THE EARLIEST PERIOD TO THE END OF THE PERSIAN WAR. New Edition. 2 vols. Demy 8vo. price 36s.

THE MYTHOLOGY OF THE ARYAN NATIONS. New Edition. Demy 8vo. price 16s.

A GENERAL HISTORY OF GREECE FROM THE EARLIEST PERIOD TO THE DEATH OF ALEXANDER THE GREAT, with a sketch of the subsequent History to the present time. New Edition. Crown 8vo. price 7s. 6d.

TALES OF ANCIENT GREECE. New Edition. Small crown 8vo. price 6s.

SCHOOL HISTORY OF GREECE. New Edition. With Maps. Fcp. 8vo. price 3s. 6d.

THE GREAT PERSIAN WAR FROM THE HISTORY OF HERODOTUS. New Edition. Fcp. 8vo. price 3s. 6d.

A MANUAL OF MYTHOLOGY IN THE FORM OF QUESTION AND ANSWER. New Edition. Fcp. 8vo. price 3s.

AN INTRODUCTION TO THE SCIENCE OF COMPARATIVE MYTHOLOGY AND FOLK-LORE. Crown 8vo. cloth, price 9s.

COX (*Rev. Sir G. W.*) *M.A., Bart., and* **JONES** (*Eustace Hinton*)— POPULAR ROMANCES OF THE MIDDLE AGES. Second Edition, in 1 vol. Crown 8vo. cloth, price 6s.

COX (*Rev. Samuel*)—SALVATOR MUNDI; or, Is Christ the Saviour of all Men? Seventh Edition. Crown 8vo. price 5s.

THE GENESIS OF EVIL, AND OTHER SERMONS, mainly expository. Second Edition. Crown 8vo. cloth, price 6s.

A COMMENTARY ON THE BOOK OF JOB. With a Translation. Demy 8vo. cloth, price 15s.

CRAUFURD (*A. H.*)—SEEKING FOR LIGHT: Sermons. Crown 8vo. cloth, price 5s.

CRAVEN (*Mrs.*)—A YEAR'S MEDITATIONS. Crown 8vo. cloth, price 6s.

CRAWFURD (*Oswald*)—PORTUGAL, OLD AND NEW. With Illustrations and Maps. New and Cheaper Edition. Crown 8vo. cloth, price 6s.

CROZIER (*John Beattie*) *M.B.*—THE RELIGION OF THE FUTURE. Crown 8vo. cloth, price 6s.

CYCLOPÆDIA OF COMMON THINGS. Edited by the Rev. Sir GEORGE W. COX, Bart., M.A. With 500 Illustrations. Large post 8vo. cloth, price 7s. 6d.

DALTON (*John Neale*) *M.A., R.N.*—SERMONS TO NAVAL CADETS. Preached on board H.M.S. 'Britannia.' Second Edition. Small crown 8vo. cloth, price 3s. 6d.

DAVIDSON (Rev. Samuel) D.D., LL.D. — The New Testament, translated from the Latest Greek Text of Tischendorf. A New and thoroughly revised Edition. Post 8vo. price 10s. 6d.

Canon of the Bible : Its Formation, History, and Fluctuations. Third and revised Edition. Small crown 8vo. price 5s.

DAVIES (Rev. J. L.) M.A.—Theology and Morality. Essays on Questions of Belief and Practice. Crown 8vo. price 7s. 6d.

DAWSON (Geo.) M.A.—Prayers, with a Discourse on Prayer. Edited by his Wife. Seventh Edition. Crown 8vo. price 6s.

Sermons on Disputed Points and Special Occasions. Edited by his Wife. Third Edition. Crown 8vo. price 6s.

Sermons on Daily Life and Duty. Edited by his Wife. Third Edition. Crown 8vo. price 6s.

The Authentic Gospel. A New Volume of Sermons. Edited by George St. Clair. Second Edition. Crown 8vo. cloth, price 6s.

DE REDCLIFFE (Viscount Stratford)—Why am I a Christian Fifth Edition. Crown 8vo. price 3s.

DESPREZ (Philip S.) B.D.—Daniel and John ; or, the Apocalypse of the Old and that of the New Testament. Demy 8vo. cloth, price 12s.

DOWDEN (Edward) LL.D.—Shakspere : a Critical Study of his Mind and Art. Sixth Edition. Post 8vo. price 12s.

Studies in Literature, 1789–1877. Large post 8vo. price 12s.

DREWRY (G. O.) M.D.—The Common-Sense Management of the Stomach. Fifth Edition. Fcp. 8vo. price 2s. 6d.

DREWRY (G. O.) M.D., and BARTLETT (H. C.) Ph.D., F.C.S.
Cup and Platter : or, Notes on Food and its Effects. New and Cheaper Edition. Small 8vo. price 1s. 6d.

DUFFIELD (A. J.)—Don Quixote : his Critics and Commentators. With a brief account of the minor works of Miguel de Cervantes Saavedra, and a statement of the aim and end of the greatest of them all. A handy book for general readers. Crown 8vo. cloth, price 3s. 6d.

DU MONCEL (Count)—The Telephone, the Microphone, and the Phonograph. With 74 Illustrations. Second Edition. Small crown 8vo. cloth, price 5s.

EDEN (Frederick)—The Nile without a Dragoman. Second Edition. Crown 8vo. price 7s. 6d.

EDGEWORTH (F. Y.)—Mathematical Psychics. An Essay on the Application of Mathematics to Social Science. Demy 8vo. cloth, 7s. 6d.

EDIS (Robert W.) F.S.A. &c.—Decoration and Furniture of Town Houses : a Series of Cantor Lectures, delivered before the Society of Arts, 1880. Amplified and Enlarged. With 29 Full-page Illustrations and numerous Sketches. Second Edition. Square 8vo. cloth, price 12s. 6d.

Educational Code of the Prussian Nation, in its Present Form. In accordance with the Decisions of the Common Provincial Law, and with those of Recent Legislation. Crown 8vo. cloth, price 2s. 6d.

EDUCATION LIBRARY. Edited by PHILIP MAGNUS :—
> AN INTRODUCTION TO THE HISTORY OF EDUCATIONAL THEORIES. By OSCAR BROWNING, M.A. Second Edition. Cloth, price 3s. 6d.
>
> JOHN AMOS COMENIUS : his Life and Educational Work. By Prof. S. S. LAURIE, A.M. Cloth, price 3s. 6d.
>
> OLD GREEK EDUCATION. By the Rev. Prof. MAHAFFY, M.A. Cloth, price 3s. 6d.

ELSDALE (*Henry*)—STUDIES IN TENNYSON'S IDYLLS. Crown 8vo. price 5s.

ELYOT (*Sir Thomas*)—THE BOKE NAMED THE GOUERNOUR. Edited from the First Edition of 1531 by HENRY HERBERT STEPHEN CROFT, M.A., Barrister-at-Law. With Portraits of Sir Thomas and Lady Elyot, copied by permission of her Majesty from Holbein's Original Drawings at Windsor Castle. 2 vols. Fcp. 4to. cloth, price 50s.

ERANUS. A COLLECTION OF EXERCISES IN THE ALCAIC AND SAPPHIC METRES. Edited by F. W. CORNISH, Assistant Master at Eton. Crown 8vo. cloth, 2s.

EVANS (*Mark*)—THE STORY OF OUR FATHER'S LOVE, told to Children. Fifth and Cheaper Edition. With Four Illustrations. Fcp. 8vo. price 1s. 6d.
> A BOOK OF COMMON PRAYER AND WORSHIP FOR HOUSEHOLD USE, compiled exclusively from the Holy Scriptures. Second Edition. Fcp. 8vo. price 1s.
>
> THE GOSPEL OF HOME LIFE. Crown 8vo. cloth, price 4s. 6d.
>
> THE KING'S STORY-BOOK. In Three Parts. Fcp. 8vo. cloth, price 1s. 6d. each.
>
> **** Parts I. and II. with Eight Illustrations and Two Picture Maps, now ready.

FELKIN (*H. M.*)—TECHNICAL EDUCATION IN A SAXON TOWN. Published for the City and Guilds of London Institute for the Advancement of Technical Education. Demy 8vo. cloth, price 2s.

FIELD (*Horace*) B.A. Lond.—THE ULTIMATE TRIUMPH OF CHRISTIANITY. Small crown 8vo. cloth, price 3s. 6d.

FLOREDICE (*W. H.*)—A MONTH AMONG THE MERE IRISH. Small crown 8vo. cloth, price 5s.

FOLKESTONE RITUAL CASE : the Arguments, Proceedings, Judgment, and Report. Demy 8vo. price 25s.

FORMBY (*Rev. Henry*)—ANCIENT ROME AND ITS CONNECTION WITH THE CHRISTIAN RELIGION : An Outline of the History of the City from its First Foundation down to the Erection of the Chair of St. Peter, A.D. 42-47. With numerous Illustrations of Ancient Monuments, Sculpture, and Coinage, and of the Antiquities of the Christian Catacombs. Royal 4to. cloth extra, £2. 10s ; roxburgh half-morocco, £2. 12s. 6d.

FRASER (*Donald*)—EXCHANGE TABLES OF STERLING AND INDIAN RUPEE CURRENCY, upon a new and extended system, embracing Values from One Farthing to One Hundred Thousand Pounds, and at rates progressing, in Sixteenths of a Penny, from 1s. 9d. to 2s. 3d. per Rupee. Royal 8vo. price 10s. 6d.

FRISWELL (J. Hain)—THE BETTER SELF. Essays for Home Life. Crown 8vo. price 6s.

GARDINER (Samuel R.) and J. BASS MULLINGER, M.A.—INTRODUCTION TO THE STUDY OF ENGLISH HISTORY. Large crown 8vo. cloth, price 9s.

GARDNER (Dorsey)—QUATRE BRAS, LIGNY, AND WATERLOO. A Narrative of the Campaign in Belgium, 1815. With Maps and Plans. Demy 8vo. cloth, 16s.

GARDNER (J.) M.D.—LONGEVITY: THE MEANS OF PROLONGING LIFE AFTER MIDDLE AGE. Fourth Edition, revised and enlarged. Small crown 8vo. price 4s.

GEBLER (Karl Von)—GALILEO GALILEI AND THE ROMAN CURIA, from Authentic Sources. Translated with the sanction of the Author, by Mrs. GEORGE STURGE. Demy 8vo. cloth, price 12s.

GEDDES (James)—HISTORY OF THE ADMINISTRATION OF JOHN DE WITT, Grand Pensionary of Holland. Vol. I. 1623—1654. With Portrait. Demy 8vo. cloth, price 15s.

GENNA (E.)—IRRESPONSIBLE PHILANTHROPISTS. Being some Chapters on the Employment of Gentlewomen. Small crown 8vo. cloth, price, 2s. 6d.

GEORGE (Henry)—PROGRESS AND POVERTY: an Inquiry into the Causes of Industrial Depressions, and of Increase of Want with Increase of Wealth. The Remedy. Second Edition. Post 8vo. cloth, price 7s. 6d.

GILBERT (Mrs.)—AUTOBIOGRAPHY AND OTHER MEMORIALS. Edited by Josiah Gilbert. Third and Cheaper Edition. With Steel Portrait and several Wood Engravings. Crown 8vo. price 7s. 6d.

GLOVER (F.) M.A.—EXEMPLA LATINA. A First Construing Book with Short Notes, Lexicon, and an Introduction to the Analysis of Sentences. Fcp. 8vo. cloth, price 2s.

GODWIN (William)—WILLIAM GODWIN: HIS FRIENDS AND CONTEMPORARIES. With Portraits and Facsimiles of the Handwriting of Godwin and his Wife. By C. KEGAN PAUL. 2 vols. Large post 8vo. price 28s.

THE GENIUS OF CHRISTIANITY UNVEILED. Being Essays never before published. Edited, with a Preface, by C. Kegan Paul. Crown 8vo. price 7s. 6d.

GOLDSMID (Sir Francis Henry) Bart., Q.C., M.P.—MEMOIR OF. With Portrait. Crown 8vo. cloth, price 5s.

GOODENOUGH (Commodore J. G.)—MEMOIR OF, with Extracts from his Letters and Journals. Edited by his Widow. With Steel Engraved Portrait. Square 8vo. cloth, price 5s.

*** Also a Library Edition with Maps, Woodcuts, and Steel Engraved Portrait. Square post 8vo. price 14s.

GOSSE (Edmund W.)—STUDIES IN THE LITERATURE OF NORTHERN EUROPE. With a Frontispiece designed and etched by Alma Tadema. Large post 8vo. cloth, price 12s.

GOULD (Rev. S. Baring) M.A.—THE VICAR OF MORWENSTOW: a Memoir of the Rev. R. S. Hawker. With Portrait. Third Edition, revised. Square post 8vo. price 10s. 6d.

GERMANY, PRESENT AND PAST. New and Cheaper Edition. Large crown 8vo. cloth, price 7s. 6d.

GOWAN (Major Walter E.) — A. IVANOFF'S RUSSIAN GRAMMAR. (16th Edition.) Translated, enlarged, and arranged for use of Students of the Russian Language. Demy 8vo. cloth, 6s.

GRAHAM (William) M.A. — THE CREED OF SCIENCE, Religious, Moral, and Social. Demy 8vo. cloth, price 12s.

GRIFFITH (Thomas) A.M. — THE GOSPEL OF THE DIVINE LIFE: a Study of the Fourth Evangelist. Demy 8vo. cloth, price 14s.

GRIMLEY (Rev. H. N.) M.A. — TREMADOC SERMONS, CHIEFLY ON THE SPIRITUAL BODY, THE UNSEEN WORLD, AND THE DIVINE HUMANITY. Third Edition. Crown 8vo. price 6s.

GRÜNER (M. L.) — STUDIES OF BLAST FURNACE PHENOMENA. Translated by L. D. B. GORDON, F.R.S.E., F.G.S. Demy 8vo. price 7s. 6d.

GURNEY (Rev. Archer) — WORDS OF FAITH AND CHEER. A Mission of Instruction and Suggestion. Crown 8vo. price 6s.

HAECKEL (Prof. Ernst) — THE HISTORY OF CREATION. Translation revised by Professor E. RAY LANKESTER, M.A., F.R.S. With Coloured Plates and Genealogical Trees of the various groups of both plants and animals. 2 vols. Second Edition. Post 8vo. cloth, price 32s.

    THE HISTORY OF THE EVOLUTION OF MAN. With numerous Illustrations. 2 vols. Post 8vo. price 32s.

    FREEDOM IN SCIENCE AND TEACHING. With a Prefatory Note by T. H. HUXLEY, F.R.S. Crown 8vo. cloth, price 5s.

HALF-CROWN SERIES :—

    SISTER DORA : a Biography. By MARGARET LONSDALE.

    TRUE WORDS FOR BRAVE MEN : a Book for Soldiers and Sailors. By the late CHARLES KINGSLEY.

    AN INLAND VOYAGE. By R. L. STEVENSON.

    TRAVELS WITH A DONKEY. By R. L. STEVENSON.

    A NOOK IN THE APENNINES. By LEADER SCOTT.

    NOTES OF TRAVEL : being Extracts from the Journals of Count VON MOLTKE.

    LETTERS FROM RUSSIA. By Count VON MOLTKE.

    ENGLISH SONNETS. Collected and Arranged by J. DENNIS.

    LYRICS OF LOVE. FROM SHAKESPEARE TO TENNYSON. Selected and Arranged by W. D. ADAMS.

    LONDON LYRICS. By F. LOCKER.

    HOME SONGS FOR QUIET HOURS. By the Rev. Canon R. H. BAYNES.

HALLECK'S INTERNATIONAL LAW ; or, Rules Regulating the Intercourse of States in Peace and War. A New Edition, revised, with Notes and Cases, by Sir SHERSTON BAKER, Bart. 2 vols. Demy 8vo. price 38s.

HARTINGTON (The Right Hon. the Marquis of) M.P. — ELECTION SPEECHES IN 1879 AND 1880. With Address to the Electors of North East Lancashire. Crown 8vo. cloth, price 3s. 6d.

HAWEIS (*Rev. H. R.*) *M.A.*—CURRENT COIN. Materialism—The Devil — Crime — Drunkenness — Pauperism — Emotion — Recreation — The Sabbath. Fourth and Cheaper Edition. Crown 8vo. price 5s.

ARROWS IN THE AIR. Fourth and Cheaper Edition. Crown 8vo. cloth, price 5s.

SPEECH IN SEASON. Fifth and Cheaper Edition. Crown 8vo. price 5s.

THOUGHTS FOR THE TIMES. Twelfth and Cheaper Edition. Crown 8vo. price 5s.

UNSECTARIAN FAMILY PRAYERS. New and Cheaper Edition. Fcp. 8vo. price 1s. 6d.

HAWKINS (*Edwards Comerford*)—SPIRIT AND FORM. Sermons preached in the Parish Church of Leatherhead. Crown 8vo. cloth, price 6s.

HAYES (*A. H.*), *Junr.*—NEW COLORADO AND THE SANTA FÉ TRAIL. With Map and 60 Illustrations. Crown 8vo. cloth, price 9s.

HEIDENHAIN (*Rudolf*) *M.D.*—ANIMAL MAGNETISM: PHYSIOLOGICAL OBSERVATIONS. Translated from the Fourth German Edition by L. C. WOOLDRIDGE, with a Preface by G. R. ROMANES, F.R.S. Crown 8vo. price 2s. 6d.

HELLWALD (*Baron F. Von*)—THE RUSSIANS IN CENTRAL ASIA. A Critical Examination, down to the Present Time, of the Geography and History of Central Asia. Translated by Lieut.-Col. THEODORE WIRGMAN, LL.B. With Map. Large post 8vo. price 12s.

HINTON (*J.*)—THE PLACE OF THE PHYSICIAN. To which is added ESSAYS ON THE LAW OF HUMAN LIFE, AND ON THE RELATIONS BETWEEN ORGANIC AND INORGANIC WORLDS. Second Edition. Crown 8vo. price 3s. 6d.

PHILOSOPHY AND RELIGION. Selections from the MSS. of the late JAMES HINTON. Edited by CAROLINE HADDON. Crown 8vo. cloth, 5s.

PHYSIOLOGY FOR PRACTICAL USE. By Various Writers. With 50 Illustrations. Third and Cheaper Edition. Crown 8vo. price 5s.

AN ATLAS OF DISEASES OF THE MEMBRANA TYMPANI. With Descriptive Text. Post 8vo. price £6. 6s.

THE QUESTIONS OF AURAL SURGERY. With Illustrations. 2 vols. Post 8vo. price 12s. 6d.

CHAPTERS ON THE ART OF THINKING, AND OTHER ESSAYS. With an Introduction by SHADWORTH HODGSON. Edited by C. H. HINTON. Crown 8vo. cloth, price 8s. 6d.

THE MYSTERY OF PAIN. New Edition. Fcp. 8vo. cloth limp, 1s.

LIFE AND LETTERS. Edited by ELLICE HOPKINS, with an Introduction by Sir W. W. GULL, Bart., and Portrait engraved on Steel by C. H. JEENS. Fourth Edition. Crown 8vo. price 8s. 6d.

HOOPER (*Mary*)—LITTLE DINNERS: HOW TO SERVE THEM WITH ELEGANCE AND ECONOMY. Thirteenth Edition. Crown 8vo. price 5s.

COOKERY FOR INVALIDS, PERSONS OF DELICATE DIGESTION, AND CHILDREN. Second Edition. Crown 8vo. price 3s. 6d.

EVERY-DAY MEALS. Being Economical and Wholesome Recipes for Breakfast, Luncheon, and Supper. Third Edition. Crown 8vo. cloth, price 5s.

HOPKINS (Ellice)—LIFE AND LETTERS OF JAMES HINTON, with an Introduction by Sir W. W. GULL, Bart., and Portrait engraved on Steel by C. H. JEENS. Fourth Edition. Crown 8vo. price 8s. 6d.

HORNER (The Misses)—WALKS IN FLORENCE. A New and thoroughly Revised Edition. 2 vols. Crown 8vo. Cloth limp. With Illustrations.
    VOL. I.—Churches, Streets, and Palaces. Price 10s. 6d.
    VOL. II.—Public Galleries and Museums. Price 5s.

HOSPITALIER (E.)—THE MODERN APPLICATIONS OF ELECTRICITY. Translated and Enlarged by JULIUS MAIER, Ph.D. With 170 Illustrations. Demy 8vo. cloth, price 16s.

HOUSEHOLD READINGS ON PROPHECY. By A LAYMAN. Small crown 8vo. cloth, price 3s. 6d.

HUGHES (Henry)—THE REDEMPTION OF THE WORLD. Crown 8vo. cloth, price 3s. 6d.

HULL (Edmund C. P.)—THE EUROPEAN IN INDIA. With a Medical Guide for Anglo-Indians. By R. S. MAIR, M.D., F.R.C.S.E. Third Edition, Revised and Corrected. Post 8vo. price 6s.

HUNTINGFORD (Rev. E.) D.C.L.—THE APOCALYPSE. With a Commentary and Introductory Essay. Demy 8vo. cloth, 9s.

HUTTON (Arthur) M.A.—THE ANGLICAN MINISTRY: its Nature and Value in relation to the Catholic Priesthood. With a Preface by His Eminence Cardinal Newman. Demy 8vo. cloth, price 14s.

JENKINS (E.) and RAYMOND (J.)—THE ARCHITECT'S LEGAL HANDBOOK. Third Edition, Revised. Crown 8vo. price 6s.

JENKINS (Rev. R. C.) M.A.—THE PRIVILEGE OF PETER and the Claims of the Roman Church confronted with the Scriptures, the Councils, and the Testimony of the Popes themselves. Fcp. 8vo. price 3s. 6d.
    ALFONSO PETRUCCI, Cardinal and Conspirator. An Historical Tragedy in Five Acts. Small crown 8vo. cloth, 3s. 6d.

JENNINGS (Mrs. Vaughan)—RAHEL: HER LIFE AND LETTERS. With a Portrait from the Painting by Daffinger. Square post 8vo. price 7s. 6d.

JERVIS (Rev. W. Henley)—THE GALLICAN CHURCH AND THE REVOLUTION. A Sequel to the History of the Church of France, from the Concordat of Bologna to the Revolution. Demy 8vo. cloth, 18s.

JOEL (L.)—A CONSUL'S MANUAL AND SHIPOWNER'S AND SHIPMASTER'S PRACTICAL GUIDE IN THEIR TRANSACTIONS ABROAD. With Definitions of Nautical, Mercantile, and Legal Terms; a Glossary of Mercantile Terms in English, French, German, Italian, and Spanish; Tables of the Money, Weights, and Measures of the Principal Commercial Nations and their Equivalents in British Standards; and Forms of Consular and Notarial Acts. Demy 8vo. cloth, price 12s.

JOHNSTONE (C. F.) M.A.—HISTORICAL ABSTRACTS: being Outlines of the History of some of the less known States of Europe. Crown 8vo. cloth, price 7s. 6d.

JONES (Lucy)—PUDDINGS AND SWEETS; being Three Hundred and Sixty-five Receipts approved by experience. Crown 8vo. price 2s. 6d.

JOYCE (P. W.) LL.D. &c.—OLD CELTIC ROMANCES. Translated from the Gaelic. Crown 8vo. cloth, price 7s. 6d.

KAUFMANN (Rev. M.) B.A.—SOCIALISM: Its Nature, its Dangers, and its Remedies considered. Crown 8vo. price 7s. 6d.

UTOPIAS; or, Schemes of Social Improvement, from Sir Thomas More to Karl Marx. Crown 8vo. cloth, price 5s.

KAY (Joseph)—FREE TRADE IN LAND. Edited by his Widow. With Preface by the Right Hon. JOHN BRIGHT, M.P. Sixth Edition. Crown 8vo. cloth, price 5s.

KEMPIS (Thomas à)—OF THE IMITATION OF CHRIST. Parchment Library Edition, 6s.; or vellum, 7s. 6d. The Red Line Edition, fcp. 8vo. cloth, red edges, price 2s. 6d. The Cabinet Edition, small 8vo. cloth, red edges, price 1s. 6d. The Miniature Edition, 32mo. cloth, red edges, price 1s.
⁂ All the above Editions may be had in various extra bindings.

KENT (C.)—CORONA CATHOLICA AD PETRI SUCCESSORIS PEDES OBLATA. DE SUMMI PONTIFICIS LEONIS XIII. ASSUMPTIONE EPIGRAMMA. In Quinquaginta Linguis. Fcp. 4to. cloth, price 15s.

KERNER (Dr. A.) Professor of Botany in the University of Innsbruck.—FLOWERS AND THEIR UNBIDDEN GUESTS. Translation edited by W. OGLE, M.A., M.D. With Illustrations. Square 8vo. cloth, price 9s.

KETTLEWELL (Rev. S.)—THOMAS À KEMPIS AND THE BROTHERS OF COMMON LIFE. 2 vols. With Frontispieces. Demy 8vo. cloth, 30s.

KIDD (Joseph) M.D.—THE LAWS OF THERAPEUTICS; or, the Science and Art of Medicine. Second Edition. Crown 8vo. price 6s.

KINAHAN (G. Henry) M.R.I.A., of H.M.'s Geological Survey.—THE GEOLOGY OF IRELAND, with numerous Illustrations and a Geological Map of Ireland. Square 8vo. cloth.

KINGSFORD (Anna) M.D.—THE PERFECT WAY IN DIET. A Treatise advocating a Return to the Natural and Ancient Food of Race. Small crown 8vo. cloth, price 2s.

KINGSLEY (Charles) M.A.—LETTERS AND MEMORIES OF HIS LIFE. Edited by his WIFE. With Two Steel Engraved Portraits, and Illustrations on Wood, and a Facsimile of his Handwriting. Thirteenth Edition. 2 vols. Demy 8vo. price 36s.
⁂ Also the Eleventh Cabinet Edition, in 2 vols. Crown 8vo. cloth, price 12s.

ALL SAINTS' DAY, and other Sermons. Edited by the Rev. W. HARRISON. Third Edition. Crown 8vo. price 7s. 6d.

TRUE WORDS FOR BRAVE MEN. A Book for Soldiers' and Sailors' Libraries. Eighth Edition. Crown 8vo. price 2s. 6d.

KNIGHT (Professor W.)—STUDIES IN PHILOSOPHY AND LITERATURE. Large post 8vo. cloth, price 7s. 6d.

KNOX (Alexander A.)—THE NEW PLAYGROUND; or, Wanderings in Algeria. Large crown 8vo. cloth, price 10s. 6d.

LAURIE (S. S.)—THE TRAINING OF TEACHERS, and other Educational Papers. Crown 8vo. cloth, price 7s. 6d.

LEE (Rev. F. G.) D.C.L.—THE OTHER WORLD; or, Glimpses of the Supernatural. 2 vols. A New Edition. Crown 8vo. price 15s.

LEWIS (Edward Dillon)—A DRAFT CODE OF CRIMINAL LAW AND PROCEDURE. Demy 8vo. cloth, price 21s.

LINDSAY (W. Lauder) M.D., F.R.S.E., &c.—MIND IN THE LOWER ANIMALS IN HEALTH AND DISEASE. 2 vols. Demy 8vo. cloth, price 32s.
Vol. I.—Mind in Health. Vol. II.—Mind in Disease.

LLOYD (*Walter*)—THE HOPE OF THE WORLD: An Essay on Universal Redemption. Crown 8vo. cloth, 5*s*.

LONSDALE (*Margaret*)—SISTER DORA: a Biography. With Portrait. Twenty-fifth Edition. Crown 8vo. cloth, price 2*s*. 6*d*.

LORIMER (*Peter*) *D.D.*—JOHN KNOX AND THE CHURCH OF ENGLAND. His Work in her Pulpit, and his Influence upon her Liturgy, Articles, and Parties. Demy 8vo. price 12*s*.

JOHN WICLIF AND HIS ENGLISH PRECURSORS. By GERHARD VICTOR LECHLER. Translated from the German, with additional Notes. New and Cheaper Edition. Demy 8vo. price 10*s*. 6*d*.

LOWDER (*Charles*)—A BIOGRAPHY. By the Author of 'St. Teresa.' Sixth Edition. Large crown 8vo. With Portrait. Cloth, price 7*s*. 6*d*.

MACHIAVELLI (*Niccoli*)—THE PRINCE. Translated from the Italian by N. H. T. Small crown 8vo. printed on hand-made paper, cloth, bevelled boards, 6*s*.

MACKENZIE (*Alexander*)—HOW INDIA IS GOVERNED. Being an Account of England's work in India. Small crown 8vo. cloth, 2*s*.

MACLACHLAN (*Mrs.*)—NOTES AND EXTRACTS ON EVERLASTING PUNISHMENT AND ETERNAL LIFE, ACCORDING TO LITERAL INTERPRETATION. Small crown 8vo. cloth, price 3*s*. 6*d*.

MACNAUGHT (*Rev. John*)—CŒNA DOMINI: An Essay on the Lord's Supper, its Primitive Institution, Apostolic Uses, and Subsequent History. Demy 8vo. price 14*s*.

MAGNUS (*Mrs.*)—ABOUT THE JEWS SINCE BIBLE TIMES. From the Babylonian Exile till the English Exodus. Small crown 8vo. cloth, price 5*s*.

MARRIAGE AND MATERNITY; or, Scripture Wives and Mothers. Small crown 8vo. cloth, price 4*s*. 6*d*.

MAIR (*R. S.*) *M.D., F.R.C.S.E.*—THE MEDICAL GUIDE FOR ANGLO-INDIANS. Being a Compendium of Advice to Europeans in India, relating to the Preservation and Regulation of Health. With a Supplement on the Management of Children in India. Second Edition. Crown 8vo. limp cloth, price 3*s*. 6*d*.

MANNING (*His Eminence Cardinal*)—THE TRUE STORY OF THE VATICAN COUNCIL. Crown 8vo. price 5*s*.

MARKHAM (*Capt. Albert Hastings*) *R.N.*—THE GREAT FROZEN SEA: A Personal Narrative of the Voyage of the *Alert* during the Arctic Expedition of 1875-6. With Six Full-page Illustrations, Two Maps, and Twenty-seven Woodcuts. Fifth and Cheaper Edition. Crown 8vo. cloth, price 6*s*.

A POLAR RECONNAISSANCE: being the Voyage of the 'Isbjörn' to Novaya Zemlya in 1879. With 10 Illustrations. Demy 8vo. cloth, price 16*s*.

MARTINEAU (*Gertrude*)—OUTLINE LESSONS ON MORALS. Small crown 8vo. cloth, price 3*s*. 6*d*.

McGRATH (*Terence*)—PICTURES FROM IRELAND. New and Cheaper Edition. Crown 8vo. cloth, price 2*s*.

MEREDITH (*M. A.*)—THEOTOKOS, THE EXAMPLE FOR WOMAN. Dedicated, by permission, to Lady AGNES WOOD. Revised by the Venerable Archdeacon DENISON. 32mo. limp cloth, 1*s*. 6*d*.

MERRITT (Henry)—ART-CRITICISM AND ROMANCE. With Recollections and Twenty-three Illustrations in *eau-forte*, by Anna Lea Merritt. 2 vols. Large post 8vo. cloth, price 25s.

MILLER (Edward)—THE HISTORY AND DOCTRINES OF IRVINGISM; or, the so-called Catholic and Apostolic Church. 2 vols. Large post 8vo. price 25s.

THE CHURCH IN RELATION TO THE STATE. Large crown 8vo. cloth, price 7s. 6d.

MILNE (James)—TABLES OF EXCHANGE for the Conversion of Sterling Money into Indian and Ceylon Currency, at Rates from 1s. 8d. to 2s. 3d. per Rupee. Second Edition. Demy 8vo. cloth, price £2. 2s.

MINCHIN (J. G.)—BULGARIA SINCE THE WAR: Notes of a Tour in the Autumn of 1879. Small crown 8vo. cloth, price 3s. 6d.

MOCKLER (E.)—A GRAMMAR OF THE BALOOCHEE LANGUAGE, as it is spoken in Makran (Ancient Gedrosia), in the Persia-Arabic and Roman characters. Fcp. 8vo. price 5s.

MORELL (J. R.)—EUCLID SIMPLIFIED IN METHOD AND LANGUAGE. Being a Manual of Geometry. Compiled from the most important French Works, approved by the University of Paris and the Minister of Public Instruction. Fcp. 8vo. price 2s. 6d.

MORSE (E. S.) Ph.D.—FIRST BOOK OF ZOOLOGY. With numerous Illustrations. New and Cheaper Edition. Crown 8vo. price 2s. 6d.

MUNRO (Major-Gen. Sir Thomas) Bart. K.C.B., Governor of Madras. SELECTIONS FROM HIS MINUTES AND OTHER OFFICIAL WRITINGS. Edited, with an Introductory Memoir, by Sir ALEXANDER ARBUTHNOT, K.C.S.I. C.I.E. 2 vols. Demy 8vo. cloth, price 30s.

NELSON (J. H.) M.A.—A PROSPECTUS OF THE SCIENTIFIC STUDY OF THE HINDŪ LAW. Demy 8vo. cloth, price 9s.

NEWMAN (J. H.) D.D.—CHARACTERISTICS FROM THE WRITINGS OF. Being Selections from his various Works. Arranged with the Author's personal Approval. Fifth Edition. With Portrait. Crown 8vo. price 6s.

** A Portrait of the Rev. Dr. J. H. Newman, mounted for framing, can be had, price 2s. 6d.

NEW WERTHER. By LOKI. Small crown 8vo. cloth, price 2s. 6d.

NICHOLSON (Edward Byron)—THE GOSPEL ACCORDING TO THE HEBREWS. Its Fragments Translated and Annotated with a Critical Analysis of the External and Internal Evidence relating to it. Demy 8vo. cloth, price 9s. 6d.

A NEW COMMENTARY ON THE GOSPEL ACCORDING TO MATTHEW. Demy 8vo. cloth, price 12s.

THE RIGHTS OF AN ANIMAL. Crown 8vo. cloth, price 3s. 6d.

NICOLS (Arthur) F.G.S., F.R.G.S.—CHAPTERS FROM THE PHYSICAL HISTORY OF THE EARTH: an Introduction to Geology and Palæontology. With numerous Illustrations. Crown 8vo. cloth, price 5s.

NUCES: EXERCISES ON THE SYNTAX OF THE PUBLIC SCHOOL LATIN PRIMER. New Edition in Three Parts. Crown 8vo. each 1s.

** The Three Parts can also be had bound together in cloth, price 3s.

OATES (*Frank*) F.R.G.S.—MATABELE LAND AND THE VICTORIA FALLS. A Naturalist's Wanderings in the Interior of South Africa. Edited by C. G. OATES, B.A. With numerous Illustrations and 4 Maps. Demy 8vo. cloth, price 21s.

OGLE (*W.*) M.D., F.R.C.P.—ARISTOTLE ON THE PARTS OF ANIMALS. Translated, with Introduction and Notes. Royal 8vo. cloth, 12s. 6d.

O'MEARA (*Kathleen*)—FREDERIC OZANAM, Professor of the Sorbonne: His Life and Work. Second Edition. Crown 8vo. cloth, price 7s. 6d.

HENRI PERREYVE AND HIS COUNSELS TO THE SICK. Small crown 8vo. cloth, price 5s.

OTTLEY (*Henry Bickersteth*) THE GREAT DILEMMA : Christ His own Witness or His own Accuser. Six Lectures. Crown 8vo. cloth, price 3s. 6d.

OUR PUBLIC SCHOOLS—ETON, HARROW, WINCHESTER, RUGBY, WESTMINSTER, MARLBOROUGH, THE CHARTERHOUSE. Crown 8vo. cloth, price 6s.

OWEN (*F. M.*)—JOHN KEATS : a Study. Crown 8vo. cloth, price 6s.

OWEN (*Rev. Robert*) B.D.—SANCTORALE CATHOLICUM; or, Book of Saints. With Notes, Critical, Exegetical, and Historical. Demy 8vo. cloth, price 18s.

AN ESSAY ON THE COMMUNION OF SAINTS. Including an Examination of the Cultus Sanctorum. Price 2s.

OXENHAM (*Rev. F. Nutcombe*)—WHAT IS THE TRUTH AS TO EVERLASTING PUNISHMENT. Part II. Being an Historical Enquiry into the Witness and Weight of certain Anti-Origenist Councils. Crown 8vo. cloth, 2s. 6d.

* Parts I. and II. complete in one volume, cloth, 7s.

PARCHMENT LIBRARY. Choicely printed on hand-made paper, limp parchment antique, 6s. each ; vellum, 7s. 6d. each.

SHAKSPERE'S WORKS. Now publishing in Twelve Monthly Volumes.

EIGHTEENTH CENTURY ESSAYS. Selected and Edited by AUSTIN DOBSON. With a Miniature Frontispiece by R. Caldecott, R.A.

Q. HORATI FLACCI OPERA. Edited by F. A. CORNISH, Assistant Master at Eton. With a Frontispiece after a design by L. ALMA TADEMA. Etched by LEOPOLD LOWENSTAM.

EDGAR ALLAN POE'S POEMS. With an Essay on his Poetry by ANDREW LANG, and a Frontispiece by Linley Sambourne.

SHAKSPERE'S SONNETS. Edited by EDWARD DOWDEN, Author of 'Shakspere : his Mind and Art,' &c. With a Frontispiece etched by Leopold Lowenstam, after the Death Mask.

ENGLISH ODES. Selected by EDMUND W. GOSSE, Author of ' Studies in the Literature of Northern Europe.' With Frontispiece on India paper by Hamo Thornycroft, A.R.A.

OF THE IMITATION OF CHRIST. By THOMAS À KEMPIS. A revised Translation. With Frontispiece on India paper, from a Design by W. B. Richmond.

TENNYSON'S THE PRINCESS : a Medley. With a Miniature Frontispiece by H. M. Paget, and a Tailpiece in Outline by Gordon Browne.

PARCHMENT LIBRARY—continued.

POEMS : Selected from PERCY BYSSHE SHELLEY. Dedicated to Lady Shelley. With Preface by RICHARD GARNET and a Miniature Frontispiece.

TENNYSON'S 'IN MEMORIAM.' With a Miniature Portrait in *eau-forte* by Le Rat, after a Photograph by the late Mrs. Cameron.

PARKER (Joseph) D.D.—THE PARACLETE : An Essay on the Personality and Ministry of the Holy Ghost, with some reference to current discussions. Second Edition. Demy 8vo. price 12s.

PARR (Capt. H. Hallam, C.M.G.)—A SKETCH OF THE KAFIR AND ZULU WARS: Guadana to Isandhlwana. With Maps. Small crown 8vo. cloth, price 5s.

PARSLOE (Joseph) — OUR RAILWAYS. Sketches, Historical and Descriptive. With Practical Information as to Fares and Rates, &c., and a Chapter on Railway Reform. Crown 8vo. price 6s.

PATTISON (Mrs. Mark)—THE RENAISSANCE OF ART IN FRANCE. With Nineteen Steel Engravings. 2 vols. Demy 8vo. cloth, price 32s.

PAUL (C. Kegan)—WILLIAM GODWIN: HIS FRIENDS AND CONTEMPORARIES. With Portraits and Facsimiles of the Handwriting of Godwin and his Wife. 2 vols. Square post 8vo. price 28s.

THE GENIUS OF CHRISTIANITY UNVEILED. Being Essays by William Godwin never before published. Edited, with a Preface, by C. Kegan Paul. Crown 8vo. price 7s. 6d.

MARY WOLLSTONECRAFT. Letters to Imlay. New Edition with Prefatory Memoir by. Two Portraits in *eau-forte* by ANNA LEA MERRITT. Crown 8vo. cloth, price 6s.

PEARSON (Rev. S.)—WEEK-DAY LIVING. A Book for Young Men and Women. Second Edition. Crown 8vo. cloth, 5s.

PENRICE (Maj. J.) B.A.—A DICTIONARY AND GLOSSARY OF THE KO-RAN. With Copious Grammatical References and Explanations of the Text. 4to. price 21s.

PESCHEL (Dr. Oscar)—THE RACES OF MAN AND THEIR GEOGRAPHICAL DISTRIBUTION. Large crown 8vo. price 9s.

PETERS (F. A.)—THE NICOMACHEAN ETHICS OF ARISTOTLE. Translated by. Crown 8vo. cloth, price 6s.

PIDGEON (D.)—AN ENGINEER'S HOLIDAY; or, Notes of a Round Trip from Long. 0° to 0°. 2 vols. large crown 8vo. cloth, price 16s.

PINCHES (Thomas) M.A.—SAMUEL WILBERFORCE: FAITH—SERVICE—RECOMPENSE. Three Sermons. With a Portrait of Bishop Wilberforce (after a Portrait by Charles Watkins). Crown 8vo. cloth, price 4s. 6d.

PLAYFAIR (Lieut.-Col.) Her Britannic Majesty's Consul-General in Algiers.

TRAVELS IN THE FOOTSTEPS OF BRUCE IN ALGERIA AND TUNIS. Illustrated by facsimiles of Bruce's original Drawings, Photographs, Maps, &c. Royal 4to. cloth, bevelled boards, gilt leaves, price £3. 3s.

POLLOCK (Frederick)—SPINOZA, HIS LIFE AND PHILOSOPHY. Demy 8vo. cloth, price 16s.

POLLOCK (W. H.)—LECTURES ON FRENCH POETS. Delivered at the Royal Institution. Small crown 8vo. cloth, price 5s.

POOR (Laura E.)—SANSKRIT AND ITS KINDRED LITERATURES. Studies in Comparative Mythology. Small crown 8vo. cloth, price 5s.

PRESBYTER—UNFOLDINGS OF CHRISTIAN HOPE. An Essay shewing that the Doctrine contained in the Damnatory Clauses of the Creed commonly called Athanasian is Unscriptural. Small crown 8vo. price 4s. 6d.

PRICE (Prof. Bonamy)—CURRENCY AND BANKING. Crown 8vo. Price 6s.

CHAPTERS ON PRACTICAL POLITICAL ECONOMY. Being the Substance of Lectures delivered before the University of Oxford. New and Cheaper Edition. Large post 8vo. price 5s.

PROTEUS AND AMADEUS. A Correspondence. Edited by AUBREY DE VERE. Crown 8vo. price 5s.

PULPIT COMMENTARY (THE). Edited by the Rev. J. S. EXELL and the Rev. Canon H. D. M. SPENCE.

   GENESIS. By Rev. T. WHITELAW, M.A.; with Homilies by the Very Rev. J. F. MONTGOMERY, D.D., Rev. Prof. R. A. REDFORD, M.A., LL.B., Rev. F. HASTINGS, Rev. W. ROBERTS, M.A. An Introduction to the Study of the Old Testament by the Rev. Canon FARRAR, D.D., F.R.S.; and Introductions to the Pentateuch by the Right Rev. H. COTTERILL, D.D., and Rev. T. WHITELAW, M.A. Sixth Edition. One vol. price 15s.

   EXODUS. By the Rev. GEORGE RAWLINSON. With Homilies by Rev. J. ORR, Rev. D. YOUNG, Rev. C. A. GOODHART, Rev. J. URQUHART, and Rev. H. T. ROBJOHNS. Price 16s.

   LEVITICUS. By the Rev. Prebendary MEYRICK, M.A. With Introductions by Rev. R. COLLINS, Rev. Professor A. CAVE, and Homilies by Rev. Prof. REDFORD, LL.B., Rev. J. A. MACDONALD, Rev. W. CLARKSON, Rev. S. R. ALDRIDGE, LL.B., and Rev. MCCHEYNE EDGAR. Second Edition. Price 15s.

   NUMBERS. By the Rev. R. WINTERBOTHAM, LL.B.; with Homilies by the Rev. Professor W. BINNIE, D.D., Rev. E. S. PROUT, M.A., Rev. D. YOUNG, Rev. J. WAITE, and an Introduction by the Rev. THOMAS WHITELAW, M.A. Third Edition. Price 15s.

   JOSHUA. By Rev. J. J. LIAS, M.A.; with Homilies by Rev. S. R. ALDRIDGE, LL.B., Rev. R. GLOVER, Rev. E. DE PRESSENSÉ, D.D., Rev. J. WAITE, B.A., Rev. F. W. ADENEY, M.A.; and an Introduction by the Rev. A. PLUMMER, M.A. Third Edition. Price 12s. 6d.

   JUDGES AND RUTH. By the Right Rev. Lord A. C. HERVEY, D.D., and Rev. J. MORRISON, D.D.; with Homilies by Rev. A. F. MUIR, M.A., Rev. W. F. ADENEY, M.A., Rev. W. M. STATHAM, and Rev. Professor J. THOMSON, M.A. Third Edition. Price 10s. 6d.

   1 SAMUEL. By the Very Rev. R. P. SMITH, D.D.; with Homilies by Rev. DONALD FRASER, D.D., Rev. Prof. CHAPMAN, and Rev. B. DALE. Fourth Edition. Price 15s.

   1 KINGS. By the Rev. JOSEPH HAMMOND, LL.B. With Homilies by the Rev. E. DE PRESSENSÉ, D.D., Rev. J. WAITE, B.A., Rev. A. ROWLAND, LL.B., Rev. J. A. MACDONALD, and Rev. J. URQUHART. Third Edition. Price 15s.

   EZRA, NEHEMIAH, AND ESTHER. By Rev. Canon G. RAWLINSON, M.A.; with Homilies by Rev. Prof. J. R. THOMSON, M.A., Rev. Prof. R. A. REDFORD, LL.B., M.A., Rev. W. S. LEWIS, M.A., Rev. J. A. MACDONALD, Rev. A. MACKENNAL, B.A., Rev. W. CLARKSON, B.A., Rev. F. HASTINGS, Rev. W. DINWIDDIE, LL.B., Rev. Prof. ROWLANDS, B.A., Rev. G. WOOD, B.A., Rev. Prof. P. C. BARKER, LL.B., M.A., and Rev. J. S. EXELL. Fifth Edition. One vol. price 12s. 6d.

PUNJAUB (THE) AND NORTH-WESTERN FRONTIER OF INDIA. By an Old Punjaubee. Crown 8vo. price 5s.

RABBI JESHUA. An Eastern Story. Crown 8vo. cloth, price 3s. 6d.

RADCLIFFE (Frank R. Y.)—THE NEW POLITICUS. Small crown 8vo. Cloth, price 2s. 6d.

RAVENSHAW (John Henry) B.C.S.—GAUR: ITS RUINS AND INSCRIPTIONS. Edited by his Widow. With 44 Photographic Illustrations, and 25 facsimiles of Inscriptions. Royal 4to. cloth, price £3. 13s. 6d.

READ (Carveth)—ON THE THEORY OF LOGIC: An Essay. Crown 8vo. price 6s.

REALITIES OF THE FUTURE LIFE. Small crown 8vo. cloth, price 1s. 6d.

RENDELL (J. M.)—CONCISE HANDBOOK OF THE ISLAND OF MADEIRA. With Plan of Funchal and Map of the Island. Fcp. 8vo. cloth, 1s. 6d.

REYNOLDS (Rev. J. W.)—THE SUPERNATURAL IN NATURE. A Verification by Free Use of Science. Second Edition, revised and enlarged. Demy 8vo. cloth, price 14s.

THE MYSTERY OF MIRACLES. By the Author of 'The Supernatural in Nature.' New and Enlarged Edition. Crown 8vo. cloth, price 6s.

RIBOT (Prof. Th.)—ENGLISH PSYCHOLOGY. Second Edition. A Revised and Corrected Translation from the latest French Edition. Large post 8vo. price 9s.

HEREDITY: A Psychological Study on its Phenomena, its Laws, its Causes, and its Consequences. Large crown 8vo. price 9s.

ROBERTSON (The late Rev. F. W.) M.A., of Brighton.—LIFE AND LETTERS OF. Edited by the Rev. Stopford Brooke, M.A., Chaplain in Ordinary to the Queen.
    I. Two vols., uniform with the Sermons. With Steel Portrait. Crown 8vo. price 7s. 6d.
    II. Library Edition, in demy 8vo. with Portrait. Price 12s.
    III. A Popular Edition, in 1 vol. Crown 8vo. price 6s.

SERMONS. Four Series. Small crown 8vo. price 3s. 6d. each.

THE HUMAN RACE, and other Sermons. Preached at Cheltenham, Oxford, and Brighton. Large post 8vo. cloth, price 7s. 6d.

NOTES ON GENESIS. New and Cheaper Edition. Crown 8vo. price 3s. 6d.

EXPOSITORY LECTURES ON ST. PAUL'S EPISTLES TO THE CORINTHIANS. A New Edition. Small crown 8vo. price 5s.

LECTURES AND ADDRESSES, with other Literary Remains. A New Edition. Crown 8vo. price 5s.

AN ANALYSIS OF MR. TENNYSON'S 'IN MEMORIAM.' (Dedicated by Permission to the Poet-Laureate.) Fcp. 8vo. price 2s.

THE EDUCATION OF THE HUMAN RACE. Translated from the German of Gotthold Ephraim Lessing. Fcp. 8vo. price 2s. 6d.
    The above Works can also be had, bound in half-morocco.
    *** A Portrait of the late Rev. F. W. Robertson, mounted for framing, can be had, price 2s. 6d.

RODWELL (G. F.) F.R.A.S., F.C.S.—ETNA: A HISTORY OF THE MOUNTAIN AND ITS ERUPTIONS. With Maps and Illustrations. Square 8vo. cloth, price 9s.

ROLLESTON (T. W. H.) B.A.—The Encheiridion of Epictetus. Translated from the Greek, with a Preface and Notes. Small crown 8vo. cloth, price 3s. 6d.

Rosmini's Philosophical System. Translated, with a Sketch of the Author's Life, Bibliography, Introduction, and Notes by Thomas Davidson. Demy 8vo. cloth, 16s.

ROSS (Alexander) D.D.—Memoir of Alexander Ewing, Bishop of Argyll and the Isles. Second and Cheaper Edition. Demy 8vo. cloth, price 10s. 6d.

SALTS (Rev. Alfred) LL.D.—Godparents at Confirmation. With a Preface by the Bishop of Manchester. Small crown 8vo. cloth limp, price 2s.

SALVATOR (Archduke Ludwig)—Levkosia, the Capital of Cyprus. Crown 4to. cloth, price 10s. 6d.

SAMUEL (Sydney M.)—Jewish Life in the East. Small crown 8vo. cloth, price 3s. 6d.

SAYCE (Rev. Archibald Henry)—Introduction to the Science of Language. 2 vols. Large post 8vo. cloth, price 25s.

Scientific Layman. The New Truth and the Old Faith: are they Incompatible? Demy 8vo. cloth, price 10s. 6d.

SCOONES (W. Baptiste)—Four Centuries of English Letters: A Selection of 350 Letters by 150 Writers, from the Period of the Paston Letters to the Present Time. Second Edition. Large crown 8vo. cloth, price 9s.

SCOTT (Robert H.)—Weather Charts and Storm Warnings. Second Edition. Illustrated. Crown 8vo. price 3s. 6d.

SHAKSPEARE (Charles)—Saint Paul at Athens. Spiritual Christianity in relation to some aspects of Modern Thought. Five Sermons preached at St. Stephen's Church, Westbourne Park. With a Preface by the Rev. Canon Farrar.

SHELLEY (Lady)—Shelley Memorials from Authentic Sources. With (now first printed) an Essay on Christianity by Percy Bysshe Shelley. With Portrait. Third Edition. Crown 8vo. price 5s.

SHILLITO (Rev. Joseph)—Womanhood: its Duties, Temptations, and Privileges. A Book for Young Women. Third Edition. Crown 8vo. price 3s. 6d.

SHIPLEY (Rev. Orby) M.A.—Church Tracts: or, Studies in Modern Problems. By various Writers. 2 vols. Crown 8vo. price 5s. each.

Principles of the Faith in Relation to Sin. Topics for Thought in Times of Retreat. Eleven Addresses delivered during a Retreat of Three Days to Persons living in the World. Demy 8vo. cloth, price 12s.

Sister Augustine, Superior of the Sisters of Charity at the St. Johannis Hospital at Bonn. Authorised Translation by Hans Tharau, from the German 'Memorials of Amalie von Lasaulx.' Second Edition. Large crown 8vo. cloth, price 7s. 6d.

SMITH (Edward) M.D., LL.B., F.R.S.—Health and Disease, as Influenced by the Daily, Seasonal, and other Cyclical Changes in the Human System. A New Edition. Post 8vo. price 7s. 6d.

Practical Dietary for Families, Schools, and the Labouring Classes. A New Edition. Post 8vo. price 3s. 6d.

Tubercular Consumption in its Early and Remediable Stages. Second Edition. Crown 8vo. price 6s.

SPEDDING (*James*)—REVIEWS AND DISCUSSIONS, LITERARY, POLITICAL, AND HISTORICAL NOT RELATING TO BACON. Demy 8vo. cloth, price 12s. 6d.

> EVENINGS WITH A REVIEWER; or, Bacon and Macaulay. With a Prefatory Notice by G. S. VENABLES, Q.C. 3 vols. demy 8vo. cloth, price 18s.

STAPFER (*Paul*)—SHAKSPEARE AND CLASSICAL ANTIQUITY: Greek and Latin Antiquity as presented in Shakspeare's Plays. Translated by EMILY J. CAREY. Large post 8vo. cloth, price 12s.

ST. BERNARD. A Little Book on the Love of God. Translated by MARIANNE CAROLINE and COVENTRY PATMORE. Cloth extra, gilt top, 4s. 6d.

STEPHENS (*Archibald John*) LL.D.—THE FOLKESTONE RITUAL CASE. The Substance of the Argument delivered before the Judicial Committee of the Privy Council on behalf of the Respondents. Demy 8vo. cloth, price 6s.

STEVENSON (*Rev. W. F.*)—HYMNS FOR THE CHURCH AND HOME. Selected and Edited by the Rev. W. Fleming Stevenson.

> The most complete Hymn Book published.
> The Hymn Book consists of Three Parts:—I. For Public Worship.—II. For Family and Private Worship.—III. For Children.
> *** Published in various forms and prices, the latter ranging from 8d. to 6s. Lists and full particulars will be furnished on application to the Publishers.

STEVENSON (*Robert Louis*)—VIRGINIBUS PUERISQUE, and other Papers. Crown 8vo. cloth, price 6s.

STRACHEY (*Sir John*) G.C.S.I., and *Lieut.-Gen. Richard* STRACHEY, R.E., F.R.S.—THE FINANCES AND PUBLIC WORKS OF INDIA, FROM 1869 TO 1881. Demy 8vo. cloth, price 18s.

STRECKER-WISLICENUS—ORGANIC CHEMISTRY. Translated and Edited, with Extensive Additions, by W. R. HODGKINSON, Ph.D., and A. J. GREENAWAY, F.I.C. Demy 8vo. cloth, price 21s.

SULLY (*James*) M.A.—SENSATION AND INTUITION. Demy 8vo. price 10s. 6d.

> PESSIMISM: a History and a Criticism. Second Edition. Demy 8vo. price 14s.

SYME (*David*)—OUTLINES OF AN INDUSTRIAL SCIENCE. Second Edition. Crown 8vo. price 6s.

> REPRESENTATIVE GOVERNMENT IN ENGLAND. Its Faults and Failures. Second Edition. Large crown 8vo. cloth, 6s.

TAYLOR (*Algernon*)—GUIENNE. Notes of an Autumn Tour. Crown 8vo. cloth, price 4s. 6d.

THOMSON (*J. Turnbull*)—SOCIAL PROBLEMS; OR, AN INQUIRY INTO THE LAWS OF INFLUENCE. With Diagrams. Demy 8vo. cloth, price 10s. 6d.

TIDMAN (*Paul F.*)—GOLD AND SILVER MONEY. Part I.—A Plain Statement. Part II.—Objections Answered. Third Edition. Crown 8vo. cloth, 1s.

TODHUNTER (*Dr. J.*)—A STUDY OF SHELLEY. Crown 8vo. cloth, price 7s.

TWINING (*Louisa*)—WORKHOUSE VISITING AND MANAGEMENT DURING TWENTY-FIVE YEARS. Small crown 8vo. cloth, price 3s. 6d.

UPTON (Major R. D.)—GLEANINGS FROM THE DESERT OF ARABIA. Large post 8vo. cloth, price 10s. 6d.

VAUGHAN (H. Halford)—NEW READINGS AND RENDERINGS OF SHAKESPEARE'S TRAGEDIES. 2 vols. demy 8vo. cloth, price 25s.

VIATOR (Vacuus)—FLYING SOUTH. Recollections of France and its Littoral. Small crown 8vo. cloth, price 3s. 6d.

VILLARI (Professor)—NICCOLO MACHIAVELLI AND HIS TIMES. Translated by Linda Villari. 2 vols. Large post 8vo. price 24s.

VYNER (Lady Mary)—EVERY DAY A PORTION. Adapted from the Bible and the Prayer Book, for the Private Devotions of those living in Widowhood. Collected and Edited by Lady Mary Vyner. Square crown 8vo. extra, price 5s.

WALDSTEIN (Charles) Ph.D.—THE BALANCE OF EMOTION AND INTELLECT; an Introductory Essay to the Study of Philosophy. Crown 8vo. cloth, price 6s.

WALLER (Rev. C. B.)—THE APOCALYPSE, reviewed under the Light of the Doctrine of the Unfolding Ages, and the Relation of All Things. Demy 8vo. price 12s.

WALPOLE (Chas. George)—HISTORY OF IRELAND FROM THE EARLIEST TIMES TO THE UNION WITH GREAT BRITAIN. With 5 Maps and Appendices. Crown 8vo. cloth, 10s. 6d.

WALSHE (Walter Hayle) M.D.—DRAMATIC SINGING PHYSIOLOGICALLY ESTIMATED. Crown 8vo. cloth, price 3s. 6d.

WATSON (Sir Thomas) Bart., M.D.—THE ABOLITION OF ZYMOTIC DISEASES, and of other similar Enemies of Mankind. Small crown 8vo. cloth, price 3s. 6d.

WEDMORE (Frederick)—THE MASTERS OF GENRE PAINTING. With Sixteen Illustrations. Crown 8vo. cloth, price 7s. 6d.

WHEWELL (William) D.D.—HIS LIFE AND SELECTIONS FROM HIS CORRESPONDENCE. By Mrs. STAIR DOUGLAS. With a Portrait from a Painting by SAMUEL LAURENCE. Demy 8vo. cloth, price 21s.

WHITE (A. D.) LL.D.—WARFARE OF SCIENCE. With Prefatory Note by Professor Tyndall. Second Edition. Crown 8vo. price 3s. 6d.

WHITNEY (Prof. William Dwight)—ESSENTIALS OF ENGLISH GRAMMAR, for the Use of Schools. Crown 8vo. price 3s. 6d.

WICKSTEED (P. H.)—DANTE: Six Sermons. Crown 8vo. cloth, price 5s.

WILLIAMS (Rowland) D.D.—PSALMS, LITANIES, COUNSELS, AND COLLECTS FOR DEVOUT PERSONS. Edited by his Widow. New and Popular Edition. Crown 8vo. price 3s. 6d.

STRAY THOUGHTS COLLECTED FROM THE WRITINGS OF THE LATE ROWLAND WILLIAMS, D.D. Edited by his Widow. Crown 8vo. cloth, price 3s. 6d.

WILLIS (R.) M.D.—SERVETUS AND CALVIN: a Study of an Important Epoch in the Early History of the Reformation. 8vo. price 16s.

WILLIAM HARVEY. A History of the Discovery of the Circulation of the Blood: with a Portrait of Harvey after Faithorne. Demy 8vo. cloth, price 14s. Portrait separate.

WILSON (*Sir Erasmus*)—EGYPT OF THE PAST. With Chromo-lithograph and numerous Illustrations in the text. Second Edition, Revised. Crown 8vo. cloth, price 12*s*.

WILSON (*H. Schütz*)—THE TOWER AND SCAFFOLD. A Miniature Monograph. Large fcp. 8vo. price 1*s*.

WOLLSTONECRAFT (*Mary*)—LETTERS TO IMLAY. New Edition, with Prefatory Memoir by C. KEGAN PAUL, author of 'William Godwin: His Friends and Contemporaries,' &c. Two Portraits in *eau-forte* by Anna Lea Merritt. Crown 8vo. cloth, price 6*s*.

WOLTMANN (*Dr. Alfred*), and WOERMANN (*Dr. Karl*)—HISTORY OF PAINTING. Edited by Sidney Colvin. Vol. I. Painting in Antiquity and the Middle Ages. With numerous Illustrations. Medium 8vo. cloth, price 28*s*.; bevelled boards, gilt leaves, price 30*s*.

WOOD (*Major-General J. Creighton*)—DOUBLING THE CONSONANT. Small crown 8vo. cloth, price 1*s*. 6*d*.

WORD WAS MADE FLESH. Short Family Readings on the Epistles for each Sunday of the Christian Year. Demy 8vo. cloth, price 10*s*. 6*d*.

WREN (*Sir Christopher*)—HIS FAMILY AND HIS TIMES. With Original Letters, and a Discourse on Architecture hitherto unpublished. By LUCY PHILLIMORE. Demy 8vo. With Portrait. Price 14*s*.

WRIGHT (*Rev. David*) *M.A.*—WAITING FOR THE LIGHT, AND OTHER SERMONS. Crown 8vo. price 6*s*.

YOUMANS (*Eliza A.*)—AN ESSAY ON THE CULTURE OF THE OBSERVING POWERS OF CHILDREN, especially in connection with the Study of Botany. Edited, with Notes and a Supplement, by Joseph Payne, F.C.P., Author of 'Lectures on the Science and Art of Education,' &c. Crown 8vo. price 2*s*. 6*d*.

FIRST BOOK OF BOTANY. Designed to Cultivate the Observing Powers of Children. With 300 Engravings. New and Cheaper Edition. Crown 8vo. price 2*s*. 6*d*.

YOUMANS (*Edward L.*) *M.D.*—A CLASS BOOK OF CHEMISTRY, on the Basis of the New System. With 200 Illustrations. Crown 8vo. price 5*s*.

THE INTERNATIONAL SCIENTIFIC SERIES.

I. FORMS OF WATER: a Familiar Exposition of the Origin and Phenomena of Glaciers. By J. Tyndall, LL.D., F.R.S. With 25 Illustrations. Eighth Edition. Crown 8vo. price 5*s*.

II. PHYSICS AND POLITICS; or, Thoughts on the Application of the Principles of 'Natural Selection' and 'Inheritance' to Political Society. By Walter Bagehot. Fifth Edition. Crown 8vo. price 4*s*.

III. FOODS. By Edward Smith, M.D., LL.B., F.R.S. With numerous Illustrations. Seventh Edition. Crown 8vo. price 5*s*.

IV. MIND AND BODY: the Theories of their Relation. By Alexander Bain, LL.D. With Four Illustrations. Seventh Edition. Crown 8vo. price 4*s*.

V. THE STUDY OF SOCIOLOGY. By Herbert Spencer. Tenth Edition. Crown 8vo. price 5*s*.

VI. ON THE CONSERVATION OF ENERGY. By Balfour Stewart, M.A., LL.D., F.R.S. With 14 Illustrations. Fifth Edition. Crown 8vo. price 5*s*.

VII. ANIMAL LOCOMOTION; or, Walking, Swimming, and Flying. By J. B. Pettigrew, M.D., F.R.S., &c. With 130 Illustrations. Second Edition. Crown 8vo. price 5*s*.

VIII. RESPONSIBILITY IN MENTAL DISEASE. By Henry Maudsley, M.D. Fourth Edition. Crown 8vo. price 5s.

IX. THE NEW CHEMISTRY. By Professor J. P. Cooke, of the Harvard University. With 31 Illustrations. Sixth Edition. Crown 8vo. price 5s.

X. THE SCIENCE OF LAW. By Professor Sheldon Amos. Fifth Edition. Crown 8vo. price 5s.

XI. ANIMAL MECHANISM: a Treatise on Terrestrial and Aerial Locomotion. By Professor E. J. Marey. With 117 Illustrations. Second Edition. Crown 8vo. price 5s.

XII. THE DOCTRINE OF DESCENT AND DARWINISM. By Professor Oscar Schmidt (Strasburg University). With 26 Illustrations. Fourth Edit. Crown 8vo. price 5s.

XIII. THE HISTORY OF THE CONFLICT BETWEEN RELIGION AND SCIENCE. By J. W. Draper, M D., LL.D. Fifteenth Edition. Crown 8vo. price 5s.

XIV. FUNGI: their Nature, Influences, Uses, &c. By M. C. Cooke, M.D., LL.D. Edited by the Rev. M. J. Berkeley, M.A., F.L.S. With numerous Illustrations. Second Edition. Crown 8vo. price 5s.

XV. THE CHEMICAL EFFECTS OF LIGHT AND PHOTOGRAPHY. By Dr. Hermann Vogel (Polytechnic Academy of Berlin). Translation thoroughly revised. With 100 Illustrations. Third Edition. Crown 8vo. price 5s.

XVI. THE LIFE AND GROWTH OF LANGUAGE. By William Dwight Whitney, Professor of Sanscrit and Comparative Philology in Yale College, Newhaven. Third Edition. Crown 8vo. price 5s.

XVII. MONEY AND THE MECHANISM OF EXCHANGE. By W. Stanley Jevons, M.A., F.R.S. Fifth Edition. Crown 8vo. price 5s.

XVIII. THE NATURE OF LIGHT. With a General Account of Physical Optics. By Dr. Eugene Lommel, Professor of Physics in the University of Erlangen. With 188 Illustrations and a Table of Spectra in Chromo-lithography. Third Edition. Crown 8vo. price 5s.

XIX. ANIMAL PARASITES AND MESSMATES. By Monsieur Van Beneden, Professor of the University of Louvain, Correspondent of the Institute of France. With 83 Illustrations. Second Edition. Crown 8vo. price 5s.

XX. FERMENTATION. By Professor Schützenberger, Director of the Chemical Laboratory at the Sorbonne. With 28 Illustrations. Third Edition. Crown 8vo. price 5s.

XXI. THE FIVE SENSES OF MAN. By Professor Bernstein, of the University of Halle. With 91 Illustrations. Third Edition. Crown 8vo. price 5s.

XXII. THE THEORY OF SOUND IN ITS RELATION TO MUSIC. By Professor Pietro Blaserna, of the Royal University of Rome. With numerous Illustrations. Second Edition. Crown 8vo. price 5s.

XXIII. STUDIES IN SPECTRUM ANALYSIS. By J. Norman Lockyer, F.R.S. With six photographic Illustrations of Spectra, and numerous engravings on Wood. Crown 8vo. Second Edition. Price 6s. 6d.

XXIV. A HISTORY OF THE GROWTH OF THE STEAM ENGINE. By Professor R. H. Thurston. With numerous Illustrations. Second Edition. Crown 8vo. cloth, price 6s. 6d.

XXV. EDUCATION AS A SCIENCE. By Alexander Bain, LL.D. Fourth Edition. Crown 8vo. cloth, price 5s.

XXVI. THE HUMAN SPECIES. By Prof. A. de Quatrefages. Third Edition. Crown 8vo. cloth, price 5s.

XXVII. MODERN CHROMATICS. With Applications to Art and Industry. By Ogden N. Rood. With 130 original Illustrations. Second Edition. Crown 8vo. cloth, price 5s.

XXVIII. THE CRAYFISH: an Introduction to the Study of Zoology. By Professor T. H. Huxley. With 82 Illustrations. Third Edition. Crown 8vo. cloth, price 5s.

XXIX. THE BRAIN AS AN ORGAN OF MIND. By H. Charlton Bastian, M.D. With numerous Illustrations. Second Edition. Crown 8vo. cloth, price 5s.

XXX. THE ATOMIC THEORY. By Prof. Wurtz. Translated by G. Cleminshaw, F.C.S. Third Edition. Crown 8vo. cloth, price 5s.

XXXI. THE NATURAL CONDITIONS OF EXISTENCE AS THEY AFFECT ANIMAL LIFE. By Karl Semper. With 2 Maps and 106 Woodcuts. Second Edition. Crown 8vo. cloth, price 5s.

XXXII. GENERAL PHYSIOLOGY OF MUSCLES AND NERVES. By Prof. J. Rosenthal. Second Edition. With Illustrations. Crown 8vo. cloth, price 5s.

XXXIII. SIGHT : an Exposition of the Principles of Monocular and Binocular Vision. By Joseph le Conte, LL.D. With 132 Illustrations. Crown 8vo. cloth, price 5s.

XXXIV. ILLUSIONS : a Psychological Study. By James Sully. Second Edition. Crown 8vo. cloth, price 5s.

XXXV. VOLCANOES: WHAT THEY ARE AND WHAT THEY TEACH. By Professor J. W. Judd, F.R.S. With 92 Illustrations on Wood. Second Edition. Crown 8vo. cloth, price 5s.

XXXVI. SUICIDE : an Essay in Comparative Moral Statistics. By Prof. E. Morselli. With Diagrams. Crown 8vo. cloth, price 5s.

XXXVII. THE BRAIN AND ITS FUNCTIONS. By J. Luys. With Illustrations. Crown 8vo. cloth, price 5s.

XXXVIII. MYTH AND SCIENCE : an Essay. By Tito Vignoli. Crown 8vo. cloth, price 5s.

XXXIX. THE SUN. By Professor Young. With Illustrations. Second Edition. Crown 8vo. cloth, price 5s.

XL. ANTS, BEES, AND WASPS : a Record of Observations on the Habits of the Social Hymenoptera. By Sir John Lubbock, Bart., M.P. With 5 Chromolithographic Illustrations. Crown 8vo. cloth, price 5s.

MILITARY WORKS.

ANDERSON (Col. R. P.)—VICTORIES AND DEFEATS : an Attempt to explain the Causes which have led to them. An Officer's Manual. Demy 8vo. price 14s.

ARMY OF THE NORTH GERMAN CONFEDERATION : a Brief Description of its Organisation, of the Different Branches of the Service and their rôle in War, of its Mode of Fighting, &c. Translated from the Corrected Edition, by permission of the Author, by Colonel Edward Newdigate. Demy 8vo. price 5s.

BARRINGTON (Capt. J. T.)—ENGLAND ON THE DEFENSIVE ; or, the Problem of Invasion Critically Examined. Large crown 8vo. with Map, cloth, price 7s. 6d.

BLUME (Maj. W.)—THE OPERATIONS OF THE GERMAN ARMIES IN FRANCE, from Sedan to the end of the War of 1870-71. With Map. From the Journals of the Head-quarters Staff. Translated by the late E. M. Jones, Maj. 20th Foot, Prof. of Mil. Hist., Sandhurst. Demy 8vo. price 9s.

BOGUSLAWSKI (Capt. A. von)—TACTICAL DEDUCTIONS FROM THE WAR OF 1870-1. Translated by Colonel Sir Lumley Graham, Bart., late 18th (Royal Irish) Regiment. Third Edition, Revised and Corrected. Demy 8vo. price 7s.

BRACKENBURY (Col. C. B.,) R.A., C.B.—MILITARY HANDBOOKS FOR REGIMENTAL OFFICERS. I. Military Sketching and Reconnaissance, by Lieut.-Col. F. J. Hutchison, and Capt. II. G. MacGregor. Fourth Edition. With 15 Plates. Small 8vo. cloth, price 6s. II. The Elements of Modern Tactics Practically applied to English Formations, by Lieut.-Col. Wilkinson Shaw. Fourth Edition. With 25 Plates and Maps. Small cr. 8vo. cloth, price 9s.

BRIALMONT (Col. A.)—HASTY INTRENCHMENTS. Translated by Lieut. Charles A. Empson, R.A. With Nine Plates. Demy 8vo. price 6s.

CLERY (C.) Lieut.-Col.—MINOR TACTICS. With 26 Maps and Plans. Fifth and revised Edition. Demy 8vo. cloth, price 16s.

DU VERNOIS (Col. von Verdy)—STUDIES IN LEADING TROOPS. An authorised and accurate Translation by Lieutenant H. J. T. Hildyard, 71st Foot. Parts I. and II. Demy 8vo. price 7s.

GOETZE (Capt. A. von)—OPERATIONS OF THE GERMAN ENGINEERS DURING THE WAR OF 1870-1. Published by Authority, and in accordance with Official Documents. Translated from the German by Colonel G. Graham, V.C., C.B., R.E. With 6 large Maps. Demy 8vo. price 21s.

HARRISON (Lieut.-Col. R.) — THE OFFICER'S MEMORANDUM BOOK FOR PEACE AND WAR. Third Edition. Oblong 32mo. roan, with pencil, price 3s. 6d.

HELVIG (Capt. H.)—THE OPERATIONS OF THE BAVARIAN ARMY CORPS. Translated by Captain G. S. Schwabe. With Five large Maps. In 2 vols. Demy 8vo. price 24s.

TACTICAL EXAMPLES: Vol. I. The Battalion, price 15s. Vol. II. The Regiment and Brigade, price 10s. 6d. Translated from the German by Col. Sir Lumley Graham. With nearly 300 Diagrams. Demy 8vo. cloth.

HOFFBAUER (Capt.)—THE GERMAN ARTILLERY IN THE BATTLES NEAR METZ. Based on the Official Reports of the German Artillery. Translated by Captain E. O. Hollist. With Map and Plans. Demy 8vo. price 21s.

LAYMANN (Capt.) — THE FRONTAL ATTACK OF INFANTRY. Translated by Colonel Edward Newdigate. Crown 8vo. price 2s. 6d.

NOTES ON CAVALRY TACTICS, ORGANISATION, &c. By a Cavalry Officer. With Diagrams. Demy 8vo. cloth, price 12s.

PARR (Capt H. Hallam) C.M.G.—THE DRESS, HORSES, AND EQUIPMENT OF INFANTRY AND STAFF OFFICERS. Crown 8vo. cloth, price 1s.

SCHAW (Col. H.)—THE DEFENCE AND ATTACK OF POSITIONS AND LOCALITIES. Second Edition, revised and corrected. Crown 8vo. cloth, price 3s. 6d.

SCHELL (Maj. von)—THE OPERATIONS OF THE FIRST ARMY UNDER GEN. VON GOEBEN. Translated by Col. C. H. von Wright. Four Maps. demy 8vo. price 9s.

THE OPERATIONS OF THE FIRST ARMY UNDER GEN. VON STEINMETZ. Translated by Captain E. O. Hollist. Demy 8vo. price 10s. 6d.

SCHELLENDORF (Major-Gen. B. von) —THE DUTIES OF THE GENERAL STAFF. Translated from the German by Lieutenant Hare. Vol. I. Demy 8vo. cloth, price 10s. 6d.

SCHERFF (Maj. W. von)—STUDIES IN THE NEW INFANTRY TACTICS. Parts I. and II. Translated from the German by Colonel Lumley Graham. Demy 8vo. price 7s. 6d.

SHADWELL (Maj.-Gen.) C.B.—MOUNTAIN WARFARE. Illustrated by the Campaign of 1799 in Switzerland. Being a Translation of the Swiss Narrative compiled from the Works of the Archduke Charles, Jomini, and others. Also of Notes by General H. Dufour on the Campaign of the Valtelline in 1635. With Appendix, Maps, and Introductory Remarks. Demy 8vo. price 16s.

SHERMAN (Gen. W. T.)—MEMOIRS OF GENERAL W. T. SHERMAN, Commander of the Federal Forces in the American Civil War. By Himself. 2 vols. With Map. Demy 8vo. price 24s. *Copyright English Edition.*

STUBBS (Lieut.-Col. F. W.) — THE REGIMENT OF BENGAL ARTILLERY. The History of its Organisation, Equipment, and War Services. Compiled from Published Works, Official Records, and various Private Sources. With numerous Maps and Illustrations. 2 vols. Demy 8vo. price 32s.

STUMM (Lieut. Hugo), German Military Attaché to the Khivan Expedition.— RUSSIA'S ADVANCE EASTWARD Based on the Official Reports of. Translated by Capt. C. E. H. VINCENT, With Map. Crown 8vo. price 6s.

VINCENT (*Capt. C. E. H.*)—ELEMENTARY MILITARY GEOGRAPHY, RECONNOITRING, AND SKETCHING. Compiled for Non-commissioned Officers and Soldiers of all Arms. Square crown 8vo. price 2s. 6d.

VOLUNTEER, THE MILITIAMAN, AND THE REGULAR SOLDIER, by a Public Schoolboy. Crown 8vo. cloth, price 5s.

WARTENSLEBEN (*Count H. von.*)—THE OPERATIONS OF THE SOUTH ARMY IN JANUARY AND FEBRUARY, 1871. Compiled from the Official War Documents of the Head-quarters of the Southern Army. Translated by Colonel C. H. von Wright. With Maps. Demy 8vo. price 6s.

THE OPERATIONS OF THE FIRST ARMY UNDER GEN. VON MANTEUFFEL. Translated by Colonel C. H. von Wright. Uniform with the above. Demy 8vo. price 9s.

WICKHAM (*Capt. E. H., R.A.*)—INFLUENCE OF FIREARMS UPON TACTICS: Historical and Critical Investigations. By an OFFICER OF SUPERIOR RANK (in the German Army). Translated by Captain E. H. Wickham, R.A. Demy 8vo. price 7s. 6d.

WOINOVITS (*Capt. I.*) — AUSTRIAN CAVALRY EXERCISE. Translated by Captain W. S. Cooke. Crown 8vo. price 7s.

POETRY.

ADAMS (*W. D.*— LYRICS OF LOVE, from Shakespeare to Tennyson. Selected and arranged by. Fcp. 8vo. cloth extra, gilt edges, price 3s. 6d.

ADAM OF ST. VICTOR—THE LITURGICAL POETRY OF ADAM OF ST. VICTOR. From the text of Gautier. With Translations into English in the Original Metres, and Short Explanatory Notes. By Digby S. Wrangham, M.A. 3 vols. Crown 8vo. printed on hand-made paper, boards, price 21s.

ANTIOPE: a Tragedy. Large crown 8vo. cloth, price 6s.

AUBERTIN (*J. J.*)—CAMOENS' LUSIADS. Portuguese Text, with Translation by. Map and Portraits. 2 vols. Demy 8vo. price 30s.

SEVENTY SONNETS OF CAMOENS. Portuguese Text and Translation, with some original Poems. Dedicated to Capt. Richard F. Burton. Printed on hand made paper, cloth, bevelled boards, gilt top, price 7s. 6d.

AUCHMUTY (*A. C.*)—POEMS OF ENGLISH HEROISM: From Brunanburgh to Lucknow; from Athelstan to Albert. Small crown 8vo. cloth, price 1s. 6d.

AVIA—THE ODYSSEY OF HOMER. Done into English Verse by. Fcp. 4to. cloth, price 15s.

BANKS (*Mrs. G. L.*)—RIPPLES AND BREAKERS: Poems. Square 8vo. cloth, price 5s.

BARNES (*William*)—POEMS OF RURAL LIFE, IN THE DORSET DIALECT. New Edition, complete in one vol. Crown 8vo. cloth, price 8s. 6d.

BENNETT (*Dr. W. C.*)—NARRATIVE POEMS AND BALLADS. Fcp. 8vo. sewed, in Coloured Wrapper, price 1s.

SONGS FOR SAILORS. Dedicated by Special Request to H.R.H. the Duke of Edinburgh. With Steel Portrait and Illustrations. Crown 8vo. price 3s. 6d.

An Edition in Illustrated Paper Covers, price 1s.

SONGS OF A SONG WRITER. Crown 8vo. price 6s.

BEVINGTON (*L. S.*)—KEY NOTES. Small crown 8vo. cloth, price 5s.

BILLSON (*C. J.*)—THE ACHARNIANS OF ARISTOPHANES. Crown 8vo. cloth, price 3s. 6d.

BOWEN (*H. C.*) *M.A.*—SIMPLE ENGLISH POEMS. English Literature for Junior Classes. In Four Parts. Parts I. II. and III. price 6d. each, and Part IV. price 1s.

BRYANT (*W. C.*)—POEMS. Red-line Edition. With 24 Illustrations and Portrait of the Author. Crown 8vo. cloth extra, price 7s. 6d.
    A Cheap Edition, with Frontispiece. Small crown 8vo. price 3s. 6d.

BYRNNE (*E. Fairfax*)—MILICENT: a Poem. Small crown 8vo. cloth, price 6s.

CALDERON'S DRAMAS: the Wonder-Working Magician—Life is a Dream—the Purgatory of St. Patrick. Translated by Denis Florence MacCarthy. Post 8vo. price 10s.

CLARKE (*Mary Cowden*)—HONEY FROM THE WEED. Verses. Crown 8vo. cloth, 7s.

COLOMB (*Colonel*)—THE CARDINAL ARCHBISHOP: a Spanish Legend. In 29 Cancions. Small crown 8vo. cloth, price 5s.

CONWAY (*Hugh*)—A LIFE'S IDYLLS. Small crown 8vo. cloth, price 3s. 6d.

COPPÉE (*Francois*)—L'EXILÉE. Done into English Verse, with the sanction of the Author, by I. O. L. Crown 8vo. vellum, price 5s.

DAVIES (*T. Hart*)—CATULLUS. Translated into English Verse. Crown 8vo. cloth, price 6s.

DE VERE (*Aubrey*)—THE FORAY OF QUEEN MEAVE, and other Legends of Ireland's Heroic Age. Small crown 8vo. cloth, 5s.
    ALEXANDER THE GREAT: a Dramatic Poem. Small crown 8vo. price 5s.
    THE INFANT BRIDAL, and other Poems. A New and Enlarged Edition. Fcp. 8vo. price 7s. 6d.
    LEGENDS OF THE SAXON SAINTS Small crown 8vo. cloth, price 6s.
    THE LEGENDS OF ST. PATRICK, and other Poems. Small cr. 8vo. price 5s.
    ST. THOMAS OF CANTERBURY: a Dramatic Poem. Large fcp. 8vo. price 5s.
    ANTAR AND ZARA: an Eastern Romance. INISFAIL, and other Poems, Meditative and Lyrical. Fcp. 8vo. price 6s.
    THE FALL OF RORA, THE SEARCH AFTER PROSERPINE, and other Poems, Meditative and Lyrical. Fcp. 8vo. 6s.

DOBELL (*Mrs. Horace*)—ETHELSTONE, EVELINE, and other Poems. Crown 8vo. cloth, 6s.

DOBSON (*Austin*)—VIGNETTES IN RHYME, and Vers de Société. Third Edition. Fcp. 8vo. price 5s.
    PROVERBS IN PORCELAIN. By the Author of 'Vignettes in Rhyme.' Second Edition. Crown 8vo. price 6s.

DOROTHY: a Country Story in Elegiac Verse. With Preface. Demy 8vo. cloth, price 5s.

DOWDEN (*Edward*) LL.D.—POEMS. Second Edition. Fcp. 8vo. price 5s.
    SHAKSPERE'S SONNETS. With Introduction. Large post 8vo. cloth, price 7s. 6d.

DOWNTON (*Rev. H.*) M.A.—HYMNS AND VERSES. Original and Translated. Small crown 8vo. cloth, price 3s. 6d.

DUTT (*Toru*)—A SHEAF GLEANED IN FRENCH FIELDS. New Edition, with Portrait. Demy 8vo. cloth, 10s. 6d.
    ANCIENT BALLADS AND LEGENDS OF HINDUSTAN. With an Introductory Memoir by Edmund W. Gosse. Small crown 8vo. printed on hand-made paper, price 5s.

EDWARDS (*Rev. Basil*)—MINOR CHORDS; or, Songs for the Suffering: a Volume of Verse. Fcp. 8vo. cloth, price 3s. 6d.; paper, price 2s. 6d.

ELDRYTH (*Maud*)—MARGARET, and other Poems. Small crown 8vo. cloth, price 3s. 6d.

ELLIOT (*Lady Charlotte*)—MEDUSA and other Poems. Crown 8vo. cloth, price 6s.

ELLIOTT (*Ebenezer*), The Corn Law Rhymer.—POEMS. Edited by his son, the Rev. Edwin Elliott, of St. John's, Antigua. 2 vols. crown 8vo. price 18s.

ENGLISH ODES. Selected, with a Critical Introduction by EDMUND W. GOSSE, and a miniature frontispiece by Hamo Thornycroft, A.R.A. Elzevir 8vo. limp parchment antique, price 6s.; vellum, 7s. 6d.

EPIC OF HADES (THE). By the Author of 'Songs of Two Worlds.' Thirteenth Edition. Fcp. 8vo. price 7s. 6d.
    *** Also an Illustrated Edition, with seventeen full-page designs in photo-mezzotint by George R. Chapman. 4to. cloth, extra gilt leaves, price 25s.; and a Large Paper Edition with Portrait, price 10s. 6d.

EVANS (Anne)—POEMS AND MUSIC. With Memorial Preface by ANN THACKERAY RITCHIE. Large crown 8vo. cloth, price 7s.

GOSSE (Edmund W.)—NEW POEMS. Crown 8vo. cloth, price 7s. 6d.

GREENOUGH (Mrs. Richard)—MARY MAGDALENE: a Poem. Large post 8vo. parchment antique, bevelled boards, price 6s.

GROTE (A. R.)—RIP VAN WINKLE: a Sun Myth; and other Poems. Small crown 8vo. printed on hand-made paper, limp parchment antique, price 5s.

GURNEY (Rev. Alfred)—THE VISION OF THE EUCHARIST, and other Poems. Crown 8vo. cloth, price 5s.

GWEN: a Drama in Monologue. By the Author of the 'Epic of Hades.' Third Edition. Fcp. 8vo. cloth, price 5s.

HAWKER (Robt. Stephen)—THE POETICAL WORKS OF. Now first collected and arranged. With a Prefatory Notice by J. G. Godwin. With Portrait. Crown 8vo. cloth, price 12s.

HAWTREY (Edward M.)—CORYDALIS: a Story of the Sicilian Expedition. Small crown 8vo. cloth, price 3s. 6d.

HELLON (H. G.)—DAPHNIS: a Pastoral Poem. Small crown 8vo. cloth, price 3s. 6d.

HICKEY (E. H.)—A SCULPTOR, and other Poems. Small crown 8vo. cloth, price 5s.

HOLMES (E. G. A.)—POEMS. First and Second Series. Fcp. 8vo. price 5s. each.

INCHBOLD (J. W.)—ANNUS AMORIS: Sonnets. Fcp. 8vo. price 4s. 6d.

JENKINS (Rev. Canon)—THE GIRDLE LEGEND OF PRATO. Small crown 8vo. cloth, price 2s.

    ALFONSO PETRUCCI, Cardinal and Conspirator: an Historical Tragedy in Five Acts. Small crown 8vo. cloth, price 3s. 6d.

KING (Edward)—ECHOES FROM THE ORIENT. With Miscellaneous Poems. Small crown 8vo. cloth, price 3s. 6d.

KING (Mrs. Hamilton)—THE DISCIPLES. Fourth Edition, with Portrait and Notes. Crown 8vo. price 7s. 6d.

    ASPROMONTE, and other Poems. Second Edition. Fcp. 8vo. price 4s. 6d.

LANG (A.)—XXXII BALLADES IN BLUE CHINA. Elzevir 8vo. parchment. price 5s.

LEIGH (Arran and Isla)—BELLEROPHÔN. Small crown 8vo. cloth, price 5s.

LEIGHTON (Robert)—RECORDS AND OTHER POEMS. With Portrait. Small crown 8vo. cloth, price 7s. 6d.

LOCKER (F.)—LONDON LYRICS. A New and Revised Edition, with Additions and a Portrait of the Author. Crown 8vo. cloth elegant, price 6s.

LOVE SONNETS OF PROTEUS. With Frontispiece by the Author. Elzevir 8vo. cloth, price 5s.

LOWNDES (Henry) — POEMS AND TRANSLATIONS. Crown 8vo. cloth, price 6s.

LUMSDEN (Lieut.-Col. H. W.)—BEOWULF: an Old English Poem. Translated into Modern Rhymes. Small crown 8vo. cloth, price 5s.

MACLEAN (Charles Donald)—LATIN AND GREEK VERSE TRANSLATIONS. Small crown 8vo. cloth, 2s.

MAGNUSSON (Eirikr) M.A., and PALMER (E. H.) M.A.—JOHAN LUDVIG RUNEBERG'S LYRICAL SONGS, IDYLLS, AND EPIGRAMS. Fcp. 8vo. cloth, price 5s.

MEREDITH (Owen) [The Earl of Lytton]—LUCILE. With 160 Illustrations. Crown 4to. cloth extra, gilt leaves, price 21s.

MIDDLETON (The Lady)—BALLADS. Square 16mo. cloth, price 3s. 6d.

MOORE (Mrs. Bloomfield)—GONDALINE'S LESSON: The Warden's Tale, Stories for Children, and other Poems. Crown 8vo. cloth, price 5s.

MORICE (Rev. F. D.) M.A.—THE OLYMPIAN AND PYTHIAN ODES OF PINDAR. A New Translation in English Verse. Crown 8vo. price 7s. 6d.

MORSHEAD (E. D. A.)—THE HOUSE ATREUS. Being the Agamemnon, Libation-Bearers, and Furies of Æschylus. Translated into English Verse. Crown 8vo. cloth, price 7s.

MORTERRA (Felix)—THE LEGEND OF ALLANDALE, and other Poems. Small crown 8vo. cloth, price 6s.

NADEN (Constance W.)—SONGS AND SONNETS OF SPRING TIME. Small crown 8vo. cloth, price 5s.

NICHOLSON (Edward B.) Librarian of the London Institution—THE CHRIST CHILD, and other Poems. Crown 8vo. cloth, price 4s. 6d.

NOAKE (Major R. Compton) — THE BIVOUAC; or, Martial Lyrist. With an Appendix: Advice to the Soldier. Fcp. 8vo. price 5s. 6d.

NOEL (The Hon Roden)—A LITTLE CHILD'S MONUMENT. Second Edition. Small crown 8vo. cloth, 3s. 6d.

NORRIS (Rev. Alfred)—THE INNER AND OUTER LIFE POEMS. Fcp. 8vo. cloth, price 6s.

ODE OF LIFE (THE). By the Author of 'The Epic of Hades' &c. Fourth Edition. Crown 8vo. cloth, price 5s.

O'HAGAN (John) — THE SONG OF ROLAND. Translated into English Verse. Large post 8vo. parchment antique, price 10s. 6d.

PAUL (C. Kegan)—GOETHE'S FAUST. A New Translation in Rhyme. Crown 8vo. price 6s.

PAYNE (John)—SONGS OF LIFE AND DEATH. Crown 8vo. cloth, price 5s.

PENNELL (H. Cholmondeley)—PEGASUS RESADDLED. By the Author of 'Puck on Pegasus,' &c. &c. With Ten Full-page Illustrations by George Du Maurier. Second Edition. Fcp. 4to. cloth elegant, price 12s. 6d.

PFEIFFER (Emily)—GLAN ALARCH: His Silence and Song: a Poem. Second Edition. Crown 8vo. price 6s.

GERARD'S MONUMENT and other Poems. Second Edition. Crown 8vo. cloth, price 6s.

QUARTERMAN'S GRACE, and other Poems. Crown 8vo. cloth, price 5s.

POEMS. Second Edition. Crown 8vo. cloth, price 6s.

SONNETS AND SONGS. New Edition. 16mo. handsomely printed and bound in cloth, gilt edges, price 4s.

UNDER THE ASPENS: Lyrical and Dramatic. Crown 8vo. with Portrait, cloth, price 6s.

PIKE (Warburton)—THE INFERNO OF DANTE ALIGHIERI. Demy 8vo. cloth, price 5s.

RHOADES (James)—THE GEORGICS OF VIRGIL. Translated into English Verse. Small crown 8vo. cloth, price 5s.

ROBINSON (A. Mary F.)—A HANDFUL OF HONEYSUCKLE. Fcp. 8vo. cloth, price 3s. 6d.

THE CROWNED HIPPOLYTUS. Translated from Euripides. With New Poems. Small crown 8vo. cloth, price 5s.

SHELLEY (Percy Bysshe) — POEMS SELECTED FROM. Dedicated to Lady Shelley. With Preface by Richard Garnett. Printed on hand-made paper, with miniature frontispiece, Elzevir 8vo. limp parchment antique, price 6s.; vellum, price 7s. 6d.

SIX BALLADS ABOUT KING ARTHUR. Crown 8vo. cloth extra, gilt edges, price 3s. 6d.

SKINNER (James)—COELESTIA. The Manual of St. Augustine. The Latin Text side by side with an English Interpretation in Thirty-six Odes with Notes, *and a plea for the* study *of* Mystical Theology. Large crown 8vo. cloth, 6s.

SONGS OF TWO WORLDS. By the Author of 'The Epic of Hades.' Seventh Edition. Complete in one Volume, with Portrait. Fcp. 8vo. cloth, price 7s. 6d.

SONGS FOR MUSIC. By Four Friends. Containing Songs by Reginald A. Gatty, Stephen H. Gatty, Greville J. Chester, and Juliana Ewing. Square crown 8vo. price 5s.

STEDMAN (Edmund Clarence)—LYRICS AND IDYLLS, with other Poems. Crown 8vo. cloth, price 7s. 6d.

STEVENS (William)—THE TRUCE OF GOD, and other Poems. Small crown 8vo. cloth, price 3s. 6d.

SWEET SILVERY SAYINGS OF SHAKESPEARE. Crown 8vo. cloth gilt, price 7s. 6d.

TAYLOR (Sir H.)—Works Complete in Five Volumes. Crown 8vo. cloth, price 30s.

TENNYSON (*Alfred*) — Works Complete:—

THE IMPERIAL LIBRARY EDITION. Complete in 7 vols. Demy 8vo. price 10s. 6d. each; in Roxburgh binding, 12s. 6d.

AUTHOR'S EDITION. In Seven Volumes. Post 8vo. cloth gilt; or half-morocco. Roxburgh style.

CABINET EDITION. 13 Volumes. Each with Frontispiece. Fcp. 8vo. price 2s. 6d. each.

CABINET EDITION. 13 vols. Complete in handsome Ornamental Case.

THE ROYAL EDITION. In 1 vol. With 25 Illustrations and Portrait. Cloth extra, bevelled boards, gilt leaves, price 21s.

THE GUINEA EDITION. Complete in 13 vols. neatly bound and enclosed in box. Cloth, price 21s.; French morocco or parchment, price 31s. 6d.

SHILLING EDITION. In 13 vols. pocket size, 1s. each, sewed.

THE CROWN EDITION. Complete in 1 vol. strongly bound in cloth, price 6s.; cloth, extra gilt leaves, price 7s. 6d.; Roxburgh, half-morocco, price 8s. 6d.

*** Can also be had in a variety of other bindings.

TENNYSON'S SONGS SET TO MUSIC by various Composers. Edited by W. J. Cusins. Dedicated, by express permission, to Her Majesty the Queen. Royal 4to. cloth extra, gilt leaves, price 21s.; or in half-morocco, price 25s.

Original Editions :—

BALLADS, and other Poems. Fcp. 8vo. cloth, price 5s.

POEMS. Small 8vo. price 6s.

MAUD, and other Poems. Small 8vo. price 3s. 6d.

THE PRINCESS. Small 8vo. price 3s. 6d.

IDYLLS OF THE KING. Small 8vo. price 5s.

IDYLLS OF THE KING. Complete. Small 8vo. price 6s.

THE HOLY GRAIL, and other Poems. Small 8vo. price 4s. 6d.

GARETH AND LYNETTE. Small 8vo. price 3s.

TENNYSON (*Alfred*)—cont.

ENOCH ARDEN, &c. Small 8vo. price 3s. 6d.

IN MEMORIAM. Small 8vo. price 4s.

HAROLD : a Drama. New Edition. Crown 8vo. price 6s.

QUEEN MARY : a Drama. New Edition. Crown 8vo. price 6s.

THE LOVER'S TALE. Fcp. 8vo. cloth, 3s. 6d.

SELECTIONS FROM THE ABOVE WORKS. Super royal 16mo. price 3s. 6d. ; cloth gilt extra, price 4s.

SONGS FROM THE ABOVE WORKS. 16mo. cloth, price 2s. 6d.; cloth extra, 3s. 6d.

IDYLLS OF THE KING, and other Poems. Illustrated by Julia Margaret Cameron. 2 vols. folio, half-bound morocco, cloth sides, price £6. 6s. each.

HORÆ TENNYSONIANÆ sive Eclogæ e Tennysono Latine Redditæ Cura A. J. Church, A.M. Small crown 8vo. cloth, price 6s.

TENNYSON FOR THE YOUNG AND FOR RECITATION. Specially arranged. Fcp. 8vo. 1s. 6d.

THE TENNYSON BIRTHDAY BOOK. Edited by Emily Shakespear. 32mo. cloth limp, 2s.; cloth extra, 3s.

*** A superior Edition, printed in red and black, on antique paper, specially prepared. Small crown 8vo. cloth, extra gilt leaves, price 5s.; and in various calf and morocco bindings.

THOMPSON (*Alice C.*)—PRELUDES : a Volume of Poems. Illustrated by Elizabeth Thompson (Painter of 'The Roll Call'). 8vo. price 7s. 6d.

THRING (*Rev. Godfrey*), B.A.—HYMNS AND SACRED LYRICS. Fcp. 8vo. price 3s. 6d.

TODHUNTER (*Dr. J.*) — LAURELLA, and other Poems. Crown 8vo. 6s. 6d.

FOREST SONGS. Small crown 8vo. cloth, price 3s. 6d.

THE TRUE TRAGEDY OF RIENZI : a Drama. Cloth, price 3s. 6d.

ALCESTIS : a Dramatic Poem. Extra fcp. 8vo. cloth, price 5s.

A STUDY OF SHELLEY. Crown 8vo. cloth, price 7s.

TRANSLATIONS FROM DANTE, PETRARCH, MICHAEL ANGELO, AND VITTORIA COLONNA. Fcp. 8vo. cloth, price 7s. 6d.

TURNER (Rev. C. Tennyson)—SONNETS, LYRICS, AND TRANSLATIONS. Crown 8vo. cloth, price 4s. 6d.

COLLECTED SONNETS, Old and New. With Prefatory Poem by ALFRED TENNYSON; also some Marginal Notes by S. T. COLERIDGE, and a Critical Essay by JAMES SPEDDING. Fcp. 8vo cloth, price 7s. 6d.

WALTERS (Sophia Lydia)—THE BROOK: a Poem. Small crown 8vo. cloth, price 3s. 6d.

A DREAMER'S SKETCH BOOK. With 21 Illustrations by Percival Skelton, R. P. Leitch, W. H. J. BOOT, and T. R. PRITCHETT. Engraved by J. D. Cooper. Fcp. 4to. cloth, price 12s. 6d.

WATERFIELD (W.) — HYMNS FOR HOLY DAYS AND SEASONS. 32mo. cloth, price 1s. 6d.

WAY (A.) M.A.—THE ODES OF HORACE LITERALLY TRANSLATED IN METRE. Fcp. 8vo. price 2s.

WEBSTER (Augusta) — DISGUISES: a Drama. Small crown 8vo. cloth, price 5s.

WET DAYS. By a Farmer. Small crown 8vo. cloth, price 6s.

WILKINS (William)—SONGS OF STUDY. Crown 8vo. cloth, price 6s.

WILLOUGHBY (The Hon. Mrs.)—ON THE NORTH WIND—THISTLEDOWN: a Volume of Poems. Elegantly bound, small crown 8vo. price 7s. 6d.

WOODS (James Chapman)—A CHILD OF THE PEOPLE, and other Poems. Small crown 8vo. cloth, price 5s.

YOUNG (Wm.)—GOTTLOB, ETCETERA. Small crown 8vo. cloth, price 3s. 6d.

YOUNGS (Ella Sharpe)—PAPHUS, and other Poems. Small crown 8vo. cloth, price 3s. 6d.

WORKS OF FICTION IN ONE VOLUME.

BANKS (Mrs. G. L.)—GOD'S PROVIDENCE HOUSE. New Edition. Crown 8vo. cloth, price 3s. 6d.

BETHAM-EDWARDS (Miss M.)— KITTY. With a Frontispiece. Crown 8vo. price 6s.

BLUE ROSES; or, Helen Malinofska's Marriage. By the Author of 'Véra.' New and Cheaper Edition. With Frontispiece. Crown 8vo. cloth, price 6s.

FRISWELL (J. Hain)—ONE OF TWO; or, The Left-Handed Bride. Crown 8vo. cloth, price 3s. 6d.

GARRETT (E.)—BY STILL WATERS: a Story for Quiet Hours. With Seven Illustrations. Crown 8vo. price 6s.

HARDY (Thomas)—A PAIR OF BLUE EYES. Author of 'Far from the Madding Crowd.' New Edition. Crown 8vo. price 6s.

THE RETURN OF THE NATIVE. New Edition. With Frontispiece. Crown 8vo. cloth, price 6s.

HOOPER (Mrs. G.)—THE HOUSE OF RABY. Crown 8vo. cloth, price 3s. 6d.

INGELOW (Jean)—OFF THE SKELLIGS: a Novel. With Frontispiece. Second Edition. Crown 8vo. cloth, price 6s.

MACDONALD (G.)—MALCOLM. With Portrait of the Author engraved on Steel. Sixth Edition. Crown 8vo. price 6s.

THE MARQUIS OF LOSSIE. Fourth Edition. With Frontispiece. Crown 8vo. cloth, price 6s.

ST. GEORGE AND ST. MICHAEL. Third Edition. With Frontispiece. Crown 8vo. cloth, 6s.

MASTERMAN (J.)—HALF-A-DOZEN DAUGHTERS. Crown 8vo. cloth, price 3s. 6d.

MEREDITH (George) — ORDEAL OF RICHARD FEVEREL. New Edition. Crown 8vo. cloth, price 6s.

THE EGOIST: A Comedy in Narrative. New and Cheaper Edition, with Frontispiece. Crown 8vo. cloth, price 6s.

PALGRAVE (W. Gifford)—HERMANN AGHA: an Eastern Narrative. Third Edition. Crown 8vo. cloth, price 6s.

PANDURANG HARI; or, Memoirs of a Hindoo. With an Introductory Preface by Sir H. Bartle E. Frere, G.C.S.I., C.B. Crown 8vo. price 6s.

PAUL (Margaret Agnes)—GENTLE AND SIMPLE: A Story. New and Cheaper Edition, with Frontispiece. Crown 8vo. price 6s.

SAUNDERS (John) — ISRAEL MORT, OVERMAN: a Story of the Mine. Crown 8vo. price 6s.

ABEL DRAKE'S WIFE. Crown 8vo. cloth, price 3s. 6d.

HIRELL. Crown 8vo. cloth, price 3s. 6d.

SHAW (Flora L.)—CASTLE BLAIR; a Story of Youthful Lives. New and Cheaper Edition, with Frontispiece. Crown 8vo. price 3s. 6d.

STRETTON (Hesba) — THROUGH A NEEDLE'S EYE: a Story. New and Cheaper Edition, with Frontispiece. Crown 8vo. cloth, price 6s.

TAYLOR (Col. Meadows) C.S.I., M.R.I.A.
SEETA: a Novel. New and Cheaper Edition. With Frontispiece. Crown 8vo. cloth, price 6s.

TIPPOO SULTAUN: a Tale of the Mysore War. New Edition, with Frontispiece. Crown 8vo. cloth, price 6s.

RALPH DARNELL. New and Cheaper Edition. With Frontispiece. Crown 8vo. cloth, price 6s.

A NOBLE QUEEN. New and Cheaper Edition. With Frontispiece. Crown 8vo. cloth, price 6s.

THE CONFESSIONS OF A THUG. Crown 8vo. price 6s.

TARA: a Mahratta Tale. Crown 8vo. price 6s.

THOMAS (Moy)—A FIGHT FOR LIFE. Crown 8vo. cloth, price 3s. 6d.

WITHIN SOUND OF THE SEA. New and Cheaper Edition, with Frontispiece. Crown 8vo. cloth, price 6s.

BOOKS FOR THE YOUNG.

AUNT MARY'S BRAN PIE. By the Author of 'St. Olave's.' Illustrated. Price 3s. 6d.

BARLEE (Ellen)—LOCKED OUT: a Tale of the Strike. With a Frontispiece. Royal 16mo. price 1s. 6d.

BONWICK (J.) F.R.G.S.—THE TASMANIAN LILY. With Frontispiece. Crown 8vo. price 5s.

MIKE HOWE, the Bushranger of Van Diemen's Land. New and Cheaper Edition. With Frontispiece. Crown 8vo. price 3s. 6d.

BRAVE MEN'S FOOTSTEPS. By the Editor of 'Men who have Risen.' A Book of Example and Anecdote for Young People. With Four Illustrations by C. Doyle. Seventh Edition. Crown 8vo. price 3s. 6d.

CHILDREN'S TOYS, and some Elementary Lessons in General Knowledge which they teach. Illustrated. Crown 8vo. cloth, price 5s.

COLERIDGE (Sara)—PRETTY LESSONS IN VERSE FOR GOOD CHILDREN, with some Lessons in Latin, in Easy Rhyme. A New Edition. Illustrated. Fcp. 8vo. cloth, price 3s. 6d.

D'ANVERS (N. R.)—LITTLE MINNIE'S TROUBLES: an Every-day Chronicle. With 4 Illustrations by W. H. Hughes. Fcp. cloth, price 3s. 6d.

PARTED: a Tale of Clouds and Sunshine. With 4 Illustrations. Extra fcp. 8vo. cloth, price 3s. 6d.

PIXIE'S ADVENTURES; or, the Tale of a Terrier. With 21 Illustrations. 16mo. cloth, price 4s. 6d.

NANNY'S ADVENTURES: or, the Tale of a Goat. With 12 Illustrations. 16mo. cloth, price 4s. 6d.

DAVIES (G. Christopher) — RAMBLES AND ADVENTURES OF OUR SCHOOL FIELD CLUB. With Four Illustrations. New and Cheaper Edition. Crown 8vo. price 3s. 6d.

C

DRUMMOND (*Miss*)—TRIPP'S BUILDINGS. A Study from Life, with Frontispiece. Small crown 8vo. price 3s. 6d.

EDMONDS (*Herbert*) — WELL SPENT LIVES: a Series of Modern Biographies. New and Cheaper Edition. Crown 8vo. price 3s. 6d.

EVANS (*Mark*)—THE STORY OF OUR FATHER'S LOVE, told to Children; Fourth and Cheaper Edition of Theology for Children. With Four Illustrations. Fcp. 8vo. price 1s. 6d.

FARQUHARSON (*M.*)
I. ELSIE DINSMORE. Crown 8vo. price 3s. 6d.
II. ELSIE'S GIRLHOOD. Crown 8vo. price 3s. 6d.
III. ELSIE'S HOLIDAYS AT ROSELANDS. Crown 8vo. price 3s. 6d.

HERFORD (*Brooke*)—THE STORY OF RELIGION IN ENGLAND: a Book for Young Folk. Cr. 8vo. cloth, price 5s.

INGELOW (*Jean*) — THE LITTLE WONDER-HORN. With Fifteen Illustrations. Small 8vo. price 2s. 6d.

JOHNSON (*Virginia W.*)—THE CATSKILL FAIRIES. Illustrated by ALFRED FREDERICKS. Cloth, price 5s.

KER (*David*) — THE BOY SLAVE IN BOKHARA: a Tale of Central Asia. With Illustrations. New and Cheaper Edition. Crown 8vo. price 3s. 6d.

THE WILD HORSEMAN OF THE PAMPAS. Illustrated. New and Cheaper Edition. Crown 8vo. price 3s. 6d.

LAMONT (*Martha MacDonald*)—THE GLADIATOR: a Life under the Roman Empire in the beginning of the Third Century. With 4 Illustrations by H. M. Paget. Extra fcp. 8vo. cloth, price 3s. 6d.

LEANDER (*Richard*) — FANTASTIC STORIES. Translated from the German by Paulina B. Granville. With Eight Full-page Illustrations by M. E. Fraser-Tytler. Crown 8vo. price 5s.

LEE (*Holme*)—HER TITLE OF HONOUR. A Book for Girls. New Edition. With a Frontispiece. Crown 8vo. price 5s.

LEWIS (*Mary A.*)—A RAT WITH THREE TALES. New and Cheaper Edition. With Four Illustrations by Catherine F. Frere. Price 3s. 6d.

MC CLINTOCK (*L.*)—SIR SPANGLE AND THE DINGY HEN. Illustrated. Square crown 8vo. price 2s. 6d.

MAC KENNA (*S. J.*)—PLUCKY FELLOWS. A Book for Boys. With Six Illustrations. Fifth Edition. Crown 8vo. price 3s. 6d.

AT SCHOOL WITH AN OLD DRAGOON. With Six Illustrations. New and Cheaper Edition. Crown 8vo. price 3s. 6d.

MALDEN (*H. E.*)—PRINCES AND PRINCESSES: Two Fairy Tales. Illustrated. Small crown 8vo. price 2s. 6d.

MASTER BOBBY. By the Author of 'Christina North.' With Six Illustrations. Fcp. 8vo. cloth, price 3s. 6d.

NAAKE (*J. T.*) — SLAVONIC FAIRY TALES. From Russian, Servian, Polish, and Bohemian Sources. With 4 Illustrations. Crown 8vo. price 5s.

PELLETAN (*E.*)—THE DESERT PASTOR. JEAN JAROUSSEAU. Translated from the French. By Colonel E. P. De L'Hoste. With a Frontispiece. New Edition. Fcp. 8vo. price 3s. 6d.

REANEY (*Mrs. G. S.*)—WAKING AND WORKING; or, From Girlhood to Womanhood. New and Cheaper Edition. With a Frontispiece. Cr. 8vo. price 3s. 6d.

BLESSING AND BLESSED: a Sketch of Girl Life. New and Cheaper Edition. Crown 8vo. cloth, price 3s. 6d.

ROSE GURNEY'S DISCOVERY. A Book for Girls. Dedicated to their Mothers. Crown 8vo. cloth, price 3s. 6d.

ENGLISH GIRLS: Their Place and Power. With Preface by the Rev. R. W. Dale. Third Edition. Fcp. 8vo. cloth, price 2s. 6d.

JUST ANYONE, and other Stories. Three Illustrations. Royal 16mo. cloth, price 1s. 6d.

SUNBEAM WILLIE, and other Stories. Three Illustrations. Royal 16mo. price 1s. 6d.

SUNSHINE JENNY and other Stories. 3 Illustrations. Royal 16mo. cloth, price 1s. 6d.

ROSS (Mrs. E.), ('Nelsie Brook')—DADDY'S PET. A Sketch from Humble Life. With Six Illustrations. Royal 16mo. price 1s.

SADLER (S. W.) R.N.—THE AFRICAN CRUISER: a Midshipman's Adventures on the West Coast. With Three Illustrations. New and Cheaper Edition. Crown 8vo. price 2s. 6d.

SEEKING HIS FORTUNE, and other Stories. With Four Illustrations. New and Cheaper Edition. Crown 8vo. 2s. 6d.

SEVEN AUTUMN LEAVES FROM FAIRY LAND. Illustrated with Nine Etchings. Square crown 8vo. price 3s. 6d.

STOCKTON (Frank R.)—A JOLLY FELLOWSHIP. With 20 Illustrations. Crown 8vo. cloth, price 5s.

STORR (Francis) and TURNER (Hawes). CANTERBURY CHIMES; or, Chaucer Tales retold to Children. With Six Illustrations from the Ellesmere MS. Second Edition. Fcp. 8vo. cloth, price 3s. 6d.

STRETTON (Hesba)—DAVID LLOYD'S LAST WILL. With Four Illustrations. New Edition. Royal 16mo. price 2s. 6d.

THE WONDERFUL LIFE. Sixteenth Thousand. Fcp. 8vo. cloth, price 2s. 6d.

SUNNYLAND STORIES. By the Author of 'Aunt Mary's Bran Pie.' Illustrated. Second Edition. Small 8vo. price 3s. 6d.

TALES FROM ARIOSTO RE-TOLD FOR CHILDREN. By a Lady. With 3 Illustrations. Crown 8vo. cloth, price 4s. 6d.

WHITAKER (Florence)—CHRISTY'S INHERITANCE. A London Story. Illustrated. Royal 16mo. price 1s. 6d.

ZIMMERN (H.)—STORIES IN PRECIOUS STONES. With Six Illustrations. Third Edition. Crown 8vo. price 5s.